Interventions for Students with Emotional Disorders

Advisory Editor

Michael Bender, Ed.D.
Vice President of Educational Programs,
The Kennedy Institute;
Professor of Education,
The Johns Hopkins University,
Joint Appointment, Department of Pediatrics,
The Johns Hopkins School of Medicine,
Baltimore, Maryland

Interventions for Students with Emotional Disorders

Sharon R. Morgan, Ph.D.

Jo Ann Reinhart, M.A.
El Paso Independent School District,
El Paso, Texas

pro·ed

8700 Shoal Creek Boulevard
Austin, Texas 78757

Library of Congress Cataloging in Publication Data
Main entry under title:

Morgan, Sharon R., 1942–
    Interventions for students with emotional disorders / Sharon R. Morgan, Jo Ann Reinhart.
        p.   cm.
    Includes bibliographical references.
    ISBN 0-89079-296-8
    1. Problem children—Education.   2. Mentally ill children—Education.
    3. Behavior disorders in children.   4. Special education.   I. Reinhart, Jo Ann.
    II. Title.
    LC480.M597   1990
        371.94—dc20   89-29103
                                                                                              CIP

Printed in the United States of America

pro·ed

8700 Shoal Creek Boulevard
Austin, Texas 78757

3   4   5   6   7   8   9   10   97   96   95

Contents

7. Interpersonal Qualities 191
Sharon R. Morgan

Background
Sample MBTI Items
The Prototype of the Empathic Teacher
The Interaction of Personality, Educational Preparation, and Burnout
The Struggle for Control
Conclusion
References

To lighten the affliction of insanity by all human means is not to restore the greatest of the divine gifts; and those who devote themselves to the task do not pretend that it is. They find their sustainment and reward in the substitution of humanity for brutality, kindness for maltreatment, peace for raging fury; in the acquisition of love instead of hatred; and in the acknowledgement that, from such treatment, improvement and hope of final restoration will come, if hope be possible. It may be little to have abolished from the madhouse all that is abolished, and to have substituted all that is substituted. Nevertheless, reader, if you can do a little in any good direction—do it. It will be much, some day.

Charles Dickens,

"A Curious Dance Around A Curious Tree"
Household Words, January, 1852

Preface

This is a methods book for teachers of children who have emotional disorders. The approach is eclectic and not biased toward any particular theory. The rationale for this type of approach is precisely because so many methods texts are biased and based on one theory alone. This text is strictly a "how to" book with little presentation of etiological theory. It does not, as many other books do, include extensive material explaining the causes and theory behind the behavior of children who are considered emotionally disturbed. There is a minimum of discussion about related methodological research. We wanted this text to talk directly and plainly to teachers and to clearly explain how to set up a classroom from the first day and carry through with the interventions on a daily basis. Certain interventions that have only been talked about in other texts are explained, in a step by step fashion, in such a way that teachers should be able to learn them well enough to implement them easily.

There is controversy over the use of the label "severely emotionally disturbed" or "behaviorally disordered," and we do not care for either one. We would rather use the term "socioemotional disorders." Both terms represent only two of the five major classes of DSM III-R disorders in infancy, childhood, and adolescence, and to use one or the other is limiting and obsolete. Nevertheless, throughout this book we have chosen to use the term "children with emotional disorders" because it is in keeping with the current federal terminology.

Many of the theoretical texts on the market refer to or structure their books based on the DSM III. While the DSM III-R is in now, it will soon be out with the forthcoming DSM IV, in which a number of disorders will simply no longer exist. We do not know where these disorders went. Individuals still suffer from the same problems but in the new manual the contributors do not see them as problems anymore. It seems that from time to time, some disorders are classified and then they are not, leaving the impression that some problems are just fads. So much for the importance of labels; time and again we have seen labels change.

In the real classroom, however, children have very definite problems, and the teacher cannot be concerned if it "fits" with what is in vogue. Teachers still must work with youngsters and their perception of reality, their behavior, their failures, and whatever is bothering them.

Both as professor and practitioners we have been concerned for quite some time with the one-dimensional approach that many methods books present. While they may discuss other approaches, nearly all of the actual "how to" material is based predominately on one theory or another. Teaching students with emotional disorders is a complex task and the youngsters in such a classroom present widely divergent problems and needs. And yet, the prospective teacher is usually confronted with instruction that implies that one type of approach or technique is the answer for all the students that might appear in a special education classroom with the title behaviorally disordered or emotionally disturbed.

Teacher trainees are often presented with choices that are supposedly in diametric opposition to one another, such as humanistic education or behavior modification. We do not believe in this opposition but instead believe that they can be blended to form a very strong program. We know that it takes many skills to work effectively with these students. Some of the youngsters have intradisturbances (emotional) and need help at a deeper level to resolve their conflicts so that they can grow emotionally and attain happiness and success; some of the youngsters need retraining because they have learned that using the most unpleasant and inappropriate behaviors (social) will often get them what they want even though it is not good for them; and some of the youngsters may be going through transient crises (social and emotional) and need a chance to get their behavior in order and to be maintained academically during this period so that they do not become lifelong failures.

In this book we have attempted to integrate many theories, allowing the teacher to take a multidimensional approach to educating students with various emotional disorders. We do not expect that all teachers will use all of the techniques all of the time. While one of us is primarily a professor and the other is primarily a practitioner, we are both, from time to time, practitioner trainers. Therefore, we are aware that some people are simply not comfortable with certain techniques even when they know how to use them.

In the training situation a common concern of teachers is, "I am afraid if I do such and such or say this or that, it will make the child worse—that I could do them even greater harm." They do not yet realize just how resilient these youngsters are and that the only thing that could cause more damage (aside from abusing them) is not being empathetic, genuine, and caring. In other words, attempting to implement interventions they do not really believe in and are not comfortable with is asking for failure and trouble. So, even though we believe that this approach is most powerful when used in its entirety, we also expect that teachers can be highly successful even if they pick and choose and do not use everything in the book. We do believe, however, that teachers need more than one way of doing things. Teachers most likely to have difficulties are those who rely on one approach exclusively.

In **Chapter 2** the philosophical basis and biases for this book are laid out. According to somebody's old saying, "You have to know where you are coming from before you can get to where you are going." From experience, we have found that many teachers have never taken the time, before acting, to pull together and consolidate their thoughts and beliefs. What do they really believe are the purposes and goals of having a special class for this type of student? How do they feel about these students? Should they have feelings or be totally objective? What expectations do they have for themselves as teachers of this type of handicapped student? What are their expectations for the students? And so forth. We think that **not** establishing a philosophical foundation for what one does is at least one of the factors contributing to teacher failure and teacher burnout. So our hope is that you agree with and believe what is said in Chapter 2. We are not necessarily trying to sell a total package, but we are definitely trying to sell love and empathy as the basic foundation for all classroom activity. One of the intentions of Chapter 2 is to assist prospective teachers in developing their own philosophical basis before they start teaching. Perhaps some will be in total agreement, some will only partially agree, and others might reflect and completely divert.

We are not just playing with words throughout this book. We have made very conscious and deliberate selections in our vocabulary usage because we intend, with considerable effort, to influence and hopefully change teachers' attitudes toward the work that they do with students who are experiencing emotional pain. So, in this book we talk about **correction** and not **punishment**. That is, after all, what improving mental health is all about. When a youngster does something that is not helping them to succeed and be happy, then what they need is correction and what we do is teach until they understand, and re-teach until it becomes internalized. The students learn what they have been doing or not doing that contributes to their own misery, and they re-learn more appropriate ways to handle situations so that they can be productive, loveable, and appreciated by more people than just their **special** teacher.

Chapter 3 focuses on the concept of teacher empathy and its importance in teaching these students. As adults, no matter our ages, nearly all of us can remember a wonderful teacher who made us feel good and want to be in school, and we can remember the battle-axes that did awful things to us, making us feel bad about ourselves, and spoiling school for a period of time. There is much to be learned from this material because, in crises situations, when teachers become emotionally over-extended, they often do in their classrooms what was done to them by their teachers. It is important to explore some of those past experiences, bring them back to a conscious level, and compare what we do now with what was done to us back then.

Most university students, especially those who are already teachers, are often surprised and shocked to find they are repeating the past, negatively and positively, in their classrooms. This experience highlights the power of modeling.

A model of teacher empathy is presented with illustrations of how each component of the model affects the functioning of the teacher and the students. The empathy of the teacher is demonstrated in concrete ways, which shows insight into the problems of the students. It is a necessary condition that makes the interventions work whether they are behavior modification or psychoeducational. The emphasis of this chapter is more on the teacher than the student. We believe that teachers must possess this affective quality in order to understand the students to such a degree that they can assist them in developing their own insight. The teacher's empathy and the student's insight is what differentiates this book from others and, we believe, makes this a most effective program.

It is insufficient to reach the "Oh now I understand" stage and then stop. "Oh now that they understand what are they going to do about it," is one purpose of this text: this is accomplished through a variety of interventions, at primarily the verbal level. The other major emphasis of this book is on academics, however, it continues to go hand in hand with affective development. The insight, the communication, and the learning do not have to be separate activities; they can be intertwined in such a way as to strengthen the students' cognitive and affective domains, and meet the requirements of the educational system that employs the teacher.

Over the years the authors have learned what we are sharing from many sources: the children we have worked with, our professors, our supervising teachers, our university students, books, and colleagues. We have received handouts at inservices, workshops, and presentations that had many helpful hints from teachers, counselors, psychologists, and other professionals. We have incorporated something from all of these sources. Most of these techniques are not new but have been discussed in a variety of textbooks and articles. What we have done, in many cases, is reconstituted some techniques in ways that we have found to be most effective, leaving some things out and adding a new twist here and there. Therefore, the reader will find in this book long passages without citations because, for the most part, we are talking about practices that are common knowledge. Where we can and when we know for sure, we reference those who originally created a particular intervention.

S.R.M.
J.A.R.

CHAPTER 1

Defining Emotional Disorders

SHARON R. MORGAN

There are a number of fine books on the market devoted to defining the varied emotional disorders of children and adolescents. Some of these follow the Diagnostic and Statistical Manual of Mental Disorders III or Diagnostic and Statistical Manual of Mental Disorders III-Revised in describing the specific disorders. Students who wish to have a greater understanding of the characteristics and descriptions of certain disorders should consult other books and consult the DSM III-R. A thorough understanding of childhood psychopathology, distinct from adult pathology, is necessary since children present unique differences and dilemmas. Although much of the terminology may sound the same there are often different indications and meanings for those terms in reference to children. Childhood psychopathology is different from adult psychopathology for several reasons.

1. Children are not constant. They change unpredictably, depending on circumstances and their feelings about the people who interview, test, or assess them. Children rarely refer themselves. The results of their assessments will often vary with the experience and personality of the examiner.
2. Children are immature. Constant change is normal as the child grows and matures. Diagnoses are not always final since the child may leave the family that is the source of the problem or a family member who is the source of the problem may leave.

3. A child's personality is not fixed. Classical forms of neuroses do not exist in children because they are still growing, changing, and maturing. Therefore, a fully-formed neurosis has not yet crystallized.
4. Children are still under the influence of their families. They are affected by the reality their parents provide, which makes it critical that the diagnostic process include the parents. In adults, external factors may exacerbate their disturbances, but the factors do not determine the kind or type of disturbance they have. Children, on the other hand, are influenced by external factors that may determine the kind or type of disturbance they develop. Their disturbances may be determined by the environment and by the child's own fluctuating personality.

It is important to establish a definition of the children we are proposing to help. In 1962, Kanner conducted a review and found that there was no discrete definition of the condition of emotional disturbance. He found that the term included children with behavioral problems as well as children with psychotic conditions. At one time, gifted children were considered deviant; some in our society wanted them sterilized. People, in general, believed that precocious children were gifted only for a short time and that eventually they would become insane or would turn to criminal behavior. An old axiom used to describe gifted children was "early to ripe, early to rot."

More recently, Morgan (1987) and Morgan and Wholeben (1984) found that different professional groups who work with children could not agree on the characteristics that indicated emotional disturbance. Regular teachers who had not taken even one special education class and school counselors identified certain behaviors as indicators of emotional disturbance. But these behaviors were predominantly representative of conduct disorders and behaviors that were disturbing to others. Special education teachers and clinical psychologists agreed on the behaviors that indicated emotional disturbance and put less emphasis on conduct-disorder behaviors. Regular teachers who had some training in special education were in a somewhat better position to identify behaviors indicating emotional disturbance. Overall, the groups were divided into those who could and those who could not distingush between disturbing and disturbed behaviors.

People are deviant if a society defines them as such. That is, if an individual deviates from the norm or what people expect, then that person will be negatively labeled. There is little room for differences in our society. Advertising tells us what we are supposed to like and what we are supposed to *be* like: neither too short nor too tall; well groomed; white; young; strong and assertive but not aggressive; industrious (willing to work around the clock seven days a week); family-oriented and from an intact family; intelligent; patriotic; at least moderately wealthy; sexy and thinking about sex most of the time; polite; helpful; well behaved; and thin. You simply cannot be "overweight" in this society, and by the looks of some of the models, there is no such a thing as being too thin. This is a strange, contradictory message to young girls who are emotionally disturbed and manifest their disturbances through anorexia nervosa. It is also a good example of the arbitrariness of defining emotional disturbances. Some of those models may indeed be anorexic, but because they have jobs that require extreme thinness and are highly paid for this very characteristic they are not considered emotionally disturbed. Girls and young women who are not in the business of modeling but who may be just as thin (and anorexic) are considered emotionally disturbed.

Cultures differ in what they consider aberrant behavior. In other words, certain behaviors are tolerated in some societies but not in others. For example, in some Latin American countries, noisier and more active children are tolerated to a greater extent than in the United States. Latin American children are allowed to be more dependent longer than children in this country. Noisy, active children in the United States will receive close scrutiny and probably become candidates for referral to some type of special education class. European societies differ in their expectations of children also. An acquaintance of mine lived in Germany for some time and had a son who was "active" and placed in special education for the behaviorally disordered. The parents took the child out of school and sent him to Belgium, where he was not considered a behaviorally disordered child and was placed in a regular class.

In this country, certain behaviors would be cause for concern and the individual in question would be labeled mentally ill or insane. Yet, in other countries the same behaviors may result in the individual's being considered blessed with special powers and worthy of prestige.

All of this means that deviance is a subjective concept that cannot be defined to fit children worldwide. It does not, however, negate the importance of a society's attempt to define what is considered aberrant. We have developed certain rules and laws so that we can live together in harmony and achieve certain societal goals. People who deviate from their society's standards do not live happily or peacefully with their immediate surroundings, are not productive, lack forward thrust, and have limited futures. Therefore, it is important to define what is unacceptable behavior in several contexts: home, community, and school.

DEFINITION

Several years ago, Bower (1969) developed a definition that could be used in all contexts but was especially important to educators. Bower's definition is used by the federal government with some modifications. From the Office of the Federal Register (1985) serious emotional disturbance is defined as such:

(i) The term means a condition exhibiting one or more of the following characteristics over a long period of time and to a marked degree, *which adversely affects educational performance*:

(A) An inability to learn which cannot be explained by intellectual, sensory, or health factors;

(B) An inability to build or maintain satisfactory relationships with peers and teachers;

(C) Inappropriate types of behavior or feelings under normal circumstances;

(D) A general pervasive mood of unhappiness or depression; or

(E) A tendency to develop physical symptoms or fears associated with personal or school problems.

(ii) *The term includes children who are schizophrenic. The term does not include children who are socially maladjusted, unless it is determined that they are seriously emotionally disturbed.* (p. 13)

Going through the definition step by step with examples may be helpful in understanding and using this definition to determine emotional disturbance in youngsters. The opening to the definition (i) states that:

. . . term means exhibiting one or more of the following characteristics . . .

Generally, the more characteristics involved, the more seriously disturbed the youngster. However, a child needs to manifest only one characteristic to be labeled, and multiplicity of symptoms should not be the exclusive criterion to judge the extent of a child's psychopathology. One symptom can work so efficiently that all of a child's anxieties are taken care of at once. School phobia is an example. In this case, the child is happy at home to an extent but has all of the problems bound up in one phobic situation with no spillage into other areas. Such children could be extensively disabled by one phobic symptom because they have many repercussions in terms of academic learning, peer relationships, social learning, the turmoil that is created at home surrounding the struggle to get the children to school, and how that affects family relationships. So, even though children may manifest one symptom, it may be so powerful that he or she is more disabled than other children manifesting more than one symptom (Clarizio & McCoy, 1983). There are other more straightforward examples of when one symptom, characteristic, or behavior may be observed that indicates a seriously troubled youngster: an attempted suicide, for example.

The last half of (i) states that the characteristic(s) must be

. . . over a long period of time . . .

This means it is a chronic behavior. According to the DSM III-R (1987), many symptoms must be observed at least six months, although some are given only one month. (Pica and bulimia are just two examples of the allowance of a 1-month duration.) Whether the time span for chronicity is 1 month or 6 months has to do with whether the behavior is life-threatening or not. For example, if the child is diagnosed as having Pica (eating animal droppings, paint, plaster, dirt, rocks, etc.), it would not be very sensible to wait 6 months to determine if the child has a problem that would cause concern and be considered an emotional disturbance. It does not take more than 1 month to make that determination.

School phobia, which according to the DSM III-R falls under Separation Anxiety Disorder, allows only 2 weeks duration. This period of time is not unreasonable considering the number of symptoms that cause the youngster excessive distress and the implications that this problem has in the school setting. It would not be reasonable to wait 6 months since doing so would mean the child would have missed almost the entire school year. It should be clear that the duration or chronicity of a problem as delineated in the DSM III-R is subjective, but the decisions have been made using reasonable considerations.

The next part of the definition states:

. . . to a marked degree . . .

which means acute. This refers to the level of seriousness of the disorder, including the impact on the child's ability to function, how many symptoms are involved, and how much distress the child is experiencing. In other words, how much interference is involved in the child's total life experience? Do the symptoms disable the child in all arenas of life (home, school, and community) and to what extent is the child disabled? The diagnostician must determine that the behaviors and emotions are seen at a significantly greater rate and/or intensity than would be normal in the youngster's peer group. The dysfunctional behaviors must be seen across different environments instead of being situation specific. Finally, the behaviors seen in the seriously emotionally disturbed child should occur infrequently in the nonhandicapped population. In many instances, adults are in the position to determine how acute a symptom is, and whether they think it requires intervention. Some children are able to make that determination also, but for the most part it is determined for them.

The definition continues:

. . . which adversely affects educational performance . . .

This means that the child's emotional disturbance should always result in lowered achievement, lowered grades, and/or dysfunctional behavior in academic situations. Evidence must be provided that demonstrates the child's disturbance interferes with classroom performance. It must be judged against a standard of reasonable progress, *not* optimal progress (Texas Education Agency, 1988).

The heart of this definition continues with a list of five general characteristics that will be elaborated upon with specific examples.

A. An inability to learn which cannot be explained by intellectual, sensory, or health factors;

This means the children are not learning at a reasonable rate for reasons unrelated to mental retardation, blindness, deafness, or severe health impairment. One example that cues the diagnostician or teacher that a child is emotionally disturbed—and not suffering from some other handicapping condition—is that on one day the child understands a math lesson perfectly and can do the work and on the next day acts as if the material has never been taught.

These youngsters are not good test takers. Generally, their anxiety is out of control under testing situations, and they will score quite poorly. Given the same tasks or problems under less stressful circumstances, where they feel it is not an evaluative process, they can perform.

Psychotic children are so out of touch with reality they are usually poor students in all academic subjects, although there are some severely disturbed students who latch onto one subject and do very well. Mathematics was chosen as the example subject, however, because if there are going to be academic difficulties they are usually in math. Reading is the second academic area in which these students have great difficulty. Much of this is attributed to their inability to sustain concentration, and reading and math require a clear mind. These students have minds cluttered with their personal emotional problems and are often overwhelmed with anxiety, which interferes to a very large extent with their ability to concentrate and think abstractly. Many people within the educational system are under the impression that youngsters with emotional disorders are mentally retarded. There are a number of reasons for this misconception. Some literature cites the group mean IQ and achievement test scores that these students have attained. With cross-categorical placement that is prominent in many school districts, the classrooms (self-contained and resource) that are for children labeled behaviorally disordered include children who are mildly/moderately mentally retarded and those whose primary disorder is learning disabilities. Naturally, if the scores of all these different handicapped students are taken as a group, then the youngsters with emotional disorders do appear to be low functioning intellectually. In cases in which there has been strict diagnoses and placement, many of these youngsters score low on IQ tests because of their emotional interferences. Their learning is inhibited for the same reason. In the right setting with the teacher running interference for their emotional interference, the students make great academic gains. Some of these students are, in fact, gifted and talented.

B. An inability to build or maintain satisfactory interpersonal relationships with peers and teachers;

There are some students (schizophrenic) who isolate themselves and never interact with peers or teachers. These are much easier to identify than the severely emotionally disturbed student who is seen interacting occasionally with peers and teachers. Some youngsters appear to make friends and may declare one day that certain children are their best friends and then turn around and do something so obnoxious to their "best friends" that those youngsters abandon the student and refuse to interact, or fights with others. These youngsters may have acquaintances, but these relationships are not permanent or as intense as friendships. Relationships with teachers should be viewed in terms of the adequacy of the student's relationship with the majority of the regular classroom teachers. These children may, however, be able to maintain a relationship with a teacher who has special training for working with emotionally disturbed students and who can accommodate their behavior and special needs.

C. Inappropriate types of behavior or feelings under normal circumstances;

Inappropriate behavior can be withdrawn, deviant, or bizarre behavior, not just aggressive or acting-out behavior. Some severely emotionally disturbed children express their inappropriate behavior or feelings through confused verbalizations, fantasizing, preoccupation with emotional conflicts in their artwork, written expressions, or other outlets.

The following is an example from my own experience with emotionally disturbed children in a classroom. Near the beginning of the school year, the principal visited the room. In regular classrooms, when the principal visits, the typical behavior of normal students is to put on their portraits of perfect angels. They raise their hands and are anxious to answer the teacher's questions and show their best sides to the principal. Not in my room. When the principal entered the class, Steve jumped to his feet and said, "What are you doing in my room, f—in' a——le?" Greg fell out of his desk to the floor and began crying. Sally got out of her desk and started dancing around the room, turning her backside to the principal and shaking it. Dale picked up the globe and threw it out of the window. Ricky ran to the closet to hide. And Timmy, who was already under his desk, began to slither around the floor and hiss like a snake. The principal left without a word. These are all prime examples of inappropriate behavior under normal circumstances.

D. A general pervasive mood of unhappiness or depression; or

Depression in children is often manifested with hyperactivity or anxiety behavior; however, some children seldom act out and appear always unhappy and depressed. The youngster never expresses joy or happiness. Another real life example would be the student Susan. Susan was hypersensitive and cried over innocuous statements or events. She cried copiously if her work was imperfect. Even an eraser smudge would bring torrents of tears. If the teacher made a general statement that the room was getting pretty messy, Susan would collapse with grief. Her unhappiness was general and pervasive and occurred over most, if not all, of her life situations. It was so marked that it impaired her academic functioning because she could rarely finish her work for fear of making a mistake.

The depressive mood should be atypical for the student's age. Adolescents tend to go through more periods of depression and with greater intensity than elementary school-age children. The extent of the depression should be judged in comparison with youngsters of the same chronological age.

E. A tendency to develop physical symptoms or fears associated with personal or school problems.

Many of these students manifest their emotional disturbances through physical symptoms. This is the most intricate part of the definition and requires sensitive awareness of what is really going on with the youngster. Some of these children have real physical problems that have been created by their disturbances. These are called psychophysiological disorders and include such things as ulcers, colitis, skin disorders, migraine headaches, and so forth. These are very real physical problems, and the teacher should consult the school nurse and the pediatrician. On the other hand, many of these children somatize their fears and problems and seem to have something that bothers them almost daily. They often use their physical complaints in order to avoid work. These children characteristically have senseless complaints. On one day, their ear lobes hurt along with aching toes. The next day their elbows feel "funny," and they complain of being sick to their stomachs. The physical symptoms appear intermittently, and there is the tendency to respond to stress with physical complaints, which become an habitual and persistent behavior pattern.

Other students manifest their emotional disturbance through fearful and withdrawn behavior. These youngsters may be unusually or pathologically anxious and fearful in all settings, to the extent that attendance and/or achievement are affected.

ii. The term includes children who are schizophrenic . .

Schizophrenic children are classified as psychotic because of their thought disorders, which are overly confused thought patterns, and impairments in reality testing where they have trouble separating reality from fantasy.

. . . The term does not include children who are socially maladjusted, unless it is determined that they are seriously emotionally disturbed.

This part of the definition excludes children who exhibit antisocial or delinquent behavior unless it can be demonstrated that these behaviors stem from serious emotional disturbance. For example, stealing may be a symptom of emotional disturbance, or it can be a straightforward delinquent act.

Children steal for more than one reason. One child may steal from the teacher because he or she really likes that teacher and wants something belonging to the teacher. They do not know how to let the teacher know their feelings in an appropriate way or may be afraid the teacher does not return their feelings.

Some children carry a feeling of emptiness or a sense of being disconnected. They often steal because they think that possessing some *thing* is going to take away that empty feeling. This feeling is seen frequently in emotionally disturbed children. Other children steal so they can give presents to classmates or teachers in order to be liked. They have low self-esteem and feel the only way they will be liked is if they give gifts to people. Finally, socially maladjusted, nondisturbed youngsters steal just because they want something they do not have and do not have the money to buy. The socially maladjusted youngster has no boundaries. Your posessions are theirs: They see it, they want, so they take it. Stealing and other antisocial acts are probably acceptable standards of behavior in their peer groups, homes, and neighborhood environments. Father deals drugs, mother sells herself for drugs, the peer group steals to buy drugs. These youngsters grow up with an entirely different value system than the general population and are usually only remorseful if caught and punished.

TEACHER CONSIDERATIONS

Before being placed in special classrooms, all children must have a diagnosis from the DSM III-R. However, there are considerations that a teacher may note before agreeing in a meeting to a special education placement. In observing the child, there are three areas that need to be attended to.

INTERFERENCE WITH SELF GROWTH, DEVELOPMENT, AND LEARNING

The teacher must observe and note if the behaviors exhibited are interfering with normal growth and developmental patterns and with the child's ability to learn. You ask yourself whether the child is growing (physically, intellectually, socially) and whether he or she is going through the normal developmental sequences. Is this child learning at an acceptable rate and making reasonable academic progress? If the answer to these questions is no, then the youngster is a candidate for a more thorough diagnostic workup and probably will need a special placement.

INTERFERENCE WITH THE GROWTH, DEVELOPMENT AND LEARNING OF OTHERS

In a classroom, all children must be taken into account. Perhaps the child in question is growing, developing, and learning, but that child's behavior is interfering with the growth, development, and learning of others in the class. Assuming that the teacher has tried to alleviate the situation, then this cannot be allowed to go on. A youngster is a candidate for a special

placement if he or she is interfering with other's growth (physical, intellectual, social) and the attainment of normal developmental sequences and
other children are experiencing interference with their ability to handle
academic work to where they are not making reasonable progress.

INTERFERENCE WITH TEACHERS' ABILITY TO FUNCTION AND DO THEIR JOB

This should only be a consideration if every attempt has been made to
alleviate the child's problem *and* the teacher has attempted to change in
some way to be more accommodating, accepting, understanding, and
helpful to the child. In other words, some behaviors are just plain irksome
to a teacher but the behaviors are not truly significant or serious enough to
warrant putting a child in a special placement. However, if all the possibilities have been exhausted and the teacher cannot do the best job possible
with all of the children, then it is necessary to consider a special placement
or a different placement for the child.

OTHER CRITERIA FOR CONSIDERATION

Other investigators (Clarizio & McCoy, 1983; Jessor & Jessor, 1977; Quay &
Werry, 1979) have proposed additional criteria that indicate disturbance
and would necessitate referral for a more complete diagnostic workup.

AGE DISCREPANCY

Most children outgrow some habits and behaviors by certain ages. Even
though children stop these behaviors at different ages, there is not a great
gap in ages at which children stop most of these behaviors. For instance,
clinging, soiling, and public masturbation are seen in very young children
(before the age of 5), and these behaviors are not considered unusual or
devient. However, by the time they reach school age, most have stopped
these behaviors, and to observe such things in an older, school-age child is
cause for concern.

FREQUENCY OF OCCURRENCE OF SYMPTOM(S)

Under great stress, many children will regress to previous patterns of
behavior (e.g., bed wetting). The child would not be considered emotionally disturbed if the behavior is isolated and recovery is quick. We become

concerned if symptoms occur under minimal stress, which, considering the times we live in, means often (e.g., if a child over the age of 5 or 6 begins to wet during the day). This might happen each time the teacher begins the math lesson, if the child is called upon to read out loud, or if the child is not chosen to play with a group.

NUMBER OF SYMPTOMS

Usually, the more symptoms a child has, the more disturbed the child. However, the multiplicity of symptoms should not be the only criteria to judge the extent of the child's disturbance. As mentioned earlier, one single symptom (school phobia) can bind together all of the anxieties a child has and cause the child to be severely disturbed.

DEGREE OF SOCIAL DISADVANTAGE

It must be determined if there is a cycle of secondary situations occurring that strengthen and perpetuate the symptoms. For example, one child may be so aggressive that he or she angers others, which consequently continues to precipitate fights. Others with school phobias, become so far behind in their work that they fear returning to school and then the phobia becomes even stronger. Other children who have the problem of day wetting or soiling become very unpopular and alienated from other children, and thus have extreme difficulty developing peer relationships.

INNER SUFFERING

These are children who feel ashamed and embarrassed about secret behaviors and are most often overlooked because they do not bother others. Many times we learn about their secret sufferings when they reveal their problems to someone they have gotten to know well. Here, we should refer back to the teacher consideration of whether the child is growing, developing, and learning. These children are usually in trouble in one of those areas, if not all three.

INTRACTABILITY OF BEHAVIOR

The consideration here is how persistent the behavior is despite efforts of the child and others to change them. Some children work hard to change their problem habits and behaviors, and they may have had teachers, counselors, and parents working with them without success in changing the behaviors. The behavior is considered intractable or unmanagable if they have received help and the behavior(s) do not change.

GENERAL PERSONALITY APPRAISAL

The first six criteria concern symptoms. This category refers to general adjustment rather than isolated symptoms. We are viewing children generally to observe whether or not they have developed relationships with family, peers, and authority figures. Their relationships should contain affection and give pleasure. Next, we observe if youngsters are generally satisfied with who they are. We are concerned if they are not receiving gratification from school work. Finally, we need to know if they are growing, developing, progressing, and whether their behavior is changing.

ETIOLOGY

One of the most common questions that people ask about emotionally disturbed children is, "How did they get that way?" This is not a book of theories, but a few words about cause or etiology might be useful before launching into the interventions that should be successful in working with emotionally disturbed children. Behavior is multidirectional, and no one theory can explain completely the different types of emotional problems that children have. The causes can be grouped into six basic areas:

CONSTITUTIONAL FACTORS

This refers to traits that are present at birth that affect behavior. They are the factors related to genetic influence and the child's physical health. Every child is born with a different temperament. This is something that any mother or neonatal nurse can tell you. Even as newborns they are given discriptors about their temperament (personality). Some are described as naturally fussy, happy, restless, quiet, good, or difficult. To illustrate what this can mean in terms of an infant's future: A child may be born with an insatiable hunger drive due to a difference in physiological functioning of the body. The child may develop a sense of distrust and dissatisfaction with the environment and fail to form the necessary dependent and close relationship with the parents. The parents may become increasingly frustrated in trying to meet the demands of the child and reject or develop some other negative reactions toward their child, thus producing a disturbance.

Another example would be the hypersensitive child who finds pain rather than pleasure in being touched. This causes some parents to abandon efforts to establish a relationship with the child.

Some hyperactive children receive overstimulation from their own bodies and find it hard to relate satisfactorily to the environment. These children may attempt to handle strong impulses and may develop rigid controls over their feelings and activities, thus losing the quality of flexibility of personality.

Different tendencies equal different effects on parental reaction, depending greatly on behaviors valued by the parents. The innate constitutional differences affect such things as their ability to adjust to change, to resist change, their sensitivity to stimulation, the ability to concentrate, and the length of attention span.

BRAIN SYNDROMES AND BIOCHEMICAL DIFFERENCES

In this area are the children who fall into the categories of disabling conditions such as autism, schizophrenia, and other types of psychotic conditions. The causes are related to impairment of brain tissue brought on by traumatic accidents, illnesses, and disturbances in physical functioning of the metabolism and/or body chemistry, as well as deficiencies in nutrition.

The severity of the condition is not always due to the extent of the damage. It is sometimes related to how the child and/or the family interprets the disorder, as well as the child's basic personality patterns.

REACTIONS TO LIFE SITUATIONS

This area concerns disrupting crises that bring about strong emotional reactions in the child. It includes situations such as separation and divorce; the loss of emotional availability of the parents because of death, physical or mental illness; losses of siblings, friends, classmates, teachers, and other significant individuals; parental alcoholism and/or drug abuse; latch-key children; children from nontraditional families, adopted children, parental child stealing, and so forth.

FAMILY BEHAVIOR PATTERNS

This category includes families where there is a lack of close, dependable, warm relationships between the child and the parents, and/or between the parents themselves. In these families, there often exist the major types of child abuse (physical, sexual, emotional). It is not uncommon that the parents lack a cohesive relationship. In fact, the relationship is frequently pathological presenting too much dependency, great hostility, scapegoating, and so on.

SOCIOLOGICAL PATTERNS

This area includes families that are struggling to make adaptations to poverty situations which tend to foster lifestyles related to depression, poor impulse control, aggression, and surrender to the overwhelming odds against them. The major styles of these families revolve around drugs, alcohol, prostitution, welfare existence, and absence of a family life involving sharing and consideration for the well-being of family members.

ECOLOGICAL AND ECONOMIC STRESS

This area refers to the pressures imposed on people by the environment meaning that, for whatever reasons, they have few or not enough coping skills to manage these stressors. Environmental stressors such as crowded urban life and the factors related to city living; air, water, and noise pollution; chronic illnesses; continuing financial pressure; frequent moving; difficult jobs, changing jobs, and losing jobs. These affect some more than others, creating emotional problems, because we all have different tolerance and frustration levels for stress.

SUMMARY

This chapter noted that normality/abnormality is a subjective concept. However, since we must have structure and rules in society, there must be some standard by which we can all live and function harmoniously. Therefore, the attempt was made to thoroughly explain the current accepted definition provided by the Office of Special Education and Rehabilitation. Included in this chapter are other considerations the teacher must attend to and other criteria that help to explain (not necessarily define) emotional disturbance. A brief account of different etiological factors were discussed to provide a background to the different types of intervention strategies that will follow. The following chapters attempt to provide interventions that will be most suitable for working with children who have different types of emotional disorders.

REFERENCES

American Psychiatric Association. (1987). *Diagnostic and statistical manual of mental disorders.* Revised. Washington, D.C.: American Psychological Association.

Bower, E. M. (1969). *Early identification of emotionally handicapped children in school.* (2nd ed.) Springfield, ILL: Charles C. Thomas.

Clarizio, H. F., & McCoy, G. F. (1983). *Behavior disorders in children.* (3rd ed.) New York: Harper & Row.

Jessor, R., & Jessor, S. (1977). *Problem behavior and psychosocial development: A longitudinal study of youth.* New York: Academic Press.

Kanner, L. (1962). Emotionally disturbed children: A historical review. *Child Development, 33,* 97–102.

Morgan, S. R. (1987). The ability of teachers to distinguish disturbed from disturbing behavior. *Journal of Instructional Psychology, 14*(3), 118–124.

Morgan, S. R., & Wholeben, B. E. (1984). Psychologists', counselors', and teachers' ratings of emotional problems in children. *Journal of Human Behavior & Learning, 1*(2), 19–26.

Office of the Federal Register National Archives and Records Administration. (1985). Code of federal regulations. Washington, D.C.: U.S. Government Printing Office.

Quay, H. C., & Werry, J. S. (1979). *Psychopathological disorders of childhood.* New York: Wiley.

Texas Education Agency and Texas Department of Mental Health and Mental Retardation Joint Tast Force On Emotional Disturbance. (1988). *Guidelines for assessment of emotional disturbance.* Austin, TX.

CHAPTER 2

Assertive Love

SHARON R. MORGAN

*Love is being on the side of
the other person. Love is
approval. I know that
children learn slowly that
freedom is something
totally different from
license. But they can learn
this truth and do learn it.
In the end, it works
—nearly every time.*
A. S. NEILL (1951)

ORIENTATION TO THE BOOK

After this opening statement, some will immediately assume that this is a book that follows completely the principles of "open" education or "humanistic" education. Others will be disappointed to learn that I do not reside in one camp or another. There is no adherance reflected here to one line of thought or one theoretical approach in working with children who have emotional disorders. Morse (1984) has said that:

When any human riddle becomes too complex for satisfactory comprehension, we reduce it to simplistic terms and superficial explanations. Our credulity dispels the actual ambiguity and produces psycho-religion. . . . Those who are the most uneasy about the ultimate truth of their beliefs want to prevent the challenge of contrary ideas. . . . the truth will eventually be distilled out over time . . . everything works and nothing works. [pp. 107 & 108]

This text is for teachers who need many skills for working with this difficult population of youngsters. The strategies derived from one theoretical approach do not always work with all children all of the time. Occasionally, there are some children who do not respond to any teaching intervention. This book is an eclectic approach to teaching these youngsters because that is the only reasonable way to effectively reach and help most of them. It is only reasonable that the teacher uses whatever works, whether interventions come from behavioral, psychoeducational, humanistic, psychodynamic, psychoanalytic, gestalt, or grandma's theory. I realize some of the potential dangers of eclecticism; teachers can become jacks of all trades but masters of none. We attempt here to present the best of all worlds in the most useful way. Many techniques grounded in any particular theory are not worth learning and cannot be put to use in a classroom. So there is very little value in being "purists."

Eclecticism is valid because behavior is multidirectional. Emotional disorders can spring from several sources: Some are from internal psychological dynamics; some are from genetic and biochemical differences; some are from innate constitutional differences; some are learned through reinforcement; some are from external forces that even the adults in the children's lives do not understand; and some are from combinations of two or more of these reasons.

Behaviorists have been the most adept at presenting their techniques so systematically that they can be easily understood and used by most teachers. One area where the field has fallen short is in the precise teaching of the complex methods that are referred to as psychoeducational, psychological, and humanistic interventions. Most texts describe these interventions but do not explain them. By now, it should be obvious that I think there is merit in all of the theories in terms of explaining causation and using certain interventions. Therefore, unabashedly, I will state that this book is *eclectic*!

GENERAL AMNESTY AMONGST OURSELVES

Over the years, behaviorists, humanists, psychoeducationalists, and others have been at odds with one another, each trying to dominate the field with their theories and interventions. My proposition is that they all have made tremendous contributions to the understanding and treatment of children with emotional problems. However, no one theory alone provides the woof and warp for the education of these students. Some things from the behavioristic approach work with some children some times, and the same can be said for the humanistic and psychoeducational approaches.

Eclecticism is a dirty word to some people, and yet the most experienced and knowledgable teachers know that it takes more than one approach and many techniques to be fully effective with our clientele. But something happens to these teachers when they go to graduate school. People begin to play mind games with them, and when experienced teachers say what they know is true, that they use a bit of everything, that everything has something of value, that they are eclectic, then they are derided and accused of coping out. With that kind of pressure, it is not long before they begin to declare I am a this or a that and anything else isn't worth the time.

If we could really be honest with ourselves we would admit that, in fact, behavioral interventions are wasted efforts if the child never develops insight, internal control, and the ability to communicate. In fact, you cannot even begin to use psychoeducational interventions to develop insight and communication when children are swinging from the rafters or on the floor biting your ankles. In fact, humanistic interventions to build self-esteem will not take hold when the child still cannot read or write a simple paragraph. So, can we call a general amnesty and admit that we all have things of value to offer and that not one of us alone has the panacea? We need to get back to what our purpose really is: to help the students that need and depend on us.

PHILOSOPHY OF THIS BOOK

A philosophy and rationale should exist for the choices we make in terms of how we will work with children. The philosophy of this book starts with the premise that you must love these children to work effectively with them. It used to be that when students made application to be educated as teachers they were asked, "Do you like kids? " It used to be that when an individual made application for a teaching position they were asked, "Do you like kids?" I have not heard of that question being asked for quite some time now. It is an important question and should be asked before anything else. The teacher must truly and deeply care about these students and be able to show it in concrete, empathic ways.

I agree with many of the things Buscaglia (1982) has written on love because he has dealt with a number of truths; however, I know it is not enough to tell teachers that love is important. It certainly is not enough to suggest that all we really need to do is look at each other, touch each other, listen to each other, and hug each other. So even though I believe you must love children, I am also in agreement with a statement Bettelheim (1949) made years ago through the title of one of his books: *Love Is Not Enough*. And while love is **not** enough, there isn't anything that takes the place of its power, so it is the necessary prerequisite to teaching.

There is an old story about a child psychiatrist who comes home to his newly paved driveway and finds his neighbor's child tromping through the wet cement. Irately, he screams and scolds the boy for what he has done. The child's mother hearing that her son is being scolded yells to the doctor, "You sir, of all people, should love and understand children! " The psychiatrist shouts back at his neighbor, "I do, Madam, in the abstract, but not in the concrete!"

When teachers leave the university they often find themselves in the same dilemma. They have read a great deal about children, looked at films, and listened to their professors talk about them. These children are portrayed in a variety of ways. So some teachers leave the university having learned how to love them in the abstract but not in the concrete. The theories which at one time inspired them, now seem to have abandoned them as they discover that children do not respond well to theories. As some students tromp through the classrooms, with seemingly little concern for others, teachers find that it is quite difficult to love them hour after hour, and day after day. Love in the abstract is easy, but love in the concrete—that requires skills.

To love appropriately and nonartificially comes naturally to some people but not to others. Some may feel love for a child but do not know how to show it. These are people who confuse love with being a buddy to the child. They think that it is not professional and does not fit the **role** of teacher. So, they fear that they would lose their authority and the control over students that they have. This book has nothing to do with all of the saccharin, trendy prescriptions that were passed around in the 1970's.

WHAT IS ASSERTIVE LOVE?

Generally, parents have children and love them totally, unconditionally, and irrationally. Teachers, on the other hand, choose to love and to give a great deal to children who are not their own. A teacher's love for students is more structured, more directed, and more rational than parental love, which is why it is called assertive love. At the core of assertive love is the teacher's genuine caring and absolute determination to make the children more competent learners and to improve their mental health status.

To demonstrate assertive love, the teacher must know:

1. How to assist a youngster in gaining self-control.
2. How to listen and empathize.
3. How to build self-esteem.
4. How to communicate and teach youngsters to become realistic, academically competent, and productive.

This is part of what is meant by assertive love. Providing appropriate love for these children requires precise skills, which can be taught and learned the same way that other skills are taught and learned.

Assertive love includes another component, which are the teachers' feelings for their work. Teaching is not an all-giving proposition, because to prosper (in the sense of professional success) and to flourish (in the sense of mental health and happiness) teachers must be getting something out of it that is most satisfying. Teachers who are there to give something of lasting value to their students *and* to get something in return expend tremendous energy. These teachers are not on power trips; rather, they are child advocates. They are in this field to work with human beings and the human condition, and not just to teach a favorite subject. They do not feel like they have to work with others who have less of something so that they can feel that they are more. They love to teach and do not use it as a stepping stone because they believe that what they are doing is already the most important and exciting work that one can do. It is this assertive love for what they do that distinguishes one teacher who just has a job from a teacher who has become elevated to a true professional. Administrators know that the best teachers they have are the ones who love the kids and love their work.

A teacher who practices assertive love is one who teaches others to love. In some cases, such teachers even teach parents how to love their own children. They teach the students to love themselves, to love each other, to love their classroom, and to love their work (or to find work that they can love). These teachers create an environment in which kids learn love.

WHAT ASSERTIVE LOVE IS NOT

Assertive love is not a program without structure and limits. It is not an "open" education program in the sometimes-misunderstood sense that the children can or cannot do whatever they want whenever they want. Young people want and need structure in their lives, and although they frequently pretend quite the opposite, they want and need limits on their behavior. So, while this program advocates love, it does not imply license to do whatever comes to mind.

Assertive love is not assertive discipline because I do not adhere to the frame of mind that the classroom belongs only to the teacher. All of the rules of assertive discipline do not apply to the students we are trying to help. Assertive love is not tough love because we cannot count on a whole community of people to help us with our students when things get tough and when we feel very angry. Aside from that, I believe that it is important for our students to see how a rational adult copes with intense feelings. All of the passionate feelings of human beings cannot be eliminated no matter how much we would like it that way sometimes; they are a fact of life. I do not believe in cool, calculated punishment. Instead, I think that a reasonably planned program of correction is the most effective way to cope with inappropriate activity or inactivity. Assertive love is not a scared straight tactic because I do not believe in terror; I believe in teaching.

THE NEED TO TALK ABOUT LOVE

To write about love was not something that I took on lightly. It is a considerable risk to present this to the professional community at a time when it is so engrossed in becoming scientific. I chose to talk about it anyway because relatively few, if any, in our field really believe that there is no place for love in education.

The decision to talk about love is also partly a reaction to the strenuous attempts to present education as if it were a science where teachers should and can control everything, as if they were in laboratory situations functioning as technicians. Teaching teachers that the classroom is *their* kingdom where they are the bosses is another idea with which I do not agree. Presenting the classroom to teachers as a laboratory or a kingdom is a mistake. Attempting to make them believe that they are scientific technicians or royal rulers is misleading. Either role implies that everything is totally within the control of the teacher, and it is not. For instance, I know that in some cases there is little we can do about our students' home situations or their status in their communities —both of which have a tremendous impact on their lives.

Teachers who believe they can control all are then saddled with the responsibility of *trying* to control everything for all of their students, as well as control all the factors that affect their own personal lives. That is a burden few teachers can withstand. Many of today's management systems call for teachers to manipulate and control others by using their authority and suggesting they take charge as the boss. How quickly we learn that our students do not respond well to bosses and that what we thought we manipulated did not transfer to other situations and settings and did not last as long as expected.

The astute teacher learns that these children are a lot like us; they respond to people who are authentic and caring. They want, just as we do, to know that people care about them, first as a person and not just a piece of behavior occupying space in somebody else's classroom.

My philosophy is that teachers have a leadership role that enables them to provide an environment in which students can learn what they need to learn. Therefore, a teacher's authority is used not to control everything and everybody, but to facilitate for others so that the things that *need* to be done *can* be.

It is unfortunate, that as a professional group, we have been so maligned and unappreciated that we feel pressured to become something we can never truly be, scientists. We are not, of course, artists either; we are a hybrid of both. What we have to offer, and have been offering, is not pap and because unknowledgable people accuse us of that does not make it so. We have a scientific basis for what we do, and we take those laws and principles and implement them with our creativity and talents. Attempting to deny this only takes us farther away from what we really do best, and then we actually do become second-rate professionals.

Another reason for my giving this attention to love is out of a reaction to developing attitudes that suggest teaching these children is a negative venture. For example, books on the issue use in their titles terms such as *conflict* and *survival*. Phrases are used such as being "on the front line," or "in the trenches." These words express an attitude and give an impression that teachers are in an adversary role with everyone in their environment; teaching emotionally disturbed children is like being at war with the world. The choice of words conveys a certain mentality and attitude that one has toward people. Even if we start out with different feelings about individuals we work with, but continue using a certain vocabulary day after day, then over time our feelings begin to coincide with the terminology. After all, isn't that what Michenbaum's (1977) Cognitive Behavior Modification is really all about? Say something enough, reinforce ourselves when we say it, and eventually the behavior or attitude will be internalized and we believe what we are saying.

This is a great concern because out of this attitude has come the proliferation of " techniques" that are basically punitive and born out of hostility. One underlying assumption of these interventions is that children with emotional disorders cannot be communicated with so that they learn to take charge of themselves and act appropriately. Another assumption is that these students have no understanding of adult expectations, concerns, needs, or feelings. Their posture toward youngsters who have been placed in special classes because of their social or psychological transgressions is that they really are the undesirables of the world. For example, one author (Grossman, 1972) entitled his book *Nine Rotten Lousy Kids*.

Some systems in public schools treat these youngsters as if they were criminals instead of students with a handicapping condition. They are brought into the special class, immediately put in cubicles, sometimes referred to as "isolation," or "time-out," or any number of other euphemisms. They are given no privileges (this means not being able to go to the bathroom or get a drink), and the youngster has to work his or her way up to getting these privileges (or, in other words, earn the right to being treated like a human being). Through this system, teachers have become jailers. An even more pressing example of the current punitive and hostile attitudes that some educators have toward youngsters took place in a school in Texas during the spring of 1985. A 13-year-old boy was "suspected" of possessing marijuana (he did not) and the principal allowed a school guard to strip and conduct a body-cavity search of the youngster. This vulgar treatment was perpetrated on a child in a public school, not on a hardened, dangerous criminal in a prison.

Other "systems" currently in vogue instruct teachers to become tougher: "These are *my* expectations in *my* classroom. Once—you've been warned, and twice—you're out. " Putting all the "don'ts" on a bulletin board is fair warning. Educators become wardens who make the final decision on the disposition of the child's case: short-term suspension or expulsion. The classroom becomes a place for the teacher, and students really are not participants in the educational process. We have practically returned to an earlier concept where education was thought of as being for the privileged and not a right for all children. The privileged, of course, are those who do not have emotional problems, or those who are so terrified of people in the environment they dare not even look sideways. You have to wonder how much learning goes on in these classrooms, or at the very least, if there is any joy left in learning or in teaching.

One of the major problems with these negative, punitive approaches to youngsters (aside from the killing of the spirit) is that teachers get back what they expect. If you treat them as criminals, expecting them to act like criminals, they will act like criminals. If you take everything away from them at the outset, then there is nothing to lose by acting inappropriately and seemingly very little to gain that is of real value. Another misunderstanding is that some believe that these youngsters cannot recognize the things that are of real value. I have not found that to be true. Indeed, these youngsters behave in certain ways and think about some things quite differently so that they appear to be "human riddles." Doubtless, they present us with many puzzles, but they are human and capable of more than they are often credited with.

More importantly, these negative approaches to children never deal with more than surface behavior. If these are special classrooms, then shouldn't these youngsters be getting something special? Any good teacher can be taught surface-management techniques. So, if that is all that we are committed to offering children with emotional disorders, then we should just leave them in regular classes, for there is no need for specialized, highly educated teachers. Obviously, I do believe there should be special teachers who do something special. It is my contention that the teachers of these children are obligated and have the responsibility to provide more and do more than what is presently going on in many classrooms across the nation.

WHO WANTS TO BE A TEACHER AND WHY?

Prospective teachers have declared a variety of interesting reasons for why they wish to enter education. Some of the most intriguing statements have come from the individuals who think they want to teach youngsters with emotional disorders.

Most of the prospective teachers who come to us for education in this very exciting and dynamic field of special education are uniquely gifted and creative people who can do more than train youngsters to sit in their seats and raise their hands. But by virtue of the education they received, or lack of it, or because their school district demands they implement a "canned" program, that is what most of them end up doing. Teachers did not enter into this particular branch of special education to learn only that.

These children are exciting and dynamic, and the people who are attracted to them are exciting and dynamic individuals as well. Most who enter this area of special education do so because it is intriging and the students are captivating—they do present many riddles to be solved. Teachers knew there was more to it than any other area of education. I believe teachers want more from us in their education so that they can give more to their students.

One wonders why anybody would want to be a teacher these days when there are so many criticisms of education and so many apparent unresolved issues. For instance, there is obvious widespread concern over the issue of managing children's behavior in all contexts: the classroom, at home, and in the community. This is evident by the number of books on the market for educators addressing the topics of discipline, management, and control. I believe there is a pervasive problem in the schools. I have asked myself just what has gone wrong in education. Why is there such a preoccupation with classroom discipline and management? Most university teacher preparation programs have at least one course pertaining to behavior management. Yet, whenever teachers are asked for topics they would like to have presented in inservices, behavior management is nearly always at the top of the list. Professionals are criss-crossing the country, presenting their work on discipline, management and control, and garnering handsome compensation for repeating most of what teachers have already heard or instinctively knew and did in the first place. I have wondered why it is that teachers never seem to get enough information on this subject so that they finally feel satisfied that they can interact competently with youngsters who have difficulty being appropriate.

I have used the term *interact competently* rather than manage or control. This language represents the attitudes and philosophy I have about working with children. If we know how to interact competently with another human being, of any age, then management and control seldom becomes an issue of great concern. I suspect that this is one of the reasons why teachers apparently never feel comfortable in their abilities to work with students who have more than just surface behavior problems.

FROM THIS POINT ON

Although I admire Canter for his work on discipline, and Buscaglia for his work on love, this book is not a comprise or a co-mingling of their work; neither is it totally new. It is the regeneration of interventions that have proved useful in helping children with emotional disorders. Some of the interventions in this text have been discussed briefly in other books. In general, they are not described well enough for teachers to learn how to use them. Other interventions, for the most part, are not even presented in books for teachers; they have been reserved for psychologists or counselors. Over the years, I have adapted them so that they can be useful classroom techniques that teachers can learn and successfully implement.

I am not attempting to change the nature of teachers or give them new titles. If we can contribute to their preparation as better and more effective helpers, their titles hardly matter except for when they apply for jobs. Hobbs (1981) has referred to the most effective special teachers as teacher-counselors and says that they are the ones who operate outside of the usual teacher role. There is no reason that teachers cannot learn to use these interventions effectively in a classroom. Whatever one wishes to call these helpers: teacher-counselors, teacher-therapist, special teachers, or teacher-teachers is not really important; if they are prepared properly they are teaching and being therapeutic. Psychologists and other mental health facilitators are the ones who really should bear in mind that what they are doing in the therapeutic process is functioning as teachers. They are helping their clients learn more about themselves and teaching them how to cope. All of the psychotherapy approaches are really teaching strategies. Although therapists would be loath to admit it or be named or labeled as such, they are, in every sense of the word, teachers.

Even though I know there will not be consensus in how I perceive the teacher's role, I have no hesitation in stating that I think therapeutic intervention is a major function of teachers of students with emotional disorders. The intent of this book then is to put together some of the best interventions for bringing structure to a classroom and facilitating the academic and affective development of children and adolescents. The emphasis of this book will be on how to implement these interventions that are the components of what I have called assertive love, which requires empathy. I want teachers to learn how to interact competently and empathically.

PRECAUTIONS

There are two promises I will not make in this book. I do not promise that if you use every single intervention in this book all youngsters will eventually respond and "get well. " There will always be some children who do not respond to anything. Their behaviors and feelings are intractible. That is a hard fact that you will have to face sooner or later. These youngsters may someday, later in their lives, for some unknown reason, turn out okay, or they may not. They may grow up, and through a series of encounters with significant people, or by having gone through psychotherapy, or winning a lottery, or for no particular rhyme or reason become responsible, healthy adults. A study by Lewis (1965) demonstrated that 70% of the children who remained on a waiting list for therapy became better without intervention. Others may be incapacited and atypical for their entire lives. You will probably never know the final outcome of any of the youngsters you have worked with. That is another hard fact you will have to accept. It goes with the territory of teaching and is probably one of the reasons that teaching is a difficult profession. It is not like being an architect where you sit in an office and design shopping malls and then some day later, when it is completed, go out look at what you designed, and walk away satisfied that you did your job just the way it was intended. You seldom get to see the final results of your work as the children grow and move out of your life.

The second promise I will not make is that you are going to like all of your students. Unless you are a computer in disguise, there will be youngsters whom you simply cannot abide, no matter how hard you " try." The reasons we do not like certain children are not always clear. The child you do not like may pick his/her nose, throw tantrums, and spit on you, but then there are other children who do the same things and you still do like them. Sometimes, it is just the "persona" of a particular child that makes him /her unlikable to you, and nothing that child does seems acceptable. When we were children we tried to like liver but trying did not change the taste. The only reason we ate liver was because our parents made us eat liver. And that was that. Every bite went down agonizingly slow and threatened to come back up. But, if we were obedient children we ate the stuff anyway. Now we are adults and we don't have to eat liver if we don't want to, but we have jobs where we have to teach children we don't like whether we want to or not. There will be days when the very thought of facing a particular child will bring back the familiar feeling that something is threatening to come back up, and you are just going to have to swallow it and go to work anyway. You can still learn to use assertive love and **interact competently** with that child.

In the following chapters, I will give you some ideas of how to better cope with these two issues. However, I still am not promising that I can help you to overcome these frustrations every time—maybe just some of the time.

REFERENCES

Bettelheim, B. (1949). *Love is not enough*. New York: Free Press.
Buscaglia, L. (1982). *Living, loving, and learning* . New York: Fawcett Columbine.
Grossman, H. (1972). *Nine rotten lousy kids*. New York: Holt, Rinehart, & Winston.
Hobbs, N. (1981). The role of insight in behavior change: A commentary. *American Journal of Orthopsychiatry* , 51(4), 632–635.
Lewis, W. W. (1965). Continuity and intervention in emotional disturbance: A review. *Exceptional Children* , 31(9), 465–475.

Meichenbaum, D. B. (1977). *Cognitive behavior modification*. New York: Plenum Press.

Morse, W. C. (1984). Personal perspective. In B. Blatt & R. Morris (Eds.), *Perspective in special education: Personal orientations* (pp. 101–124). Glenview, ILL: Scott, Foresman and Company.

Neill, A. S. (1951). *Summerhill: A radical approach to child rearing*. New York: Hart Publishing Company.

CHAPTER 3

The Fundamental Element of the Teaching Process: Empathy

SHARON R. MORGAN

Empathy is critical to good teaching, especially to teaching emotionally disturbed students. We work with youngsters who perceive their worlds differently than most people do. Teachers who work with these children must have insight and understanding. Empathy provides the ability to know the students' world in the way that they live it, to interpret that understanding back to the student, and then provide boundaries of reality so that they can function more competently. In a classroom, the teacher must possess empathy and demonstrate it, and the children must learn to demonstrate empathy with others.

The first part of this chapter discusses the components of teacher empathy: It is a model of what goes into being an empathic teacher for emotionally disturbed children. This is followed by some concrete examples of what empathy is and is not and an activity to help develop sensitivity or enhance empathy. Later in the chapter is an example of classrooms that seem to be more conducive to developing empathy in emotionally disturbed children. Other chapters in this book are related to the components of the teacher empathy model.

WHAT IS EMPATHY AND WHERE DOES IT COME FROM?

There are several unanswered questions about empathy. Is empathy something we gain through experience? Are we all born with empathy that either grows or diminishes over time? If empathy is not there in the first place, can we develop it? Hoffman (1978) wrote a lengthy article on empathic arousal and development. He believes it exists in infants where it begins through conditioning. Empathetic and sympathetic distress occur along with a feeling of guilt, which becomes the motivational base for prosocial behavior. No one knows whether this is true. We have seen films of very young abused children (toddlers) interacting with their abusing mothers and becoming very attentive to their mothers' distress and trying to provide comfort. Whether empathy is there from birth or comes along some time later is an unanswered question. I do believe that if empathy is there to any degree, it can be enhanced with knowledge and experience. Further, I believe that sensitivity can be developed.

I have seen empathic gestures in very young children which suggests that empathy can be present from very early on. For instance, on an occasion when a class of preschoolers was being observed, one young child who did not have full use of his hands was standing in front of an easel during art time. Another child was watching this child and quietly walked over, picked up the paint brush, and put it in his hands and closed his fingers to a grip. The helpful child did not say a word or try to help the other child do his own painting. He quietly walked away and then came back when the other child had finished his art work, released his grip, and put the paint brush back in the tray—all without one word. I would call this a nonverbal demonstration of empathy. The helpful child saw that there was a need —that the other little boy could not pick up and grip the paint brush without some help—but at the same time the helpful child did not overstep boundaries. He realized that the art work needed to be the creation of the other little boy and that to do more would be assuming him to be more helpless than he was.

There is another example from an old Wediko film, *Johnny*, in which a summer camp for emotionally disturbed youngsters is over and the children are boarding the bus to go home. One child hesitated and asked the camp counselor if he could stay just one more day. Clearly, he did not want to leave. A child standing in line behind this boy responded, "One more day or one more summer?" This child knew instantly how the other boy was feeling and responded with a verbal empathic interpretation/ clarification of the other child's exact feelings and thoughts. These two illustrations show that empathy is seen at an early age and can be demonstrated both verbally and nonverbally.

In his earliest writings, Piaget (1972) focused almost exclusively on the parallel, irreducible nature of the affective and the cognitive. He made several important observations on the interaction of cognition and affect. Piaget talked about the development of all children, but it is apparent in his writing that working in the two domains is especially imperative for teachers of emotionally disturbed students. The special education teacher is compelled to teach the academics and the behaviors necessary for healthy affective development. This cannot be accomplished without empathy.

Empathy is difficult to discuss until it has been defined. There are many definitions of empathy. It has been talked about more in the fields of counseling and psychotherapy than in education. In the fields of counseling and psychotherapy, empathy is discussed as a verbal behavior. In other words, it is measured by how much the therapist understands what the client is feeling and responds verbally in a way that shows the therapist understands.

Teachers, on the other hand, work in an entirely different arena. They do not have the luxury of a 50-minute hour with each student, and they have different tasks to accomplish. They are there to teach their students, both in the cognitive and the affective domains. A teacher of emotionally disturbed students cannot neglect or favor one domain over the other.

One definition of teacher empathy (Aspy, 1972) suggests that empathy is demonstrated verbally just as it is in psychotherapy. Aspy said:

Empathy in the classroom is seen as being the teacher's understanding of the meaning to the student of the classroom experience in which they are mutually engaged. This understanding is reflected in the learning interaction by the way in which the teacher responds to the students [p. 54].

Aspy's method of discovering the empathic teacher is to listen to verbal interactions that take place in the classroom between the teacher and the student. In the following section, we shall see that empathy in teachers of emotionally disturbed students is much more than verbal interactions, although verbal interactions are an important component.

AN EMPATHY MODEL FOR TEACHERS OF DISTURBED STUDENTS

Empathy is what we say it is. It appears to be one of the personality dimensions that we know when we see it or experience it from someone else but have difficulty defining. It is much easier to describe because most of us have had the experience of encountering someone who made us feel that we were understood and cared about, and we think of that person as empathic.

On the other hand, most of us have had an experience in which we encountered someone who seemed totally lacking in empathy. Their behavior was such that we felt they did not know or care how we felt about something that was extremely important to us. For example, at least some of us have had the experience of going to the doctor for an examination, and we have been asked to take off our clothes and sit on a hard, cold table in a cold room and wait for the doctor. Sometimes our wait is long and we are cold and feel uncomfortable, nervous, and rather silly while we are trapped in our most humble condition, nakedness. We know we have not experienced empathy from the doctor or nurse under these conditions. In contrast, we may have gone to another doctor who treats patients differently. The examination itself and the way it is conducted is a different experience. The doctor or nurse does not have to verbalize anything to us. These are all nonverbal empathic behaviors. We are not left to be cold and uncomfortable, and feeling vulnerable because we are naked. During the examination only the necessary parts are exposed and we are treated very gently. We are treated as human beings with feelings and not just as patients with conditions that need diagnosis and treatment. We leave feeling we have been treated empathically. So even though it is difficult to define, we know empathy when we experience it.

It is Morgan's (1979) contention that empathy is expressed differently by different professional groups because they have certain responsibilities to perform inherent to their work. For example, physicians, nurses, and dance instructors all have tasks to perform, and it is not their work to talk for an hour with their patients or students. Again, different professionals can express empathy in different nonverbal ways. Teachers interact with their students both verbally and nonverbally (probably in equal proportions) and can and should be able to express empathy through both modalities.

To talk about teacher empathy, however, we first must present a definition and then try to establish the behaviors that reflect this personality dimension. As adults we can tell if we have received good—empathic —treatment. We know for ourselves what is good versus what is not good. Morgan (1979) believed that emotionally disturbed children were capable of determining and discussing good teachers, empathic teachers. She interviewed emotionally disturbed children and normal children discussing their views of a good teacher. The word *empathy* was not used because of the obvious difficulty in explaining its meaning to children. Instead, there were several behaviors and situations predetermined as representative of empathic behavior that were discussed.

The children were asked to describe their favorite teacher and tell what those people did or said that made them good teachers. The discussion questions were designed to obtain information about verbal, nonverbal, and actual helping behaviors. The questions used are grouped in the following categories: (1) How are academic activities structured for students to help them cope with their emotions? (2) What do teachers do to create a therapeutic environment? (3) What do teachers do and say that indicates they know the students' unspoken feelings? (4) What do teachers do and say that helps the student cope with feelings? (5) How are these teachers described? What traits do the students identify as important?

The students were asked if the teacher knew how they felt even when they did not describe their feelings and how they knew the teacher knew their real feelings. They were asked whether their teacher still liked them if they did something wrong and how they knew they were still liked. There was some opposition to conducting this study because people felt these emotionally disturbed students were "too crazy" to give appropriate responses and that they would prefer undemanding teachers. To offset this notion, the children were asked how would they like it if they had a teacher who let them play games all day and do anything they wanted to do?

As it turned out, these students were capable of discussing good teaching, and their responses were consonant with the research on effective teaching. In response to the question of how they would like having a teacher who let them play games all day and do anything they wanted, only one child responded "Great!" Others responded "That would not be a good teacher," "That teacher would not like us," and one child just began rocking and moaning with anxiety.

The following responses of the students fell into four categories that became both the definition of and working model of empathic teachers of emotionally disturbed students:

1. Management of instruction
2. Organization of the environment
3. Responses to feelings and emotional well-being
4. Interpersonal qualities

Each of these components has specific examples that are presented for clarification and use in the classroom.

MANAGEMENT OF INSTRUCTION

The students described a teacher who helped them learn academics; who stayed with them until they understood; and who minimized failures. This is a teacher who brings the students along; who will teach and re-teach as much as necessary until the students understand and are competent. Such teachers are careful to provide successful experiences for the students and mindful that too many failures can be destructive to emotionally disturbed students. The described teacher provided many opportunities and ways for the students to learn their lessons. They had a wide variety of approaches to teaching a subject and used many commercial and individually created materials. Work is tailored to each student's needs. The teacher personalized lessons and devised legitimate reasons to change an activity when the student becomes frustrated.

ORGANIZATION OF THE ENVIRONMENT

Emotionally disturbed students prefer an organized environment. From their responses, it appears that they need to know where things that are needed are kept. The room is tidy and the teacher knows where everything is.

One of the teachers who received very high marks from her students had a most businesslike atmosphere. The room was meticulous. She was friendly but professional. At first glance, the room appeared cold and sterile, but the students did not experience it that way. To them, it provided a much-needed orderly atmosphere. This makes sense when we consider the students' condition. These are youngsters whose lives are disorderly and who have difficulty making sense out of the world around them. So clearly they need an environment that provides what they do not have internally and, perhaps, what is missing at home. The environment must be predictable and structured. Each student was given a time and a place to be alone and quiet. In this environment the student was never sent to someone else for correction or punishment.

In contrast, another teacher who was not viewed by her students as a good teacher had a most unusual classroom. At first glance, it seemed that the classroom was set up with children in mind. There were plants, a fish tank (dripping water), a big old car seat where the students could go to read a book of their choice, materials (books, workbooks, worksheets) stacked everywhere. The teacher herself was exuberant and friendly. For the disturbed student, however, it appears that this room was too chaotic. To the students, a teacher seems disorganized when materials are stacked everywhere in the room. The teacher did not appear professional and, perhaps in the students' eyes, was perceived as too exuberant or overly friendly, not teacher enough. It could be that she was a teacher who left things too open-ended, with too many choices for the students to make when they were not yet capable of making many good choices about what work they wanted to do and what they wanted to do with their free time. The key concept here is structure versus not enough structure.

RESPONSES TO FEELINGS AND EMOTIONAL WELL-BEING

This is primarily the verbal component of the model. It is the teacher's ability to observe and listen to a child and *know* the real or deeper feelings of the student. In the study (Morgan, 1979), the emotionally disturbed youngsters said their favorite (good teacher) knew how they felt even when they would not say what was wrong or that something was wrong. The teacher could sense when the student was on the verge of getting into trouble and offered help before it was requested, or before a blow-up occurred. These teachers were able to identify for the students their real feelings that they themselves were unable to verbalize. They also stayed physically close to the youngsters and lavished reassurances consistently.

This also requires insight into the *real* meaning or motives of a child's behavior and the ability to make verbal responses that accurately reflect knowledge and understanding of the situation. In Morgan's (1979) study, the emotionally disturbed students identified the empathic teacher as one who knew their *real* feelings. One child in the study said his teacher knew his real feelings because she said, "Why are you faking? You're acting silly when you really feel sad." According to Egan (1982), this would be an example of what he refers to as Accurate Empathy. He explains that empathic responses can be at the feeling level or the content level. In the example given, the teacher has responded at the feeling level. Responding to both affect and content is relating to both feelings and the experiences and behaviors underlying the feelings. From the example the child gave, we do not know if the teacher continued and responded to the content.

The following example of an interaction one of the authors had with an emotionally disturbed student is intended to illustrate empathic responses to both affect and content.

Robert

Robert was an 11-year-old who had been in special education for two years. He was what today is called a latch-key kid. His parents left for work before he went to school. Robert had to get himself up in the morning and off to school. No one was there when he got home from school; frequently, he was alone until late in the evening, fending for himself for dinner, and sometimes getting himself to bed. He was often left alone for long periods of time on the weekends as well. When he came into special education, he frequently got into fights, had no friends, and could not get along with others. He was barely able to read and was 2 years behind in most of his school work. For the most part, he would not complete his assignments in class or at home. By the end of the first semester of his second year in special education, Robert had made great strides both academically and behaviorally. It was clear that he would be ready to return to regular class the following year. The wish to be back in regular class ("and not in this retard room ") was one of his frequent declarations.

I had started a slow transition toward regular placement by first sending him down the hall to the regular classroom for reading, then for math, and so on, until he was spending most of the day in a regular classroom and only a small part of the day with me. I began to make references to next year when he would be out of special education and back in a regular classroom. Things were going smoothly until late spring of that year when Robert made a sudden turnaround in his behavior. He balked when it was time to go to the regular class, fell behind in his work, and started fighting again. On one of these occasions of misbehavior, I walked over to him and commented that he had changed quite a bit. I asked how he expected to go to the regular class if he continued to act as he was. The interaction begins:

Robert: Go away! I hate you! [He grabs my arm and tears roll down his face.]

SRM: You tell me to go away but I think you want me to stay close by. You said an angry thing but it seems that you are more sad than angry. [feelings]

Robert: I don't want you to go away. I love you. I don't want to go to regular next year.

SRM: It looked like you were enjoying the time you have been spending in regular class but now you seem sad about leaving this class. Maybe it is a bit scary to think about being in regular class permanently. Your reports have been very good. So we know you can do it. What do you think is scary? [feelings]

Robert: I do the work okay but the teacher doesn't pay much attention to you. You just have to do it [the work] you know. She doesn't talk to us or help us the way you do.

SRM: So you don't get a lot of attention the way you do here. You are just expected to do your work. The teacher expects you to act more grown up —like you can take care of yourself. That kind of sounds like the way things are for you at home. [content]

Robert: Sometimes at night I hear noises. Maybe its burglars or murderers.

SRM: And that is real scary when there isn't anyone at home to protect you if something happens. [feelings] In the special class there is always someone to help you when you don't know what to do, but in regular you kind of have to figure out what to do for yourself, and that is scary, like being home alone. [feeling and content] In some ways it's easier if you know you will be taken care of when things go wrong. But that isn't growing up. Being taken care of—isn't that why you call this the retard room? Because sometimes everybody in this class doesn't always act like they are as big or as old as they really are. [content] Maybe growing up is just a little bit scary too. [feelings and content]

Robert: What will I do if I don't know what to do in regular? The others will call me retardo. The teacher won't like me.

SRM: In the regular classes you go to now, do any of the other kids ever ask the teacher questions or ask for help?

Robert: Yes.

SRM: And what happens?

Robert: She answers or helps them.

SRM: So, it is not exactly like being at home alone. If you ask for help it sounds to me like the teacher will help. Nobody can do everything by themselves. Even grown-ups need help sometimes. I am a grown-up. Have you ever heard me ask for help?

Robert: Before when you were bringing in boxes.

SRM: What did I say? Do you remember?

Robert: You said, would you help me carry these boxes?

SRM: And what happened?

Robert: Some of us helped.

SRM: So, I needed help and someone helped me. It seems that even a grown-up can get help when they really need it. That there is always someone who can help and we are not totally alone when we have a problem or something to figure out. Does that seem to be the way it really is?

Robert: Un-huh. So I can ask the regular teacher for help?

SRM: Un-huh.

Robert: And I could call you and you would come over to help?

SRM: Would you really want your special teacher to come to your regular class to help you?

Robert: That would be like a real baby—huh?

SRM: It would mean that for a little while you got real scared.

Robert: Then you won't come to my new school?

SRM: Well I will be here at this school helping kids who can't work —the way you used to be before you got more grown up. But you can stop by after school when I am here and I would be real happy to see you. Would that work?

Robert: Uh-huh. You would be happy to see me?

SRM: Uh-huh. Real!

Notice that in this encounter the original feeling that Robert manifested was anger, but that underneath that was sadness, and even deeper underneath the sadness was fear. During this interchange, the teacher responds to the child's feelings (sadness and fear) and to the content (growing up and becoming responsible for ourselves). In Robert's case, he has had to be responsible for himself at much too young an age. That is why he was sad to leave the protective and nurturing environment of the special class and so fearful of the regular class. In this event, Robert had the opportunity to work through his real feelings, and when they were recognized he learned how to handle them (at least at school). In the final resolution, he decided for himself again that he really did want to grow up, and most importantly, he learned that there are always options.

INTERPERSONAL QUALITIES

In this component, the emotionally disturbed students made reference to certain personality traits of their empathic teachers. They were teachers who had a sense of humor. They were warm, caring individuals who could openly show affection to the students. They were described as people who smiled frequently, spoke softly, and appeared calm and relaxed. Many of the responses of the emotionally disturbed students, when describing the interpersonal qualities of their teachers, were in harmony with previous findings. Wakefield and Crowl (1974) studied the personality characteristics of special educators and found that:

> . . . the ideal teacher is one who has the desire to analyze the behavior and motives of others, to predict how others will act . . . to sympathize and show affection for the sick and hurt . . . has relatively little need to display anger, feel depressed by inability to handle difficult situations [p. 87].

In a later study (Morgan, 1984), teachers of emotionally disturbed students who were rated high on verbal empathy were found to be moderate in sensitivity to their own needs and feelings and were able to express their feelings behaviorally. They were not fearful of being spontaneous. Their feelings of self-worth and self-regard were balanced. They do not deny feelings of anger or aggression when they have them, but those feelings are not incited easily. These teachers have no difficulty establishing warm, interpersonal relationships. They are sensitive to others' needs but not to the interference of their own well-being. As teachers, they are sensitive to the psychological needs of the children but not so overwhelmed by them that they cannot function in the classroom. Knowing that they are meeting the emotional needs of the children gives them their greatest sense of satisfaction. These teachers do not view emotionally disturbed children as that much different from other children.

Most would say that the first two components of the model represent what is considered good teaching; this is true to an extent. Unfortunately, many people stop once instruction and environmental control are covered in the teacher education curriculum. But that is only half of good teaching, and stopping with these two components does not complete the interaction that creates the empathic process. The emotionally disturbed students thought the components of responses to feelings and emotional well-being and interpersonal qualities were as important as instruction and environment.

For emotionally disturbed students, the relationship with the teacher embodies more than a business affiliation. The cluster of the disturbed students' needs creates and shapes a necessarily different type of teacher. We must design a therapeutic environment as a place of recovery and re-learning. For many emotionally disturbed students, the teacher embodies the "therapy": The teacher is the surrogate parent, the adult model, as well as the "real life teacher."

ENHANCING TEACHER EMPATHY

When we find ourselves in highly emotionally charged situations, it is natural to fall back on experience. We tend to do to our students what teachers and parents did to us, which is why it is important to learn specific intervention techniques for working with the emotionally disturbed student. Even when we have learned new techniques, things can fall apart when a student (especially one we dislike) pushes us to our limit. Many teachers resort to some punishment or type of behavior that they experienced when they were young students. This makes it extremely important that we are functioning at all times in a totally conscious manner and that we are empathic. In other words, we must be completely and keenly aware of what we are doing and why we have chosen to do what we do as well as aware of what the student is doing and why.

As we get older, we tend to forget what it is like to be a child. We forget how children think and how easily some things can hurt a child's feelings. Things that seem small and insignificant to us can be events of gargantuan importance to a child and something they do not forget for the rest of their lives.

At the beginning of every methods course I teach, it includes a relaxation exercise in which participants recall two types of teachers: the battle-ax and the wonderful teacher. The battle-ax and the wonderful teacher can be young or old, male or female. We recall specific incidents that happened to us as children. In the case of the battle-ax, we recall something that was done or said to us that did not make us feel good about ourselves and made us feel as though we did not want to be in school. In the case of the wonderful teacher, we recall what it was about that teacher that made us feel good about ourselves, that school was a nice place to be, and that we had a place in the classroom. The purpose of this exercise is to try to remember what it is like to be a child and to remember how things that happened to us in school, no matter how small they seem now, were significant to us then.

In all the years that this exercise has been conducted in the methods course, there has never been a teacher or prospective teacher who could not remember a specific event with a battle-ax or a specific event with a wonderful teacher. Depending on the age of the teacher, or prospective teacher, these events happened fifteen to forty years ago and they were never forgotten. So, you can see what a powerful impact some incidents have on us. They stay with us all of our lives. We never forget the Battle-Ax or the Wonderful Teacher.

ACTIVITY

Relax and remember back to when you were a child in school and had a teacher who did or said something to you that made you feel awful; made you feel like you wished you were not in school—that you could just disappear; that made you hate that teacher—the battle-ax. Recall all or as many of the details as you can remember surrounding the incident and recall the feelings that went along with the incident. It is most important to try to remember how you *felt* and what you thought at the time. Write it down.

When you have finished recalling the incident with the battle-ax, then it is time to remember that wonderful teacher you had. What was it about the wonderful teacher that made you feel good about yourself; like you belonged to the class; and made you feel good about being in school? Again, try to recall as many of the details surrounding the incident as possible. Most importantly, try to remember the *feelings* that accompanied the incident.

There are common themes and descriptions that recur when the teachers and prospective teachers talk about their battle-axes and wonderful teachers.

THE TWO TYPES OF TEACHERS

Battle-Axes make children feel alienated, embarrassed, humiliated, betrayed, lonely, fearful, anxious, unimportant, non-existent, stupid, ugly, angry, and resentful.

Wonderful Teachers make children feel they are as important as anyone else in the class; that they are smart, capable, calm, safe; that they have a special place in the classroom; that they are special; that the teacher understands their predicament and it is alright and not peculiar; that they belong; and that they are loved, or at the very least the teacher cares about what is best for them.

Many incidents involving the Battle-Ax and the Wonderful Teacher could be recounted here but only two poignant examples will be used. These are opposite extremes of how similar incidents were handled by the two types of teachers.

The Battle-Ax. One student remembered a time in the second grade when she got into trouble over some minor incident that took place in the bathroom during the lunch hour. She was sent back to her classroom before her turn to use the bathroom. Class started again and she needed to go to the bathroom but the Battle-Ax would not let her go. More time passed and the need to use the bathroom became more urgent but still the Battle-Ax would not let her go. This went on until the child could not hold it any longer, and finally, the ultimate humiliation occured —the child wet her pants. All the other children in the class knew what had happened and teased her, and the Battle-Ax scolded her for her accident and called her a baby.

Thirty-nine years later this student remembers the sting of humiliation, the feeling of being an outsider in her own classroom, and the hatred she felt (and still feels) for that teacher. As a result of that incident this student, who is a teacher now, is highly sensitive to children who express a need to go to the bathroom during class time, and she always lets them go when they ask, even when she is not sure they really have to. In her words, "better safe than sorry." So there are times when some children may use that excuse as a means to get out of class or temporarily get away from some work they do not want to do, but I agree with the better safe than sorry attitude. These bathroom trips can be time limited so the child does not miss much class or much of the lesson, and what was missed can be gone over again with the particular child. The time missed is far less serious than creating a situation where a child is likely to have an accident in class and suffer humiliation.

This teacher has taken an event that happened to her as a young child and vowed that it would never happen to any of her pupils. She has an empathic sensitivity to such situations and to children's feelings about such things. However, it could have worked the other way, and in an emotionally-charged classroom this woman could have been a teacher who would become just as insensitive and thoughtless as the second grade teacher she had. She might have become a teacher who refuses to "buckle under" the pressure of the pupils' needs. When all of the children have their hands up and want something, she might have become the type who refused to attend to any of their needs when she felt pressured. But she did not become that kind of teacher. She remembers vividly how it feels to be humiliated, to feel like the teacher hates you, to feel alienated from one's peers, to feel like going home and never coming back to school, to feeling like a stupid baby, and to feeling physically miserable.

The Wonderful Teacher. Now an example of the same theme as told by a student who is now a teacher. This student remembers a time in the third grade when she needed to use the bathroom during class time but was too embarrassed to raise her hand and ask the teacher to be excused. She put it off and put it off until it was too late and she started to wet her pants. She left her seat and started for the door leaving a small wet trail behind her.

Her wonderful teacher saw immediately what was happening and quickly got the watering can used for the plants in the room and followed behind her spilling small amounts of water on the floor so the other children would not know what was really happening—they just thought the teacher was spilling water from the can as she walked along, and they had no idea that the little girl was wetting her pants. What a wonderful teacher! That was truly an empathic gesture. That teacher was very sensitive to children, and a quick and clever thinker. It has been over twenty years since this incident happened and the student has never forgotten that teacher's kindness, sensitivity, and loving regard she had for children. She has never forgotten that teacher's name either. As a teacher now it has made her always try to remember what it is like to be a child and to be ever sensitive and vigilant to events where she can come to the children's rescue and help them save face.

There are good things to be learned from the good and wonderful teachers we have had, but we can also learn from our bad experiences with battle-axes. From the battle-axes we can learn what never to do to children and what does not work. We can learn how ineffective we can become by approaching situations in a negative and thoughtless manner. The point to conducting such an exercise is to sensitize ourselves to the way children think and experience the world. If we can capture this ability then we have taken the first step in developing sensitivity, or building on and enhancing the empathy we already have.

Empathy is a necessary condition to implement the interventions successfully that are presented in the chapters to follow. For instance, without empathy you cannot conduct a worthwhile life space interview, or do story telling, and you cannot moderate role playing or class discussion in any meaningful way. Empathy is such a necessary condition that even the straight teaching of academics cannot be conducted successfully without some level of empathy.

UNBALANCED EMPATHY

When you feel no empathy for a child, it may be for several reasons. Perhaps you are too focused on the student's surface behavior and are not looking for the underlying reasons. In order to be empathic, we must know what motivates these children; that is, where the behavior comes from and how it develops. Take the example of swearing, which these youngsters seem to do to excess. There is more than one reason for swearing. A child may swear because that is a way to get attention. Heads certainly turn when a string of four-letter obscenities come out of the mouth of an 8-year-old. If it is done for attention, then you should ask yourself why this child is so desperate for attention. Some youngsters swear because they hurt inside. It is not so unnatural to swear when hurt. For example, you are hanging a picture on the wall, the hammer misses the nail and hits your thumb. What is your instant reaction? Usually, it is anger because you feel pain. Few of us just stare at our poor bruised thumbs and mumble, "Oh doo doo! Golly darn! That sure hurts!" Some of us yell expletives with great gusto. Consider that some of these students are in constant emotional pain and they are expressing their pain. Empathy comes from understanding the experience of being a child. That is why I think the battle-ax and wonderful teacher exercise is important. If you can see beyond the surface and relate to the experience, then you can be empathic.

Some teachers have complained (burned out) of feeling too much empathy. Empathy does not necessarily mean feeling the same feelings. In fact, you do not want to become caught up in the same feelings. Recognize those feelings, understand the meaning underneath the feeling, relate in some way to the feeling, but do not feel the feelings. If you are feeling the same feelings, then you have gone past empathy and you are in a symbiotic intertwining with the student, which will render you helpless. Stop and examine your own psychological workings. Are you reliving something of your own past that is similar to the student's experience? If so, then you have gone within yourself and lost sight of the child. Focus on the child. There may be similar things in your background but yours and theirs is not exactly the same. There are differences and you must pull out of yourself and listen to how it is for the student. If you remain caught up in the feelings, then look for a sensitive and appropriate time to disengage in your discussion with the student and gently turn to other activities.

Teachers of emotionally disturbed students must be individuals who are in touch with themselves. You must know the issues that still cause you pain and distress and seek ways to alleviate those for yourself. Sooner or later, you are going to bump into a student who has issues very much like your own. You cannot help the student if you become caught up in those issues. In the long run, it is damaging to yourself and you may not last long in the profession. Because you still have unresolved issues does not mean you cannot be a successful teacher of emotionally disturbed students. Few of us have come through life emotionally unscathed. But if your issues are intense, then they must be resolved or harnessed in some way. Think about therapy for yourself. It is nothing to be ashamed of and you can take pride in helping yourself grow.

DEVELOPING EMPATHY IN STUDENTS

In one way or another, educational systems are forced to attend to the affective development of children. Affective disturbances occur in many situations at various levels: episodes of violence in relation to cultural and social conflicts; children who suffer in a quiet internal way; and children whose emotional suffering causes others in their environment to suffer as well. If we hope to be successful teachers of emotionally disturbed students, then clearly it is just as important that we attempt to at least develop sensitivity or enhance empathy in our students as it is for us to be empathic.

Hogan (1969) referred to empathy as a role-taking ability that is the main element in social and moral development. By taking the moral point of view, people should be able to consider the consequences of their actions regarding the welfare of others. The willingness or ability to put oneself in another's place and change one's own behavior as a result is considered an important aspect of moral growth. As teachers, we are responsible for the moral growth of our students. In teaching emotionally disturbed young-sters, we are concerned that they learn to consider the consequences of their actions and eventually change their own behavior. It is important that our students learn how to create (within themselves and in their own class-rooms) a climate of warmth, trust and understanding and to know how to keep channels of communication open between each other —child to child.

One study (Morgan, 1983) explored the development of empathy in children and attributed greater empathy in emotionally disturbed children to the type of classroom environment in which they were placed and the classroom techniques. In this study, empathy in children was defined in terms of observable behaviors that were classified as *help-giving* . Already, we have seen that empathy is a multifacted concept; the strict psychother-apy definition of verbalizing understanding is a limited view of empathy. Others (Barnett, Darcie, Holland, & Kobashigawa, 1982; Hoffman, 1978; Hook, 1982; Peterson, 1983; Weiss, 1982) have considered help-giving gestures as examples of altruism, which these researchers understand to be generated by the condition of empathy.

Defined and understood in this way, empathy is especially logical in reference to children in particular, whose cognitive and language skills are not sophisticated nor as well developed as an adult's verbal abilities.

Classrooms where empathy was found to be greatest in emotionally disturbed students were eclectic: There, teachers attended to developing *responsibility* (acquiring academic skills); *self-control* (not fighting, staying in seats, raising hands, not shouting out); and *help-giving behavior* (showing kindness, understanding). The teachers' methods were varied: Behavior modification was used for the development of *responsibility* and *self-control*. The strategies that differentiate this type of classroom from a strictly behavior modification classroom and develop the help-giving behaviors were activities most commonly associated with the psychoeducational or humanistic approach. They included group meetings to work on each other's "problems"; group meetings to discuss how certain behaviors made others feel; peer tutoring activities; and role playing. Activities that are directed toward building self-esteem, self-understanding, and understanding of the meaning of another's behavior were integral parts of the curriculum that took place on a daily basis.

Upcoming chapters (4 and 5) present behavior modification interventions for the development of responsibility and self-control (management of instruction and organization of the environment). Chapter 6 will explain how to conduct life space interviewing and group meetings, do role playing, and implement a variety of other interventions for the development of help-giving behavior.

REFERENCES

Aspy, D. (1972). *Toward a technology for humanizing education.* Champaign, ILL: Research Press.

Barnett, K., Darcie, G., Holland, C., & Kobashigawa, A. (1982). Children's cognitions about effective helping. *Developmental Psychology, 18,* 267–277.

Egan, G. (1982). *The skilled helper.* Monterey, CA: Brooks/Cole Publishing Co.

Hoffman, M. L. (1978). Toward a theory of empathetic arousal and development. In M. Lewis & L. Rosenblum (Eds.), *The development of affect.* New York: Plenum Press.

Hogan, R. (1969). Development of an empathy scale. *Journal of Consulting and Clinical Psychology, 33,* 205–212.

Hook, J. (1982). Development of equity and altruism in judgments of reward and damage allocation. *Developmental Psychology, 8,* 825–834.

Morgan, S. R. (1984). An illustrative case of high empathy teachers. *Journal of Humanistic Education and Development, 22*(4), 143–148.

Morgan, S. R. (1983). Development of empathy in emotionally disturbed children. *Journal of Humanistic Education and Development, 22*(2), 70–79.

Morgan, S. R. (1979). A model of the empathic process for teachers of emotionally disturbed children. *American Journal of Orthopsychiatry, 49*(3), 446 196453.

Peterson, L. (1983). Influence of age, task competence, and responsibility focus on children's altruism. *Developmental Psychology, 19,* 141–148.

Piaget, J. (1979). The relation of affectivity to intelligence in the mental development of the child. In S. Harrison & J. McDermott (Eds.), *Childhood psychopathology* (pp. 156–182). New York: International Universities Press.

Wakefield, W., & Crowl, T. (1974). Personality characteristics of special educators. *Journal of Experimental Education, 43*, 86–89.

Weiss, R. (1982). Understanding moral thought: Effects on moral reasoning and decision making. *Developmental Psychology, 18*, 852–861.

CHAPTER 4

Organization of the Environment

JO ANN REINHART

PREPARING THE ENVIRONMENT FOR LEARNING

Emotionally disturbed students like and need an organized environment. In preparing the learning environment for these students, the key consideration is structure versus not enough structure. These students require a classroom environment in which the teacher behaves professionally; students are safe from each other and from themselves; classroom routines are predictable and appropriate; individual rights are respected and privacy is allowed; consequences and correction are fair and systematic; and materials and supplies are organized and accessible.

A classroom in which the teacher has carefully thought out and responded to these considerations is generally pleasant but businesslike. In this classroom, students have a sense of ownership of the environment and belonging to the class as a group. The climate is supportive and safe even during emotionally difficult moments. Emotional well-being has priority in this class. This means that the learning process includes affective as well as cognitive development at all times and that students are well aware of this. Classwork is not only reading, writing, and arithmetic, but also self-awareness, problem solving, self-control, and empathy toward self and others. The teacher of a self-contained class for emotionally disturbed students can make some choices in setting up the classroom that will provide the structure and consistency required by these students.

FURNITURE ARRANGEMENT

When emotionally disturbed students first come to our classrooms, they usually do not get along well with others. They are often clumsy and may be very poorly organized, even to the point of being messy. Desks placed in rows do not allow adequate space or privacy for these students. With this in mind, the teacher should look for a way to provide a personal space for each student within the classroom, a personal space for the aide and the teacher, and space for small and large group activities.

In order to accomplish this, it may be necessary to select and arrange furniture creatively. Individual "offices" can be created by using school furniture such as bookcases, chart boards, easels, coatracks, filing cabinets, and any other piece of furniture that can block off a small space around the student. These offices should separate one student from the next but must still provide a clear view of all students to the teacher. Student desks should be flat-topped small tables whenever possible. Desk tops that slant and that provide only enough surface for writing in a notebook can be frustrating for these students because books, papers, and pencils slide off and there is not enough room to keep all materials on the desk top at once. The student's individual office should have adequate storage for books, papers, pencils, and other school supplies.

The teacher and the aide should each have a space with a storage area also. Students learn that each individual in the class is entitled to an area for which they alone are responsible and which they may organize for their own needs. Students should not be allowed in the teacher's or aide's space without permission. This eliminates problems with students getting access to items that the teacher has organized, such as lesson preparations or things placed off limits, such as sharp scissors, pins, confiscated toys, and so forth. Conversely, the teacher and aide should be mindful when entering a student's space not to disturb the student's organization without the student's permission. Respect for individual space is an important concept in learning to get along with others.

If a "quiet room" is not built into the classroom, one can be created in the same way as the student offices. This area should be as closed off from the view of members of the class as possible. This room is used for privacy at times when emotional outbursts occur and a student either needs to be alone or needs to talk privately with another person. It may also be used for individualized teaching during times when the rest of the class is doing quiet work at their desks.

When a student begins to perform sucessfully in getting along with others and demonstrating self-control, the student should be moved to seating that is more like the regular classroom. This may be achieved by placing a small grouping of student desks in the middle of the room facing the blackboard, either in rows or in an arrangement as similar to the regular classroom as possible.

There should be at least one large table for group work. This table should be able to seat every member of the class including the teacher and the aide. It should be placed in a central area of the room, as far away from student offices as possible. Chairs should be kept around this table. Students should not be dragging chairs from their offices to the group table. This table is used frequently throughout the school day, and transitions to and from group work sessions need to be efficient and effortless.

If space permits, smaller tables may be placed in other areas of the room for learning centers, listening centers, computer work stations, or small group work centers. Strategically placed tables encourage and allow for cooperative learning. Working cooperatively is another key concept in learning to get along with others.

Figure 4-1 provides a sample floor plan of a room arrangement that allows for the considerations just discussed.

Fig. 4-1. An example room arrangement

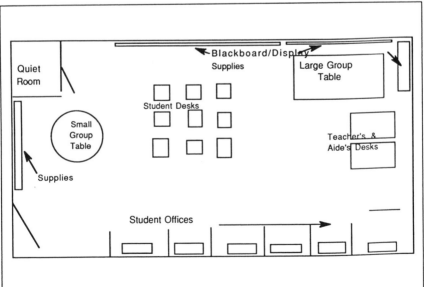

MANAGING SUPPLIES AND MATERIALS

Throughout the school day, students need access to certain supplies and materials. The teacher must decide what the students may keep in their offices, what will be available to use in a common area such as the group table or small group work centers, what is to be used only under supervision, and what is strictly off-limits. Depending on the age and maturity of the students, the teacher may need to consider carefully what is allowable and what is not and under what circumstances certain items may be used. For instance, one student I knew chewed on her pencils. This was not a particular problem until one day the student came to school with an ink-pen and went home with ink-stained clothes, hands, and mouth. Obviously, teacher supervision was required from then on while this student learned to use an ink pen.

Other items need to be carefully considered by the teacher for their potentially dangerous qualities. Some school supplies should be stored in a safe place by the teacher and should only be used by students under supervision. Any school item that can be abused, misused, or turned into a projectile or a weapon should be placed on this list: sharp scissors, compasses, pins, tacks, staplers, rubber bands, liquid paper, glues, and so on. Some items such as knives, superglue, glass bottles, should not be allowed in a classroom for emotionally disturbed students and should be confiscated by the teacher and returned to the student's parents.

Emotionally disturbed children need to know that they are safe in their classroom from others and from themselves. Both the teacher and the aide must be vigilant at all times. Students must clearly know which items they may use and under what conditions. Confiscation of items that are dangerous or misused by the student will be necessary in this classroom.

DEVELOPING A DAILY SCHEDULE

Emotionally disturbed students require consistency and predictability. They need to know the classroom routines and what to expect; they need to know what is expected of them. In designing the daily classroom schedule, the teacher must consider the following factors:

1. Time must be provided for both affective and cognitive development within the curriculum.
2. Initially, time on task will be quite short for the emotionally disturbed student; the schedule may change throughout the school year to accommodate improving attention spans.
3. Time for reinforcement must be built into the schedule.

4. Time for all subjects should be built into the schedule; although core subjects should be taught daily, the weekly schedule should reflect some time for art, music, PE, library, science, and social studies.
5. Emotionally disturbed children in the elementary grades require a supervised recess period in the morning and in the afternoon.
6. Lunch and break time for the aide and the teacher need to be designed into the daily schedule.

A sample schedule might be arranged as follows:

Minutes	Activity
5	Opening Exercises
30	Sharing/Group Meeting
45	Individualized Work Folders (Reading, Writing, Math)
15	Recess [Aide covers then takes a 15 minute break]
45	Individualized Work Folders
30	Whole Group Lessons (Social Studies, Science, Cursive, etc.) [Aide's Lunch Period]
45	Lunch/Recess
25	Story
20	Journals
45	Whole Group Lessons (Art, Music)
45	Self-Selected Activity
15	Closure (Preparations for Dismissal)

Figure 4-2 is a chart for developing a class schedule. It is designed in 15-minute increments, which allows for flexible scheduling, particularly in classrooms where individual students are going in and out for other services such as speech, physical therapy, and counseling. This chart presents a weekly schedule since some time periods may be assigned different activities on different days: that is, science on Monday, Wednesday; social studies on Tuesday, Thursday. Friday, the time might be used to extend a class project or to provide additional reinforcement time.

The daily or weekly schedule should be posted somewhere in the classroom. It may be written on the chalkboard, tacked up on the bulletin board, or taped to the students' desks. Individual students who have outside activities on certain days (such as speech) should have their schedules taped to their desks. These children cannot cope with surprises. We need to let them know what to expect in as much detail as possible, and we need to keep these expectations as constant as possible. The daily schedule lets the students know what is expected of them throughout the school day. Assuring that students know specifically what is expected of them is the first step in helping them accept responsibilty and develop self-control.

56

	MONDAY	TUESDAY	WEDNESDAY	THURSDAY	FRIDAY
8:30 - 8:45					
8:45 - 9:00					
9:00 - 9:15					
9:15 - 9:30					
9:30 - 9:45					
9:45 - 10:00					
10:00-10:15					
10:15-10:30					
10:30-10:45					
10:45-11:00					
11:00-11:15					
11:15-11:30					
11:30-11:45					
11:45-12:00					
12:00-12:15					
12:15-12:30					
12:30-12:45					
12:45 - 1:00					
1:00 - 1:15					
1:15 - 1:30					
1:30 - 1:45					
1:45 - 2:00					
2:00 - 2:15					
2:15 - 2:30					

Fig. 4-2. Worksheet for Developing a Daily Schedule

A word of caution about becoming rigidly attached to the daily schedule is in order. In a classroom for emotionally disturbed students, the primary goal is to help the children achieve balance and emotional well-being. Although academics are important, we must recognize that there will be times when serious emotional problems will have to take priority and the daily schedule of academic activities will be postponed, canceled, or altered. Our students cannot be expected to maintain concentration on reading, writing, and math in the midst of extreme anxiety attacks, extreme anger, or severe depression. A well thought out schedule is necessary to provide the basic structure for the day's activities, but it is not written in granite. It may be changed whenever necessary or appropriate. There may even be times when you are all tired, have worked hard, and just choose to dump the schedule and watch a filmstrip or go out for an extra recess. Relaxation is also part of teaching our children balance in their lives.

PREPARING STUDENTS FOR LEARNING

There are no recipes or formulas for the art of great teaching. We must be willing to think, experiment, and discover the best answers for particular times and situations. The techniques that are presented in this book have been selected because they work most of the time. However, the teacher for emotionally disturbed children will learn quickly that at times nothing works with a particular child or for a particular situation. Then, it is essential to think, experiment, and sometimes simply "wait it out" with as much patience and consistency as possible.

DEVELOPING CLASS IDENTITY

The issues of individual rights, fairness, control, and respect are crucial to emotionally disturbed students. Often, these issues do not exist for these students outside of the classroom. More than most, these children need to belong to a group in which these issues are a priority. If these children are ever to experience emotional well-being, it will most likely have to be in the classroom.

This can only occur if the teacher acts as a facilitator of individual contributions to the group process. From the first day of class, the teacher can assure that students are aware of this through activities that involve the students in classroom decision making. Ownership of the classroom must be shared if a sense of belonging is going to develop.

One of the first and simplest decisions that can be shared is room arrangement. Although it is the responsibility of the teacher to select furniture items

and make certain considerations about room arrangement, the students as a group may decide on placement of furniture, selection of offices, individual and group areas of the classroom, use of storage areas, and display and bulletin boards. This may be accomplished in a class meeting at the group table. If students are not yet ready for this, seating should be assigned by the teacher and students may provide input from their assigned seats.

The next decision that should be shared by the group is the rights of individuals in the classroom. This discussion should lead to a short list (no more than five) of responsibilities for behavior in this class. This is preferable to the posting of class rules. As soon as the word "rules" is used, it invokes the concept of "breaking the rules" in many children's minds. The following poem was copied from a poster in a second grade classroom in Albuquerque, New Mexico many years ago. The source is unknown to this author, but the message is so timeless that it is impossible not to want to pass it on the teachers everywhere. This poem has been used by this author to establish classroom rights and responsibilities with students from grades one through twelve.

I have a right to be happy, and to be treated with kindness in this room.
This means that no one will laugh at me, ignore me, or hurt my feelings.

I have a right to be safe in this room.
This means that no one will hit me, kick me, push me or pinch me.

I have a right to hear and be heard in this room.
This means that no one will yell, scream, or shout
and my opinions will be considered in any plans we make.

I have a right to be myself in this room.
This means that no one will treat me unfairly because
I am fat or thin, fast or slow, boy or girl.

Once rights and responsibilities have been established, there follows an introduction to the concept of consequences. This should not be a detailed response to every imaginable kind of infraction. Rather, it should introduce the concept that when rights are breached or responsibilities ignored, people get hurt and there are certain consequences for these behaviors. These discussions may need to be done over a number of days in short sessions. This is usually a more difficult group meeting to manage, but it is an excellent way to help children understand that they are going to belong in this room and that they are going to have a role in this group.

A third group issue is developing an understanding of what kind of class this is and what kind of work is done in this class. This discussion must be supportive and based on the understanding that this is a community with

a common goal: emotional well-being. Students should realize from the start that they will be able to help each other in achieving this goal. They should be allowed to decide how they will deal with outside perceptions of the class and what they want to tell other children about their class. Although everyone knows this is a special class, the students may prefer that it not be posted outside their classroom door or announced in any public way.

Two things occur simultaneously in order for the students to experience belonging in the classroom: (1) each individual is valued for his/her strengths, characteristics and talents and (2) the group functions as a support system while facilitating the personal growth efforts of its members. Emotionally disturbed students will not automatically know how to make this happen. The teacher must act as a facilitator, teaching students the behaviors which allow them to hold group discussions and come to consensus or agreement on issues that are important to them.

Once students become aware that their input in discussions and decision making can make a difference, then the move to class meetings and discussions of personal growth issues is much easier. Students should be allowed input in decisions that affect them. This is the second step in facilitating the acceptance of responsibility and the development of self-control.

THE CLASSROOM AS A MODEL WORKPLACE

If children hate school, it is because we as educators are doing something wrong. Learning is the child's work, and school is the child's workplace. If you have ever experienced a time in your life when you were out of work or looking for work, you may already realize how important work is for most people. Through our work we feel valued, competent, and get a great deal of our life's satisfaction. At work, we contribute, exchange our ideas and our energy, make a difference, and, most importantly, feel a belonging to the society in which we live. For most teachers, work is far more than a paycheck; it demands love and dedication. Teachers who stay in teaching generally "love" their work. It is this love of work that we need to transmit and share with our students.

Our goal must be to create a classroom that is as close to a model workplace as possible. To achieve this, we need to first examine what it is about work that is satisfying and then make our classrooms the kind of workplaces that best enhance that feeling of satisfaction for the children and for ourselves.

What is it that teachers love about their work? Undoubtedly, we love children. Working with children allows us to be creative and to grow with our students. No teacher can teach children without learning something new. The children model what we do, allowing us to see ourselves through their eyes. Through this process, we are forced to constantly hone our skills and rethink our approaches. There are no recipes, no standard answers in teaching. Teaching permits us to continue to experience the joy of learning and the excitement of mental stimulation beyond our years of formal education. We are reminded daily that "we don't know it all." This is what we model for our students. Students require models of competence, happiness, and self-control in order to internalize behaviors associated with these desired states of being.

SOFT B-MOD: GETTING THEM TO COOPERATE

Behavior modification is a technique that is unquestionably useful in the management of surface behaviors. Surface behavior problems are those with which every teacher must deal to some degree. These are those obviously irritating behaviors such as talking out, getting up without permission, and so on. However, unless these problems are managed, learning cannot take place. For students with emotional disorders, these behaviors are more frequent and more severe. They are called "surface" behavior problems because they are manifestations of deeper problems. The deeper problems take time and insight to discover and even more time to change. Since real cognitive and affective work cannot be done in a chaotic environment, we must first establish sanity, order, and consistency for the student. To do this effectively, we need to elicit the support and involvement of the students.

"Soft" behavior modification implies a cooperative effort between the student and the teacher rather than having the teacher simply apply authoritative decisions in the treatment of the student. It is primarily a feedback system that allows the student to know if a behavior is appropriate or not. It is also a teaching tool in that a student may learn self-control through modeling, discussion, practice, and consequences. As a student learns new behaviors, there are immediate responses built into the procedures that reward the student for measured improvement toward the target behaviors. If the student does not make an honest effort, then these rewards are diminished or withheld.

"Soft" behavior modification involves a classroom feedback system that is used to help students behave appropriately so that affective and cognitive learning may take place. A good feedback system will have four basic components: (1) a way for the student to know when behavior is appropriate, (2) a way for the student to self-correct inappropriate behavior, (3) a way for the student to receive consequences for not correcting inappropriate behavior, and (4) a way for the teacher and the student to chart "real" progress.

FEEDBACK SYSTEMS

Emotionally disturbed students do not or cannot distinguish behavior that is appropriate from that which is inappropriate. At any given time, they may not know if they are doing well or doing poorly. They must be taught to recognize and evaluate their own behaviors. This is the first step in teaching self-control. Feedback on behavior must be given constantly throughout the day and for every activity in which the student participates, including lunch and recess. In behavior modification, appropriate behaviors are reinforced at regular time intervals with points or tokens. At the end of a given time period the points or tokens are tallied and exchanged for a tangible or intangible reward. In cases in which the inappropriate behavior is extreme, rewards are given as soon as the appropriate behavior occurs. This is the positive reinforcement aspect of behavior modification.

Before developing a point system, the target behaviors must be designated. This can be done by the teacher or, better yet, in collaboration with the students. If the teacher is going to designate the target behaviors, the following questions should be reviewed first:

1. Are the behaviors to be changed for the benefit of the students or for the convenience of the teacher?
2. What kind of behaviors really do interfere with learning opportunities for others and which are just personally annoying to the teacher?
3. How much freedom should be allowed?
4. Are any of the target behaviors primarily due to cultural differences? Is there a discrepancy between your personal values and the cultural values of the student?

If selecting target behaviors is going to be a collaborative effort, these questions may still be valuable to consider. Selecting appropriate behaviors with the students may be the topic of class meeting one day. Basically, this is comparable to developing a set of student rights and responsibilities. Have the students brainstorm a list of all the behaviors that they feel will make the class a safe, healthy working environment. Keep the students focused on the idea that these are their responsibilities. Perhaps use the poem "This Room" to once again remind students of individual rights within the classroom. When the list is complete, have each student rank order the five items they see as the most important. There may need to be some discussion of items prior to selecting five. Tally the student responses and select no more than five behaviors for the final list. This list becomes the criteria by which students may judge their behavior as being appropriate and by which they will receive their reinforcement points. This may be called the list of student responsibilities rather than rules, which have a more negative and authoritative connotation. Developing this list is clearly an important task and should not be taken lightly by any member of the class, including the teacher and the aide.

A similar list may be developed by each student to target individual behaviors that the student wishes to improve. This system may be reinforced through bonus points added to the daily point tally or through contracting for a specific reward. The individual target behaviors should also be developed with teacher assistance. Students often select behaviors that are too vague and not easily measured, or behaviors that are currently too demanding and would put undue pressure on the student.

For most of our students, a daily reinforcement system is adequate. This means that they earn and save points throughout the day for appropriate behavior. If there are students whose behavior is severe, the system may need to respond every few minutes or at least once an hour with smaller rewards (i.e., a piece of fruit, nuts, stickers). Points earned are individually recorded by the teacher and the aide on point sheets. Figure 4-3 is an example of a point sheet used in an elementary school class. The points are earned during the various activities and are noted at the end of each work period. Assigning points is based upon the list of responsibilities developed by the students and the teacher. Bonus points may be given for individual target behaviors, for ignoring other inappropriate behaviors, for being a role model for other students, or for doing something special such as helping a friend. At the end of the day, the points are tallied and may be spent in store or saved. The teacher or the aide records the accrued points in a notebook or on a chart where students can see how many points they have earned and spent.

There are two types of rewards: tangible and intangible. When beginning to work with emotionally disturbed students, and especially the younger ones, you will need to give tangible rewards. At the end of each day, the store should be open for students to spend their points on items such as small toys, school supplies, paints, clay, candy, ice cream, and soda. Be sure to find things for store which the students will want to buy and can afford on an average day's earnings. Price articles according to their demand and how much students are earning on average. Inflate the prices as the students do better in class and earn more points. (Take this as an opportunity to do some teaching about the capitalist system, the supply and demand market place, and the causes of inflation. Never let the student borrow

POINT SHEET

Name : _____   Date : _____

	POINTS POSSIBLE	POINTS EARNED	BONUS
Sharing	10		
Reading	10		
Spelling	10		
Math	10		
Science	10		
Social Studies	10		
Art/Music	5		
Library	5		
P.E.	5		
SSR	5		
Story	5		
Recess AM	5		
PM	5		
Bus AM	10		
PM	10		
Lunch	10		

BONUS

◯ ◯ ◯ ◯
◯ ◯ ◯ ◯

Total _____

Comments :

Fig. 4-3. An example of a Point Sheet

against future points). Intangible rewards work well with older students and with students who are on the road to understanding more instrinsic rewards through academic and social successes. For these students, earning time for self-selection activities, a pass to the library, a visit to someone special in the school (kids often adore the custodian and want to spend hours with this person), or going out to lunch with the teacher are appropriate motivators.

A number of point systems on the market may be implemented in the classroom. In designing or choosing a point system keep in mind several concerns:

Avoid systems which require that you and your aide stop and assign points every 10 or 15 minutes. This disrupts the academic process and for the most part is unnecesary. Rarely will we have a student so severe that that kind of monitoring is required. If so, then do it just for that one student.

Avoid systems that target more than five behaviors at once. It is too difficult to observe and rate more than five, and it is overwhelming to the student. Most students cannot consciously work on more than five behaviors at once.

Avoid systems that require marking scores of points one at a time. One system on the market requires that the teacher mark over 200 boxes within one day, and that is for just one student. If a cumulative number of points is possible for one activity, design your system so that the number of points earned is written as a whole number.

Set up the point sheet so that it can easily be tallied at the end of each day. Neither you nor your aide will have a lot of time to do this since the sheets are collected after the day's activities are over and the students are getting ready to go home. The tallied points may be quickly recorded and the point sheet sent home to the parents as a record of the day's achievements.

A second kind of feedback system is contracting. Contracting is usually done with individual students for personal target behaviors. It is used for motivating and charting long-term behavior changes. To implement a contract, both the teacher and the student agree to certain target behaviors; then they set a timeline that must be adhered to. The terms of observation, recording, and successful completion are negotiated and written into the contract. The reward for completion of the terms of the contract is determined and agreed upon; it too is written into the contract. The teacher, the student, and a witness sign and date the contract, which makes it binding.

Date _____

CONTRACT

This is an agreement between _____
Student's Name

and _____. This contract begins on
Teacher's Name

_____ and ends on _____. It will be
Date   Date

reviewed on _____.
Date

The terms of the agreement are :

Student will : _____ _____

_____

_____

_____

Teacher will : _____

_____

_____

_____

If the student fulfills the terms of this contract, an agreed upon reward of

_____

will be awarded the student.

Student's Signature _____

Teacher's Signature _____

Witness _____

Fig. 4-4. An example of a Contract

If a contract is broken it becomes null and void, in which case the student may renegotiate a new contract. Figure 4-4 shows a sample contract format.

Both contracting and point systems may be applied to the class as a whole. When the individual students are ready to work for the good of the group in pursuit of a common reward, then a group contract may be written. The number of points necessary and the reward upon successful completion are negotiated before implementation of the contract. One such contract might target bus behaviors. Each day that there are no bus reports, the whole class earns one point on a special point sheet. For this one, you might draw a bus on poster board and mark off the number of squares agreed upon in the contract. Each day at the end of sharing time one square is colored yellow until all of the squares are filled in and there is a picture of a yellow bus. The reward must be implemented as soon after this point as possible and it should be more than store—perhaps a field trip to the zoo on the bus or a walk to the local ice cream shop.

CORRECTION, NOT PUNISHMENT

The purpose of the point system is to keep the student aware of when behavior is appropriate. Correction is the way to let the student know when behavior is inapporpriate, to provide instruction in appropriate behaviors, and to allow the opportunity for self-correction. Correction implies that learning has not yet taken hold and that reteaching and additional practice are necessary. We are often so quick to judge student misbehavior and to remedy it with immediate consequences that we sometimes forget our true purpose as a teacher is to teach. In the classroom for emotionally disturbed children, teaching includes instruction in affect as well as academics. Correction is different from punishment. Punishment implies first that the student is misbehaving on purpose and second that we can permanently stop the misbehavior through fear, pain, or intimidation. Our students are not always misbehaving on purpose. In fact, much of the time they are simply acting out the turmoil that is going on inside themselves without much regard for what it looks like from the outside. Sometimes, they cannot stop what they are doing and sometimes they simply don't know how. We must find ways to teach them new, more appropriate behaviors, then provide the support and time for practice until the new behavior replaces the old.

Correction must be applied consistently and fairly. It works in conjunction with the reinforcement system of earning points. When a student does not earn all possible points for an activity, the teacher tells the student specifically which behaviors resulted in the loss of points. At the same time, the teacher should suggest ways to change the behavior and correct the problem. Ideas for correction may also be elicited from other students who are successful with that behavior. Once the student has been made aware of the problem behavior and given alternatives to try and models to observe, then the teacher or a trusted peer may prompt the student when the misbehavior begins. If there is some event in particular that sets off the behavior, the student should be made aware of this also. When a student is able to self-correct, bonus points should be given immediately. This is an important step that we want the student to feel very good about.

CONSEQUENCES

Correction is the first step we take with a child who is misbehaving. Sometimes stronger measures are required. Built into the system must be a way for students to receive fair and consistent consequences for not correcting inappropriate behaviors. Consequences must be carefully thought out by the teacher and discussed with the students. Get feedback from the students on what they think is fair. Match the consequence to the degree of misbehavior and student awareness of the misbehavior. There are some important guidelines for what not to do in deciding consequences.

Consequences must **never** be physical (i.e., corporal punishment). Many emotionally disturbed students are abused children. Hitting or paddling them reinforces the idea that adults may hit and may hurt those who are smaller and more helpless than themselves, that they may force their will upon children through brute force.

Consequences must never interfere with rewards that a child has previously earned. There are programs available that tell the teacher to remove points a child has earned or to lower a child's status in the class along with a total loss of points. This is certainly not fair and will be perceived as unjust by the student.

Consequences must never include restrictions of basic human needs, (i.e., going to the bathroom, eating lunch, feeling and being safe). These are human rights that no one should be allowed to threaten or remove.

Consequences must never involve humiliating a child, either publicly or privately. Our students already have poor self-esteem. One event in which we do something humiliating can destroy trust and our ability to reach that student for a long time.

Consequences must never involve extra school work. Education is a privilege that we take for granted in this country, so much so that we put it down as something children should hate to do. In our classrooms, we want our students to feel privileged and good about school work. We do not want to use the child's work as negative reinforcement.

Consequences must be immediate or as soon after the misbehavior as possible. Do not carry over consequences to the next day. Allow the student to begin each new day with a clean slate.

The very best consequence for a child who misbehaves is boredom. At the end of each day, there should be at least 30 minutes scheduled for self-selection activities. (More will be said about what happens during this time later in this chapter.) During work periods, students who are misbehaving or who are not on task should lose the same amount of time they are wasting from their self-selection time. So for every minute they are misbehaving, the teacher may take a minute from the student's time. Then while all the other children are enjoying themselves, the student must pay back the minutes lost. This they do by sitting in their seats doing nothing. They may not read, write, or talk. Use timers and stop watches to clock the exact time. At the end of the paying-back period, if their assignments are still not completed, they remain in their seats and complete their assigned work. If the student has had a particularly bad day and no work was done, then the teacher should select an appropriate assignment that can be completed within the given time.

When students fail to complete their work because they are not on task, use recess time or half of the lunch period to have them finish their work. Do not let them participate in any nonacademic activities until their work is completed satisfactorily. Make decisions carefully about what will be satisfactory. That does not necessarily mean everything that was assigned. Perhaps too much was assigned and that was the reason for the off-task behavior. Perhaps the student didn't really understand the assignment and requires more instruction. Always look for a reason for the misbehavior before jumping to conclusions about the consequences. They are only consequences if the student perceives them as being fair and matching the degree of misbehavior. Otherwise, they are punishment and will breed hostility and more uncooperative behavior.

Sometimes misbehavior is more serious than simply being off-task or disturbing other students in the class. A student sometimes actually loses control and behaves in such a way that someone could be physically hurt. When there is a total loss of control, students may try to punch, kick, throw furniture, books, or whatever is around them. They may scream obscenities, try to verbally attack another student to get a fight going, or defy and talk back to the teacher. This kind of behavior requires much stronger and more immediate consequences. Above all, this is a time for calm on the part of the teacher. Talk in an even, firm voice to the student. Move close to the student. Proximity to someone in control will sometimes calm the child enough to get the out-of-control behaviors to stop. Firmly tell the student to go to the quiet room to calm down. If it seems appropriate, go with the child and begin the process of working through the feelings. If the student cannot be calmed and is an actual threat to the safety of the other students and yourself, then move everyone away and out of danger, even if this means leaving the room.

Physical restraint is the final measure that may be taken; in some cases, it must be taken. If you can manage the child yourself, hold from behind the child, crossing the child's arms and holding at the wrists. Continue talking in an even, calm voice until you feel the child start to release the muscle tension. Let go of one arm at a time slowly while continuing to talk in a soothing voice. When the child has regained some control, immediately begin the process of working through the feelings. If the child is too big, get some help. It is a good idea to have a contingency plan. Know who you are going to call upon to help. Be sure that person knows what to do and what will be your role in the process of calming the out-of-control student.

Most of our students have spent their lives being in some kind of trouble. Some of them seem to no longer care if they are in trouble. They are no longer sensitive to feelings of guilt and shame. In fact, they don't know what it feels like not to be in trouble. Most of all, they have no idea how to get out of trouble. We must assure that our students know that there is always a way to get out of trouble and that we will show them exactly how. Then we will teach them behaviors that will keep them out of trouble. There must always be a way in our system for the child to recover from misbehavior: to pay back the time, to complete the assignment, to apologize to someone, to fix things that they've broken, to pay the consequences and wipe the slate clean. The system should provide ways to do this as quickly as possible. It is best to send the student home with a clean slate at the end of each day.

CHARTING PROGRESS

The system of points, correction, and consequences will lead to improved student behavior. Students need to know how much progress they are making. Using the components of the feedback system, we can create a structure of levels that shows a student's progress and how they are functioning in the system. There are some basic guidelines for creating this structure.

There should be no more than five levels. A student begins on level 1 and works through to level 5.

The teacher should establish how much time must be spent on each level. A reasonable minimum amount might be 30 days.

The teacher sets the criteria for moving to the next level. These may include the number of points earned, academic performance standards, minutes lost for off-task behaviors, and so on.

The teacher (with the students cooperation and input) should establish the rights, responsibilities, and consequences for each level. Level 1 will have far fewer rights than level 5. Students on the upper levels will be preparing for mainstreaming and should have many more rights and responsibilities. You may also want to include the self-selection activities students may be allowed at each level. This provides one extra motivator to move up in the level system.

The teacher and the students should establish how the system will deal with regression. There must be a way for students to be placed back on an earlier level if they cannot maintain the behaviors demanded at a higher level.

In the classroom, there should be some kind of display that shows where the students are in the level system. This may be a simple chart or a bulletin board on which each student is represented (e.g., by balloons climbing higher into the sky as they move up the levels).

The importance of having a good feedback system in place will become readily apparent to you as soon as you begin working with these children. They require a highly structured, organized environment. An effective feedback system frees the students and the teacher to focus on the important work of the classroom, developing emotional well-being and learning academics. Once the system is in place, the teacher must learn to rely on it to manage surface behavior problems. Use the system consistently. Do not change the rules the first time a student gets out of control and you feel upset and confused. Stay with your system. Calmly continue to remove minutes from self-selection time. Calmly remind the student that points cannot be earned while this behavior continues and that minutes are being taken from self-selection time. Tell the student exactly how to stop this process and get back on task. Be specific in your directions. If you are feeling angry, let the aide work the system with the student. Do not change the rules because the system doesn't seem to be working. It does work when it is used consistently and fairly.

NONACADEMIC ACTIVITIES

Throughout the school day, there are several nonacademic activities scheduled including recess, lunch, and self-selection activity time. During these activities, there is no direct instruction of academic material. However, in the classroom for emotionally disturbed students, these activities provide some of the most important teaching and learning opportunities. During these activities, true social learning takes place in a natural setting. This is not just free time. It is time for playing together, talking, and sharing meals. During these activities, a strong sense of group and belonging may develop and students truly learn how to get along with each other.

RECESS

There should be 15-minute recesses scheduled in the morning, after lunch, and in the afternoon. Recess time should be spaced throughout the daily schedule to provide a break following on task periods. Recess should be supervised but not highly structured. The aide needs to go to the playground and supervise as the children play together. The children should be allowed to make choices during recess about what they want to play. The teacher can provide ideas and sports equipment such as volleyballs, jump ropes, and so on. If the children cannot decide who to play with or what to play, a chart can be put up in the room letting them sign up for the week for the activities that they want and the team they would like to be on. Do not allow the children to play games in which betting occurs or they are playing for keeps, as in marbles. Be alert to games that become very competitive. If this becomes a problem, it should be discussed during class meeting.

Recess is usually a time when the children will want to go outside to the playground and play physical games. However, there are some students who would prefer to be inside playing board games, reading, or doing art work. This is a 15-minute break time for the teacher, so if you wish to allow students the choice of going out with the aide or staying in with the teacher, recognize that you must give up your break time to supervise those who are inside. Decide what works best for you. You may need a break from them and you should allow yourself that time to regroup. There will be times when you will have to give up this break to stay with students who are using recess to complete unfinished work. This is not particularly imposing since they should be working quietly to finish their assignments.

If problems occur during recess (and this is a time when they are most likely to), immediately hold a class meeting to discuss what happened, what resulted, what might have been done that would have averted the problem, what can be done if the situation happens again, and what consequences are appropriate. Our students need to learn that problems can be dealt with and resolved quickly. They need to learn that there are ways to get out of trouble and deal with what they did to get into trouble in the first place. This way, they can begin to change their behaviors with the help and support of the teacher and their peers.

LUNCH

It is likely that many of our students do not learn how to eat together as a family at home. They come to school with absolutely no table manners. They eat with their fingers since they do not know how to use eating utensils. Some will even stick their faces in the plate and eat like animals. They do not know how to carry a conversation at the table. You will hear them talking in detail about blood and guts movies while eating their food. They will throw food, use food as bribes, trade food, or just not eat what they should. They don't eat together and so want to leave the table at different times to go out and play. This pressures the slower eaters to eat too fast or to leave food on their plates even though they are still hungry. Obviously, there is a lot of teaching we can do at the lunch table.

At first, it will be most unpleasant eating with them. Don't count on getting a lot to eat yourself. Plan on finishing your lunch during the after lunch recess when the aide is with them. Begin by working on two or three table manners at a time. For instance, have them all bring their trays to the table, sit down and wait for the others before starting to eat. Show them how to place the napkin in their laps. When they can do this, then work on utensils, appropriate conversation, and so on. Set up some ground rules if necessary. This is a good topic for class meeting. Together with the students decide if they should be allowed to share food. Determine the five most important manners at the table. Write them on poster board and put them up in the room by the door where they can be seen before going to the cafeteria for lunch. Keep the students aware that certain social behaviors are expected of us during eating. After several months, you will find that they are actually pleasant to be with during lunch. They can be more open and relaxed. They will talk about things at lunch that they wouldn't in the formality of the classroom. If possible, take them on several field trips to restaurants to practice their new manners.

SELF-SELECTION

Self-selection should be scheduled for at least 30 to 45 minutes daily. This is a time in which the students select their own activities. These activities should be predominantly social and require interaction among students. A wide variety of board games and card games should be available. Students may choose to do puzzles, art projects, or listen to music or taped stories in a listening center. Use class meeting time to find out what kinds of activities the students would most like available for self-selection. When a new game is introduced to the class, the teacher will need to play with the students several times until they are able to follow the rules and participate appropriately. Always teach the students the rules that come with the game. Once they have learned the official rules, then let them know that they may change the rules as long as everyone who is playing agrees to the changes. The teacher will always need to be available during self-selection to be a mediator. There will be disagreements over rules, playing pieces, cheating, and who may play with whom. From time to time, the teacher and the aide should play with the students to provide models and sometimes just to have fun and relax with the students.

Self-selection is used as part of the feedback system. When students do not complete their work because of off-task behavior or lose minutes for disruptive behavior which is not self-corrected, they must pay back that time during self-selection. Either they will stay in their seats until the work is done, or if paying back minutes, they will sit and do nothing. Self-selection may also be tied to the level system. In a class meeting, the students may help determine which activities should be allowed on different levels. For example, a student on level one might be able to select from five activities, whereas a student on level five would be allowed to select from all available activities.

Self-selection provides a time for students to relax and interact with each other in a natural play setting. It is appropriate for older students as well. The kinds of games will be somewhat different but the value of the time spent interacting with each other will be the same.

SPECIAL EVENTS

Throughout the school year, there will be holidays and student birthdays to celebrate. Planning and preparing for parties, being host to relatives and friends are important learning experiences for our students. All student birthdays should be celebrated. There should be a party with a cake with the student's name on it. Our children have such poor self-esteem that they generally do not feel valued or that they belong. Acknowledging their birthdays makes them know that they are special. The teacher's and the aide's birthdays should also be celebrated with a party and cake. This is for the purpose of modeling. Our students do not know how to behave when they are being honored or praised.

Celebrating holidays such as Halloween, Valentine's Day, and Thanksgiving gives the children the opportunity to work together to plan an event around a theme. For holidays, the students will want to make decorations and special invitations to family and friends. They may write poems, stories, or prepare a play to perform or a song to sing. Parties are another way to have students learn to interact in a natural setting.

BUILDING AND MAINTAINING A SUPPORT SYSTEM

Children spend most of their time and certainly much of their energy in school. A child may actually spend more time with the teacher and with classmates than with family members. Our students come to rely on the support system that is in place for them at school. As the child's teacher, it is our responsibility to assure that this support system works for the benefit of the child. This means that we must maintain the channels of communication with the child's parents and with all the other professionals who work with the child.

GETTING PARENT SUPPORT

The parents of emotionally disturbed children are generally not comfortable coming to school and do not communicate well with school personnel. Many times, they are dealing with serious problems of their own. Getting their support will be something that you must consciously set out to do.

When children are placed in special education classes, the parents are sent a letter telling them to come to a staffing meeting in order to place their child. They walk into this meeting alone to be greeted by sometimes as many as nine or ten school professionals, each with a report about their child, usually in terms of weaknesses and problems rather than strengths and successes. This is a very intimidating experience for many parents, and after this they are not anxious to go to the school again for any reason. If we are going to get them back to school, we will have to find ways to do so that are nonthreatening. There are some things we can do that will allow parents to know that we value their support and welcome them in our classroom.

At the beginning of the school year, prepare a letter to go home welcoming the child to your classroom and inviting the parents to come and visit their child's classroom. You may want to develop a class handbook in which you could include a description of the program, a daily schedule, a description of the behavior management system, a calendar of school holidays and special events, a list of pertinent school personnel and phone numbers, a bibliography of books for parents, and a floor plan of the classroom. A nice touch is to then mount a picture of their child with the teacher and the aide on the front of the handbook.

Invite parents to attend special events parties. Plan these parties for late afternoon or over the lunch hour so that parents who work can get away for a while to attend. Send home a student-made invitation that invites them to come join the class in celebrating a special event. The first time you may even wish to follow up with a phone call just to let them know that you really would like them to attend. Be sure that parents who do attend feel a part of the celebration. Have enough chairs for all to sit comfortably. Teach the children how to be good hosts at the party. Be sure there is enough food or that you divide it up so that everyone may be served. Once parents have attended one party and had a nice time, it will be easy to get them back for another. Talk to the parents at these parties about their child's successes in the class. Do not use this time for conferencing about problems. Keep it nonthreatening. Most of these parents feel helpless to do anything about their child's problems anyway. They can learn to feel better about their child if they hear what the child is able to do well.

Invite parents to chaperone class field trips. Usually the children are lots of fun on a field trip, and this can be a very positive experience for the parents. Furthermore, you will need the help. Let them know that you genuinely appreciate their help.

Send home daily or weekly behavior reports. After the point sheet tallies have be recorded, send the point sheet itself home to the parent. Ask them to look it over each evening then sign or initial it and have the child return it the next morning. When appropriate, write comments but try to keep them positive. These parents generally don't have any answers for their child's misbehavior and will actually do more good if they start to respond to positive characteristics in their child. You may prefer to have a weekly report that is sent home every Friday. A similar report can be made for the week looking at the overall behavior for that week. You may want to include how well the student did with the personal target behaviors during the week. Grades should be reported on the regular report card with a notice of the student's averages sent home about midway between report cards.

Allow parents to check out books and games from the classroom to do with their child at home. Show them how they might best use the materials.

Teach parents how to use a simple system of rewards and consequences with the child at home. Sometimes parents don't know how to praise and reward their child. Often, they were not praised or rewarded as children themselves. They were constantly put down and so now they put their children down. Help them to break this pattern by suggesting alternative behaviors.

Maintain confidentiality with the parents. Let parents know that you will not discuss what they have said to you with anyone without their permission. Be sure that if you are ever going to release information about a child to anyone the parents have signed a permission to release confidential information form and specifically stated to whom the information may be released.

WORKING WITH OTHER PROFESSIONALS

In school, our students work not only with the special education teacher and the aide but also with many other school professionals such as regular education teachers, counselors, school psychologists, diagnosticians, the nurse, and the speech therapist. They come into daily contact and often befriend school staff members such as bus drivers, cafeteria workers, and custodians. Occasionally, the child is sent to an outside agency such as a psychologist, a psychiatrist, or a pediatrician. The teacher is the key person in coordinating and communicating with all of these support personnel for the benefit of the child.

In communicating with other professionals, there are also some important guidelines to be aware of:

- Always be conscious of confidentiality. When releasing records or confidential information to outside agencies, be sure that there is a Permission to Release Confidential Information signed by the parents. Check this form to see to whom the information may be released and which information may be given out.

- When consulting with other school personnel about a student, remain positive about that student. Badmouthing our kids only confirms what most people tend to think, that our students are the school's "bad" ones.

- If other school personnel are working with our students (i.e., counselors, music specialists) take responsibility for behavior management during that time. Either the teacher or the aide should stay with the students keeping the feedback system in place and removing behavior problem students immediately so that the others may participate.

- Maintain contact with the regular teachers in your building. Be on the lookout for potential teachers for mainstreaming. Look for teachers with high empathy who will be willing to go the distance with you to successfully mainstream our students.

In summary, our students want an orderly atmosphere, a friendly but professional teacher, an environment that is structured and predictable, and to know they will not be sent out of this safe environment for correction and punishment. The empathic teacher can provide this and much more simply by considering the topics in this chapter and by continuing to ask students what they need.

CHAPTER 5

Management of Instruction
JO ANN REINHART

USING ACADEMICS AS THE MEDIUM

In a classroom for emotionally disturbed students, the focus is primarily on affective development and emotional well-being. This does not mean, however, that cognitive development should be ignored or relegated to a secondary position. In fact, cognitive development or academic instruction becomes the medium through which the teacher establishes structure and substance with these students. All students understand that they come to school to learn. This includes students in special education classes, no matter what their handicapping condition. They all expect to be taught, and they all expect to learn. *How* they learn is what makes them different from other students. These students may require alternative methods of instruction, adapted materials, and creative forms of evaluation and assessment.

Students with emotional problems often are not challenged academically. Teachers and adults in the child's life become more concerned with trying to control the child's surface behavior problems. Real academic instruction takes a secondary role, and, in some cases, does not occur at all. We can get so focused on having the children in their seats, being quiet, and behaving that we provide them with "junk" seat work and then punish them if they aren't interested enough to finish their work. This does not have to be the case. Teachers can select and present real school work in such a way that the child's emotional life becomes an integral part of what the student is being asked to learn. In other words, both cognitive and affective domains of learning may be addressed simultaneously.

PRESENTATION OF ACADEMIC WORK

How well our students learn is certainly a result of how well we plan and present lessons to them while taking into account their emotional well-being. In developing the model of the empathic process for teachers of the emotionally disturbed, Morgan (1979) asked the students questions about how the teacher structured academic activities for them to help them cope with their emotions. Student responses to these questions give us some clear guidelines that we need to consider in planning lessons and teaching if we are to help our students cope with and better understand their emotions and also learn academics.

1. **The empathic teacher provides successful experiences for the students.** Too many failure experiences can be destructive to emotionally disturbed students. According to the students, the good teacher minimizes failures, stays with the student until there is understanding, brings the student along slowly, and teaches and reteaches until the student understands and is competent. We can do this through diagnostic teaching, reteaching, relearning, and providing built-in reinforcers in our lessons.

Diagnostic Teaching: Use the goals and objectives of the Individualized Educational Plan (IEP). Carefully examine each objective in terms of the tasks involved in accomplishing it successfully. Nothing should be taken for granted. Even the simplest task may not yet be mastered by the student and may be the cause of failure. Assure that when a sequence of tasks is required to learn a particular skill the student has actually mastered the earlier tasks of the sequence. This kind of task analysis during lesson planning allows the teacher to do diagnostic teaching while working with the child. This means that the teacher responds to mistakes by diagnosing and reteaching immediately. In this way, student success is assured.

Reteaching: Reteaching literally means to "teach again." If a student does not understand a concept or process, we must continue to teach until there is understanding and competence. It may be necessary to consider an alternative approach if simply teaching again does not help the child grasp the concept or process.

Relearning: Relearning is what the students must do when learning has occurred but the student's performance is inadequate for other reasons. Students must know that no matter how poorly they do on a given assignment, there is a procedure within the classroom structure that allows them to improve their performance and their grade. Give students the opportunity to redo their work for a better grade. Point out specifically what is inadequate with the work. Always check on learning first, and be sure that reteaching is not required. If emotional problems are interfering with academic performance, stop the school work and help the student deal with emotions first.

Built-in reinforcement: Although students are constantly being monitored through a point system, academic rewards should be built into lessons whenever possible. The teacher can provide for immediate responses to student work either by assessing the work as soon as it is done or through peer review procedures and activities. Students should be made aware of progress and successful mastery through the use of charts and graphs, bulletin boards for best work, and tangible rewards such as stickers given daily for best work papers. Rewards may be designed and built into certain kinds of long-term activities. For instance, when a student successfully learns all the times tables, a certificate and a calculator may be rewarded. Or a student who reads a certain number of books may receive a certificate worth a dollar toward the purchase of a book at the school book fair. (More detail will be given for these activities later in this chapter.)

2. **The empathic teacher provides many opportunities and ways for students to learn their lessons.** This teacher uses a wide variety of approaches to teaching a subject and tailors work to each student's needs. Lessons are personalized by the teacher. Responding to each student's individual needs requires that we take into account childrens' learning styles. Through different grouping models, we can provide more opportunities for students to learn from each other and develop their skills of cooperation.

Learning Styles: Lessons that provide for learning styles and personal differences will be more effective. There are a number of factors that we now know can affect learning. In the instructional environment, students will show learning preferences that concern the level of sound, lighting, room temperature, seating design, modality input, student grouping, time of day, and the need for mobility (Dunn, Beaudry, & Klavas, 1989). Lack of knowledge and consideration of learning styles forces us to teach from our own learning-style preferences. These are not necessarily compatible for all the students in our classes and may actually inhibit learning. Therefore, we should investigate our own learning styles as well as our students'. There are a number of good instruments for discovering learning-style preferences. In some districts now, the learning style of the student has become part of the comprehensive assessment for special education placement.

Grouping Models: Lessons and classroom procedures during work periods should allow students to work in a variety of grouping modes. There are basically four grouping modes that the teacher should consider: student and teacher; small group; whole group; and students pairs. Much of the teaching and learning in this type of class is based on the goals and objectives of the IEP. Most of the learning activities related to the IEP require individualized or small group instruction. These are the common grouping modes for this type of class. Whole group instruction is so difficult with these students that it is generally not attempted until later in the academic year when most of the students are much better at self-control and on-task behaviors. It may also be used when several students in the class are being prepared for mainstreaming.

Emotionally disturbed students have a particular need to learn to work together. Often, they are intelligent and quite competent in their work and yet unable to get along with their peers. If these patterns of behavior continue into their adult lives, they will be unable to keep jobs for very long or experience success in their careers. Having students work together in pairs or very small groups may not be possible in the beginning but should be a goal right from the beginning. Students may be encouraged to work together simply by being allowed to ask each other questions or to ask for assistance related to their work during on task periods. A low level of noise within a classroom is often a sign of a healthy working environment. Students with learning problems in addition to emotional problems must be taught to rely on peers to edit and check their work when necessary. These skills of cooperation must be taught to the students by the teacher. Teachers should not take for granted that a student knows how to ask for assistance, knows what to ask, can select the best person to ask, knows how to accept the feedback, and knows how to show appreciation for help given. Conversely, students must be taught how to give assistance without giving an answer or doing the work for another. They must learn to do this without getting haughty or putting the other student down.

When students are able to help each other appropriately, the teacher may try cooperative learning (Bergk, 1988). This model places the student in an environment in which interpersonal forms of learning naturally occur. Students learn to combine individual and social activities during the process of accomplishing a common academic objective. Cooperative learning is a particularly good model for students who are writing stories and books, performing science experiments, doing projects in art, social studies, theatre arts, solving math word problems, and any subject in which students are being asked to think logically.

3. The empathic teacher devises legitimate reasons to change an activity when the student becomes frustrated. Emotionally disturbed students become frustrated easily when trying to concentrate on work that is difficult or new to them. In addition, there will be at least one student in every class who has developed a phobia about a certain subject such as math or reading. In the same class will be at least one student with an unusually short attention span. These students will reach their frustration levels quickly. With this in mind, we can plan their lessons according to some simple guidelines that will help ease this frustration.

Minilessons: For these students, the amount of material presented will make a difference. Work should be given in very small doses, usually no more than one page at a time. Concepts should be taught one at a time. Before beginning to teach a new concept, spend some time checking to see if the student has maintained mastery of background skills. Reteach when necessary. Shorten the length of time that these students are expected to remain on task. Increase on-task time slowly over the course of the year. Stay with the student through the initial stages of frustration, but if it continues, stop or change the learning activity and return to it later.

Alternative mediums: Allow students to do their work through mediums other than traditional paper and pencil: for example, on the chalkboard, on the overhead, on a computer, orally, by using manipulatives or role playing a problem or situation, or by taping a response to an assignment.

Mobility Preferences: Some students may prefer to work standing up or sitting on the floor. Others require more freedom to move around while concentrating. If these alternatives help the student stay on task and complete acceptable work, then they should certainly be considered and the teacher should find appropriate ways to allow for these preferences.

4. The teacher uses a wide variety of commercial and individually created materials. Although we generally do not need to use alternative materials with our students, we should consider how to make the materials fit the learning needs of our students. Careful selection of materials and lessons in textbooks for teaching our students is essential. Tailoring these lessons to the student requires that we know something about current trends in instructional methodologies. In addition, we need to consider the effects of traditional evaluation and testing procedures on our students and look for alternative procedures for assessing learning and achievement.

Focus on Process: Lesson objectives and planning should focus on process—not product. The process of learning has recently become the focus of a great deal of research in education. It has produced a new field of thinking about learning called *metacognition* (Palinscar & Brown, 1987). The focus of metacognition is to teach students how to develop strategies that promote and monitor learning. Students are taught to think about how they are learning while they are learning—process. This is different from the traditional teaching model in which the teacher instructs the students in a discrete set of skills, then tests the students to see if they have synthesized those skills into learning—product.

In teaching processes, initially the teacher assumes full responsibility for modeling a strategy and providing an explanation of how the strategy works (Gordon, 1985). In other words, the teacher actually talks through the mental processes that are occurring during an academic task. As the student begins to understand and apply the process, the teacher gradually shifts the responsibility to the student through guided practice. Finally, teacher and student explore how the strategy may be generalized to other uses and situations.

Evaluation and Testing: We must take into account the fragile nature of some of our students with regard to being judged. Many of our students come from backgounds in which they were or are being physically and/or emotionally abused, neglected, ignored, or unwanted. They have learned to defend themselves from this in a number of ways, most of which are considered socially inappropriate. Any form of evaluation or judging of them or their work may set off a defense mechanism that can disturb the student and disrupt everyone in the environment. When planning assessment of learning, it is especially wise to take this into account. For these students, paper and pencil testing will not yield an accurate accounting of what has been learned. Alternative methods will have to be used if the teacher really wants to know what this student has learned and retained.

Diagnostic teaching is probably the best way to get at assessing learning in this student. This is done one-to-one with the student. A problem is presented and the student is asked to answer, talking through the steps being used to arrive at the answer. If the student gets stuck at any point, the teacher may prompt the student. The student should be allowed to use mediums other than paper and pencil, such as the chalkboard, and so on. Often, a student who would have torn up a lesson sheet on paper will complete all the problems on the chalkboard. Students should be allowed to present projects or role play an activity for the purpose of grading.

The strategies and activities presented in the remainder of this chapter are for adapting methods and materials for the emotionally disturbed student. It is not intended to be a curriculum framework nor a scope and sequence. There is no need to develop an alternative curriculum for these students if the teacher is willing to become a decision maker about the kind of teaching and learning that will take place within this type of classroom. I have used these strategies and activities successfully. More importantly, they incorporate what the children tell us about being good, empathic teachers with our responsibility to provide a sound academic program.

READING AND WRITING

There are different philosophies and approaches to the teaching of reading and writing. All have merit and all can prove that they successfully teach students to become literate. Ultimately, there is no substitute for good teaching, direct instruction, time on task, appropriate opportunities for application of learning, and the reinforcement of successful learning. With our students, the development of language skills must be used to enhance interpersonal learning and communication skills. This can be achieved by using activities from many different sources and philosophies. In other words, we need to be eclectic and open minded. As teachers, we need to be strong decision makers about what works with our students.

APPROACHES TO TEACHING READING AND WRITING

Basal Reading Approach

Reading in the elementary school is traditionally taught with a commercial basal reading program. Basal readers present reading as a carefully sequenced set of skills that are mastered over the course of elementary school years. The modern basal readers provide an anthology of stories, poems, and articles—much of which is award-winning children's literature. The basal readers are age- and grade-specific. The introduction of vocabulary is carefully controlled and presented through direct instruction. Reinforcement of new words and new skills is provided through paper and pencil activities from the basal readers, dittos, and workbooks. This approach is sometimes called a *bottom up approach*, in which learning moves from specific skills to the whole process called reading.

Literature-Based Approach (Whole Language)

In many school districts, the basal approach to reading instruction is being replaced by a whole language- or literature-based approach (Goodman, 1986). This is a holistic approach to teaching reading and writing. Students are taught the skills or parts of language within the context of natural, whole, meaningful language. Whole language teaching is based on the premise that children should learn to read and write in the same natural way they learned to speak. This approach is often called a *top down approach*, in which learning moves from the whole to the part. Skills are taught within the context of reading and writing with emphasis being primarily on process.

Basal Language Arts Approaches

In a *basal language arts program*, the principle is that specific writing skills may be taught independently and then, as the student matures, these skills will be applied to meaningful writing. This is similar to the bottom up approach of the basal reading program. The identified skills are taught every year with increasing degrees of complexity and difficulty as the student progresses through the program.

Writing Process Approach

The writing process approach to teaching language arts is part of the whole language approach. The student learns how to manipulate language through the composition process. The emphasis is on the five phases of writing: prewriting, drafting, revising, editing, and postwriting or publishing. By teaching students to work through this process in different forms of writing, proponents believe that they will learn what they need to know about the written language. This approach is part of the top down approach in which learning moves from the whole to the parts.

ACTIVITIES FOR READING AND WRITING

Reading and writing are interactive processes. In the classroom, they are best taught as integrated subjects rather than in isolation. When they are taught as a series of skills and subskills, students rarely synthesize these skills into actual learning. Teaching reading and writing as integrated processes allows for more interpersonal forms of learning. In other words, our students can relate their own experiences to their own learning. They can grow as they learn from their new experiences and the sharing of these experiences with others in school and at home.

Our classrooms have reading and writing activities that enhance the interpersonal learning experiences of our students. The activities discussed in this chapter have been adapted by this author and used in classrooms for emotionally disturbed students. They are particularly appropriate to our students since they support and enhance affective expression. They are appropriate for students of all ages.

Oral Activities

Before we learn to read and write, we first listen; then we speak. If we expect students to read and write well, we must provide opportunities for them to practice organization of thought through oral language. Emotionally disturbed students are less effective communicators than their nonhandicapped peers. They have difficulty primarily in informal conversation situations. They have been shown to talk in shorter sentences, contribute information that is not relevant to the topic and does not maintain communication. Also, they cannot maintain coherent, fluent interactions with others (McDonough, 1989). Remediation of social communication is best achieved in activities that motivate personal expression in a natural setting. Some activities that will help students do this follow.

Sharing Time. This is adapted from the old "Show and Tell." It works best when done first thing in the school day, although it may be done at the beginning of any class period. Students gather together in a circle or around a group table. Each member of the group must be able to see all the other members. Students are allotted a certain amount of time in which to share something that is current in their lives. It will take some time before all students participate. Some will simply listen at first. The teacher must act as facilitator monitoring time and assisting the students in feeling comfortable with sharing. This is done through words of encouragement, modeling active listening, asking questions, and encouraging other students to ask questions or make comments on the topic. As the school year progresses and students become more comfortable and trusting with each other, they will begin to share personal experiences. Be prepared to hear about sleepless nights while parents fought or a drunken relative wrecked havoc in the home, and much much more. This activity permits a catharsis for our students. Following sharing time, students are usually able to settle down and attend to academic tasks.

Prereading Activities. Prior to reading, students should be prepared for reading. This is done by having the students talk about what they think the topic is and discussing any information they may already know about the topic. Students are asked to predict what will be new in the passage or how the story might evolve. The purpose of these pre-reading activities is to get the students in touch with knowledge they already possess and how that knowledge might affect the comprehension of the passage or story. Within this process, the students are given the opportunity to get in touch with what they think about a topic and how that topic relates to them.

Prewriting Activities. Just as students prepare for reading, they must prepare for writing. In writing, the process is reversed since now the student becomes the author. This requires that students decide on a topic, gather appropriate information with which to write about the topic, get in touch with the audience for whom they are writing, and determine the organization of the writing. All of this is may be done orally before a first draft is written. Initially, these activities are teacher directed. As students become more competent in discussing prewriting activities, they may work in pairs or individually.

Reading Activities

Reading begets reading. The way to help children read better is to provide lots of different kinds of reading opportunities for them. The classroom must become a community of readers. In other words, the teacher, the aide, the students, everyone in the classroom participates in reading activities. It is essential that the classroom become a reading community. We need to share the joys and pleasures, the information and knowledge that we get from reading with our students. If we are highly motivated readers, then we can teach our students how to become highly motivated readers.

Through reading, we communicate deeply with other human beings. We may share the full range of human emotions. We come to realize how much we are alike and how much we are each different from one another. We learn from one another. We relate in a quiet, personal way through reading. Getting our students in touch with the power of reading is essential. This is best done through reading of real literature and whole books. The following activities have been used successfully for this purpose.

Sustained Silent Reading (SSR). SSR is a well known activity. It is just what it says it is: a sustained period of time over which silent reading takes place. During this period, the classroom becomes the reading community. Everyone in the classroom participates, even visitors. The purpose of SSR is to provide time for and encourage reading for pleasure. In order to have a successful SSR activity with emotionally disturbed students, however, there are certain guidelines that the teacher should keep in mind.

- Begin with a very short time period, probably no more than 5 to 10 minutes. Work toward the goal of 20 to 30 minutes of SSR.

- Allow students to select what they want to read. Remember, reading begets reading. Students only benefit from reading silently if they are reading materials at their independent reading level. At this level, the student should be able to read nearly 100% of the words with fluency and full comprehension. Allow students to read books, magazines, newspapers, and so on. Allow limited English proficient students to read materials in their native language if available. Allow older students to read easy readers if they wish. Allow poor readers to read along with a taped book or story or to read wordless picture books. Students must be allowed to read materials that they have selected and that they are comfortable reading.

• Be sure that everyone reads, especially the teacher. If the teacher is grading papers or out in the hall talking to another teacher, the students infer that this time for reading really isn't very important.

• Do not allow students to use SSR time to complete homework or to finish other academic work. This is a time for reading for pleasure. It is not a study hall.

• Become a reading consultant. Use SSR time to read those books that are appropriate to the student population that you are teaching. Use your school librarian to help you select award-winning books or books on special topics. Librarians also have updates of the latest books on the market. Knowing about the books in the school library will enable you to help students select books that they might like or that may provide a message for their problems. For more on this topic, see the section on Bibliotherapy in Chapter 6.

• If possible, set up a classroom library. Include books and stories that will address different reading and interest levels. Include basal readers from earlier grades and wordless picture books. If you are willing to spend some of your own money and time, you can amass a nice library of children's books by visiting used paperback book stores, flea markets, and garage sales. Try to get multiple copies of books so several students may read the same book at the same time and share their thoughts about the book. Include joke books, karate and motorcycle books, books about alcohol and drug abuse, and any topic or genre that you know may interest your students. Read all the books yourself, especially the novels.

Book Club. Book Club is, in a sense, an extension of SSR. There is generally no evaluation of what the students have read during SSR. Book Club can provide a way for students to share their books. Tell the students that there will be a classroom book club that anyone may join. In the beginning, the poor readers will be the most antagonistic to the idea. Set up a bulletin board on which the Book Club will post its member's names and a display of the books each member has read. Members may enter a book into the Book Club by presenting the book orally to the other members of the club. Basically, this is a book report by "any other name." The teacher must provide the format and the form for this presentation. Students prepare to answer the questions posed in the format by either writing in the answers or simply preplanning in their minds. Questions on this form might include:

- What is the title of the book?

- Who is the author? Is this a pseudonym? If so, what is the author's real name?

- What other books has this author written?

- Is this book part of a series? If so, what are the other books in the series?

- Is this an award-winning book?

- Who are the main characters? What is the setting? Tell about the antagonist.

- Give a synopsis of the story.

- What is the solution or resolution to the story?

The student must then be asked to express opinions about the book?

- What made you want to read this book?

- Would you recommend this book to a friend? Why or why not?

- Do you feel that this book was well written? Why or why not?

The student should then be asked to rate the book: on a scale of 1 to 10, awarding stars, and so forth. Students and teacher may agree on some kind of rating scale.

When a student is ready to present a book to the Book Club, a form with at least the student's name, date, and title of the book to be submitted must be turned into the teacher or Book Club President. Each day during an alloted time, these presentations can be made. Often they will have to be limited to no more than two presentations a day, since each will take about 5 to 10 minutes. A good time for Book Club presentations is directly following SSR. The teacher or president may assist with the presentation by posing the questions on the form to the presenter to keep the presentation within the boundaries of the format. When the student has finished the presentation, the members of the Book Club may pose questions. There may be more they wish to know about the book or questions related to the flow of the story as told in the synopsis. The purpose of these questions is to assure the other members that the member submitting the book to Book Club did, indeed, read the book. Remember that the teacher and the aide are also members of the Book Club and as such may also ask questions and submit books through oral presentation to the other members. Finally, when all the questions are satisfied, the total members vote on whether to allow the book to be submitted or not. Generally, books are approved by the membership. On occasion, one will not be approved. This is usually because the presenter really didn't show through the synopsis and follow-up questions a true understanding of the story. In this case, the member is encouraged to reread the story in order to answer the questions that were asked and to resubmit the book at a later date.

A book that has been accepted is then posted on the bulletin board. Members are rewarded for books accrued. In one classroom, for every ten books read, students received a $1.00 certificate toward the purchase of a book at the school book fair. Another teacher provided gift certificates to a local book store for students who had read a predetermined number of books. In most self-contained classrooms, there is a small budget for reinforcers which may be used to pay for Book Club rewards. Often, PTA will be happy to provide money to support this kind of classroom effort.

Story Time. During Story Time, the teacher or aide reads out loud to the students. This may last from 10 minutes a day for very young children to 30 minutes daily for older students. Although it is entertaining, reading out loud to students has some very real academic benefits. First and most importantly, it provides children with a model of reading for pleasure, reading for meaning, and reading beyond reading. Second, it allows students to experience a whole piece of literature that they themselves might not be able to read or might read so poorly as to not experience the true meaning of the literature. Reading out loud provides an environment in which everyone shares the experiences and emotions that the author intends to elicit in the reader. If you don't believe this, read *Where the Red Fern Grows* to students of any age. If you don't know this book, a pre-reading is highly recommended before trying to read it out loud to a class. Even then, you will probably need a box of kleenex to get through the ending. Finally, if students are involved in the selection of the books for Story Time, this process will help them learn how to decide what they want to read when they have an opportunity to select a book for themselves.

In setting up Story Time, there are some guidelines that the teacher should follow in order to assure that these benefits occur:

- Select good literature. Let students know which books are award-winning books and what that means. After they have read such a book, ask students to rate the book and support their ratings.

- Select literature in its original form. Do not read edited versions of stories from basal readers, and so on. Since Story Time occurs daily, you simply continue reading a little each day for as long as it takes to get through the book.

- Select a range of genres: mysteries, adventures, humorous, sad, and so on. Select books that you know will have special meaning to certain students in your classes. For example, *Do Bananas Chew Gum?* is a wonderful story about a boy who discovers he has learning disabilities.

- Prior to reading a book out aloud, assure that the students have the background knowledge necessary to fully enjoy the novel. In one class of predominantly Mexican American students, they chose to read *The Black Pearl* by Scott O'Dell. The students voted for this book because the setting is in Mexico and there are Spanish words used throughout the text. However, after reading only one chapter, the students lost interest and wanted to vote to discontinue reading the novel. The problem was that these were children who lived in the desert. They knew nothing about the ocean, had no idea what an oyster was, and did not know that pearls come from oysters. In other words, they had inadequate background knowledge with which to relate to the story and so lost interest quickly in the story. The solution was to spend one day of Story Time with a real oyster from the grocery store. After a discussion of oysters and pearls, a vote was taken on how many thought this oyster would contain a pearl and how many thought not. The oyster was then shucked and unfortunately, no pearl was there. But the students immensely enjoyed the rest of the novel, *The Black Pearl*.

- Involve the students in the selection of the books to be read during Story Time. This is easily accomplished by either having a class-room library or by bringing a selection of books from the library from which the students may choose a book or several books for Story Time. Spread the books out on the group table. Allow each of the students to come to the table and select one book to propose for Story Time. Show students that they may select a book to read for a number of different reasons: the cover is interesting, by reading the synopsis, by the number of pages or the number of illustrations, by the author, because the book is part of a series, the book has won an award for literature or illustrations, by the genre or topic, by the setting or types of characters, by a recommendation from someone who has read the book, and so on. Once each student has selected a book to propose, write each title on the chalkboard, overhead, or chart tablet. Be sure to underline the titles (modeling!). One by one, have the students propose the book they chose. They do this by orally presenting the book to the class, giving the title and the author, reading the synopisis (if there is one), then telling what made them select that for Story Time. They are trying to persuade others to want their book also. When all of the books have been proposed, the whole class votes on which books they would most like read aloud. Allow the students to vote as often as they wish; then eliminate the books that receive the fewest votes. Continue the process until only one or two books are left. Have the students decide in which order they would like to read the books.

• When reading a novel over a long period of time (sometimes it can take weeks to get through one book), each day have someone summarize what has happened to this point and then ask the students to try to figure out what they think will happen next. This will refocus their attention and assure greater enjoyment of the day's reading.

• With very young children, the teacher may have to do much of the selection of books. Books for young children are usually short enough that they may be read in one sitting. With these books, it is best to read them in one sitting. Sometimes, try presenting a wordless picture book and have the children make up the story. Write it down for them if you wish. Or take a book with clear illustrations and let the children make up a different story to match the illustrations.

Writing Activities

Writing is an interactive process with reading. The reader is the recipient of the message intended by the author. The reader, however, is not just a passive recipient. The reader brings to the author's message any knowledge already acquired on the topic, opinions, interest or lack of, and ability to read fluently and comprehend what is read. As an author, the student reverses this process and must consider that the reader is now the audience.

It stands to reason that if we want students to become better writers, then we must encourage them to read a lot of writers.

Writing, like reading, requires that we create a sense of community in our classrooms. In this case, we will consider ourselves a community of writers and authors. Through becoming authors, students are offered one more channel for self-expression. This is perhaps the most powerful channel because the written word may be made permanent. There are activites that will help our students achieve this act of self-expression in writing.

Interactive Journals. In learning language, we first learn to listen and discriminate sounds, then words, and, finally, meaningful communication. We then learn to speak thereby completing the communication. With instruction, we learn to read. The last and most difficult phase of language learning is learning to compose, to express our thoughts and knowledge in writing. For many students (and especially for older students), this process is poorly developed or not developed at all. One of the best ways to begin writing with students like this is to start an interactive journal with them. This is simply a spiral bound notebook in which an entry is made every day by the student. Students should be given 10 to 15 minutes during the language-arts period in which to write in their journals. Each day, the teacher reads the entries and writes a response to the student. This is what makes the journal interactive. There are some specific guidelines for these interactive entries.

- The students are allowed to write whatever they wish, regardless of ability to spell, capitalize, punctuate, or use correct grammar. As the students are writing, the teacher and the aide may be available to help with spelling or students may ask each other. However, no emphasis should be placed on these aspects of the writing. The purpose of the entry is expression and communication.

- The teacher *never* makes corrections on the student's entry. The corrections are made in the response that is written to the student. The teacher rephrases the student's message, correctly writing what the student intended. For example . . .

Student: I will go to see *Ghostbusters* last weekend. It costed four dollars. But I liked it anyway.

Teacher: I went to see *Ghostbusters* last weekend, too. It cost five dollars where I went, but I liked it also. My favorite part was when they got slimed. What part did you like best?

- Students who have difficulty getting started with the process can draw pictures for a while. Respond to them by drawing pictures also, but add dialogue or text of some kind to your pictures. When they are ready to write start by asking questions, "What did you do last weekend?" but avoid yes/no questions. You'll find that that is all some students will write.

- For students who are limited English proficient, they may be allowed to write in their native language if someone is available to read the entry. The response may be in either the student's native language or in English.

- If students wish, they may keep an interactive journal with other students in the class or with a student in another classroom. This means that two journals are exchanged and are written in on alternating days. Occasionally, the teacher should read these entries and make an entry addressed to both writers.

With patience and care in responding to the students' entries, you will see an enormous change in their writing over a period of time. One student who never capitalized or punctuated suddenly one day wrote three pages all of it correctly punctuated and capitalized; sometimes it just takes a while to ripen.

The real value of interactive journals with our students is that students will often write what they will not or cannot say; they may open up to you in their journals. Be sure that all students understand that the journals are private. Only the student and you are going to read them unless the student wants someone else to read and write in the journal. Then be sure and keep it that way.

Writing Process. The current trend in writing instruction is to teach children through the writing process. We use the student's original composition as the basis of instruction. Ideally, the student should select the topic of the composition. Ideas for topics generated by the student are kept in a writing folder to be developed or simply left to percolate for a period of time. First drafts, unfinished pieces, and ongoing research may also be kept in the writing folder.

The writing process has five basic phases. Prewriting, which has already been mentioned under oral activities, occurs as a mental activity before anything is written. Prewriting is how we organize our thinking in order to get ready to write. In this phase, we think about topics, about our opinions and how we might persuade another person, about descriptions and dialogues, about the steps we would have to give to tell someone how to do something. Students may wish to write notes or complete organizers in the prewriting phase, but much of this phase is thinking, brainstorming, and sharing.

Then comes the first draft. This is just like the entries in the interactive journals. The student writes without regard for spelling, punctuation, capitalization, or good grammar. Drafting simply gets the thoughts down on paper. From there, revisions are made. This is the third phase. Revising deals with the content, how well it is stated, if it says what was intended, if it makes sense, and whether it is clear enough. When students are in the revising phase with a composition, they may begin the peer revising/editing procedures. They may ask an outside reader to provide feedback on the writing. Again, students must be taught how to ask for and how to provide appropriate feedback. Once the author is satisfied with the content and organization of the composition, then it is time for editing.

Editing is the phase before publishing; this is the time that errors in spelling, punctuation, capitalization, and grammar are cleaned up. Naturally, students will not see all of their mistakes. If that were true, they wouldn't have made them in the first place. This is not the time to take out your red pen. In fact, if you are teaching writing process, you can throw away your red pen. Students will learn to write better without it. First have the students do peer editing. Encourage the students to get as many readers as possible to edit. There are two schools of thought on further editing by the teacher. One says that we should not interfere with the developing writer and that they don't learn anything from the corrections we make on their papers. The other side believes that the final copy of a student's work should be perfect, or publishable. You will have to make the decision for yourself and with your students as to how far to carry the editing process. No matter what your decision, it is still best not to red mark a child's creative effort. Instead, take another sheet of paper and write the total number of spelling errors, and so on that you have found. Let the student try again to edit out the remaining errors. Then if any remain, you may write them correctly on the second sheet and still allow the student to make the corrections within the text.

Writing process is personal and individual. That is its power and its appeal. It must be carefully handled by the teacher, especially with emotionally disturbed students. Like interactive journals, its value to our students lies in the motivation to express their own thoughts and emotions and to share them with others through writing. The student becomes the author, able to select the topic, write about real life experiences or how life might be.

Conflict Reports. Writing journal entries and compositions are only two of hundreds of forms of writing. Filling out forms and reports is something most of us have to do regularly. In a classroom where there may be a lot of conflict, it might be useful to develop a report form to be completed by students involved in a conflict. The form might include the following questions:

- What kind of conflict were you involved in (shouting, fighting, etc.)?

- With whom did this conflict occur?

- Describe how the problem started. Be sure to think back to anything in the past that might also be part of this problem.

- What else would you like to say or do to the person you are in conflict with?

- What have you done to try to stop the conflict?

- What else would you like to try to stop the conflict?

- Who might be able to help you to stop the conflict?

- What will happen when the conflict stops?

- Write a plan of action for stopping the conflict. Be specific. Tell who will do what when.

From this report the teacher could do some followup work with those involved in the conflict.

READING DISABILITIES

An estimated 10 to 20% of school age children have difficulty learning to read through traditional methods of instruction (Oliphant, 1979). These students are sometimes identified as *reading disabled* or *dyslexic*. Failure to learn reading in the early grades can be a major cause of behavioral and emotional problems in school. However, if the condition is mild, these children may go undiagnosed and untreated. As they progress through school, their reading problems will become more severe unless intervention takes place. Children who are unable to read or do not learn to read like other children are often told that they are slow, mentally retarded, lazy, or not living up to their potential. Rarely do these children realize that their difficulty in learning to read is through no fault of their own. As teachers, we unfortunately say these things to children because we are frustrated and unsuccessful in teaching them to read. It is a vicious cycle that can only be broken if we recognize the real cause of the reading problem.

In order to understand where the reading process fails for these children, we need to consider some of the components of the reading process. Reading requires two basic skills: decoding of individual words and sentences and comprehension. When we teach initial reading, we usually expect that a child will learn to read by remembering whole words through multiple exposures in print, both in isolation such as word lists and flashcards, and in context through either controlled exposure in the basal readers or through trade books and literature in the whole language approach. This is what is called the *sight word approach* to learning to read. We present some phonics instruction incidentally in which we focus on initial or final consonants and medial vowels beginning with the short vowels. In most phonics books and lessons, these sounds are taught in isolated words that have no realtionship to one another and no pattern of sounds such as might be found in rhyming words or words with the same beginnings or endings. For most children, the application of sound to new words comes automatically from knowledge gained in the learning of sight words and the little bit of phonics that we teach. For instance, a child learns the sight word "cat," then comes across the word "fat." Almost instantly, an association is made that this is the same word except with a different sound at the beginning. If you've ever taught kindergarten or first grade, you know that the children tell you when this revelation occurs. It delights them to unlock the door to reading new words. For children with reading disabilities, this does not occur automatically or easily.

Students with reading disabilities have a deficit in phonemic processing and in verbal retrieval (Richardson, 1984). In other words, they do not know how to use the sounds that letters and groups of letters represent to decode unknown words, and they have difficulty remembering and retrieving sight words. These students are sometimes able to retrieve a word for a day or a week; then suddenly it is gone and must be relearned. This is frustrating for both the student and the teacher. The teacher should be aware that there are some reading behaviors that are characteristic of students with reading disabilities. The reading-disabled student may exhibit the following difficulties in learning to read:

- Difficulty learning the sounds of letters and, in particular, the sounds of vowels

- Misreads function words (i.e., prepositions, pronouns, articles)

- Uses the wrong word in the same class (i.e., "little" for "small", "noise" for "sound")

- Reads slowly and laboriously as if seeing each word for the first time

- Guesses at words, using only the first or first and last letters (i.e., "fly" for "family")

- Makes up nonsense words using the letters for which sounds are known (i.e., "flamy" for "family")

- Has particular difficulty with word endings and breaking words into syllables

- Confuses letters and words with slightly different configurations (i.e., "p, b, d, q", "big - pig")

These are some of the most common characteristics. Observation of several of these behaviors during reading may indicate that a student has reading disabilties.

Without good decoding skills, the reader cannot read fluently; without fluency, comprehension is severely impaired. Both decoding skills and comprehension are essential to good reading; therefore, both must be taught at the same time. For students with reading disabilites, you will need to find a good phonetic-linguistic approach that addresses both of these areas. Do not settle for a program that promises to teach students to decode but will make no guarantees for comprehension. There are some excellent approaches on the market today. Some are relatively easy to learn to teach, whereas others require more committment in time and money. The time spent, however, is well worth it. These children may never be excellent readers and they may never love reading, but they can learn to read and they can feel good about themselves again.

What about the student who can decode well, knows all the sounds, reads fluently, and yet does not comprehend at all or comprehends minimally? This is a reading problem that we see primarily in the upper elementary and secondary grades. There are probably a number of causes for this failure. The teacher should look at the following factors when planning reading instruction for the student.

Attention Deficit Disorders (ADD): The student may have ADD, a neuro-logically based deficit in the ability to attend and concentrate for long periods of time. It may be manifested in hyperactivity, which is easily observable since the student cannot sit still and moves almost constantly, or in distractability, which is less obvious since a student may appear to be on task and yet can be light years away mentally. Both deficits may be treated medically if they are severe enough and if the physician and the parent agree that this is the best course of action. The teacher's role in the medical treatment of ADD is to report to the parent or physician any behavioral changes that are observed in the classroom and in the child's ability to succeed with schoolwork. For many of these students, however, medical treatment is not the best course of action. For some it does not work at all, and for others there may be negative side effects. If the child is not treated medically, it is up to the teacher to work with the student to help develop a conscious understanding of what is going on and to deliberately work to improve on task behaviors. This may be done through contracting, using timers, tangible rewards such as stickers and treats, or intangible rewards such as free time following a certain amount of time on task. In terms of reading comprehension, though, this student will need to be taught strategies such as selecting the main idea and key concepts, rereading, summarizing, reader generated questions, predicting, and so on.

Vocabulary Development: A student with this factor lacks in-depth vocabulary development and understanding. Often, children can decode and read words and yet have no idea what they mean. If you have ever read a medical report, you have experienced this. You can read and decode the words in the report and still have no idea what your physician is saying about your medical condition. No matter how motivated you are to understand, if you do not know the meaning of more than 50% of the words used, you will not be able to make much sense of the report. This is particularly true for our limited English proficient students or students who have just exited bilingual programs. Although they appear to speak and read English fluently, these students may not have the depth of understanding of word meaning. There are often multiple meanings of words, nuances, and idiomatic uses that are difficult to learn and only develop after years of use of the English language.

Remediated Dyslexic: A student with this factor may be dyslexic and in whom the decoding skills deficits have been remediated. This student appears to decode adequately and reads fluently, yet does not comprehend. For this student, fluent reading may still demand overfocusing on individual words in order to decode. The first reading of written material is, therefore, completely devoted to decoding the words in the passage. This student requires a second reading in order to gather information from what is written. In addition, this student may benefit from continued work in decoding skills with an emphasis on affixes, syllabification, word usage, editing, sentence combining, cloze procedures, and word meaning.

The Nonstrategic Reader: This may be the student who has not developed and has not been taught good reading strategies. This student does not know what to do before reading, how to think about what is going to be read, how to get in touch with what is already known about the topic, the personal or imposed motivation for reading, or the author's purpose in writing. During reading, this student does not look ahead and predict what might happen, summarize what has happened, use cloze procedures to understand unknown words, or pose questions as reading progresses. This student is not aware when reading is not occuring and when rereading is necessary. After reading, this student does not know how to assess the predictions that were made during reading, summarize what was read, look for key ideas and concepts, or develop opinions about the topic, the author, or how well or poorly the piece was written. This student does not know how to apply and integrate what was read with previous experiences.

When working with poor readers, you should always apply certain principles:

1. Find the student's independent, instructional, and frustration reading levels. The independent reading level is the level at which the student is able to read nearly 100% of the words with fluency and full comprehension. At the instructional level, the student should be able to read from 80 to 90% of the words and achieve full comprehension with direct teacher instruction. The frustration level is the point at which the student is able to read less than 50% of the words and has little or no comprehension. It is important to provide a lot of reading materials for the student at the independent reading level. Allow time in class for individual reading at the independent reading level.
2. Reading materials presented at the student's instructional reading level must always be through direct instruction. Materials at this level must be thoroughly explained and read out loud, then reinforced through rereading.
3. Provide plenty of oral reading activities. Read and have students read stories, plays, poems, songs, jokes, lists, journals, newspaper and magazine articles, novels, and even basal reader stories. Reading orally is a multisensory experience for the student. Reading out loud allows the child to see and hear the printed word at the same time.

4. Provide motivational activities such as SSR and Book Club. Share your joys and motivations for reading with your students. If you've read a good novel, present it in Book Club. Create a sense of community in which one of the common goals is the joy of literacy.

5. Never ask students to spell words that they cannot read and comprehend. Select spelling words from the student's independent reading level. Be sure to provide dictation in which the words appear in a meaningful context. When giving dictation, say the complete sentence to the students; then have them write. Do not break sentences into parts for the purpose of dictation. The students must learn to mentally hold a verbal string (complete sentence) long enough to write it.

In your classroom for emotionally disturbed children, there will doubtless be students with reading disabilities. This may be a secondary handicapping condition and will be noted on the IEP. It may also be missed in the diagnosis as a cause of the emotional/behavioral problems a student is having. Remediation and correction of a reading problem can often make an enormous difference in the successful treatment of an emotionally disturbed student.

MATHEMATICS

The learning of mathematics is basically linear and progressive. One skill builds on another and requires mastery of earlier skills before progressing to the next in the sequence. Most of the facts learned in math must be memorized (i.e., plus and minus facts, times tables, properties, equations, rules, and formulas). These skills must then be applied through problem solving. Problem solving requires the use of logic, the application of math facts, and an understanding of the concepts involved as well as adequate reading ability. Assessment of math skills and math problem solving is very concrete. We assume that if the student is able to arrive at the correct answer to a problem, all of these skills have been mastered. If, however, a student arrives at the wrong answer, we must look at all of the component skills to find the area in need of reteaching.

In math, there are only two kinds of answers: right and wrong. This is considerably different than most of our reading and reading-related subject areas in which answers may vary and, in fact, are encouraged. Because of the concrete nature of math, emotionally disturbed students may feel threatened or intimidated by it: that is, phobic. Even students without phobias may have a hard time with math until they realize that they are in an environment in which it is safe to make mistakes and in which they are always given an opportunity to correct their mistakes. In this environment, mistakes are considered an essential element of the learning process. Even the teacher may make mistakes and correct them without intimidation or shame. You will need to model this for the students.

To successfully teach math to these students, the teacher may refer to the following guidelines.

Begin by administering a good diagnostic skills assessment. Find out which math facts the student has not yet memorized. Refer to the IEP to find out if the student has at one time memorized the facts and since forgotten them. Use common sense about how much time to spend making children memorize math facts. Use good judgment and observation to determine whether a student is capable of retaining memorized math facts. Students with memory deficits are incapable of retaining math facts over the course of time. These students should be given calculators with which to perform these functions. It is a waste of a student's time and intelligence to force the memorization of math facts year after year.

Use manipulatives to teach math. Most of the current basal math programs incorporate manipulatives into the typical paper and pencil lessons that have dominated our math classes for so many years. If this is not done for you in the books and teacher's editions, do it for yourself and your students. Use paperclips, plastic chips, candy, pizza, three-dimensional objects, computer simulation programs, measuring tapes, measuring cups, play money, clocks with hands that can be moved, or anything that will illustrate a math concept for the student and with the student's participation.

Integrate student's real life experiences into problem solving activities. With the students' participation, rewrite story problems to include the students in the class, their families, friends, and their lives. Have students think of story problems that happened to them. Create story problems that require activities to be solved (i.e., keep a record of student heights and growth over the course of the year, then calculate the percentage of growth, etc.). Integrate math activities into other content areas, especially science and social studies. Teach students how math learning applies to all areas of learning, such as map reading, time lines, charting science projects, and so on.

Allow the students to work with mediums other than paper and pencil. Use the chalkboard, the overhead, or a chart tablet. For students who work slowly, the teacher or the aide should write the problems on the chalkboard; then the student only must work the answers.

Teach only one concept at a time, thereby assuring that the student has mastered any necessary prior concepts. Use a task analysis of the concept to determine the skills and prior concepts necessary to mastery of the concept being taught. During direct teaching of a new concept, the teacher should verbalize the steps taken to arrive at the answer, thus modeling the strategy for the student. The focus of this modeling is on the thinking processes rather than the mechanical operation. The teacher continues to do this but asks the student to verbalize some of the steps until the student can verbalize the entire procedure and apply it in independent work. Teaching the student to think aloud works for problem solving as well.

Focus on higher-order thinking skills. Do not teach only the facts and skills. We have a tendency to do this in special education because they are simply easier to teach and assess. When we are busy dealing with inappropriate behavior, we may not feel that we have the time and the concentration to teach our students to apply logic and thinking skills to problem solving. In addition, these concepts are difficult for our students to learn. The students require a great deal of repetition and practice in order to master problem solving. To cope with these factors, teach the vocabulary and reading skills required to understand math problems. Teach the key words that cue the functions required to solve the problem. In other words, teach strategies for solving math problems the same as you would teach strategies for comprehension in reading.

Teach students to use calculators. Set guidelines for when and how they may use them during math class. Calculators should not replace learning paper and pencil arithmetic. We should be reasonable, however, about how much time our students spend on performing calculations that can be done in seconds on a calculator. We also want to assess the value of having the student perform the calculations versus moving on to the application of these calculations.

Assess math learning in ways other than paper and pencil tests. Once again, you do not have to rely on traditional testing to assess mastery in math. Allow the students to work the problems on the chalkboard or the overhead; have them work one or two problems at a time; and let them go back and correct wrong answers then average the two grades together to get the final grade for that assessment. Have students do a project that involves the application of the math skills and concepts being assessed. Allow students to work together on such a project.

MATH ACTIVITIES

Math skills development requires practice. Problem solving requires that the student experiences math in everyday life and is aware of how it is meaningful. Certain activities can provide this practice and awareness and are fun for our students.

Times Masters

In the early grades, a good deal of math learning is rote memorization. Students must learn addition and subtraction facts and times tables in order to succeed with more complex calculations. Although this activity is designed for teaching times tables, the procedures described could also be applied to any sequential set of facts that must be memorized, such as plus and minus facts, time or money, and so on. To become a "Times Master," a student works through a series of flashcards, practice sheets, and tests over a period of time. The teacher will need to prepare the materials.

1. First make a complete set of times table flashcards from zeros through twelves. Although most basal arithmetic programs teach only through tens now, the students who become "Times Masters" have a much greater sense of accomplishment and pride for having learned through the twelves.
2. Prepare a practice worksheet for each of the times tables from zeros through twelves. The first sheet should contain facts for zeros, ones, and twos since less than this would not be very challenging. On each sheet in the progression, be sure to write facts from prior levels, (i.e., the fives practice sheet should contain not only the fives times table facts, but also some fours, threes, twos, ones, and zeros). You should be able to fit from 50 to 90 facts on each sheet.
3. Prepare four times mastery tests. These tests contain all of the facts from zeros to twelves. On one test, write the facts vertically; on another, write them horizontally. On the third test, write the facts so that the student must fill in the missing factor (i.e., 12 X _____ = 144. On the fourth test, do all of the above.
4. Prepare a Mastery Chart or Contract. See Figure 5.1 for an example of a Times Master Contract. On this sheet, the students keep track of where they are in the process toward becoming a "Times Master." It may take 6 weeks to achieve this goal, or it may take 6 months. The contracts and times mastery materials should be kept in one place within the classroom where they will be easily accessible.

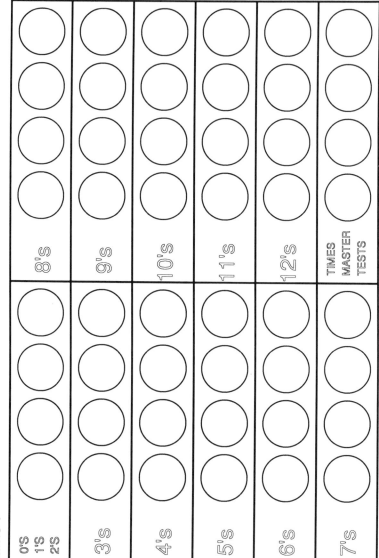

Fig. 5-1. Times Master Contract

5. Procedures: Each day (for no more that 15 to 20 minutes) have the students participating in "Times Masters" come to the group table and work with the flashcards orally. This is a good activity to have the aide do, and it allows the teacher to work with individual students not participating in "Times Masters." In the beginning, use only the cards that correspond up to the level that the students have mastered. Keep adding cards as the students progress through the times tables. When responding to the flashcards, students must take turns in a predetermined order. Allow the students to make up the rules for what will happen when an answer is missed, and so on. It is fun to let the student take the card when a correct response is given. At the end, have the students count the number of cards each had correct. The student with the most cards gets a sticker for that day. Following the flashcard round, students do one practice sheet, have it scored, and write the results on the chart. Any scores of less than 70% must be corrected in order to be used for Times Mastery. The teacher decides whether to time the practice sheets or not. Many students can perform much better when they are not being timed. When a student has worked through all of the times tables and completed at least four practice sheets for each level with at least 70% accuracy, then the four mastery tests are administered. At the completion of the contract, the student should receive a certificate awarding the status of "Times Master." Then, the student may receive other kinds of rewards such as running the flashcard activity or earning a calculator to be used at specified times within the classroom.

Other Activities Related to Math

Students unknowingly participate in school activities every day that are related to math. The following list should at least set you to thinking of the many ways your students can be made aware that math is part of our daily lives.

REAL LIFE MATH APPLICATIONS

Counting
- jumping rope
- games such as Hide-and-Seek which require counting by 2's, 5's, 10's
- finding pages in a book
- counting reinforcement points
- taking a classroom inventory—books, pencils, paint boxes, scissors, etc.

One-to-One Correspondence	• taking roll
	• passing out books, papers, pencils, etc.
	• setting up chairs around the group table
	• planning a party, figuring out how much food and drinks to bring
Classifying	• sorting papers—colored papers, assignment sheets
	• sorting supplies—pencils, crayons, pens, clips
Operations	• charting science experiments, then performing prescribed operations to glean information
	• comparing temperatures at different times
	• comparing student heights and weights
	• averaging grades and points sheets
	• keeping score in a game
	• using birthdates to calculate age
Measurement	• developing a personal time line for the academic year
	• reading schedules
	• measuring student offices—Does everyone have the same amount of space?
	• measuring student heights and weights
Using Money	• exchanging points for tangible rewards in store
	• saving points for a particular purpose
	• using checks and balancing a checking account
	• learning about inflation through price increases in the items in store
Telling Time	• writing a personal daily schedule
	• reading a schedule
	• keeping track of minutes off free time for inappropriate behaviors
Games with Numbers	• monopoly, dominoes, triominoes, uno
	• any game that uses dice such as Yahtzee
	• most card games

SCIENCE AND SOCIAL STUDIES

Teaching science and social studies to emotionally disturbed students is basically teaching reading, writing, and arithmetic. If we are successful at teaching the basics, we can integrate these content areas into daily learning activities. Many of the suggestions already given in this chapter under reading and math activities do just this. Teaching and learning in the content areas allows the student to apply higher-order thinking skills to the basic processes of reading, writing, and arithmetic. In studying science and social studies, students should be asked to analyze, synthesize, and evaluate.

The content areas lend themselves to writing process activities. Students should be taught to identify and write in the different kinds of expository text structure. This is particularly important for students in the upper elementary and secondary grades. However, even kindergarten children can work through the oral prewriting activities and write some simple ideas with the teacher's help. Students should be taught to identify and produce expository writing in the following categories:

1. *the descriptive paragraph*, which describes the topic and its specific attributes
2. *the enumerative paragraph*, which states a topic and then lists examples to support the main topic
3. *the sequence paragraph*, which states a main topic supported by details that must be given in a specific order
4. *the cause/effect paragraph*, which states a main topic supported by details that state why the topic statement is made
5. *the compare/contrast paragraph*, which gives the subjects to be compared and contrasted then tells how they are alike and how they are different
6. *the problem/solution paragraph*, which states a problem in the topic sentence and then describes the problem, its causes, and the solutions
7. *the persuasive paragraph*, which states the author's opinion on the topic and then persuades the reader through supporting statements (Piccolo, 1987).

These are all forms of expository prose that can be found in textbooks, magazines, journals, newspapers, novels, autobiographies, and nonfiction books. In preparing students to write in these different forms, pre-writing activities (oral or written) should lead to higher order thinking. Students are being asked to support statements of fact and opinion, to compare and contrast, to analyze and evaluate, to show the steps of a solution to a problem, and to analyze cause and effect relationships.

To help our students think in these terms, we should ask questions that teach this kind of thinking. Using Bloom's cognitive taxonomy, we can develop certain kinds of questions that elicit different levels of thinking (Bloom et al., 1956). The following list gives Bloom's levels with brief definitions and some examples of questions that might be asked:

QUESTIONS FOR QUALITY THINKING

Knowledge—*Identification and recall of information*
   Who, what, when, where, how _____?
   Describe _____ .
Comprehension—*Organization and selection of facts and ideas*
   Retell _____ in your own words.
   What is the main idea of _____?
Application—*Use of facts, rules, principles*
   How is _____ an example of _____?
   How is _____ related to _____?
   Why is _____ significant?
Analysis—*Separation of a whole into component parts*
   What are the parts or features of _____?
   Classify _____ according to _____?
   Outline/diagram/web _____?
   How does _____ compare/contrast with _____?
   What evidence can you present for _____?
Synthesis—*Combination of ideas to form a new whole*
   What would you predict/infer from _____?
   What ideas can you add to _____?
   How would you create/design a new _____?
   What might happen if you combined _____ with _____?
   What solutions would you suggest for _____?
Evaluation—*Development of opinions, judgements, or decisions*
   Do you agree _____?
   What do you think about _____?
   What is the most important _____?
   Prioritize _____ according to _____ .
   How would you decide about _____?
   What criteria would you use to assess _____?

In content area teaching, the question of grouping becomes more of an issue. At the beginning of the school year, most of our students are not ready to handle whole-class instruction. All work must be individualized. As our students learn to cooperate, they should be moved into working pairs and small groups. By the end of the school year (and especially when preparing for mainstreaming), some whole-group instruction needs to occur. When students are ready to work together, you might consider grouping them in reading teams (Madden, 1988). These are cooperative learning teams in which students are grouped heterogeneously, irrelevant of their reading ability. A project is assigned or determined by the students. Each member of the group is given a specific task toward the completion of the project. The teacher should assure that these tasks meet each student's needs and abilities. The teacher must also provide resource materials or access to them for the reading team. Upon completion of the project, some form of sharing is arranged (similar to the publishing phase of the writing process). This is the component that provides motivation for completion of the project. When selecting projects, be sure to include visual, auditory, and kinesthetic activities.

Content area curriculum generally is based upon a textbook. Our students tend to balk when handed a textbook and told to read certain chapters. An excellent way to motivate students to read text is to select a topic and then provide several textbooks that cover the same topic. Prepare a pre-test on the topic and administer it to the students prior to reading. Have the students read about the topic in each of the textbooks; then have them evaluate what they have read. Was it well written? How many times did you have to reread to get meaning? Which text taught you the most? Which one provided the best definitions of new words? Were important points left out of some of the texts? Which ones had the best illustrations? Did the illustrations teach and how? If you were going to teach this lesson to another student, which text would you use? What else would you do to be sure your student learned the necessary information to pass the test? If the students determine that one of the texts is poorly written and organized, have them fix it, rewrite it, develop questions and activities that would improve the lesson, and so on. Then administer the posttest.

In content area teaching, and especially in science and social studies, learning may be integrated with the basic processes of reading, writing, and arithmetic. Students should be given hands-on experiences through projects developed individually or in teams and shared with other students. Laboratory experiences should be provided whenever possible. Our students are going to learn best when they understand that learning relates to their lives and when learning is a shared experience with their peers.

ORGANIZATION AND STUDY SKILLS

Students are referred to special education classrooms because they are failing in the regular classroom. One of the underlying causes of this failure is the inability of our students to organize their materials, supplies, environments, work and most importantly, thinking. These students do not know how to access and retain the information necessary to school success. They do not know how to prepare for and cope with tests and testing situations. If we want our students to return to the mainstream and succeed in school, one of the most crucial skills we need to teach is organization.

ORGANIZING THEMSELVES

Very few of our students know how to organize their materials, books, supplies, and schoolwork. Usually, they live in disordered environments. These students have no sense of how organization of their working environment might help them do better in school. They do not see that they are often unable to get on task within reasonable amounts of time because they cannot access the materials and supplies they need to do this. Furthermore, they do not see that this is a situation over which they could have control. Instead, they will use this as an excuse and present it as something for which they are not responsible. We must provide the time and the directions for these students to learn otherwise.

At the start of school, the teacher should issue a list of supplies that each student will be required to have. This list may go home with a note letting parents know which supplies they will need to provide. A copy of this list is then posted in the room or in each of the student offices. You may wish to prioritize the items they must have such as pens and pencils, paper, paperback dictionary, from the items they may simply want to have such as a protractor, paperback thesaurus, or colored pencils.

At the end of each day, there should be at least 10 minutes in the schedule just for cleaning up and closure. During this time, students are instructed to clean their offices and around their desks. At least once a week the desks should be emptied, old papers thrown away, and everything else organized and replaced in the desks. There should be an inspection followed by some kind of acknowledgment that the job has been well done.

Each student should be asked to keep a notebook for at least one daily subject. In this notebook, there should be sections for different aspects of the course such as new vocabulary, notes and outlines, homework assignments, and tests. The teacher must decide what is appropriate to go in this notebook, and then teach the students how to set it up. There must be consistent checks for organization. The teacher may do this by collecting the notebooks and evaluating them for completeness. Or the teacher may prepare a checklist of what should be in the notebook and let the student check for completeness before turning it in to the teacher for examination.

STUDY SKILLS: ORGANIZING THINKING

Students who do not do well in school often do not know how to study. They are overwhelmed by the amount of information that they are given each day and have no idea how to organize it in their minds to retain it, use it, integrate it with other learning, and evaluate it. These students require training in these study skills. They need strategies to help them organize and retain information. This can be done through the use of organizational schemes, such as brainstorming for ideas, mapping for vocabulary and concept development, reading guides and advance organizers, and pre-writing organizers.

Brainstorming

When students first approach a topic, the teacher and the students must find out what they already know about the topic. What words and ideas come to mind when the topic is given? In brainstorming, students are asked to state these ideas out loud and everything that is said is written in a list in whatever order they are given. Do not leave anything out (not even misinformation). Keep the list in a place where the participating students can refer to it. As learning takes place on the topic, go back to the list and add new information to it while removing inaccurate information from it. Care should be taken when removing misinformation. A student took a risk and submitted that piece of information, right or wrong. One idea is to create a fiction list and place the inaccurate information on that list. Later, someone in the class may wish to write a story using words and ideas from the fiction list, such as "The Six Legged Spider." Once the study of the topic has been completed and everyone is satisfied that the list contains all of the important, accurate information about the topic, then it may be reorganized into outline form or a conceptual map. Brainstorming is also a good way to search for topics for writing. Students may want to keep a running list of brainstormed topics in their writing folders.

Mapping for Vocabulary and Concept Development

In teaching vocabulary, the goal is to have the student make semantic associations, that is, to place words in categories so that the student may examine similarities and differences and draw relationships. Semantic mapping will help the student do this: It is similar to brainstorming in that the student is asked to state words which come to mind related to a specified topic word. The words are written in a graphic form (a map) that shows their relationship to the topic word. A semantic map for the word "classroom" is illustrated in Figure 5.2. Maps or graphic forms of relationships also may be developed to show concept relationships. The graphic form or map may change according to the type of information that is being

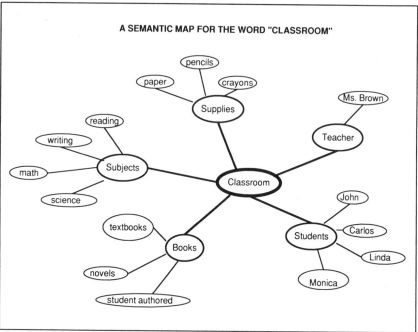

Fig. 5-2. Semantic Map for the word "Classroom"

presented. Students need to be taught to recognize and develop different kinds of maps for representing different kinds of information.

Another graphic form that is useful for helping students organize information for compare and contrast activities is a characteristics grid. In this, the vertical axis lists items and the horizontal axis lists characteristics of the items. The student works through the grid, rating items for the various characteristics. Once the grid is completed, the students will see that characteristics vary from item to item. This is then the basis for a discussion that may compare and contrast the items or look for patterns of similarities. A characteristics grid for "favorite pets" might look like this:

ITEMS			CHARACTERISTICS			
	Furry	Carnivorous	Herbivorous	Playful	Friendly	Purrs
Dog	+	+	-	+	+	-
Cat	+	+	-	+	+	+
Parakeet	-	-	+	-	-	-
Goldfish	-	+	-	-	-	-
Hamster	+	-	+	+	-	-

Reading Guides and Advance Organizers

These two activities are primarily effective in teaching comprehension and retention of information in the content areas. They are essential for our reading-disabled students who must expend so much energy in decoding a text that much of the meaning and structure is lost, even with re-reading of the text. They must both be prepared ahead of time by the teacher. In some schools, teachers using the same textbooks are accomplishing this job by preparing guides for different chapters in the same books then sharing them. The advance organizer prepares the student for reading. It is an overview of the material that is about to be read. The advance organizer should contain prereading questions that direct the student to think about the topic and what is already known. It should contain any background information required and a synopsis of the material. There should be postreading questions that focus on how the student interprets what has been read and how this new material may be incorporated into previous learning.

Reading guides are basically outlines of the material being read. The student uses the guide during reading. The reading guide directs the student to key concepts and topic statements by completing statements on a worksheet while progressing through the reading material. When the guide is complete, it may be used as a study guide for test preparation. Teacher-made tests should carefully correlate with the information on the reading guide. As with graphic organizers, the reading guide may take on different formats, depending on the type of material being read. Students should understand the reasons for this. Essentially, the reading guide teaches the student formats for note taking from textbooks. The same activities may be applied to oral instruction through lecture guides. This, however, requires that the teacher prepare the lecture and the lecture guide ahead of time and then not stray from the format during the lecture. The lecture guide provides a multisensory learning experience for our reading-disabled students in that they hear, see, and write the information at the same time.

Prewriting Organizers

Most students have difficulty writing because they do not know how to get started. They do not know how to organize their thoughts into a sequence that makes sense for the kind of writing they intend to do. Prewriting organizers help students prepare for writing. These are generally graphic and require that students fill in at least one word, phrase, or entire sentence. As with maps, prewriting organizers will take on different shapes for different kinds of writing. Figures 5.3, 5.4, and 5.5 show prewriting organizers for a paragraphing system that begins at Level 1 with just five sentences: a topic sentence, three supporting sentences, and a concluding statement. At Level 2, only three detail sentences are added (one detail sentence for each of the three supporting sentences). At Level 3, three more detail sentences are added (one more for each of the supporting sentences). Now the student has an 11-sentence paragraph, which may be rewritten in paragraph format. This organizer is excellent for expository writing of most any kind. Figure 5-6 is a story map that may be used to write the components of a narrative that the student has read or is planning to write. The following questions are asked for the components of the Story Map:

- **Setting:** Where and when did the events in the story take place?

- **Characters:** Who was involved in the story?

- **Problem:** What started the chain of events in the story?

- **Events:** What did the main character do about the problem?

- **Solution:** What happened as a result of what the main character did? How was the problem in the story solved?

Not all students require organizers in order to read and write successfully. For students who satisfactorily master learning without them, they should not be used. These kinds of activities may lock them into systems that stifle their learning style and creativity. These are for students who otherwise will not succeed due to a lack of organization and strategic planning for learning tasks.

ACCESS TO INFORMATION

If our students are to grow up and attain success in the modern world, they need to know how to access information. They must learn how to use the library not only to select books for leisure reading but also how to use reference materials. Every student should have a complete understanding of how and when to use all of the reference materials in a library by the time of high school graduation. This means that we begin in kindergarten taking children to the library and showing them the atlas and the dictionary, the encyclopedia, and the book of famous quotations. From the elementary grades on, we demand research requiring the use of reference books. We teach students how to take notes, to paraphrase (not just copy from the encyclopedia), to summarize, and to organize information. Their future

Name : _____   Date : _____

Paragraph : Level 1 Draft

Topic Sentence

Support Sentence

Support Sentence

Support Sentence

Concluding Statement

Fig. 5-3. Prewriting organizers: Level 1

118

Name : _____   Date : _____

Paragraph : Level 2 Draft

Topic Sentence

Support Sentence

Detail

Support Sentence

Detail

Support Sentence

Detail

Concluding Statement

Fig. 5-4. Prewriting organizers: Level 2

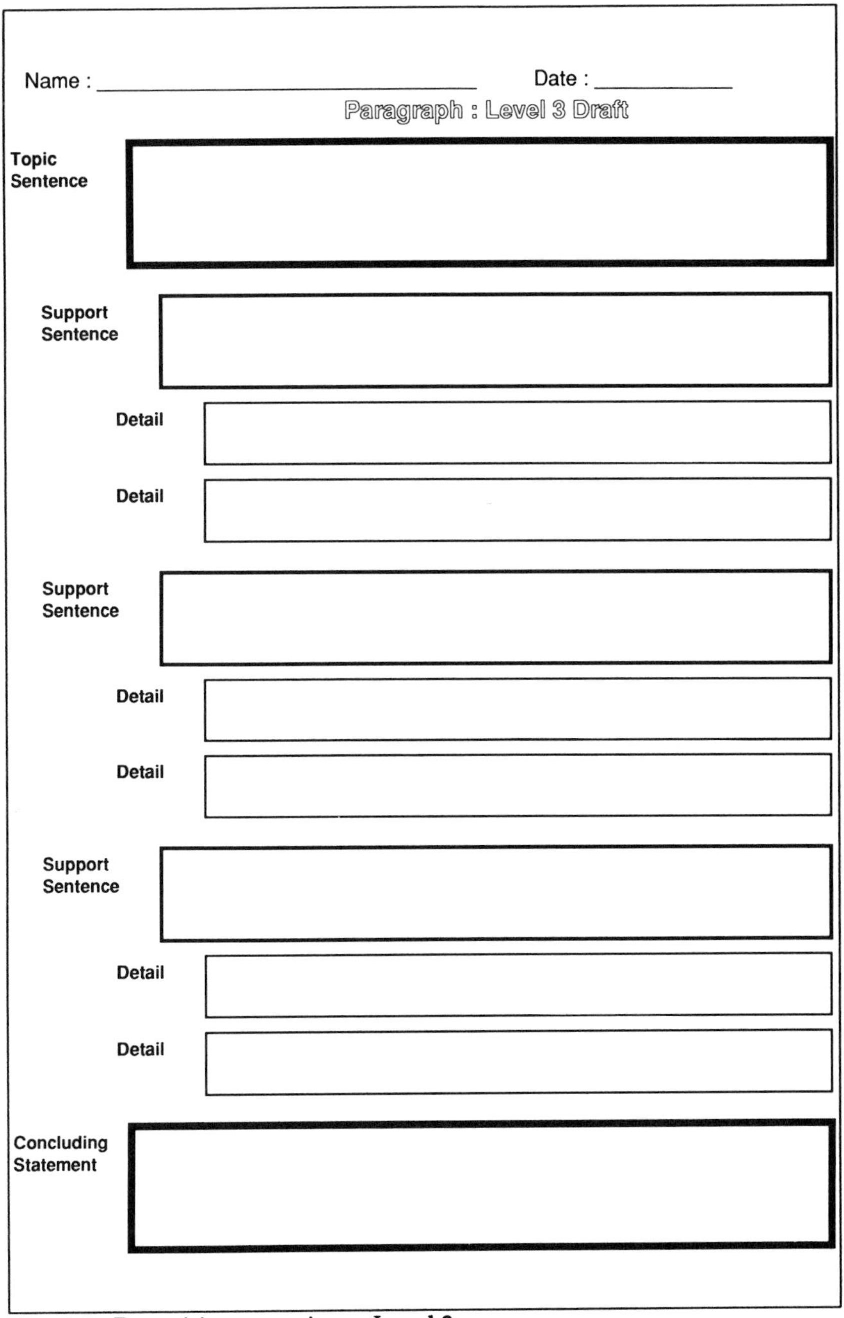

Name : _____ Date : _____

Paragraph : Level 3 Draft

Topic Sentence

Support Sentence

Detail

Detail

Support Sentence

Detail

Detail

Support Sentence

Detail

Detail

Concluding Statement

Fig. 5-5. Prewriting organizers: Level 3

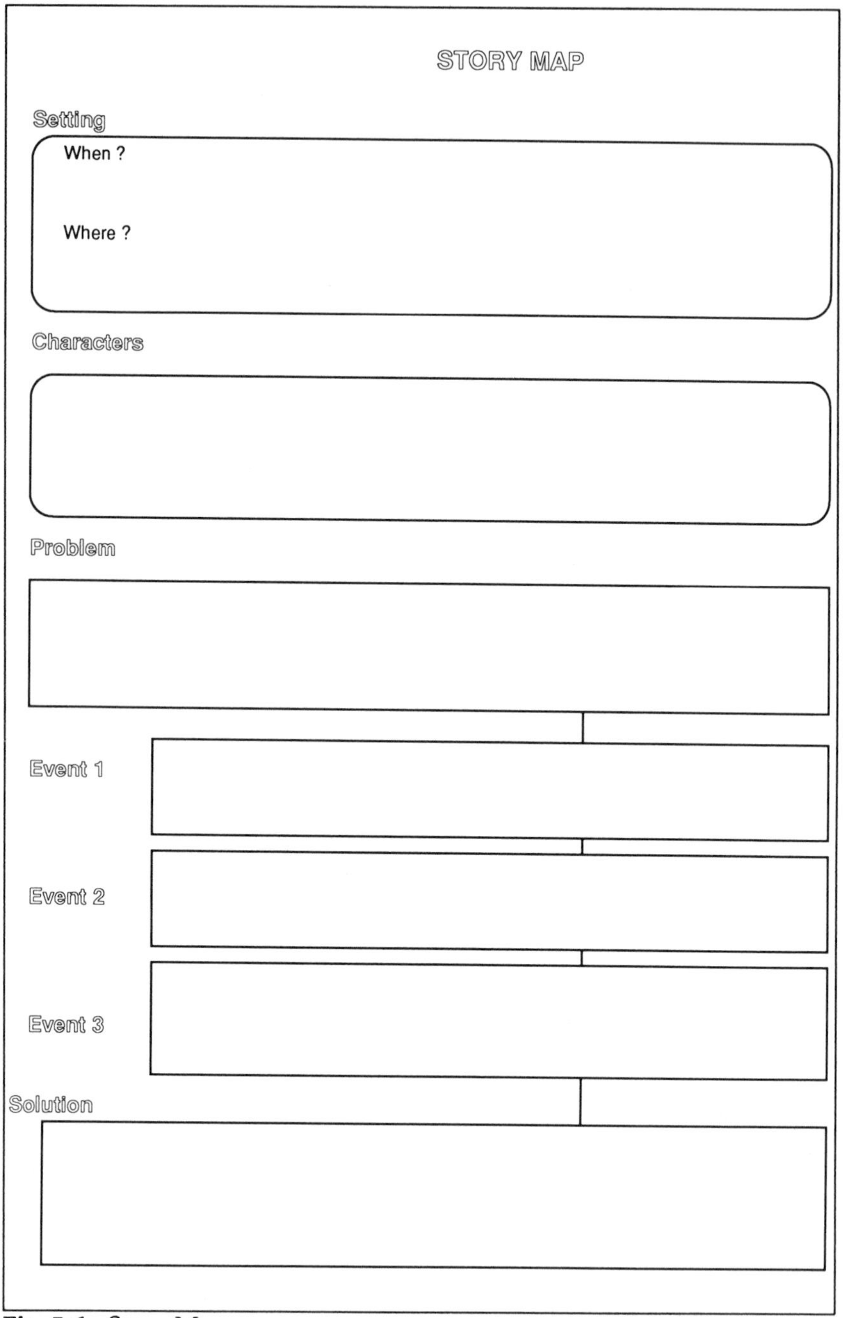

Fig. 5-6. Story Map

will depend on their ability to know how to gather information and, especially, their ability to take that information and synthesize it into meaningful communication.

Computers will be part of all of our students' futures. Even now, if you own a new car you know that in order to change the station you have to reprogram the computer chip in the car radio. The fact is that our students will not be able to escape this technological revolution. We are remiss if we do not provide the computer training now that will enable them to deal comfortably with computers in their futures. We must not allow the exclusion of our students from computer labs and computer literacy classes simply because they are in special education. On this point, we must be strong advocates. If this requires partial mainstreaming to accomplish, then we must be willing to take responsibility for behavior management within the computer lab. We must remain with our students to keep the reinforcement system intact during this training. The bottom line is that our students must be allowed access to computer training.

In some school districts, there is enough funding to purchase computers just for the special education classroom. If this is the case, then you should be sure that you get enough training to teach the students how to handle the hardware and the software, to do word processing for writing, to select appropriate instructional software, and to troubleshoot equipment malfunctions. Even if you do not have computers in your classroom, you should be computer literate. We are teaching students whose lives will probably extend another 70 or 80 years. We cannot pretend that someone else will motivate and teach our students in the technology of their generation.

PREPARING FOR TESTS

The long-term goal for special education students is to be mainstreamed successfully. In the mainstream, students are assessed through teacher made tests, through publishers tests correlated with the textbook, and through standardized national and state achievement tests. When special education students are mainstreamed, they must be prepared to take and pass these same tests. This means that they must learn to deal with test anxiety and other distractors, timed performance on tests, answer sheets and test booklets, and test-taking strategies (Scruggs & Marsing, 1987).

A number of good workbooks on the market are correlated to various national achievement tests. Classroom instruction using these materials should begin as soon as students are able to attend and perform on task behaviors for adequate periods of time. The teacher should prepare the students with appropriate relaxation activities. A timer may be used to help students get used to the pressure of a timed performance. Review of test items and correct responses should be done immediately after the student has completed the testing task. There should be a discussion of key words and item-elimination strategies. Whenever possible, students should use computer answer sheets (especially the kind where they must bubble in answers). They need to learn how to fill in these sheets and to stay in the right column on the right answer slot. Students should not be exempted from taking the actual tests unless there is *no way* that they can perform reasonably well on them. If they are insecure, administer the tests in the special education classroom. If they are getting ready for mainstreaming, have them go to the regular education classroom and take the test with their peers.

Teacher-made and publishers' tests in the content areas should be correlated to reading guides, lecture guides, organizers, or study guides. If they are not, help the student create a study guide that will organize the material effectively. Avoid giving tests that are poorly reproduced or written in cursive. Always have students focus on test directions before they begin to work on the test. Be sure the students understand the directions, (i.e., how to mark the matching answers, whether to underline, circle, or cross out). Be sure that students are aware of transitions in testing items from one format to another and know where and how to mark an answer. Be sure that they are aware of how many pages comprise the test so as not to miss any of the items. Most importantly, teach the students how to review their work when they are done so as not to have made unconscious test-taking errors.

THE END OF THE SCHOOL YEAR

The end of the school year can be very hard for emotionally disturbed students. For the first time, many of these students have experienced order, organization, consistency, tranquility, belonging, achievement, cooperation, caring, and sharing. At school, they live in a world that makes sense. Sometime around the end of April or early May, they realize that that is all about to end soon. About this time, behaviors deteriorate and regress, which will probably puzzle and frustrate you. These changes are related to separation anxiety, which means that they really love you, even though it doesn't look that way. In order to cope with separating from this strong support system, students have to find a way to reject what they really love and do not want to leave. They try to reject the class, their peers, the teacher, the aide, and their achievements. This is not a permanent condition, and you will see them go back and forth expressing love and hate.

As soon as the end of the year separation anxieties begin, it is time to begin closure activities. The purpose of these activities is to help students remember and summarize class events throughout the year, to look at how they have changed, to establish that their peers are actually their friends whom they may see over the summer, and to say farewell. Some of these activities are ongoing thorughout the school year and culminate in a closure activity.

CLOSURE ACTIVITIES

There are several activities that can help students close successfully.

1. Create a class yearbook. Mount photographs that have been taken throughout the school year. Be sure to put at least one picture of each student in the yearbook. Have the students submit drawings, poetry, stories, essays, and personal memories that they would like to see in the yearbook. Have pages for students' personal information and recollections. Some ideas might be: student birthdays; the funniest thing that happened this year; the worst thing that happened this year; my favorite days; special memories; something students liked about each person in the class (by name); my favorite jokes.

   Include a few blank pages in the yearbook, and make a copy for each student for friends' messages.

2. Academic Portfolio: Students with poor self-concepts cannot acknowledge their achievements. For these students, we provide constant feedback and reinforcement. Over time, we hope that each student internalizes the message that success is attainable through emotional well-being, hard work, on-task behaviors, and cooperation. We hope that our students will eventually learn to reinforce themselves and recognize their own successes. Developing an academic portfolio is an important activity that will help students do this for themselves.

   Students create academic portfolios based on their best work over the course of the academic year. The teacher never influences students; rather, the teacher sets up the portfolios and then allows time for students to work on them. Each student should be provided a box, bag, drawer, or expandable file folder (kept in a secure place) for their work. Students are directed to place into their portfolios learning products which they feel best represent themselves and their achievements throughout the current academic year. Talk to the students about professional portfolios, telling them that they are used to show other people our best work, the work by which we would like to be judged, the work which we feel best represents who we are and what our strengths and talents are. At first they will put in every 100 paper that they receive. The purpose of providing time to work in the portfolios is to allow students to clean out and select only the most representative pieces. What goes in or out of the academic portfolio is completely the student's decision. The contents do not have to be exclusive to academic work or just work done in school.

From time to time, students may wish to share what is in their portfolios with others. This is not requisite but should be allowed. At the end of the school year, students should inventory the contents. The student may then examine and analyze the contents in order to write a resume indicating strengths and talents; a letter of application for a job; or a narration, exposition, or poem about themselves and this academic year. This is an excellent closure activitiy. On the last day of school, students take home the portfolio.

3. Class Meetings: Class meeting time can be used to discuss the end of school, summer activities, and future plans. Students should be encouraged to express their feelings about school closing and what they think summer is going to be like. If they are unable to express themselves, tell them you are feeling sad about school ending and you know you are going to miss them a lot.

4. Summer Activities: Prepare a handbook of summer activities that are available through the schools and the community. Call the recreation department, the libraries, local universities and colleges, the YMCA and the YWCA, community centers, fine arts centers, the newspapers, church schools, and the chamber of commerce. Find out what is available for children in the age group you are teaching. Send this handbook home to the parents with enough information that they will be able to carry through on a summer program for their child. Most of our students need structure year round.

5. Last Day Party: With the students, plan a party for the last day. Make invitations for parents, friends, and school people the students want to have at the party. Be sure to have a birthday cake for all the summer birthdays. Perhaps the students would like to roast the teacher, or do oral readings of some of their best writing or favorite prose and poetry, present a play, sing some songs, or

tell jokes. Begin planning early, and be sure all of the students are involved.

Taking into account separation anxiety and planning for closure activities early enough will make a difference in how well the school year ends. On the last day, you may actually feel sad to see them go instead of glad it is finally over.

PREPARING FOR MAINSTREAMING

The irony of teaching special education students is that just when they get better, we have to let them go. No matter how much we love them, we must always remember that our long-term goal is for our students to be mainstreamed successfully. In always keeping this goal in mind, we will not lose sight of certain facts. First, we need to work with our students to keep them as close to on grade level work as possible. Second, we must provide a curriculum that matches the regular curriculum since our students will need this foundation when they return to the regular education program. We do not need to use alternative textbooks; we simply need to use alternative approaches to the textbooks. Third, we need to keep our students in touch with students in the mainstream program. We can do this by inviting other students into our classrooms for special events such as parties and presentations. We need to assure that our students are invited to all school functions such as assemblies, spelling bees, faculty-student ball games, and so on. Fourth, we should insist that our students are integrated for any subjects that they can handle as soon as possible. Our students deserve to have physical education, art, music, computer literacy, and counseling, if these are provided to regular education students. We must take responsibility for handling the behavior problems and allow our students to participate in these classes.

For the most part, mainstreaming a student will not occur quickly. It may take 2 years or more until our students will be ready for a completely mainstreamed program. Discussions about mainstreaming should occur on a regular basis during group sessions. These discussions should be positive and unpressured. Their purpose is simply to keep everyone focused on the long-term goal. In this way, a student who is ready for mainstreaming will more than likely tell you that it is time to start the process.

Mainstreaming probably will take up to a year. It should be done one subject at a time beginning with the student's strongest area. Certain considerations need to be taken into account in mainstreaming a student:

If appropriate, notify the parents that their child is about to begin the mainstreaming process. Talk to them about how this is likely to work and the kind of feedback you will be providing them. Be honest about how long you think the process will take.

Carefully assess the student's ability to handle on grade-level material in the subject area. If needed, integrate the student a year below grade level. Help the teacher modify materials and approaches for the student.

Select the teacher carefully then stay in touch, (daily, if possible). Develop a contingency plan with the teacher in case there are behavior problems or the student begins to fail. Agree on how the student will be evaluated. Set up a placement that will practically assure success for the student.

Develop a feedback system for the student. In the beginning, a daily report will be necessary. This can be a simple happy or sad face that the regular classroom teacher marks, or the reporting of a grade for that day's work. As the student gets closer to full integration the reporting of grades on the report card will become the reporting system.

Do not move a student too fast through the integration process, and do not let others pressure you into doing so. Do not be surprised if, in the midst of the process, the student regresses for a while. Simply slow up the process, wait a while, and things will more than likely return to normal. It is sometimes hard for our students to let go.

Do not mainstream a student because of a move to a new level (i.e., elementary to junior high) or a change in schools. This is a time when more support will be needed. Pass along the information that the student is ready to begin or has begun the mainstreaming process and allow the receiving teacher to make the decisions about mainstreaming in the new school.

Do all that you can to assure success of the mainstreaming process for the student. Lack of proper support can cause the process to fail; which can be devastating to the student. One student I know who was mainstreamed without these considerations ended up back in the self-contained classroom for another 2 years with a whole new set of school-related phobias.

THE PROFESSIONAL TEACHER

The ideas presented in this chapter just touch on events in teaching methodology today. It is a most exciting time for educators and especially for children, the recipients of our best and our worst ideas. This chapter took some of the best and most adaptable ideas from the current trends and presented them as an examples of what works for our students. It is now up to you, the professional teacher, to continue learning and keeping up with the research and trends in teaching methodolgies. It is up to you to get in touch with your own competencies in adapting these ideas to meet the needs of our very special students. Further, it is up to you to pursue this knowledge through reading, continuing education, workshops and in-services, and especially through listening to the children. Through listening, we keep in touch with the empathy that makes our work with these children successful. Although instructional approaches change over time, the characteristics of emotionally disturbed children and their need for an empathic teacher do not.

REFERENCES

Bergk, M. (1988). Fostering interpersonal forms of reading. *The Reading Teacher, 42*(3), 210–218.

Bloom, Benjamin S., et al., Eds. (1956). *Taxonomy of Educational Objectives, Handbook I: Cognitive Domain.* New York: David McKay.

Dunn, R., Beaudry, J.S., and Klavas, A. (1989). Survey of research on learning styles. *Educational Leadership, 46*(6), 50–58.

Goodman, K. (1986). *What's whole in whole language?* Portsmouth, N.H.: Heinemann.

Gordon, C.J. (1985). Modeling inference awareness across the curriculum. *Journal of Reading, 28,* 444–447.

Madden, L. (1988). Improve reading attitudes of poor readers through cooperative reading teams. *The Reading Teacher, 42*(3), 194–199.

McDonough, K.M. (1989). Analysis of the expressive language characteristics of emotionally handicapped students in social interactions. *Behavioral Disorders, 14*(2), 127–139.

Morgan, S.R. (1979). A model of the empathic process for teachers of emotionally disturbed children. *American Journal of Orthopsychiatry, 49*(3), 446–453.

Oliphant, G.G. (1979). Program planning for dyslexic children in the general classroom. *Bulletin of the Orton Society, XXIX.*

Palincsar, A.S., & Brown, D.A. (1987). Enhancing instructional time through attention to metacognition. *Journal of Learning Disabilities, 20,* 66–75.

Piccolo, J.A. (1987). Expository text structure: Teaching and learning strategies. *The Reading Teacher, 40*(9), 838–847.

Richardson, E. (1984). The impact of phonemic processing instruction on the reading achievement of reading-disabled children. *Annals of the New York Academy of Sciences, 433,* 97–118.

Scruggs, T.E., & Marsing, L. (1987). Teaching test-taking skills to behaviorally disordered students. *Behavioral Disorders, 13*(4), 240–244.

SUGGESTED BIBLIOGRAPHY

In addition to the books and journal articles cited in the references, there are other excellent sources that will help you continue your professional growth.

Books
Borba, C., & Borba, M. (1978). *Self-esteem: A classroom affair*. Minneapolis, MN: Winston Press.
Borba, C., & Borba, M. (1982). *Self-esteem: A classroom affair*. Vol. 2. San Francisco: Harper & Row.
Cooper, J.D. (1986). *Improving reading cmprehension*. Boston: Houghton Mifflin.
Devine, T. (1986). *Teaching reading cmprehension: From theory to practice*. Boston: Allyn and Bacon.
Graves, D.H. (1983). *Writing: Teachers and children at work*. Exeter, N.H.: Heinemann.
Harris, T.L., & Cooper, E.J. (1985). *Reading, thinking and concept development*. New York: College Entrance Examination Board.
Kreidler, W.J. (1984). *Creative conflict resolution*. Glenview, ILL: Scott, Foresman.
Langer, J.A., & Smith-Burke, M.T., Eds. (1982). *Reader meets author: Bridging the gap*. Newark, DE: International Reading Association.
McNeil, J.D. (1984). *Reading comprehension: New directions for classroom practice*. Glenview, ILL: Scott Foresman.
Pearson, P.D., & Johnson, D.D. (1978). *Teaching reading comprehension*. New York, NY: Holt Rinehart.
Readence, J.R., Bean, T.W., & Baldwin, R.S. (1985). *Content area reading: An integrated approach*. Dubuque, IA: Kendall/Hunt.
Reid, D.K., & Hresko, W.P. (1981). *A cognitive approach to learning disabilities*. New York: McGraw-Hill.

Journals
American Journal of Orthopsychiatry
Arithmetic Teacher
Behavioral Disorders
Childhood Education
Education Week
Educational Leadership
Exceptional Children
Exceptional Parent
The Exceptional Child
Gifted Child Quarterly
Instructor
Journal of Child Psychology and Psychiatry
Journal of Clinical Child Psychology
Journal of Creative Behavior
Journal of Learning Disabilities
Journal of Reading
Journal of School Psychology
Journal of Special Education
Learning

Learning Disability Quarterly
Learning Disabilities Research
Mathematics Teacher
Pointer
Psychology in the Schools
Reading Research Quarterly
Teaching Exceptional Children
The Reading Teacher
The Writing Teacher

CHAPTER 6

Responses to Feelings and Emotional Well-Being

SHARON R. MORGAN

This chapter is the component of the empathy model that is primarily the teacher's verbal and nonverbal ability to respond appropriately to the students' needs. This chapter focuses on the affective domain and covers specific interventions. All of these techniques require practice. Do not expect everything to fall in place the first time you try them. It is like anything you do that is new to you and new to the students. You do not become good at it unless you practice. The students are likely to frustrate you in the beginning by acting silly or being uncooperative. It may seem like chaos at first and you may experience the feeling of not having control of your class. But hang in there and keep working on these interventions until they become as natural as teaching any other lesson.

RELAXATION TRAINING

BACKGROUND

Relaxation exercises, first thing in the morning, are an important part of the program for disturbed students. Most of these students are extremely tense and under great stress. If you have ever taught these students, you know how chaotic the beginning of the morning can be. They hit your classroom at full speed. Some have been fighting on the bus before even reaching school. Some have had an unpleasant start at home with their parents. Maybe mother was drunk and on the floor before they left for school. Some have had the usual morning argument about going to school at all. Some have arrived without their homework and anticipate an ugly day with the teacher. Some have had nasty altercations with their siblings. Some are experiencing the anxiety that is the core of their disturbance in the first place. Stop and think how much sense it makes to launch into reading, writing, language arts, or a math lesson at 8:00 A.M. If you try it, you might as well forget teaching for the day. These students need to get into a relaxed state before beginning anything challenging. Learning academics requires the students to be able to concentrate, and concentration cannot occur without relaxing.

Another reason for relaxation training is that these children are tense and stressed and need to learn how to feel otherwise. This is a lesson just as important as math. Relaxation is something you will need to learn for yourself as well. Many teachers of disturbed students wake in the morning tense in anticipation of what all of these youngsters are going to do today; what is the administration going to do about such and such; what kind of new paper work will appear in their mail boxes; the admission, review, or dismissal meeting they have to go to; or, the parent conference they are going to have. So, relaxation exercises are a good way to start your day too.

Many of the techniques you will be using necessitate that the students are in a relaxed state. To communicate clearly requires that the students feel relaxed so that their thoughts are not jumbled and they can put things in order. If they are going to be involved in class meeting, story telling, role playing, life space interviewing, or guided fantasy they need to be relaxed. Relaxation exercises are helpful to the student who has just had an emotional upheaval. They need calming and a way to get back their equilibrium.

EXERCISES

Tense and Relax

Have you ever noticed how small can children relax easily? They can engage in vigorous activities, one minute rolling and tumbling, running and jumping, skipping and hopping, and then just falling across your lap like rag dolls, or dropping to the floor and falling fast asleep. After about the age of 5 or 6 (when children have started school), people acquire many tensions, and they must relearn relaxation. To know what relaxation feels like, the students must first be able to recognize their tensions. Although many are already tense they must experience (in a conscious way) *extreme* tension so they can feel truly relaxed. Following are a few exercises you can use in the classroom.

Begin by having the students (you do it too) sit up straight in their desks, feet flat on the floor, arms to their sides, and chin resting on their chests. Now, curl the toes under and squeeze tight; now let go. Then squeeze the muscles in the calves; now let go. Follow through with the thighs, buttocks, and tummy, each time letting go. Then pull the shoulders up tight around your neck; let go. Now, make your hands into tight fists; let go. Then tense the arms; let go. Finally, the face muscles: Squeeze the eyes tightly shut; purse the lips together tightly; clench the teeth; now let go. Follow this with stretching exercises. Stretch the muscles out as far as possible: the feet, legs, arms, and facial muscles. Hold the eyes open very wide, stretch open the jaw, stick out the tongue and stretch (kids like this since they can legally stick out their tongues at you); now relax everything. When this exercise is finished, the student, and you, should know what real tension feels like and how it feels to relax.

Breathing

Have the students practice breathing exercises for 2 or 3 minutes. This is simple and involves just taking in a deep breath until the stomach is extended, holding it for 3 or 4 seconds. Then let all the air go rushing out while telling them to blow out all the bad feelings: angry feelings, scary feelings, sad feelings, nervous feelings. They will probably get silly on you the first few times you do this; remind them what they are supposed to do. Keep bringing them back to the task. Once this has become a daily routine, the silliness will stop.

Now, practice rhythmic, steady, even, deep breathing. Tell your students to close their eyes and begin concentrating on breathing. Do it with them to show what you mean.

The Bouncing Ball

If you can, purchase a metronome or borrow one from the music teacher and tape-record the sound of a metronome. This will be used for different things (breathing exercises or just listening to the sound and relaxing). Use the sound of the metronome for a relaxation exercise.

Start the sound of the metronome and begin the students breathing (evenly, steadily, deeply) with the rhythm of that sound. Now tell them to close their eyes and picture a beach ball at the top of a flight of stairs. Then tell them you are going to slowly count from ten backwards and each time you say a number they imagine the ball slowly, slowly bouncing down to the next step. Tell them when the ball reaches the bottom to keep their eyes closed because then you will count to 10 and with each number said they will imagine the ball slowly, slowly going back up each step to the top.

Now, begin. Picture the ball at the top of the steps—breathe deeply—10—the ball slowly drops to the next step—9 . . . 8 . . . 7 . . . breathe deeply . . . 6 . . . 5 . . . 4—breathe deeply—3 . . . 2 . . . 1 . . . 0. Now relax and breathe deeply picturing the ball at the bottom of the stairs. We are going to take the ball back up the stairs very, very slowly and keep breathing nice and steady. When we get to the top you will feel very good, very relaxed, very calm, and then you can open your eyes. Okay 1—picture the ball going up to the first step very slowly—2—the ball is on the next step—3 . . . 4 . . . 5—breathe deeply—6 . . . 7 . . . 8—breathe deeply—9 . . . 10. Now you feel very good, very calm, nice and relaxed. Open your eyes and very gently stretch out your arms and legs and let out a nice deep breath.

The Rag Doll

This is a short, simple exercise that can be used after the students have practiced and incorporated the basic skills of relaxation such as tension/release and breathing. For a few minutes have them begin with tension/release and their steady, deep breathing. You may use the sound of the metronome. Then tell them we are going to let each part of the body imitate a rag doll bit by bit. First, we sit up in our desks and let our legs go loose and limp. Now, the body and the arms: Let them go loose and limp; let your head droop down, or back, or to the side, loose and limp just like a rag doll. Keep up your nice steady, deep breathing. This can be done for about 10 minutes.

Using Clay

Give the students a lump of clay and have them hold it for awhile and enjoy its feel. Tell them to rub it around in their hands, kneading, pressing, folding, and squeezing it so that it oozes between their fingers. Now they close their eyes and imagine all of the things that they could mold out of the clay. Give them about a minute to imagine these things. Then tell them to select one of those figures and mold what they want. This can be a very relaxing exercise.

Heat and Warmth

This is not a technique the student does, but it is something you can do for the youngster who has been very upset or overcome with anxiety. Extreme anxiety and tension cause the circulatory system to contract, leaving the student feeling chilled. Usually, the extremities (fingers and toes) are very cold. So it is advisable to keep in your room a small blanket, afghan, or shawl. Take the youngster who has had an emotional upset and wrap him or her in the blanket or a coat, and put the child in a seat in the sun or near a heating duct to help speed relaxation.

CONCENTRATION AND RELAXATION

Relaxing and concentrating go together. Concentrating on regular academic activities cannot be accomplished without relaxing first. However, some concentration exercises that are not academically related can bring about relaxation.

A TRIP TO THE STORE

Purchase some play money (coins, not paper money). Have the students sit quietly in their desks and let their bodies relax: Get them breathing evenly and deeply. Now give them each a coin and tell them it is worth five dollars. Then have them put it in the palm of their hands. Look at both sides of the coin and see the writing and picture on the coin. Now tell them to close their eyes and feel the coin with their other hand. Feel the bumps on the coin (remember the picture on the coin) remember what it looks like and that it is worth five dollars. Let them do this for a moment or so until the picture is clear and stays in their minds.

Tell them that we going to pretend that we are going to the store to buy something. Let someone describe the store. Is it a big store or small? What is in the front of the store? In the back? To the left? To the right? Tell them, quietly, in their own minds, to look around the store at all of the things they could buy. See something you want to buy? What color is it? What shape? What size? Look at the price: Can you buy it with your five dollars? Most children, especially the elementary age ones, will say they can buy it no matter what it is—even if in real life it costs much more than five dollars.

Now tell them to see the clerk at the checkout. Take what you have selected from the shelf, and give it to the clerk. Watch the clerk wrap it and put it in a bag. Now the clerk gives you what you have picked out. Pay the clerk. Do you get any change? Most imagine that they do get, change too. Now take what you have just bought and leave the store. Okay, now you can open your eyes. Have the students each tell the class what they bought.

PICTURES

Have the group relax and breathe. Show the class a picture. Let them look at it for about 15 seconds. Now tell them to close their eyes. Let someone describe what is on the right of the picture; someone else, what is on the left; someone else, what is at the top; and so on. Practice this exercise frequently. Later, when they have become good at this, it will help and can be worked into academic lessons in reading, science, and so forth.

NUMBERS

Get the children relaxed and breathing deeply. Put a number on the chalkboard; start with the number 5. Let them see the number for a couple of moments and then have them close their eyes. Now tell them to imagine the number that goes before 5, then the number that goes after 5; the number before 4; the number after 6; the number before 3; the number after 7; the number before 2; the number after 8, until they have reached 0 and 10. This is not an exercise to start with right away because it does require a great deal of concentration and, at first, may seem academically or task-oriented. Practice this many times; when they do it well, keep increasing the numbers by 2. Later, when concentration builds, you can work this into math lessons involving addition, subtraction, and so on.

GUIDED FANTASY

Guided fantasy is useful for several areas of work with the emotionally disturbed student. It also aids relaxing; alleviates certain problems; and enhances students' creativity. Guided fantasy was developed out of hypnosis (Levine, 1980). Although teachers are not trained in hypnosis (and I am not suggesting that hypnosis should be used in the classroom by teachers), guided fantasy is an acceptable technique for teachers to learn and use in helping their students. For this group of students, it can be used as another type of relaxation technique and to build or enhance group creativity. One-on-one, it can help a student alleviate a specific problem.

GROUP RELAXATION AND CREATIVITY ENHANCEMENT

In any guided fantasy activity, the teacher remains in control of the story the students are going to make up. As the title implies, the teacher guides the students through the fantasy to ensure they do not just ramble, tell frightening stories, or become rowdy. Although in the final end it will be their story, you will have carefully brought them through the details to the ending. Following is an example of this type of guided fantasy.

Exploring the Mountains

Begin by getting the children relaxed and breathing deeply. Tell them you all are going on a hiking trip in the mountains. Who has been to the mountains? If none of them has, select someplace appropriate to your area of the country: The forest, the lakes, the animal reserve, a city park. For this example, though, let us assume that they have been to the mountains. Start first by giving a brief reminder of what the mountains are like: they have gentle rolling slopes that go up higher and higher; there are many trees and rocks; there are wild flowers, birds, and creeks. The air smells fresh and good and feels cool. It is quiet and peaceful.

A word of caution before begining the guided fantasy. Some of these students cannot tolerate being removed from reality, so for them have them keep their eyes open and allow those that want to, to draw a picture of the story as you go along. This keeps them grounded and prevents anxiety from getting out of control. Now the guided fantasy begins.

First we are going to put on some warm clothes because it is cool in the mountains. Put on your jacket and some tough sturdy shoes so we can hike. Here we are at the trail we want to follow. I look up ahead and I see tall trees. Nickey, what color are the trees and how tall are they? Wait for the description. Then repeat what Nickey has just said. Yes, the trees have gold leaves, and some have green and greenish blue needles. They are as tall as the school building. Now go on leading them. Here we go farther up the trail. I hear birds singing. Clair, what do the birds look like? What color are their feathers? Wait for the description. Then repeat what Clair said and add to the description if you want to. How pretty! You see birds with blue feathers and birds with red feathers. I see some birds myself. They have yellow feathers and brown and green. They soar from tree to tree singing beautiful soft notes. Oh, here we are at the creek that runs down from the very top of the mountain, and there are wild flowers all over the place. Listen to the pleasant sound of the running water as it rushes over the rocks and babbles. John, tell what the flowers smell like. What color are they? Now go on as described. If someone says, I see a bear or I see a snake, then guide them back to this peaceful and safe setting by saying, "and the bear (or snake) sees you too and is afraid of people and runs away to a place where it feels safe." If someone tries to get silly by saying they smell moose doo doo, then remind them that if they want to be a part of this story they will have to stop being silly, or they will have to wait in the hall until we have finished the story. Undo, what was just said by reminding them of the beautiful smelling flowers, and the smell of the trees, and the creek. Then go on with your guided trip.

As you take them on this exploration be sure you point out all of the beautiful and peaceful things in the mountains: warm sunshine, nice sounds and smells, gentle animals such as deer and rabbits, and soft gentle breezes. After you have done all of the exploring and made the trip peaceful and safe, quickly return to the bottom of the mountain and tell them that now everybody goes home feeling very good.

Other Ideas

First have the children make a list of their favorite things: colors, food, animals, toys, activities. They can then incorporate these favorite things into the guided fantasy. A few other ideas for a guided fantasy could be:

- A trip to the moon

- A walk along the beach

- Designing a new school building so it is just as they would like it

- Developing new transportation systems

You will come up with other creative ideas and so will the students once they have tried this several times. Try to get them to bring into the guided fantasy some of the favorite things they have listed. Guide them by asking questions. What colors are the uniforms you wear on your trip to the moon? What kind of food will you eat on this long journey? What toys will you take along? What kind of activities will you do to keep from getting bored while you are traveling on this long trip?

GUIDED FANTASY TO ALLEVIATE A SPECIFIC PROBLEM

This particular intervention can be helpful to some students who are experiencing specific problems. You can help them with some of these problems directly in the classroom, and some of the problems need attention at home. Once you have learned the basics of guided fantasy, you can teach certain things to the parents so that they can work with their own child at home (as in the case of children with sleep disorders). A sleep disorder is the type of problem that you really cannot do anything about directly in the classroom, but you can teach the parents a few techniques to use at home.

For now, we will select a problem that you can work on in the classroom. For this particular technique, you will need to find a time alone with the student to teach this technique for alleviating the problem through guided fantasy. Let us use the example of a student who is extremely anxious about reading or speaking out loud in class.

Example for Students

Sit with the student alone in a quiet place and begin by asking the student to describe all of the feelings he or she has when they have to stand in front of the class and speak or read out loud. Following is an actual case:

Student: "When I think I will be asked or am asked to say or read something in front of the other kids I start to feel sick to my stomach."

Teacher: "Imagine that I have just asked you to read something out loud to the class. What other things do you feel?"

Student: "I start to sweat. My hands get real sweaty."

Teacher: "What else? Try to remember all of your feelings."

Student: "I feel sick to my stomach, my hands get sweaty, and I feel weak in my legs—like I can't stand up. I feel real shaky all over."

Teacher: "Okay. Now that you have imagined I am asking you to read out loud, do you feel all of those feelings now?'

Student: "Yes."

Teacher: "Okay. Now close your eyes and start breathing nice and deep and steady like we do when we are doing relaxation. Close your eyes. Think about a time when you felt real happy. When you were feeling good and relaxed, and safe. It may be a place you went on vacation. Or, something that you do when you are not in school that makes you feel happy, and you feel safe." Give the student some time to think about this and then go on. "Now describe that place to me. Tell me all about it. Tell me what things

> look like, sound like, smell like—tell me how you feel when you are in your happy place."

Student: "I feel happy when we go to the mountains. I don't feel scared of anything. I just feel like laying on the ground and taking a nap."

Teacher: "Good. What is it like in the mountains? Tell me what you like about it."

Student: "I like the sunshine—it feels warm and I feel warm—and the air is cool. I like to look at the lake and the sky—they are so blue. The birds sing and the flowers are pretty. You don't hear any other sounds—like cars honking and buses going by. It is just real quiet and peaceful."

Teacher: "Good. Now think about being in the mountains for awhile and imagine all of those things. Tell me how you are feeling and describe it to me again."

Have the student go through the happy experience again and, if needed, remind him or her of any of the parts left out; the sunshine or the color of the lake or sky, feeling peacful and taking a nap, and so forth. Now, tell the student to imagine speaking out loud to the class again. Ask the student to describe those feelings again. When this is done, then tell the student that you are going to hold onto his or her wrist. Take the student's arm and grip gently around the wrist like a bracelet. Next, ask the student to describe the mountains again and describe the accompanying feelings. As the student describes the mountains and the happy, safe feelings, gently tighten your grip around his or her wrist. When the story is finished, let go. Repeat the sequence of the scary event and the happy event at least one more time.

This activity needs to be done several times on different days. Each time the student describes the happy, safe place, gently squeeze his or her wrist. After you have practiced this with the student three to four times, then have the student tell the happy story again, only now have the student hold his or her own wrist and gently apply pressure while telling the story. Practice this two or three times. After this is well understood, tell the student that when asked to read out loud or recite in front of the class that when the anxious feelings start the student should hold his or her own wrist and apply the pressure to bring back the good, happy, relaxed, safe feelings experienced when in the mountains.

After much practice, the squeeze of the wrist should elicit the good feelings and overcome the anxious feelings. The gentle squeeze of the wrist should signal the body to let go of the anxious feelings and be replaced with happy feelings. This has to be practiced many times to be effective; once it is learned, though, the student can use this technique whenever anxious feelings occur.

Example for Parents

A number of emotionally disturbed students have sleep disorders; the parents may tell you about this and ask for help. Teach them a guided fantasy they can use at home with their own child. The following was used with several parents who had children experiencing this problem, and it was done successfully.

They must spend some time with their youngsters in their bedrooms before expecting them to go to sleep. Many of these parents just put their children to bed, turn off the lights, and leave the room. To be successful, they will have to take more time with their child to help alleviate the sleep disorder. Most children with sleep disorders have scary thoughts at bedtime. They imagine all of the horrible things they see in the movies and on television. They worry that there are monsters under the bed and in the closet; some are worried that the parents will abandon them once they have gone to sleep. So, parents must dispel these frightening fantasies.

First, they should go around the room with the child and look in the closets and under the bed, reassuring the youngster that there are no monsters in the room. Then they should sit on the bed with the child and ask the child to imagine something beautiful. Here they must describe something beautiful in great detail. For example, if the child cannot think of something, then suggest a bouquet of flowers. Have the youngster describe how many flowers are in the bunch, what shape are the flowers, what color, and how they smell. Every minute detail must be described. When this is finished, instruct the parents to repeat what the child has just described and comment on the beauty of the whole experience. Next, to alleviate the fear of abandonment, tell the parents to ask the child what they would like to have for breakfast in the morning. Then they should say to the child that sounds very good. In the morning when you wake up and come into the kitchen with mom and dad (or whatever the parental situation is) we will have such and such, and you can help me fix breakfast while I fix the coffee.

This exercise should put the child in a happy mood thinking about something plesant right before going to sleep. If necessary, tell the parent(s) the child can have a nightlight. Suggest that the parent(s) offer the youngster some favorite toy (teddy bear, etc.) to keep in bed with them. I have found that adolescents at first may say no to a teddy bear but then quickly take one to bed with them after all. As long as the parent(s) does not act as though it is silly, the youngster will accept the toy. The discussion about breakfast tells the child that the parent(s) is definitely going to be in the house in the morning. It gives the child a sense of security that they can look forward to the morning and their parent(s) again. You do not have to use this example, of course; other creative ideas of your own will work just as well. The main points to cover are to find ways to dispel the concern about monsters in the room and worries about being abandoned in the night. Often, this exercise is effective in clearing up the problem of nightmares. The parent(s) can be instructed to tell their child that after the happy story they should go to sleep and try to dream the happy story. Sometimes the children do just that.

INTERACTIVE COMMUNICATION

This section of the chapter contains techniques that require the teacher's ability to observe and listen to the students and know their real or deeper feelings. These interventions require insight into the real meaning and motives of a student's behavior and the ability to respond with techniques that accurately reflect knowledge and understanding of a situation. Before launching into any of these techniques, be aware that there are different types of verbal responses that have been catagorized.

TYPES OF COMMUNICATION

When we talk to people, there are at least eight types of verbal responses that can be used (Della-Piana, 1973). We should at least recognize the verbalizations we are using so that we know we are communicating exactly what we intend. It can be helpful to the teacher to tape-record interactions with the students to be played back later and see if you communicated precisely what you wanted the student to hear. Following are the eight types of communicative responses with examples.

Evaluating

This type of communication can deteriorate into scolding if not monitored carefully. It communicates a judgment of the appropriateness, the effectiveness, or the rightness of a student's thinking, feeling, or acting. It can be critical and is often used to justify authority. Too often, the emphasis in *evaluating* is placed on what ought to be rather than on what the student should do. *Evaluating* responses must be used moderately, but when it is used correctly the student will develop appropriate values.

Examples of inappropriate uses of *evaluating* would be to say to the student, "That isn't the way you are supposed to do it," "You were told not to get out of your seat," or, "Crying is not going to help."

Examples of appropriate uses of *evaluating* would be to say to the student, "The way you are supposed to do your work is like this." "We have a rule. You cannot leave your seat without permission." Or, "I can see by your crying that you are frustrated and unhappy. When you have finished your work, you will not feel so bad."

The difference between the inappropriate and appropriate use of the evaluating response is in the first case the child is simply told that he or she is wrong about something. In the other examples, the teacher lets the students know their behavior is inappropriate but explains what the student must do so he or she can correct the problem. Undoubtedly, the student has been told many times what the correct behavior should be, but in teaching these students it is necessary to teach and re-teach as many times as necessary until they are responding in the manner required and necessary.

Supportive

These are verbal responses that tell the students you are on their side. You understand, you are with them, and you will help them. These responses are meant to give the students a sense that they are not alone with their frightening or sad feelings, that they are not the only ones in the world who have ever made a mistake or had the feelings they are experiencing. The *supportive* response relieves some of the guilt which many of these students experience to excess. Of course, if you have students who seldom feel guilt for any of their transgressions, then this is not the response to use. With those types of students, you do not want to let them off the hook.

Some examples of *supportive* responses would be: "It will work out all right." "You are doing fine." "I know you feel very badly but this kind of thing happens a lot." "This can be fixed, nothing is so bad that we cannot do something to make it better." Or, "Most of the kids in this room have the same trouble but eventually we get it worked out."

Accepting

This type of communicative response is intended to provide the student with a nonthreatening, nonpunishing audience. It involves reflecting or mirroring back to the students their feelings and ideas; to show understanding and that you know how they feel.

Some examples of *accepting* responses are: "It sounds like you really feel hurt." "Right now is seems you are feeling nervous and frustrated." "It seems that you are really scared you will not be able to get all of the work done." Or, "So, that made you very angry and you felt like hurting back."

Questioning

The point to *questioning* is to get the student to clarify something or develop an issue further. *Questioning* is not to be used to grill the student but to get more information out in the open so that both the teacher and student can understand better what is going on or what happened. Some examples of the inappropriate use of *questioning* are to ask the student a question that you already know the answer to, such as, "Who stole the money?" This is a closed and unfriendly question and sets up the student to lie. If you already know the who, what, where, when of a situation then *don't* ask! Tell the student, "You stole the money. Tell me what you were going to use it for?" Another example of closed and unfriendly questions are those that can be answered with a simple yes or no. Or, "Why did you do that?" The naughty word for teachers to use is *WHY*. "Why did you steal?" "Why did you fight?" "Why won't you get your work done?" Generally, what we get back from the student to a "why" question is, "I don't know," or just a shrug of the shoulders. Quite often, they really do not know why they did what they did, and part of your job is to help them understand themselves better, to understand why they do the things they do.

Instead of asking, "Why did you do that?", say something like, "You were fighting with Dale; tell me how that happened. When you came into the room what did you do first?" "Then what happened?" "When you took the money, what were you thinking you were going to do with it?" Or, "You have a lot of trouble getting your work finished. Let's talk about what is keeping you from doing your work. Tell me what happens when you first think about doing your math (or whatever)."

Explaining

This response is used to teach the student the way things work or how things happen the way they do. It is intended to enlighten students; to help them understand why they get into so many fights, or don't get their work done, or feel that they have to steal something, and so forth.

The use of *explaining* may go something like this: "You are always late because Steve is always late coming by to walk with you. Maybe he is always late partly because you always wait for him. If you did not wait for him then you would not be late. Perhaps then if you went on without him a few time he would not be late and you would not be late anymore either." "The other kids treat you that way because you spit on them. That makes them very angry with you and then they want to hit you or they do not want to play with you, and they say ugly things to you." Or, "Robert shoved you because every time you go by you knock his books off the desk or call him a name. Those things make people really angry, and when you feel very angry you want to do something back to hurt the person who hurt you."

Directing

This communicative response is used to teach students what they need to do so that things do not go wrong. It is to instruct them how to handle particular situations. Using the example from above, you would say to the student: "Until you feel like you can go by Robert without doing something to make him mad then don't go back to your desk that way. Go down that isle instead." "The next time you feel like spitting, spit on the ground—not on people." Or, "When you are feeling very angry, don't call people names—tell them or tell me that you are feeling very angry—if we talk about what is making you feel so angry then you will feel better and you will not do something that gets you in trouble."

Distracting

For the most part, this type of response is more effective with the younger child than with older students. Many times, we have observed parents using this with their own children when they are crying and unable to follow through with something they need or want to do. In the classroom, it may be something as simple as saying to a crying, tantrumming youngster, "Look, look at what Mimi is doing! She is making a pretty picture with her paints—let's go over and see." The use of humor is a *distracting* response. Also, the use of humor can release tension surrounding an event that has taken on more importance than it should and can put things back into their proper perspective.

For example, a child in the cafeteria has just spilled a drink all down the front of his or her clothes. This can be very frustrating and lead to an angry outburst or crying. The teacher can say, "Oh, I didn't know you wanted to go swimming! This will dry soon—let's go over and get another drink." Reading this example may not sound funny to you as an adult, but this example really did happen and the child thought the idea that he had taken a swim was very funny. The seriousness of the situation was put into proper perspective with a few laughs and the simple fact that the clothes would dry and the child could get another drink immediately. Humor is effective when used before an emotion suddenly erupts. Another real life example of how humor can offset a potentially serious situation happened when one older elementary school age child lost his temper with the teacher and got out of his seat, took off his belt and started toward the teacher as if he was going to use the belt to strike her. The teacher just said, "Taking off your belt is pretty dangerous—you could lose your drawers." Here the teacher could have chosen to be more threatening to the student but humor was the better response. The student laughed uproariously, put his belt back on, and went to his seat. Humor, as a distractor, is not effective and should never be used with a child who is sad and crying. It should never, never be used to humiliate or put down a student. Only use humor when the student can also laugh at the situation. A youngster should never be made to feel like he or she is being laughed at—the use of humor should be a laughing together event.

Ignoring

Saying nothing is also a way of responding. There is communication going on in remaining silent. *Ignoring* is used to stop an inappropriate behavior because it withholds encouragement. Many times, students will say inane, silly, or naughty things just to get something going. They may be trying to distract the teacher, get the other students riled up, get attention, or make the teacher angry. Whatever the case, students will say things at times that warrant no response.

A few more real life examples are in order here. In the middle of a math lesson, the student raises his or her hand and asks, with the most serious look: "Teacher, does a bear fart in the forest? When you bend over and look at the floor, why don't your eyes fall out? Why is your butt so big?" Perhaps the student puts a hand under the armpit and makes the sound of expelling gas or forces a big belch. If you have had these experiences, you know how hard it can be sometimes to keep from laughing yourself; or, maybe it makes you angry. Regardless, it is important that you maintain your businesslike decorum and go on with the lesson, completely ignoring what was just said. Often, to comment or attend to such nonsense just spurs the student on to bigger and better silliness and becomes contagious with the other students so that they want to get in on the act. If you say anything at all, it should be to the other students who are behaving appropriately. "Sally, you are doing very well with your writing. Butch, all of your math problems are correct— you must feel proud of yourself. Mike, I like the way you are paying attention and getting your work done."

BUILDING A GOOD RELATIONSHIP

If you are going to engage the student in communicative interaction—and you will because it cannot be avoided completely—then there are some skills you will need so that you can interact competently. Your ability to learn this for yourself will serve as a model for the students so that they too will become more proficient at communicating and interacting competently. The following material contains both nonverbal as well as verbal responding techniques.

NONVERBAL ATTENDING SKILLS

The study of nonverbal communication is not an exact science, and you should be wary of people who tell you it means this when you scratch your nose, or cross your legs, or twist your hair, or so on, and so on. There are, however, some nonverbal communications that do have definite meanings. For example, if someone gives you the "okay" sign or the naughty finger, you definitely know what they are communicating. There are also some nonverbal actions that could be easily misinterpreted by another. So even though that is not what you intended to communicate, it is best to be aware of these actions and try to avoid them altogether.

Certain nonverbal responses tell students that you are really interested in hearing what they have to say, that you respect their feelings, and that you want them to learn to talk about what is going on with them. This is so important because emotionally disturbed students have many problems in school—primarily because they have not learned how to verbalize their feelings and instead they just act on those feelings. When they are angry, they fight; when they are frustrated, they say naughty things, run around the room, or tear up their schoolwork; when they are sad, they cry or tantrum or sulk. We need to help them learn how to interact competently so that they behave more appropriately and understand their feelings better. Gazda, Asbury, Balzer, Childers, and Walters (1977) have several areas of nonverbal communication modalities they list as being important to developing attending skills. Following is a discussion, with examples, that comes from their list of nonverbal attending behaviors.

Personal Space

When you are talking with a student, you need to be aware of personal space. There are differences in people in the amount of space they need between themselves and someone else when they are talking. If you stay too far away from students, they may read that as you do not really want to be near them and that you are not willing or interested in hearing their side of a story. Emotionally disturbed students are sensitive to space; until they know someone well, they require more distance from others. An arms length is generally what most people can tolerate, and this is a good guideline from which to start.

Body Posture

When students are talking, lean forward toward them. If you lean back when they are talking, it could be read that you are judging what they say as wrong or that you are not interested. When you are talking, you can lean back in your seat. Be relaxed and attentive. If you slouch, it could be misinterpreted that you find the whole conversation boring; if you sit up rigidly, that could be interpreted that you are uncomfortable with what the student is telling you or that you do not approve of them, or that you find what they say shocking. This is most important because some students may reveal some startling information, such as sexual abuse. The message you do not want to give to them is that you are so shocked or disgusted you cannot listen. Doing this will most likely cause them to clam up and feel they cannot talk about their situation. You may be the first and only one they have revealed such information to, and they need to feel they have a sensitive and caring listener, someone who will be able to help them with their problems.

Eye Contact

Keep your eye contact regular without staring. Despite what some people say, it is not necessary to make direct eye contact constantly when the student is talking. Using the example of a student talking about sexual abuse, it is all right—and more sensitive—to occasionally glance to the side and back to the student. In general, they feel embarrassed and uncomfortable talking about sexual matters. At such times, maintaining strong eye contact seems more like staring and can communicate that you think this is something bizzare, shocking, disgusting, or that you are a voyeur just dying to hear all of the juicy details. Averting your eyes momentarily says relax, you are not the only one in the world this has happened to, I have heard this before (even if you haven't), you are not so different than anyone else in the world because this has happened to you, you are not a freak to be stared at, this is not so shocking, and this can be heard and something can be done to correct what is going on.

Time

Give the students the time they need to tell their story. Do not look at the clock or at your watch. Do not interrupt with something you want to say or finish their sentences for them. Wait for a pause in the conversation and then say what you have to say. If you really intend to talk with them, then make sure that there is time. Do not seem hurried or sit there correcting or shuffling papers. If you cannot give them the time they need, tell them that you really do want to talk with them and set a time when they can have your full attention. It is better to put off the talk than to mishandle the situation. You can tell the student, "I believe you have something important to talk about and I want to hear what you have to say. Let's do that when it is a good time for both of us, say at 3:30, or lunch, or recess, or during my planning time."

Environmental Barriers

Furniture can be a barrier when talking. If you do not want someone to stay around long or talk to you, go sit behind your desk; do not make the offer for them to sit down and see what happens. They will stop talking and go away. It has probably happened to you; remember how you felt. When you are ready to listen and talk with students, sit beside them in chairs, or side by side in desks, or move to a table and sit with them there.

Facial Expressions

It is all right to let some emotion show on your face. In most instances, let the emotions be in concert with the students. You must be cautious with your facial expressions, however. If they smile, then most of the time you can smile also. But be sure you are really listening. Does their smile or laugh fit with what they have just told you? If a student just told you that his or her mom was drunk this morning and fell on the floor, and then the child laughs; don't laugh! Their laughter was nervous, sad, frightened, or angry. The incident was too serious (and probably frightening) to the youngster. You also do not need to comment on their laughter. The chances are great that they know they just laughed but did not mean it was funny. You are on target to say something such as "It is scary to see your parents so out of control. I would be mad if I thought they were so drunk they could not take care of me, or help me with my homework, or help me get ready for school", or whatever else you think this alcoholic parent is interfering with or neglecting. If a student tells you, as one student told me, about her father tying her to the bed and doing all sorts of perverted things to her, keep your facial expressions relaxed and calm. Yes, it is disgusting and shocking, but you must think of the emotions the child is experiencing. More important than how shocking and disgusting the whole matter is, is how sad it is for the child, how frightening it is for the child. The message you can allow to show on your face is your understanding of how sad it is for the child.

Vocalizing

Your voice reveals your emotions. Keep it clearly audible and neither too loud nor too soft. Pace your vocalizations at an average or somewhat slower than normal rate. Do not speak hesitantly, impatiently, or very slowly. If you are hesitant or halting it says you do not understand any of this. If you speak too slowly, it says, you are uninterested, bored, not willing to go on with this conversation. If you speak too fast or too loud, it may be interpreted that you are eager to get this over with, do not want to hear any more shocking things, or that you are angry or upset, beside yourself—whatever you are saying can sound more like you are being judgmental or accusatory.

VERBALIZING

Another thing we must be cautious about is that we do not put words in the student's mouth that may not be true or that we blurt out a definite response of what we think their feelings are. You may be exactly right in your interpretation, but you have to proceed carefully because you may not be interpreting precisely what is really going on with the child. If you have made an incorrect interpretation, it could say to the student that you do not understand them at all, or that you were not really listening. Perhaps they will interpret that as you really do not care about them. So there are some key phrases you can use to begin your sentence that will allow the student to see that you do understand and care. Or, if you were not quite right these phrases give students a chance to clarify the situation for you and also for them to gain greater insight into what they are talking about. Following are some of those key phrases to beginning a sentence.

It sounds as if, or it sounds like
The way I hear it is
What you seem to be saying is
I think you're telling me
It seems that
I have the feeling that you are saying, you are feeling, you mean, you are
    telling me, you have told me
Something tells me that

The picture I am getting is that you
What I think you just told me is that you
When things like that happen, sometimes people feel like
If that happened to me, I would feel
I imagine that you might be feeling or thinking
Could it be that you feel

The way you interact (verbally and nonverbally) comes with time and experience and, most importantly, with empathy. It may come more naturally and quickly to some than it does to others, but all of us need practice with these skills. I cannot tell you exactly how to act or exactly what to say at any given moment, for every situation or for every child. You will learn over time what is right for your situation, and it will come more naturally with experience. What I can tell you that will help you become competent in your interactions is to listen with your heart as well as your ears. Try to imagine yourself in the student's place and how you would feel in the same situation. Hear the feelings: That is the most important skill.

GROUP MEETING

After relaxation exercises in the morning there should be a group meeting that lasts 30 to 40 minutes. This serves a similar purpose as relaxation exercises. Students are not ready for academics if their minds are plagued with their personal troubles. This author's experience with running group meetings is that, if handled well, it can be the most dynamic and important experience the students will have. Initially, many youngsters do not know where to begin with group meetings, are hesitant to talk about their problems, or think this is a time to just shoot the breeze. However, some students are eager to jump right in and tell all. It is most often the teacher that hears their experiences first because, in many cases, these students do not go to therapy. So it is the teacher and the group who hears and responds to their significant and often tragic situations. Over time, the students become very comfortable with each other and eventually begin to run group meetings by themselves, with the teacher as just another member of the group instead of the moderator. Experience with this intervention technique has shown me, that if properly taught, the students can become the most empathic listeners of all and can come up with some good solutions to another peer's problems.

A group meeting can be called at any time but it is most effective when done first in the morning to clear the mind of troubles so that the student can go on and do the academics required of them. There are many good reasons for integrating group meetings as a part of the daily routine. Dreikurs, Grunwald, and Pepper (1982) have provided a number of reasons for the value of regularly scheduled group meetings. Some of their reasons include: students learn to discuss highly charged material, which is often ignored; they learn to develop values and attitudes, which can bring about lifetime changes in behavior both internally and externally; difficult issues become easier to handle and seem less overwhelming when shared with others; a peer group provides what we all need, which is a support system; students learn more constructive ways of coping with problems; it provides an opportunity to see that there are always options and we are not stuck with one way of handling problems; since these youngsters are generally segregated, it provides a first opportunity to learn how to work in a group; as in belonging to any group, this gives the students the chance to feel accepted and have a rightful place somewhere; students gain more self-direction, self-management, and the ability to make appropriate decisions and thus feel greater control over themselves and their lives. Finally, it provides the teacher with more knowledge about the students' feelings, thoughts, attitudes, and how they relate to others. Some of the following material comes from Dreikurs and Cassel (1972), some from Glasser (1969), and some material from unknown sources.

PROCEDURES

Group meeting is not just sitting together having a conversation. It is different in that there is direction and there are rules that must be followed so that group meeting becomes a constructive and reconstructive intervention. There are certain procedures to follow to set up the atmosphere for having group meeting, and you should not deviate from these.

1. Use a circle arrangement with the teacher sitting in a different place each time. This prevents the misperception that the teacher favors one student over another. It is the beginning of the teacher eventually becoming a member of the group and not always the moderator. The students have to learn from the first that this is *their* group and not the teacher's. Group meetings serve two main purposes: (1) to discuss with empathic listeners the problems they are having and to find ways to cope better with their situations and, (2) to bring to the group day-to-day school-related problems that can be handled through a democratic process.
2. Group meeting should never be used so that the teacher can impose his or her own ideas or to preach to the students about

broken rules and so forth. This time is for the students to share their ideas, right or wrong, and eventually their ideas will become more reasonable. The group will decide consequences for broken rules and misbehavior. Obviously, in the beginning the teacher will have to act as moderator. My experience is that initially the students are overly harsh with each other and can come up with some outlandish ideas for consequences and punishment. But remember, they are repeating what they have experienced and need to learn how to be just and fair. Usually in their discussions some are too lenient and some too harsh; after some debate, a moderate and reasonable solution will be found.

3. Group meeting should not be allowed to become a free-for-all where it is unstructured and unrestrained. The group needs to be kept focused on constructive thinking and not allowed to become unproductive by engaging in meaningless pratter. Often at the start many students do not know how to attend to serious matters because they do not know what to say; some students may find the material being discussed too anxiety-provoking; and some, because they need attention cannot attend well to others for long periods. These are all skills they have to learn. To stop meaningless pratter, the teacher moderates by saying something such as, "Ricky, I know you want to talk but Carol is telling the group something really important now. Soon it will be your turn to talk. For now let's listen very carefully to what Carol is saying and try to help her figure out what to do about her problem. Maybe you have had the same problem or something like it and you could share what you did about it." At times, some student will cause the discussion to stray to something that is important, but this should not be allowed either. You can bring the discussion back with comments such as, "We were talking about why Carol has so much trouble making friends. Some other time we can discuss why you have the same problem Ricky." Some will talk forever without getting to the point (i.e., telling every minute detail of a fight they had with someone). Direct them back to the original problem with specific questions, such as, "How often do you fight? Where are you when the fighting starts? What starts the fighting? What do your parents think of all this fighting?"

4. The students should not be allowed to humiliate one another. Remind them that unkind treatment of one another is not allowed. If it continues excessively, one rule might be that they cannot join group on that day. This is not the most ideal solution because they lose the opportunity to learn what they can from the group meet-

ing. Call on the group to comment. Ask, "What is the rule? Why do you suppose Sergio feels like hurting someone today?"

5. You should hold meetings for a specific duration; do not vary the length of the meetings. As the moderator, you will have to cut off the meetings at the appropriate time even if the students are engaged in a hot debate. Meetings should not drag overtime and become an excuse for avoiding other responsibilities. Sometimes, you see the same dynamic that happens in therapy where a person waits until the time is almost up to start talking about something really important. This is to avoid the issue even though they really want to talk about it. You must say to them that time is up and that they brought up something very important that needs to be discussed. Tell them that tomorrow the group will start with that issue.

6. The teacher should not interrupt the students to correct bad grammar or mild profanity. If the swearing gets out of hand, ask the group what is the rule about using dirty language.

7. Students who dominate and talk endlessly should be interrupted politely and then promised that you will return to them later. You might say, "This is all very interesting but the others need a chance to talk too because this is for the whole group. Later we will come back to you and hear what else you have to say."

8. In all cases, the teacher should not be the judge. In the first place, this is the students' group. Also, this is an opportunity where the teacher does not have to be the heavy. There are already numerous instances in these classes where, as the teacher, you have to do the correcting and disciplining. Here you are off of the hook and can be neutral. Allow the group to be the judge, especially about things such as making up stories or lying. You can say, "That sounds interesting—quite a story—what do you think group?"

PROCESS

Group meetings should be started as soon as possible but not the first day, of course. You can begin when you have all become acquainted and the students are feeling comfortable with you. There is a process that must be followed for this to become an organized group that will deal with important issues. You will need to do much of the work in the beginning and a great amount of modeling until the students arrive at the point where group runs smoothly and they are doing most of it themselves. The process necessary to get started follows:

1. These students obviously had difficulty maintaining themselves in the group structure of a regular classroom or they would not be in a segregated setting for emotionally disturbed youngsters. To set up group meetings is really the beginning of teaching them how to work in a group setting and getting back to the regular classroom. This is not going to come quickly or easily for them. Clearly, you cannot start group meetings by discussing highly emotionally charged issues. You need to start with simple ideas that they can all handle. To begin, you can bring them into a circle and invite them to give suggestions on how the room should be decorated. Planning bulletin boards is a beginning. The group should discuss their ideas, plan and organize together, and assign responsibilities. Another beginning idea would be to let them discuss and plan where they want to have group center, or time out, or where they want their desks, or perhaps even where they would like your desk to be (it should not matter to you because with these students you will be on your feet most of the day anyway). Older students may be interested in discussing what they enjoyed and what they did not like about school in the past.

2. You need a training period; it is hard to say how long this will take. It is different for each teacher and goes according to the personalities of the students you have, their disabilities, the intensity of their emotional problems, and the number of low- and high-functioning students in the group. You will know by "feel" when they are ready to discuss important issues and when they are ready to take over their group. During the training period, the teacher must be active as the moderator and model how a moderator relates to the group. Eventually, you will want each student to take turns at being the moderator. But in the beginning, you will decide on the issues to be discussed. You will clarify the plans and procedures, set the time limits, and keep them focused on the discussion.

3. You will have to establish immediately the rules for group meeting. Start first by talking about what it means to have a discussion where people have differences of opinion without getting angry. Work out guidelines that will protect everyone's rights and prevent students from being unfair and violating the rights of others. The guidelines should be simple, few in number, cooperatively planned, and agreed upon by the group.

4. Find ways to ensure total participation by encouraging all students to contribute in anyway possible within the limits of their capacity. This can be done by starting with simple issues that are of such a nature that most students have an opinion. For instance, you can

discuss playground activities, free-time activities, or snacks. Do not wait too long to draw the silent students into discussing issues. You can have a rule that everyone is allowed to pass once but that the next time they must say at least a few words. You might draw out the quiet ones by saying, "What do you think about the things that have been said? We haven't heard from James yet; let's hear what he has to say."

5. All suggestions that the students come up with should be accepted by the teacher but immediately given back to the group. Your comments should be restricted to things such as, "That's an interesting idea. There's a new thought. What does the group think?" Even if you really like the student's idea, you should not comment, "What a great idea! That's good" or "I don't think that is going to work" and so forth. You do not want to stop the thinking of the group or prejudice them with your opinion. Accept, but turn it back to the group to decide and to continue working on the issue.

6. After 1 or 2 weeks of having group meeting, you should discuss with the students the things that have been achieved, how they think things are going, what might have been poorly planned, and what needs improvement. You should ask such questions as, "What have we accomplished in group meeting? Has it been good so far? In what ways has it been good? What hasn't been so good?" Then you can add some of your observations about how group has been working. Tell them what they need to discuss more and what they are doing well.

SPONTANEOUS MEETINGS

Spontaneous meetings can be called when an incident occurs in class and you want the participation of all the students to discuss rules and consequences. They are effective, but only after the class has learned to run group meetings very well, and you are at the point where the students are the moderators. As students progress and become more reasonable and moderate in their judgments, others see them as just and fair. It is interesting to observe that students, when they have reached this point, will accept the consequences (even when they are much stiffer than yours would have been) of the group with little complaint. Again, here is a place where the onus can be lifted from the teacher as the one who is always handing out the classroom unpleasantries. It gives you much more freedom to move about the room helping with academics and passing out praises and encouragement. You become, in the eyes of the students, much more benevolent.

ROLE PLAYING

This intervention can be very helpful from time to time (Wallen & Wallen, 1978). It is linked in some ways to group meeting. Role playing is especially useful in solving relationship problems among two or more students. It is a valuable intervention for helping a youngster to stand back and look at his or her problems through the eyes of other people. It helps students understand the situation of another who might be feeling rejected, scapegoated, unloved, and unable to handle frustration in an acceptable manner. In role playing, the student is assigned roles or characters that are portrayed and interpreted according to the student's understanding. The student should not be told what to say or how to interpret the role or character that is being portrayed. There are three uses for role playing.

CLARIFYING A PROBLEM

This intervention is used to bring about recall of an incident that needs attention, such as a fight. It brings out not only the details of the incident as well as the emotions that precipitated the event. (This type of role playing is the *action* counterpart to Reality Rub-In of the Life Space Interview discussed later in this chapter). The incident (a fight) is acted out up to the point of contact. You do not, of course, allow the re-creation of a real fight.

This particular role playing serves several purposes for both the teacher and the students. You are not caught in the middle of trying to figure out the facts. The teacher does not have to try to listen and decipher who did what to whom first, who started the fight, and does not have to always end up as the judge and jury. The teacher will not have to lecture, chastize, pass judgment, or sift out the truth. You will have the group observing the role playing and discussing it afterwards. Then they will decide. To start the role playing, you declare ignorance of the event and insist that you be shown what happened. You say, "Don't tell; show!"

It is helpful for the students because they gain insight into their own behavior. Later, they learn to recognize what starts conflicts, how they became involved, and how they often create their own problems. It does not allow them to wallow around in self-pity, always blaming others for their troubles.

When this role playing is finished, the teacher recounts the details observed and turns it to the group. Something can be said such as, "Now, what did you all notice? How did that make Saul feel? What about Terry's feelings? What really happened here and what should be done this time?"

FINDING SOLUTIONS

This type of role playing is used to demonstrate to and impress upon the students that many problems have more than one solution. It is important for these youngsters to see how others feel in certain situations and to discover for themselves that certain behaviors do not solve some problems. In this type of role playing, the event or problem is acted out more than once.

For the first time, a report of what happened is made. Then a set of actors are assigned (not the students involved), and they act out the incident exactly as it was described.

This is followed by a group meeting where the teacher asks several questions to get everybody involved in finding optional solutions to problems. The teacher might start by saying, "Let's discuss what you liked about the way this problem was handled. How do you think they felt? Where were the mistakes made? What was the solution? How many think they could handle this situation in a better way?"

Next you designate a new set of actors who have to act out the same situation; but this time they must come up with a different solution. This should be followed with another group discussion asking the same questions. Also, ask the group to compare the two solutions and determine which one was most helpful. You could go for a third reenactment although it is not necessary and would be very time-consuming, as well as potentially boring the students with overkill.

GETTING IN TOUCH AND DEVELOPING EMPATHY

This type of role playing is used to help students become aware of their feelings and to recognize the impact that their emotions have on their bodies and how it affects their behavior. You begin by inventing situations that cause emotional reactions. Give them the situation and then tell them to "freeze" their facial expressions. A mirror is then passed around so that they can see how they are affected by their emotions. Point out all of the outward signs of emotion such as frowning, twisting their eyes, and turning their mouths.

This is followed by having them "freeze" their whole bodies and describe where they feel tension. Next, they should improvise a dialogue with another person and act out the situation. As in the other types of role playing, the group observes and provides other alternatives to the actors solutions. Empathy for others cannot come about until we are in touch with our own feelings first. There are a number of situations and problems that most all youngsters experience. Some are used to get in touch with their own feelings and some are used to begin developing empathy for other's feelings. Following is a list of ideas that can be used as starters:

Someone told a lie about you.
Someone tore up your paper.
Someone just hit you.
Someone shoved your books off your desk.
Someone called you a bad name.
Someone told you to shut up.
It seems like you always make a lot of mistakes.
You have just failed a test.
You stole something and now you have to face up to it.

GUIDELINES FOR ROLE PLAYING

Just as in conducting group meetings, there must be procedures, rules, and a process for role playing.

Atmosphere

There are important factors that the teacher must convey to the students and questions asked to set the tone for role playing. The teacher should let the students know that there are many problems that are not easily solved. The teacher should convey that there are many solutions to most problems and that everyone runs into difficulties from time to time.

In setting the atmosphere, the teacher presents the problem story the students are going to act out. They must be given time to think about the problem before jumping right in. The teacher asks, "What is the problem? What happened?" and then invites ideas and accepts all whether they are good or bad. This is based upon the same principle as group meeting. The students have to learn the best way to handle their problems.

Selecting the Actors

Students should not be selected as actors to portray a role that is most like them. For instance, the teacher or students should not "type cast" a particular youngster who is always fighting, swearing, awkward, and so on. Students need to be warmed up to the characters by the teacher asking, "What is Karl like? How does he feel? What do you think he thinks about such and such?"

Setting the Stage

Equipment will be needed such as table(s), chairs, and space for action to take place. The teacher will need to ask a few questions to get them into the situation that is to be enacted, such as, "Where will this take place? What time of the day is it? What are the characters supposed to be doing?"

Enactment

The teacher decides when to stop the enactment and which solutions are to be portrayed. The role playing must be kept focused when the students get silly. If this happens, then the teacher stops the enactment and asks, "Are you really playing the character? What kind of person is Tim? We're not really working on the problem, are we?"

This is not a time to scold or allow other members of the group to tell one of the actors what to do. The youngster should be allowed to work out his or her idea of the role. Keep the focus on true life and bring awareness to the different feelings and ideas.

The rest of the group should be instructed to observe and see if the actor is playing the part for real, or if what is happening could be real. Tell them to keep track of what feelings are being portrayed and what solutions come to their minds as they watch.

Discussion

When the role playing is over, the teacher opens the discussion by asking, "How do you suppose Tim felt? Why do you think his mom said that? What were the solutions? Which one seemed to work best? Where could you use what you have learned today? You all did a very good job. Thank you." These questions for discussion are to bring closure to the experience. The students should not be allowed to just finish, go back to their seats, and start working on math, and so on.

UNDERSTANDING THROUGH STORIES

There are two ways to use stories as interventions for emotionally disturbed students: bibliotherapy and mutual story telling. Stories are to be used when the group is not yet ready to analyze and understand their own behavior directly the way they will in group meeting, role playing, and life space interviewing. Bibliotherapy and mutual story telling are interventions that should be implemented on a daily basis at first. Approximately

20 minutes is often enough to allocate to this activity. It is also a natural tie to academics, which they expect in the class, but it is nonthreatening as opposed to being required to do activities in a regular reading lesson.

BIBLIOTHERAPY

A clarification of what bibliotherapy is *not* is needed. When I first started talking to teachers of emotionally disturbed students about the use of bibliotherapy, an editorial appeared in the local newspaper that stated some professor at the university was teaching teachers to conduct therapy using the Bible. Bibliotherapy has nothing to do with the Bible, or the Talmud, the I Ching, the Koran, or any other religious material, although some people might use this type of material to "cure" people.

Bibliotherapy is the use of specific books (*So You Have A New Brother (Sister)!, Mom and Dad Are Getting Divorced, If I Could Just Stay Dry*) to help students with certain problems. Common fictional stories can be used to illustrate a point. The teacher helps the group to analyze and understand behavior through stories. Using books allows students to feel free to express feelings and ideas in a situation that does not have to be threatening to them personally. Specific students are not put on the spot. A major purpose to using bibliotherapy is to help youngsters think of all the possible motivations characters might have for their actions. It is used to help bring about understanding of how one's problems affect everyone in class. And, it helps to develop empathy by demonstrating that we can be accepting that everyone makes mistakes and mistakes can be rectified.

Morgan (1976) outlines several cautions about the use of certain kinds of books with emotionally disturbed students and gives suggestions on how to conduct bibliotherapy. The selection of reading material for disturbed children is crucial. What youngsters are given to read could compound their existing state or add a new dimension to their problems. The chances are slim that no matter how many appropriate books given to read—reading alone about their problems will not be a cure. New problems, however, can be prevented, and old problems can be minimized by a thoughtfully planned reading program. There are three major areas to avoid:

1. *Fear induction.* Many of these children have a tendency to distort events and to have developed fears. Some of these fears are specific, and some have not yet been identified. Certain literature may only compound identified fears, whereas other may give a generalized fear some new shape. Stories with a central theme of abandonment, violence, and brutality should be avoided. Books about death and dying require obvious caution.

2. *Symptom exacerbation.* Common characteristics shared by disturbed children are highly enriched fantasy lives and the strong tendency toward magical thinking. For example, they have a firm belief in the existence of imaginary creatures such as those found in the popular book, *Where the Wild Things Are.* Books that tend to compound an *unreal* conceptualization of the world contain stories about characters such as talking beasts, humanized inanimate objects, giants, ghosts, witches, and goblins. Included in this example would be locations that do not exist such as "never-never land" in *Peter Pan. Alice in Wonderland* is a prime example of a most inappropriate selection. By magic, Alice is swept into a fantasy land where inanimate objects and animals are personified, a powerful female figure screams of removing heads and uses living beasts as inanimate objects. Some disturbed children would find it extremely difficult to sort disorganization and fantasy from reality.

3. *Self-esteem: Motivation Reduction.* This includes listerature with sexist and racist overtones. This material may be very subtle such as consistently depicting females as passive and nonproductive; demonstrated disapproval of boys showing emotion; or insulting misrepresentations and stereotypes of ethnic minority groups. Books that contain nonrelevant subject matter such as story after story of Caucasians only loses meaning and interest to a Black child. All male adventure stories with unimportant roles for females are boring. To be avoided altogether are the obvious characterizations of ethnic groups such as the "lazy Latin type" and Little Black Sambo stories. Any stories, fairytales, or nursery rhymes about wicked stepmothers, helpless damsels, evil witches, cruel queens, silly old spinsters, giddy girls, comical teachers, or that represent females as inferior should be left out. Finally, books that are clearly labeled for a certain age group should not be included if they do not fit with the students' age.

Follow-up discussions after the reading is an important aspect of bibliotherapy. Certain types of questions about the reading have been highlighted by Lundsteen (1972) and are similar to the methods employed by Ojemann (1961) and Gardner (1971). Some of the general questions in the dialogue that might be useful are:

What happened to the character?
What else? And then what?
How do you suppose he/she felt?

What made them do that?
What else could have caused it?
What would you do?
What if you were the main character?
How could it be done differently?
Would that make a difference? How?
What is the story trying to show?
How could you use this someplace else?

MUTUAL STORY TELLING

This intervention was created by Gardner (1971), a child psychiatrist who used this intricately in therapy with children. I have distilled the essentials that a teacher could use in the classroom with students. (It is, of course, a type of therapy). But as stated early in this book, therapy is really teaching and many therapeutic techniques can be adapted and used successfully by well-educated teachers. You do not have to delve into deep subconscious material to be effective. As in all of these interventions, the teacher *is* looking deeper than at the surface behavior and working to help the students with the feelings and motivations that precipate all of the surface behavior they present. We are not going to provide these students with anything lasting or that will carry over to the regular classroom by focusing on what is readily apparent. Our goal is to help the students understand themselves better so that the behavior improves but, more importantly, so that they are more emotionally righted.

To conduct mutual story telling, you will need to establish some rules. You should start by telling the students that the more adventure there is to the story, the more interesting it will be. They cannot tell a story about things they have read, seen on television or at the movies, or things that have really happened to them or to someone they know. This rule takes away the threatening aspect that they might reveal something about themselves to others that they really are not ready to tell. If it is make-believe, then it is not embarrassing. As they become more comfortable with story telling, they will reveal inner feelings and fears, but still in the context of pretense. The next rule is that the story must have a beginning, a middle, and an end. Lastly, after the story they should tell the moral. After they have told a story, you will tell a story and it will have a moral as well.

They will need a warm-up period. You can start by introducing the child and asking the age, address, name of school, grade, the principal's name. Then give them time to think. If students cannot produce a story right away, comment that some kids have a little trouble thinking of a story the first time, but with some help they can because they have lots and lots of stories in their heads that they do not even know about yet. If a youngster cannot come up with a story, then just drop it and comment that maybe later they will have a story. Almost always, they all will have a story.

You can start a short beginning and let them know that when you point to them they should come in and say exactly the first thing that comes to mind at that moment. Do not introduce specific phrases or words, only introductions and connections.

You need to take notes during the story because you might have to ask questions at the end for detail, such as, "Was the horse a man or a woman? Why was the boy so mad at the horse? Why did the horse do that? What did we learn from the story?"

Next, you will tell a story that has a healthier solution. Your story will be a more mature adaptation involving the same characters, setting, and situation, but it will have appropriate resolutions to the most significant parts of the story. This shows the students that there are alternatives and options, and that they are not trapped where they have to keep behaving the same way to difficult situations.

Listen carefully to their stories and try to determine which characters or animals stand for the student and which for significant others. Two or more characters could stand for parts of the student. For example, a good dog and a bad dog could both represent the youngster and the conflict the student has about being bad at times but wanting to be good. Evil characters often represent the youngster's own hostility, but you must listen carefully and keep in mind what you know about the student. Evil characters may actually be in the child's home (e.g., abusive parents). Listen to the feelings in the story. Was it a pleasant story, neutral, or terrifying? Did the child tell a frightening story in an emotionless tone? If so, these are students who need to learn how to express emotion appropriately. Listen to the moral of the story. Often, this capsulizes the whole thing in one sentence. Following is a story that was told to me by a 9-year-old boy who was hospitalized for his emotional disturbance.

Bobby

"Once upon a time there was a little kid who had a real bad broken leg. Nobody could fix it. Not his mom or dad or anybody. It hurt so bad he thought he would die. In fact, he was going to die for sure. Then they took him to the hospital and his leg was fixed but he didn't want to go from the hospital. He knew if he went he would die and everyone else was going to die too. But he was afraid to cry or tell the people at the hospital about it. Everyone thought he was too big to cry. He didn't know what to do. If he cried they would kick him out. If he left and didn't stay they would all die.

He decided to sneak around and hide so everyone wouldn't die. The moral is keep your bad feelings from showing so people won't die."

The main points in Bobby's story is that he is afraid of his own condition and afraid he isn't loved by his parents. He has doubts, at times, that his emotions can be "fixed." He is afraid if he goes home and does not do well that he would be abandoned and have no place to go. And, obviously he is afraid of his own feelings and letting others see his feelings. Next is the story I told back to Bobby.

The Teacher's Version

"Far away in another country there lived a young boy: His name was Tomu. This boy had quite an imagination. He could make up and tell wounderful stories around a campfire. But sometimes, even his own stories and imagination were so scary they even frightened him. When he told stories about spirits and ghosts, he could almost see and hear them, and sometimes he really believed his own stories.

One day, this boy hurt his leg but not so bad that it couldn't be fixed. His mom and dad loved him and cared about him so they took him to the best hospital so his leg would get the very best treatment. At the hospital, his treatment hurt pretty bad but Tomu didn't want anyone to know it hurt so he tried not to show it. He imagined a story that no one would love him if he cried and he really believed that everyone would go away or never want to see him again if he wasn't real brave and if his leg didn't get well perfectly. But the Doctor said to him, I bet that leg hurts pretty bad and this treatment hurts too. I used to think I shouldn't let anybody see me cry when I was hurt. But once I hurt my hand so bad I couldn't stop myself from crying. But you know what happened next? People were sorry that my hand hurt so bad and they helped me fix it and made me feel better. They weren't upset at all to see me cry. I was pretty surprised but glad.

Then Tomu told the Doctor that his leg was hurting pretty bad and he began to cry. Well, the Doctor fixed his leg and told him the hospital was where everyone came when they didn't feel good or was hurt, and that Tomu could come to visit whenever he needed or wanted to. That's what they were there for and someone would always be there when he came. Tomu left feeling much better. The moral of this story is that people will help if you tell them you need help and sometimes our imagination is scarier than real life."

Now, that story was a bit long, but the points that needed to be addressed for Bobby were: that he imagined most of his fears; that people can help but they have to know what is bothering someone; that if he did have more problems when he went home he would not be abandoned and could come back to the hospital until everything was fixed; and obviously, it is okay to show your feelings.

Your stories do not have to be as long as this one. The main issues you want to deal with in your story are the students' strongest feelings. Finally, you want to show in your story that there are healthy or good outcomes, and that there are solutions to problems.

THE LIFE-SPACE INTERVIEW

Many good teachers have conducted life-space interviews (LSI) with their students without knowing it had a name and that there were components to life-space interviewing that had titles. An LSI, however, is not just having a chat with a student or moralizing. It has a definite aim at a specific target. The concept of the LSI was developed by Fritz Redl (1959) and it is intended to handle problems and provide emotionally disturbed students with insights into their behavior on the spot, in their natural setting, where blowups occur.

In the LSI, the greatest amount of empathy is needed and can be maximally manifested. It is important to know the types and components of a LSI because you must be aware of what you are trying to accomplish with the student. But the teacher really does not need to memorize these titles that Redl has given to life-space interviewing. In fact, doing so can interfere with natural empathic responses.

For example, I made a supervision visit to a practicum student who was in a class for emotionally disturbed children. This graduate student was very good and had the potential to be an excellent teacher for these youngsters. When I observed her in natural interactions with the students, she was excellent; her responses were right on target and very empathic. However, when she decided "Now I am going to conduct a life-space interview," she sat down with a student and pulled out index cards that had the types and categories of LSI listed and attempted to interact with the student. It was, of course, a disaster because she was not really attending to the youngster. Instead, she was attending to her notecards to see if she was following the correct procedure. She was frustrated because she was getting nowhere with the student and the student was drifting and shifting around in his seat. Why should he pay attention? The practicum teacher was not really tuned in to him; neither person was interacting competently. You can and should tape-record your LSI and go back later to see if you accomplished with the student what you intended. But do not try to follow notes to see if you are doing the "right thing." Be natural, attend to what the student is feeling and saying, and listen. You will become proficient with time and practice.

FACETS OF CHILDREN'S NATURE

There are two primary reasons for the development of the LSI. First, while the teacher is not an analyst, many situations that come up in school cannot wait for the resolution of deeper problems solved through nondirective procedures used by a psychotherapist. Issues and situations that come up in a classroom require immediate closure. Second, human beings are not just physical organisms amenable to exact science and training; our inner emotional life needs attention, too. Before attempting to work with these students, you must realize that there are different facets to youngsters just as there are in adults. They have three aspects to their nature.

1. *Youngsters are feeling beings.* Their lives are filled with many strong emotions, such as anger, hate, hurt, fear, sadness, anxiety, love, joy, and so on. These feelings are intricately intertwined into their motivational systems. This intertwining of emotions and motivations are both at a conscious and unconscious level and have much to do with what they need and what they want, and what they need and want have a significant impact on how they feel. For instance, a student may feel rejected at home, which causes him or her to need and want recognition and attention at school. These feelings and needs can be so strong that the students will try to get recognition and attention in inappropriate ways. The consequences of the inappropriate behavior can then lead to feeling bad, stupid, and rejected. So the cycle goes on. The purpose of the LSI is to make the students aware of their feelings and motivations, realize how this has been affecting their lives, and break this cycle.

2. *Youngsters are thinking beings.* Like everyone, youngsters can be either rational and irrational. As they develop cognitive skills, they learn to organize their world. They learn to classify things and talk about them. The world then begins to take on structure according to the classifications that the youngsters use to organize. The ego is closely related to these skills and becomes the mediator between the youngster's internal and external world. The ego modulates input and output and is responsible for development of such capacities as perception and language. It is the ego that must repond to the demands and stresses accompanying development. The most important cognitive ego skills are modeling, comparison, abstraction, projection, and prediction. This is one reason that

the LSI is most useful with older elementary-school-age children and very useful with adolescents. It is not a very amenable intervention with primary-age children because they have not yet developed these sophisticated cognitive skills. They are still very primitive in their abilities and cognitive development. Since they do not have well developed language skills, or strong abilities to compare, abstract, project, and predict, their responses to their feelings are primarily behavioral reactions. They just act what they feel. Other interventions, such as behavior modification, are more appropriate for the very young child. This does not mean that you never talk to them. You must start early explaining while demonstrating what they must do, but do not expect to go very deep with them.

3. *The youngster experiences on many levels: Some they are aware of, and some they are not.* Behavior is governed by motivations and experiences, past and present, which the youngster does not always recognize. Fantasy is a significant interface between the complexities of a youngster's inner world and the concrete world of external realities. Many components of the LSI are directed at sorting out what is fantasy and part of their inner world and what is reality and part of their outer world. It is designed to make them aware when they are not aware and to understand how they may be acting in the present because of something that happened in the past. The LSI is a psychodynamic intervention; many criticize it because they believe the past is the past and only the present should be given attention. The flaw in this thinking is believing that the past is a dead issue. There is the old saying that if we do not know history we are doomed to repeat our mistakes. More importantly is the question of when is the past the past? If we are still functioning and *feeling* right now in the present based upon what happened in the past, then is it the past? That is, of course, a rhetorical question. The past is not the past if it is still motivating what we feel and do in the present. The past is only the past when it no longer has influence over our feelings, motivations, and behavior.

In the LSI, we must proceed with the basic assumption that the behavior we observe is the best solution that students have found to protect themselves from something that seems even more stressful. For example, a student cries and refuses to do some work assigned. This causes the youngster stress because there are consequences for incomplete work. Refusal to do assigned work is an outward symptom, but it is not the real problem. Perhaps the real problem is the youngster's lack of self-esteem and the fear of failure and feeling stupid. Whatever consequences the teacher implements for incomplete work assignments must surely seem less threatening to the student than the fear of failure and feeling stupid. One of the tasks in LSI is to go straight to the source of the problem and not to focus on the symptom. Why does the youngster have such low self-esteem? Why does the student fear or assume failure? What can be done to dispel this and protect the student from feeling stupid? In the LSI, you will have to decode both verbal and nonverbal communication.

VERBAL COMMUNICATION

Words can be misleading, and students will say things they do not mean. They have learned over the years that saying what you really feel or think can get you into trouble. Therefore, they often say things that are not true to mask or protect their real feelings. Teachers have to learn to pay as much attention to *how* the student speaks as to what the student says. The depressed youngster may speak hesitantly and have trouble finding words. The anxious student may speak rapidly and stutter and never reach the target. Some use talking to keep us at a distance. They may go on incessantly; if they are particularly bright and verbal, they can lead us astray. Their taking control of the talking keeps us off the necessary topic. Some talk too much because they need to talk in order to share and make us a part of them and their lives with words. Some behave like that because they think you will not otherwise pay attention, or care. You must also listen to the tone and flow of youngsters' communication; they may say the opposite of what they feel and mean. To illustrate is the example of what came out of a LSI with a student I taught.

GARY

Gary was one of those rare students we get from time to time in whom we begin to see almost immediate improvement in his behavior. Within 3 or 4 months, Gary's behavior had changed so dramatically that he was spending more time in the regular class for reading, math, science, PE, and Shop than he was in the self-contained room. It was a mistake I was not aware of at the time, but I had been making consistent comments about his success and thought by the next year he would be ready to go to the regular classroom full time. Then, rather rapidly, his behavior changed dramatically and he was in worse shape than when he first entered the self-contained room. I cannot pinpoint my own behaviors precisely now. As I look back, I realize that I had allowed, or made, Gary more dependent upon me than was healthy. Perhaps I protected him too much and had not allowed him to have some failure experiences and then worked through them with him. This may have made him too dependent upon me.

On one occasion, I approached him and commented on the change in his behavior, asking what was going on. He looked up at me and shouted, "Get out of here; don't talk to me!" I stepped back a bit, startled at this atypical reaction. Tears were rolling down his face and he grabbed my arm. We talked, and he revealed that he did not want to go to regular class next year. That he was afraid he could not do the work and keep up, and that he wanted to stay with me. That he wanted me to be his teacher forever. His original communication of, "Get out of here; don't talk to me" is an example of one of those misleading communications that mask and protect real feelings. He really meant, "I love you; don't abandon me; don't let me fail." He was given away, of course, by his nonverbal actions of the tears and grabbing my arm, but also his verbal reaction to me was so distorted and out of character to the relationship we had developed that I knew something else was going on.

NONVERBAL COMMUNICATION

A youngster's body language may suggest the opposite of what is being said or if nothing is being said at all (as in Gary's case, when he told me to get out of here but then grabbed my arm). Again, some youngsters may not verbally communicate because they have learned that certain feelings and words are reacted to with anger or disappointment. They have learned that the spoken word can be held against them. Silence, however, is a part of communication. It may mean they are embarrassed, frightened, lack trust, too upset and angry to talk, or recalling another situation that interferes with hearing what you are saying. They may not talk to keep from crying. Toughness can be a cover-up when they are afraid of their own feelings. They may be concerned that if they acknowledge your kindness, they might fall apart. Sometimes they are silent because they do not know the acceptable words to use to talk about their feelings or something they have experienced. We do not know what all body language signals, but some of the things to watch for are: messages sent with the eyes (teary, squinted and angry, looking away in embarrassment); muscles (tense and taut, slack as in depressed or feeling hopeless); skin temperature (cold, clammy hands when anxious, face flushed when angry); breathing patterns (rapid as when anxious or fearful, deep sighing as when sad and depressed); and body movement (fidgeting, snapping fingers, wiggling feet, pulling hair, rubbing face and arms—all indications of feeling nervous and apprehensive about what is being discussed).

GUIDELINES FOR LIFE-SPACE INTERVIEWING

The LSI can be conducted almost anywhere out of earshot of the other students: a corner of the room, the hall, time-out space, cafeteria, or nurse's office. Some suggest that if the teacher cannot conduct the LSI, the principal is the logical person to do this work. I do not agree with this for several reasons. First, most principals see themselves as disciplinarians in a fairly stringent manner. Most (not all) administrators have no training in LSI and frankly do not want that type of involvement with the students. Most administrators do not have nearly the knowledge of the youngster that the teacher has and do not make the same intense effort to understand them. Finally, it is the teacher who knows the student best (and who has the training) and therefore is in the position to make the LSI the most beneficial intervention for the student. If the teacher cannot conduct the LSI, then it should be forgone. It is better to let the opportunity go by than to allow someone else to make an attempt and botch it. Below are some common sense standards to go by in conducting the LSI. Some of these are suggestions by Brenner (1963), some come from my own experience, and some come from the experiences of others:

1. Be as courteous, considerate, and polite as you would to an adult. If the child has tears and a runny nose, offer a tissue. Apologize if you are distracted from the discussion. Do not answer your own questions for the child; allow time for thinking and responses. Do not finish their sentences for them if they are slow in responding. This time is for them, not you. Insure their privacy. Make them comfortable. Do not sit while they stand, or stand while they sit.
2. Do not have barriers between you.
3. Do not stand over the youngster in a position of dominance and authority. Kneel, bend down, or, preferably, have a low chair for yourself to sit on so that you are eye to eye. Never lift small children off of their feet to sit them on a desk or table. This can be frightening to children, and once again it shows your dominance, not your thoughtfulness, giving youngsters the feeling of a loss of control.
4. When you are *sure* they have done something, confront them with it immediately and do not give in to their excuses or fabrications.
5. Remember not to use the word "why."
6. Get the conversation going about the actual event. Have the youngster give a detailed description of what happened. Listen.
7. If the student is overwhelmed with guilt or shame, try to take some of the potency out of the situation. Tell them, "This doesn't

bother me very much but it is something we need to explore because it can continue to cause you problems" or, "This is not so unusual, it happens to lots of people, let's discuss it very carefully." Remember that the youngster who has no guilt or shame needs a different approach.

8. If the youngster cannot find the words to express the appropriate feelings, then supply the words. "You are feeling angry, or hurt, or disappointed, or frustrated" or whatever.

9. Do not assume that a child's thinking is like your own. What children say does not always mean what you would mean if you said the same thing. Bright youngsters give the impression through their developed vocabulary that they mean the same thing you would mean. This is not always the case.

10. Do not invalidate their feelings with comments such as, "You don't really mean that, children don't hate their mothers", or, "You should not wish someone to die." You bet that is really how they feel at the moment. Don't put a value judgment on feelings. They are what they are: Deeds are good or bad but feelings are not. Do not comment on feelings of hate and wishing someone dead. Instead, say something such as, "So and so really hurt your feelings and made you very angry. I can understand how you would feel like hurting them back" or, "I can see how you would feel like you wished you would never have to see so and so again."

11. To bring closure to the LSI, recap the main points of what was discussed and how they felt. Ask them how they are feeling now. They should leave the LSI with better feelings than when they started. Then point out how it is better to talk about feelings instead of carrying them around inside. Next, assist the student in developing a specific plan of action to change what needs to be changed. They should also leave the LSI feeling more competent in being able to handle their problems.

12. Finally, ask them if they have any questions they would like to ask you, or if there is anything they would like you to try to do to help them out.

With all of this in mind, we are ready to delve into the LSI and all of its components. Following are the types and forms of LSI. One should not get the impression that an LSI will always follow one strand but, in fact, several of the forms may take place in one LSI. All of the titles of the LSI were developed by Fritz Redl. The explanations are in my own wording, and the examples are my own.

THE CLINICAL EXPLOITATION OF LIFE EVENTS

The clinical exploitation of life events LSI is designed to zero in on a real life event that comes up in the school setting. Such an event has significant and deeper meaning for the student's emotional well-being. This type of LSI is used when we want to develop an issue that has long-range consequences in terms of actual change in youngsters' personalities and their psychopathology.

Reality Rub-In

The purpose of this form of LSI is to help students see how they are instrumental in creating some of their own problems. Some of these youngsters are unable to understand that many of their problems are not externally controlled and that people do not always just do things to them for no reason. They have to learn that they have some internal control over the events that take place. A short example would be that the teacher sees Dale go by Robert's desk and says something. Robert jumps from his desk and socks Dale. Dale screams, cries, and tells the teacher Robert is a no good so and so and should be kicked out of the room. The Reality Rub-In would go thus:

Dale: You saw him! The son-of-a-bitch hit me! Kick him out! Put him in time out! Take his points!

SRM: I know you are hurt and very angry, and I am sorry you feel that way. But let's look at what happened. I heard you say something ugly to Robert first when you went by his desk. Do you remember what you said?

Dale: All I said was fat ass. People say that all the time. Do you think he should have hit me for no reason?

SRM: Right now I am not talking about whether or not it is all right to hit people. Right now I am concerned about how you do things that get you in trouble with other people. Had you just gone to your seat and not called Robert an ugly name he would not have hit you. When you call people names that hurts their feelings, makes them angry, and then they want to hurt you back. This same thing happened between you and Ricky yesterday. You called him retard and he pushed you down. You were unhappy and crying then too. You see Dale, every time you hurt someone they want to hurt you back. That is why you are having such a difficult time making a good friend in this class. So far, you have hurt just about everyone's feelings. I am sorry you are hurt and that so far you do not have a friend. I hope you will make friends in this class. What do you need to do so that people will stop hurting you?

Dale: Stop calling names.

SRM: Yes, that will work. Later we can talk about what you can do to make friends. But first you have to remember that you start fights when you hurt people's feelings. Some kids might like to be your friend but that won't happen until you stop doing the things you do. Now a good way to end this and maybe begin to start making friends would be to tell Robert you are sorry for what you said, and he will say he is sorry for hitting you.

Symptom Estrangement

The purpose of this form of LSI is to show students that whatever goodies they think they are getting out of their misbehavior are really not worth the price they have to pay. Basically, Redl says that these students cannot accept that something is wrong with them because they have developed too many secondary gains from their psychopathology. For this form of LSI, an example would be Steve, who was prohibited from attending the math lessons in the regular class because he had taken back some of his old forms of behavior to "get along" with the others in his self-contained room. This loss of privilege was very upsetting to Steve because he was the oldest in the room and had enjoyed going to a class with kids his own age and feeling more competent by taking his math lesson in a regular classroom. What he had done to lose the privilege of time in regular class was to straddle his desk seat and push up and down with his penis while telling the other kids, "Look, I'm screwing!" This, of course, got a lot of attention and laughter and made him a part of the old gang again. The LSI that followed went like this:

Steve: I don't see what I did so bad. Everybody screws, don't they? Well, don't they?

SRM: Steve, that isn't even for discussion right now, and you know it. Everyone does not do what you did in the classroom. When you go to Mrs. Yotter's room, you do not see the other students doing those kinds of things.

Steve: That's because they are square britches.

SRM: If you really felt that way then it would not matter whether you went to Mrs. Yotter's for math with students your own age. I have a feeling that you are not completely comfortable in the regular class right now. Could it be that you have not gotten to know the other students very well, and that you do not have a real friend in that room yet?

Steve: They look at me funny when I come in—like they don't want me there.

SRM: So, right now you feel out of place there, and you are more comfortable here with the guys you know? I think they just look at you because you are new and they have not gotten to know you yet. It seems to me that you started that inappropriate behavior to keep from going to Mrs. Yotter's class so that you could stay here where you know everyone. But you are not really happy about losing your regular class time. You must be feeling kind of confused. You want to do the right thing and be in regular class and at the same time you want to be with your old friends. But you cannot have both at the same time. When you act inappropriate it costs you something you want very much: time in Mrs. Yotter's class with kids your own age. It is pretty clear that you have to give up something. What do you think?

Steve: Yeah. Well, I want to be in Mrs. Yotter's class.

SRM: Then you know how you have to act. It isn't worth losing regular class time just to get attention from the guys in this class. And, you can still be friends with some of the boys here without being inappropriate.

Massaging Numb Value-Areas

This form of the LSI is intended to bring to the surface something that is worthwhile in the student. Many, if not all, enter classes for the emotionally disturbed feeling like failures, worthless, unloved, rejected, and lacking in self-esteem. They need to have their good points emphasized, but they often cannot tolerate compliments or the appearance of a goody-goody. It isn't cool or tough, which is an important image that most feel the need to portray. On one occasion, I paid a compliment to Danny in front of the class whereupon he immediately turned and punched another student. Value areas have to be emphasized in private and also nonverbal ways of doing this can be found. Following is a short illustration of how this was done with Danny.

SRM: Can you tell me what made you feel like hitting Jon when I told you how helpful you had been by cleaning the boards?

Danny: They call me a sucky and teacher's baby.

SRM: So, it is really important to you what the others think. I guess by hitting Jon you wanted to show that you were just one of the guys. You would rather I did not say nice things out loud, even when you deserve to be told what a great job you are doing?

Danny: Well, I don't want them to call me a baby. Besides, I'm not so great. What is so great about cleaning the boards?

SRM: For one thing, it shows how responsible you are and that you can be trusted to take care of some things. You have been doing many things lately that tell me you are really improving and have some very nice behaviors inside of you. Suppose I just don't say anything in front of the group when you show this very good side of you. I think that would help, don't you? Let's make a deal. Starting tomorrow, you will collect the lunch money and take it to the cafeteria. I know I can trust you to do a good job at that. You will be in charge of that duty and bringing back change for the right people. You do that and I won't say anything in front of the group about you're doing a good job. We will just know you are doing a good job. Okay? Deal?

Danny: Deal!

New-Tool Salesmanship

This form of LSI is specific and direct. The student is told exactly what has to be changed and how to change. It involves pointing out the most obvious way to deal with problems. An example of this form involved the case of Greg and his fear of math. As soon as the group was told it was time for math, Greg would fall out of his desk to the floor and begin screaming and crying. Tears would stream down his face as he declared he could not do the work by himself. This short LSI went as follows:

SRM: I know math scares you and that you need my help to get started. I always do help you, don't I?

Greg: Yeah. But not right away. What if you don't help me?

SRM: You let your scary feelings run away with you. I always help; you are not going to fail. But I don't help you because you scream and cry. I do it because you need more help than some of the others. You have to wait a few minutes while I pass the books and papers out to the others. Look at how you feel now. You are all tired and shaky from all that screaming and crying, and you have lost some of the time you need to finish your math. Now, you have to trust me more that I am always going to help you. You must not fall out of your desk and start screaming and crying for my attention. Tomorrow, when it is time for math I want you to hold real tight to your desk and watch me give the others their books and papers. Count to yourself, one book and one paper to Dale, one book and one paper to Saul, one book and one paper to Tim, one book and one paper to Jon, until everyone has their work. Then say to yourself, now it is my turn, she is coming to help, and watch me as I come down the aisle to your desk. Try that first tomorrow instead of falling out of your desk and screaming and crying.

Manipulation of the Boundaries of the Self

Almost every group of these students will pick out a scapegoat. They manipulate them into acting out. This is done partly because there is always someone more different and less liked than anybody else, and partly because they want to get something exciting going in class but they do not want to have to pay the consequences themselves for acting out. They get a vicarious pleasure out of the hugger mugger. Scapegoated students must learn from the LSI that they are often set up to get into trouble and that they really do not have to let that happen. Dale and Ricky were particularly good at goading Timmy into throwing a punch at one of them. Then they would sit back and call attention to Timmy's transgression and watch him pay the consequences. This was often done in such clever, underhanded ways the misbehavior of Dale and Ricky could not be pinned down. Sometimes they simply made unseen gestures to Timmy that signalled recall of incidents that were provoking or embarrassing to Timmy. On one occasion, however, I overheard comments that precipitated a fist fight between Dale and Timmy. I had just complimented Timmy on his work and given him free time to work on his model car. On his way back to his desk, I overheard Dale say to Ricky, in a tone loud enough for Timmy to hear, "Hey, remember when Tim pissed his pants last week?" Ricky joined in with, "Yeah, what a coody, creepy baby. And, it was all down his leg and his pants were all wet and smelly." Timmy threw a punch. Following is an example of this form of LSI:

SRM: Timmy, do you remember how many fights you have gotten into with Dale and Ricky in the past week?

Timmy: No. Maybe three.

SRM: One every day this week and it has caused you trouble. You have lost points. Been in Time Out. Lost privileges. Do you know what I see happening? I see Dale and Ricky doing things that make you mad and then you fight and get into trouble. Know what else? Until today, they never got into trouble. Just you paid the consequences. I think they like it that way. What do you think?

Timmy: Yeah, I get into trouble but they don't, and they start it.

SRM: But do you see what they are doing? They want you to fight and to get into trouble, and you always let them sucker you in by paying attention to what they say or do. Now, you are much too smart to keep on letting them get away with that. I think that you are smart enough now to know they want you in trouble and to not let them bother you so much that you have to pay for it. Just like today, they were caught this time causing trouble and now they have to pay consequences. But I cannot always know that they have started something. So, you are going to have to stop letting them make a sucker out of you. You are going to ignore them and tell me when they do something they are not supposed to do. Other people may try the same thing with you and not everybody will always know what is really going on. You have to pay attention and realize when people are trying to get you into trouble. You will have to stop and think and cool off, and ask yourself if they are worth getting into trouble for. As soon as they realize they cannot get you into trouble they will stop teasing you. Then you can sit back and watch them get into trouble. But as long as you keep fighting, they will keep trying to get you to fight and get into trouble. Do you see what I mean?

In summarizing this section on the clinical exploitation, these forms of the LSI are intended to reach long-range goals for the students that they can transfer to different and new settings. This type of the LSI is aimed to develop skills the students will need and (hopefully) use a lifetime.

EMOTIONAL FIRST AID ON THE SPOT

The emotional first aid LSI means just what the title implies. It gives youngsters support during an emotional unheaval or crisis. It is used when emotions or situations are out of control and students need someone to empathize and sometimes sympathize with the predicament they are in.

Drain-Off of Frustration Acidity and Support for the Management of Panic, Fury, and Guilt

I have combined these two because almost always they go together. The Drain-Off form is simply allowing the youngster to ventilate frustrations. Support for the management of panic, fury, and guilt is to empathize and assist the student in putting things back into perspective and then to guide them back into a normal routine. It involves being there with the youngster to provide help through these highly emotionally charged times so that they do not go off with unresolved feelings. From these two forms, they learn that they can have strong, powerful emotional feelings and find nonphysical outlets. As an illustration, I will use an incident that occurred with the student Thomas.

Thomas had built something for his shop class and had been looking forward to it for a week. When he showed up for his shop class, the teacher had gone to an inservice session and had not warned Thomas that they would not have class that week, but in 2 weeks instead. I found Thomas at the shop teacher's door kicking, swearing, and screaming. He had damaged his project in his fury. I called Thomas to come over and sit beside me on a bench. The important point of this form of LSI was to just let Thomas drain off all of his strong feelings. I would ask an occasional question to clarify what had happened and make verbal observations regarding his disappointment, unhappiness, and anger. Moralizing and contradicting are not appropriate; neither is at this time commenting on swearing or his threats to kill the shop teacher and never go back. Since students sometimes lose sight of the incident that set them off, when they are reasonably calm you summarize the incident, point out how they handled it, and how everything is still okay. I stayed with Thomas and helped him pick up his material, while talking about how it could be repaired, or reconstructed. The LSI ended with a suggestion that we join the others in his class in the gym. The physical activities in the gym also helped to work off the tension he was feeling after such a strong emotional upheaval.

Communication Maintenance in Moments of Relationship Decay

This form of LSI is used when a student is so angry with us that they are on the verge of totally breaking off any relationship with us whatsoever. Redl talks about children who may withdraw to an autistic like state if they feel you have betrayed, abandoned, or rejected them. But some of these youngsters may withdraw from you without withdrawing into something as extreme as a classical autisticlike state. They may close the door in your face for the rest of the year, opting to put you out of their lives forever. Anything you try or have to say will go completely unnoticed. While they may interact with others, to them you are a nonperson.

This process was observed in one of my students. Dale had instigated a fight and was furious. I corrected him and leveled the consequences. I remember this incident clearly because at the time I did not know what to do, and I lost him for the rest of the year. I saw it happening and did not know how to handle the situation. (I had not read Redl then.) A look came into his eyes and covered his face, which said, "I hate you. You do not care about me, so I do not care about you. No matter what you do from now on, you are nothing to me." That is the way it ended with Dale and me. He was not particularly naughty all year. He just walked through my life as if I did not exist. There was not one thing that I could do all year to get through to Dale and help him with his greater problems. Surface behavior was managed, but nothing else.

Redl suggests that in these moments you maintain communication no matter what you have to talk about. Just keep a conversation going, and keep the youngster in touch. You can talk about the weather, the turtle in the room, the class down the hall, the color of paint on the walls, what you did on the weekend, the clothes they are wearing that day, how big elephants are, if there is life on other planets, and so forth. The point is just keep a conversation going and do not let them close the door on you.

Regulation of Behavioral and Social Traffic

This form of LSI consists of presenting the students with reminders and discussions of the rules and regulations they already know about but that are sometimes forgotten. It is most effectively used before the student has him or herself in some kind of trouble. It is important to alert students to where they are about to go wrong. As an example, you have a rule that before going out to recess they must line up, be quiet, and not interact with each other until they are outside. The following incident illustrates where prevention comes in. I had the students lined up to go outside. Mike was first in line and was in charge of taking the soccer ball to the playground. He was jerking the ball forward in Seth's face and stopping it just before it hit. I reminded him of the rule regarding this behavior. If I had allowed this behavior to persist, the temptation would have become too great to go on and allow the ball to hit Seth in the face, or Seth may have become so annoyed that he would strike Mike before being hit.

Umpire Services

This final form of LSI includes the actual refereeing of disputes, arguments, and fights, as well as overseeing any trading or swapping of articles. Trading articles or food is most common among youngsters and can become a real problem. They often take advantage of each other by making most unreasonable and unfair swaps. Some of these youngsters are real con artists and can have another kid just aching to swap a most desirable object for broken junk. Later, when he or she realizes, or the parents find out, and the youngster wants the original belonging back, a fight can ensue, or you can have angry parents at your door. The trading business must be carefully supervised.

SUMMARY

As you can see, many good teachers have been doing most of these forms of LSI without ever knowing that someone had given names to what they were doing. Some of them are obvious, common-sense interventions. Hopefully, through some of the illustrations teachers will learn to use more empathic responses.

OTHER INTERVENTIONS

This section includes an area the teacher must attend to and also some highlights of other interventions the teacher can supplement into the affective curriculum from time to time as an enhancement.

DREAM INTERPRETATION

I have not met a teacher for emotionally disturbed students who never had to listen to the children's dreams. Most teachers do not know how to respond to a child's dream because they think either that dreams do not mean anything or that they need psychoanalytic training to talk about dreams. Neither is the case.

First, dreams always have meaning, but that does not mean that teachers have to or should try to delve into the deeper meanings of dreams. Most importantly, dreams, especially "bad" dreams, highlight feelings and emotions. Most everyone can relate to how it feels to wake in the morning after a "bad" dream. If it was a particularly distressing dream, it can leave us feeling off balance all day, apprehensive, sad, and so forth. These students come to us with their dreams; it is not enough to just listen and not comment in some way.

Second, you do not have to have psychoanalytic training to respond to a youngster's dream. You do have to listen carefully to the overall emotional tone of the dream, and that is what you can respond to empathically. Do not try to interpret with a few of the common things that most people have heard about symbols in dreams, such as what snakes and spiders are supposed to mean. Dreams are complicated subconscious material, and the same symbols mean different things to different people. I am not suggesting you run out and read a book on dream analysis. I am saying that you do need to respond to the youngster.

If you do not know much about the youngsters, then all you have to do is respond to the feelings you hear expressed in the dream. You need only comment, "That dream must have frightened you very much and those feelings haven't gone away yet" or, "That must leave you feeling very sad." You can ask them what they think their dream means; do not contradict their own interpretation. Just comment on the feelings. You can suggest that they might like to draw a picture about the dream. Drawing can assist some students in working out their feelings.

The more information you have about your students the more you will be able to help them find some *feeling* resolution to their dreams. Following is an illustration of a dream told to me by an 11-year-old girl. I knew both the girl and the family situation quite well. This child, who was living with her divorced mother, who had had a sudden onset of a mental disorder. The father had visitation privileges, and the social worker was beginning to suspect that there was incestuous activity going on during these visits. The girl came to me in the morning and stood by the desk. She looked pale, was twitching, clenching her fists, frowning, and breathing shallow, rapid breaths. She was clearly anxious, told me she had a bad dream, and asked if I wanted to hear it. The dream as told to me by the child and my responses to her dream follow.

Samatha: I was in this deep, deep hole and when I tried to climb out, it was like the sides of the hole were flesh and all bloody. I kept slipping back down and I couldn't get out.

SRM: That was a very scary dream. To be trapped in a deep hole and unable to get out. You must have felt very afraid. What was up at the top of the hole? Did you know or could you see what was at the top?

Samatha: Outside, it was very beautiful. There was sunshine and birds and deer and lots of green grass. I really wanted to get up there so bad.

SRM: When you looked up at the top of the hole, could you see if there was anyone up there to help you get out of the hole?

Samatha: No, there wasn't anyone up there.

SRM: Well, besides being very scary I suppose that it made you feel lonely that there wasn't anybody up there who could help you get out of the hole. Did you shout out to make sure that there wasn't someone around who could have come and help you get out?

Samatha: No. I just didn't see anybody.

SRM: You know I don't think you will have that dream again but if you ever do or if you have one something like it—like being trapped someplace, then the next time look very carefully to see if there is someone who can help you get out, and be sure and shout out so that someone can hear you and come and help. I can see that the dream still bothers you. Would you like to draw a picture of what you would see when you got out of the hole? Why don't you draw the beautiful things you described to me?

Notice that I did not interpret one symbolic thing about that dream. What I did was only respond to her feelings of being frightened and feeling trapped and alone. The final thing I did with her dream was to try to reassure her the dream was gone but that if something like it recurred, there might be a better ending. The message I tried to give her was that when we are in situations where we feel alone, trapped, frightened, or bad in some way, we need to try to find people who will help us and there are always people who will help. Finally, to help dissipate her anxiety, I suggested she draw a picture of what was beautiful and peaceful in the dream.

Sometimes, youngsters are not telling you a real dream but a fantasy daydream. It does not matter if it was a night dream or a fantasy. They are trying to share their feelings and fears with you. You can respond to a fantasy the same as you would a night dream. It is important, however, to clarify that they are not telling you a story they saw on television or in the movies. Once the other youngsters hear you listening to dreams, they will want the same attention, and often they will tell you they had a dream when they did not. They just want to tell a story and get your undivided attention, too. Let them know that you will only listen to real dreams.

CREATIVE INTERVENTIONS

Creative intervention refers to artwork, music, and dance. These interventions are things that you might want to use now and then—not on a daily basis or even a weekly basis with older verbal youngsters. However, you might want to make them an integral part of your curriculum for working with very young emotionally disturbed children who do not have the verbal abilities to engage in some of the interventions already presented. These interventions are ways to teach students more sophisticated coping mechanisms. They help youngsters develop new skills and channels for release of tension and conflict. This section will highlight these interventions briefly.

Artwork

At one time, I had my class of emotionally disturbed students come in first thing in the morning, get their crayons and a piece of art paper, and draw a picture of themselves. They did this every morning. My purpose in doing this was to get them in their seats and working on something nonthreatening. Generally, they hit the door at 8:30 a.m. in rotten moods. Some had been fighting on the bus, some were depressed about something, and some were anxious about school and academics in general. This was a way to calm everyone down before starting the more difficult work. It also gave me a good idea of the moods they were in and what they thought about themselves. It would not be scientific enough for some people, but I found it very beneficial. For instance, one boy in my class for months would draw a picture of himself using only black and brown crayons and then he would scribble over his portrait. That told me something about his moods and what he thought of himself. One boy, for weeks, always drew a picture of himself as a monster. After a period of time, his pictures gradually started to look more like a little boy and less like a monster, and his behavior coincided with his pictures. And, one boy, for weeks, would never draw himself. He drew racing cars, planes, and rockets. When I asked him where he was in the picture he was always inside one of those objects. Gradually, he started to draw himself outside of the objects, and then later left out the objects and just drew himself.

If you are going to use artwork as an intervention, you can follow these guidelines:

1. Scribbling for a short period of time is okay. This allows the youngster to relax.

2. In the beginning, allow them to select their medium and subject matter.

3. Stress that they must create a work of art, so that they do not become overly anxious or get lost in fantasy.

4. Provide structure and supervise their work so that things do not get out of hand.

5. If they have trouble choosing a subject, start by drawing a few simple lines and have them complete the picture. Or, provide open-ended ideas such as drawing their three wishes.

6. Have them visualize a picture, describe it to you, and then produce it.

7. Don't force compulsive children to work with something that obviously repulses them, such as clay or finger paints. At some other time, they may actually enjoy and find it a release to make a mess.

8. Do not force anxious youngsters to work with a medium that requires fine motor control to do good work.

9. Do not give hostile youngsters things to work with such as scissors, compasses, tools, heating elements, and so forth.

Music

Bringing music into your classroom can be helpful to some students. It can have a quieting effect and aid in concentration by shutting out other kinds of distracting noise.

Playing certain instruments (drums, clappers) allows acceptable outlets for physical aggression while giving a feeling of success. Be cautious about playing stimulating music when you have overly active youngsters; they can become more out of control. Withdrawn youngsters may become more isolated with music that is of a "dreamy" nature. Have these youngsters draw while they listen to the music to keep them in touch.

Music is an area in which you should insist that all of the youngsters who can handle it are integrated with the music classes or band. It provides a group experience, and the music is a reason for being together. Ensemble music requires the individual to subordinate his or her own interests to the groups' if music is to result. The demand comes from the music and is objective, rather than coming from the group. This provides a feeling of being needed and having an identity in a group.

Dance

Many youngsters with extreme anxiety or psychotic children have poor motor coordination. Dance can fine-tune their muscles and improve coordination. It is another acceptable channel to release tension. Your approach is unique. There is no one technique that should be used. Following are some guidelines for using dance:

1. With reluctant youngsters, move with them beginning with the movement initiated by the child.
2. Focus on body parts and how different parts of the body move. How many ways are there to move a hand or a leg?
3. Add simpler basic locomotor movements in a dance style with music, such as the walk, run, hop, and then various combinations of these movements.
4. Use rhythms and pantomine to express emotions. The hostile youngster can express aggression to marching music.
5. In groups, most use a circle formation so the children can see each other and feel united.
6. Finally, display acceptance and give constant encouragement.

SOME FINAL TIPS AND HINTS

In conclusion, I am including some general ideas of things that I have found do and do not work with emotionally disturbed youngsters. Below is a simple laundry list:

1. Try the simplest tactic first. Sometimes just a stare with "mean" teacher eyes is enough to stop some behavior. Try putting their names on the board without saying what it means. Some sit quietly and look at their names all day wondering what it means but afraid to test it out. If they are noisy and interrupting stop your talking. Don't try talking over the noise. Sometimes moving a youngster's desk to a new spot can avert some problems.
2. Never post rules until you need them. In Assertive Discipline teachers are instructed to post a long list of rules. I think this is a mistake. You can be sure that there will be at least one little scamp in the group who looks at the list and thinks, "Hey, now there's an idea I never thought of—think I'll give it a try." With your long, long list you are inviting them for sure to try something they might never have thought of in the first place. Initially, we had

three rules: you cannot hurt other people; you cannot hurt yourself; and you cannot damage or destroy property. Rules were added as things came up. They always got one warning and one chance.

3. These students swear—a lot! Many teachers think it is just to get their attention and to shock them. There are many reasons why they swear. Some do swear to shock you but for others that is not the case. Many feel pain and anger and that is why they swear. Usually the feelings of hurt and anger go together. Let's use ourselves as an example. Suppose you are hanging a picture on the wall and you miss with the hammer and hit your thumb. Do you just drop the hammer and say, "Oh, doo, doo. That sure hurt. Golly, darn." You are a saint if that is all you say. When we feel hurt we get angry and we respond with strong reactions. Some students feel frightened and they swear. Using ourselves as an example. Suppose it is 2:00 A.M. in the morning and our youngster is not home yet—they were supposed to be home at 11:00 p.m. We are very worried. We hear sirens in the distance. Now we become frightened. We hope and pray he comes in the door so we can see his face and hug him. Finally, he walks casually in the door. How do we react? Usually with instant anger. We don't run up and throw our arms around this thoughtless rotten kid who scared the hell out of us. We say, "Damn't, where in the hell have you been?" Some swear because they do not know how else to express their feelings. My first student of the year came in the first day and walked around the room grumbling, "I don't want to be in this f——— class! I hate this f——— school and the f——— food here! I guess you're the f——— teacher! Well, I hate your f——— face!" This went on for quite some time. I listened while the student named all of the f——— things he hated. Finally, when he slowed down I said to him, "John, why don't you sit down here and tell me how your life got so f——— up?" He did. He sat down and told me quite a bit about what was going on at home. That is the only time I ever used a foul word back to a student and I did not do it to show him that I was not shocked. Although he looked shocked that I was not shocked. At the time it seemed like the best response. And it was. He was telling me that something was very wrong with his world but he did not know how to express it otherwise until asked. However, the general rule is do not use youngsters' swear words back to them to show that they cannot shock you. If swear words and obscenities are shocking to you and you intend to continue teaching these students, then go into

your bathroom and close the door and practice saying them over and over until they have no more shock value. They have to become just words with no meaning.

4. Begin changing the most important behaviors. There will be many things that need attention and you cannot attend to all of their behaviors at once. Swearing is not the most important behavior but hurting others or hurting themselves is most important. That does not mean you never comment on their swearing. Many will respond, "That's the way everone talks—even at home." You need only say in the beginning, "That is not the way we talk in this classroom. I do not care if others talk that way, or if it goes on someplace else, but in our room we do not use that language."

5. Starting with day one, take every thing away from them that could be used as a weapon (scissors, compasses, etc.), put them in a box with their name on it, and keep them in a closet only to be used at appropriate times.

6. Things that distract them from their work should be taken away (i.e., toys, and objects they play with). These can be given back at the end of the day but if they continue to bring them to school they go in the locked closet, and they do not get them back until the end of the year, or if the parents come to pick them up. Knives and other weapons become the property of the school and go the principal's office.

7. Never threaten a student with something you know you cannot follow through on, such as: "You will finish your work if we have to stay here all night!"

8. Don't impose consequences that are going to make you miserable. For instance, "If we have to stay through lunch time to get this done, we will!" Do you want to give up your lunch time or some other break period you need? Make sure that you don't impose a consequence that forces you to chauffeur the student home because of missing the bus.

9. Never argue. Say what you have to say and walk away letting the consequences fall where they may.

10. Don't demand confessions.

11. Never use physical power.

12. Do not attend to unacceptable behavior.

13. Do not ask them to do "it" for you (e.g., "Come on finish your math. Do it for me.").

14. Raising your voice is seldom useful.

15. Comparing kids doesn't help.
16. Don't offer them solutions to their own problems, instead ask them, "What can you do to make things better?"
17. Don't offer sympathy which denies their feelings such as, "I'm sorry you can't play." Instead, "I'm sure you wished you had done better."
18. Provide structure.
19. Never ridicule or humiliate a student.
20. Never give non-verbal messages which are confusing such as, smiling after you have just said no.
21. Don't give your authority to someone else such as, sending a student to the principal for punishment. This communicates two messages. It says to the youngster, "I don't know how to deal with you." And, it tells the principal you don't have control over your own classroom.
22. Don't give third chances.
23. Don't give them decisions they are not ready to make.
24. Don't allow stalling. That's a sucker's game.
25. Don't use punishment instead of known consequences.
26. Don't use the naughty word "why!"
27. Taking away privileges and suspension does not work with withdrawn children.
28. Forcing an issue with withdrawn children does not work.
29. Ignoring withdrawn children does not work.
30. Withdrawn children do not respond to peer pressure except to become more withdrawn.
31. Let the withdrawn and shy youngsters write their answers down on paper and do not force them to stand and recite or respond.
32. Provide cognitive and not moral reasons to change.
33. Make a list of successes and strengths for the withdrawn and shy child.
34. Allow withdrawn and shy youngsters do parallel activities to the groups' activities until they are ready to join.
35. Put withdrawn and shy youngsters in charge of pets and plants.
36. Make sure you have built in activities and lessons that you know the withdrawn youngster can do successfully.
37. Finally, you have to recognize that, at times, there will be limitations on your ability to deal with certain situations. This is a fact you have to live with and you cannot allow those times to make you feel unsuccessful or incompetent. Realize that all teachers come upon this problem from time to time.

REFERENCES

Brenner, M. B. (1963). Life space interview in the school setting. *American Journal of Orthopsychiatry, 33*, 717–719.

Della-Piana, G. (1973). *How to talk with children (and other people)*. New York: John Wiley & Sons.

Dreikurs, R., & Cassel, P. (1972). *Discipline without tears*. New York: Hawthorn Books.

Dreikurs, R., Grunwald, B. B., & Pepper, F. C. (1982). *Maintaining Sanity in the Classroom*. (2nd. ed.) New York: Haper & Row.

Gardner, R. A. (1971). *Therapeutic communication with children*. New York: Science House.

Gazda, G., Asbury, F., Balzer, F., Childers, W., & Walters, R. (1977). *Human relations development: A manual for educators*. (2nd ed.). Boston: Allyn & Bacon.

Glasser, W. (1969). *Schools without failure*. New York: Harper & Row.

Levine, E. S. (1980). Indirect suggestions through personalized fairy tales for treatment of childhood insomnia. *The American Journal of Clinical Hypnosis, 23*(1), 57–63.

Lundsteen, S. W. (1972). A thinking improvement program through literature. *Elementary English, (April)*, 505–512.

Morgan, S. R. (1976). Bibliotherapy: A broader concept. *Journal of Child Clinical Psychology, 1*(1), 39–42.

Ojemann, R. H. (1961). Investigations on the effects of teaching on understanding and appreciation of behavior dynamics. In G. Caplin (Ed.), *Prevention of mental disorders in children*. New York: Basic.

Redl, F. (1959). The concept of the life space interview. *American Journal of Orthopsychiatry, 29*, 1–18.

Wallen, C. J., & Wallen, L. L. (1978). *Effective classroom management*. Boston: Allyn & Bacon.

CHAPTER 7

Interpersonal Qualities
SHARON R. MORGAN

This final chapter focuses on the interpersonal qualities of teachers of emotionally disturbed students. It is the fourth component of the empathy model based on responses of emotionally disturbed youngsters regarding what they viewed as an empathic teacher. Besides this study, (Morgan, 1979) there have been others in which researchers tried to isolate the characteristics of "good" or empathic teachers.

BACKGROUND

Why is the study of interpersonal qualities so important? It is necessary to reach an understanding of the total person by learning the specific connections of affect to cognitive processes and resulting behavior. One of the most interesting facets of Piaget's (1972) work was his continual effort to reconcile two dimensions of development: cognitive and affective. Even in his earliest writings, Piaget focused almost exclusively on the parallel, irreducible nature of the affective and the cognitive aspects of development. He made several observations on the interaction of cognition and affect:

It is incontestable that affect plays an essential role in the functioning of intelligence. Without affect there would be no interest, no need, no motivation; and consequently, no intelligence. Affectivity is a necessary condition in the constitution of intelligence ... [p. 167]

Within the last few years, the role of the teacher has shifted to fit an earlier conception of educational goals for the child. Today, the educational system seeks teachers with multi-dimensional training, rather than the former training, which focused on development of the cognitive or intellective capacities of students (Lee, 1971). With this emphasis on fostering the psychosocial development of the child, we are still looking for the "better persons" to educate as teachers. This is an especially important area for teachers of emotionally disturbed youngsters where personality, attitudes, motives, and interpersonal qualities must receive attention.

Many years ago, Aichhorn (1925) expressed the idea that every teacher works with his or her personality and that specific educational methods are far less important than an attitude that brings the child in contact with reality. He also thought that educators must start with a capacity for this work because even though much could be learned through training and earnest study, an educator (especially one for the emotionally disturbed child) could not be made out of every personality.

I agree with Aichhorn. You cannot make a good teacher out of every personality. Some are suited for the work and some are *not*. Anybody with the intellectual capacity can be trained to teach. But the degree and certificate do not guarantee that good, or more importantly, empathic teachers will result.

A number of experts have warned that this speciality attracts not only mature individuals but also many who hope to work out their own problems through the job. Such teachers and prospective trainees have been referred to as "crackpots" (Dunn, 1963) or "sicker" than the children they hope to work with (Smith, 1967). Dobson (1970) suggested screening people before they became teachers of emotionally disturbed youth on the basis of personality conflicts. But conflicts are a matter of degree and extent, and moderate problems do not necessarily mean the person will be an incompetent teacher (Morgan, 1977). I have known some people in this profession had (or have) problems and conflicts, but because of these experiences they can be more empathic than others who have never had difficulties in personal functioning. On the other hand, I have also had prospective teachers in my classes who were so disturbed themselves that they could not possibly put together a realistic and rational world for themselves, let alone accomplish this task for emotionally disturbed students.

Our profession does not attract more than its share of "crackpots," but we have them in the same proportion as any other profession. Since we are more aware of psychopathology, we know how to identify it and label it accurately. Some who enter our preparation programs or who are in the schools right now are psychotics or sociopaths, and we are keenly aware of their incompetence. In other professions, however, they use other names for their disturbed professors or university students. In philosophy they may just think that they are deep in intellectual thought that others do not understand. In art, music, and theatre arts they think of them and refer to them as "excentric artists." In other professions they may think that they are so gifted or such geniuses that their behavior is bound to appear peculiar. We are in no worse shape than any other profession.

In terms of empathic teachers entering the field, I do not believe that you can *teach* someone how to be empathic. They have it or they do not, and some have it to a greater degree than others. I do believe that if they have empathy in the first place that it can be enhanced as talked about in chapter three. For those who do not seem to have it, I think that we can make some more sensitive, not necessarily empathic, but more aware and sensitive. And, there are some with whom we just cannot help to become more sensitive—their personalities do not fit the demands of teaching disturbed youngsters.

PERSONALITY TYPE INDICATOR

There is a personality type indicator test that can be useful in identifying those most suitable to teaching special population students. The Myers-Briggs Type Indicator (MBTI) (1987) separates personalities into 16 types. Myers and McCaulley (1985) present a great deal of information and research regarding these types, how they function in the educational setting, and their occupational preferences.

The MBTI has four major indices; each of those has two choices which, when combined, produce 16 basic personality types. These types affect what these individuals attend to and how they draw their conclusions about the world. The four major indices include:

1. A preference between extroversion and introversion. Extroverts (E) direct their perceptions or judgments on the outer world. Introverts (I) direct their perceptions or judgments on the inner world.
2. A preference between Sensing (S) perception and Intuitive (N) perception. Sensing types rely on reports of observable facts through the five senses. Intuitive types rely on the process of intuition that reports meanings, relationships, and possibilities that go beyond the conscious mind.
3. The third indice includes the Thinking (T) judgment type and the Feeling (F) judgment type. These are differentiated by which kind of judgment they trust and rely upon. A person (Thinking type)

may rely entirely on thinking to make impersonal decisions based on logical consequences. Others (Feeling Type) may make their decisions primarily on the basis of personal or social values.

4. The fourth indice includes the Judgment (J) type, who deals with the outer world by using Thinking or Feeling, and the Perception (P) type, who deals with the outer world by using either Sensing or Intuition.

These four indices with two types in each can come together in combinations that make up the sixteen personality types. To determine personality type, the individual takes a test that has 94 questions about attitudes toward certain things. Each of the 94 questions has two possible answers. It is a forced-choice answer-type test. Some sample items from this instrument follow.

SAMPLE MBTI ITEMS*

E/I: At parties do you always have fun or sometimes get bored?

E/I: In a large group, do you more often introduce others or get introduced?

S/N: If you were a teacher, would you rather teach fact courses or courses involving theory?

S/N: Which word appeals to you more: BUILD or INVENT?

T/F: Which word appeals to you more: COMPASSION or FORESIGHT?

T/F: Do you usually value sentiment more than logic or value logic more than sentiment?

J/P: When you go somewhere for the day would you rather plan what you will do and when or just go?

J/P: Does following a schedule appeal to you or cramp you?

Carlyn (1976) analyzed the MBTI responses of preservice teachers and found the following significant correlational relationships:

1. Feeling types were more interested in teaching the lower grades.
2. Intuitive and Perception types were more interested in using independence and creativity in teaching.
3. Extroverted and Intuitive types had more interest in planning school projects.

*Reproduced by special permission of the Publisher, Consulting Psychologists Press, Inc., Palo Alto, CA 94306. *From:* Myers-Briggs Type Indicator, by Isabel Briggs Myers & Katharine C. Briggs (1977).

4. Intuitive types received more enjoyment from working with students in small groups.
5. Extroverted and Feeling types expressed a high commitment to classroom teaching.

DeNovellis and Lawrence reported certain results of MBTI scores for elementary and middle school teachers in their 1983 study. They found that Introverted, Sensing teachers were more controlling in the choice of activities; Intuitive teachers moved more freely around the classroom; teachers high on the trait of Feeling attended to students closely, could attend to several students at the same time, and had their students centrally involved in the classroom activities. The teachers high on the Feeling dimension also provided more positive verbal and nonverbal feedback to their students. Those teachers who scored high on the combination of Intuitive, Feeling, and Perception showed more nonverbal disapproval; the high Feeling types could allow more individual activity in their classrooms, they attempted to control disorderly behavior with nonverbal negative behavior.

DeNovellis and Lawrence (1983) finally concluded that productive behavior occurred in the classrooms of all the types of teachers. However, when nonproductive behavior did occur, it was most likely to happen in hostile or aggressive acts with the Intuitive teachers. When nonproductive behavior occurred (such as withdrawal and passivity), it was most likely to happen under the teaching of those high on the combination of Sensing and Judgment.

The most fascinating study using the MBTI and teachers was conducted by Thompson (1984). This study focused on the ways teachers perceive their role, plan their work, teach their classes, evaluate their students, and perceive their own success. Thompson only used the combinations of the Sensing/Thinking; Sensing/Feeling; Intuitive/Feeling; and Intuitive/Thinking types. The results follow:

1. The Sensing/Thinking type sees teachers as role models, who set an example and share their knowledge and experience. They get their ideas from curriculum guides, textbooks, and experience. They make complete, detailed plans well in advance for the year and term, including specific objectives. The Sensing/Thinking teacher needs to follow a daily routine and direct the activities. They evaluate their students using points and percentages in a systematic way, and they feel successful as teachers if their students' grades and behavior improve.

   These teachers could be successful working with some types of emotionally disturbed children, but they might have difficulty following the intervention techniques suggested in this book. They might last in the profession for a short while. But eventually the strong need to have a daily routine, evaluate students in a stringent, systematic way, and the need to feel successful based upon changes seen in the students would eventually cause burnout.

2. The Sensing/Feeling type views the role of the teacher as one who should instruct, discipline, encourage, support, be a role model, and serve others. They get their ideas from curriculum guides, manuals, textbooks, workshops, other teachers, and experience. They design detailed plans according to the school calendar and set complete objectives while taking the students' abilities into consideration. Sensing/Feeling teachers follow orderly daily patterns adjusted for person-centered interactions. They use points and percentages and extra credit to evaluate their students. They feel successful if their students' grades and behavior improve.

These teachers are likely to be more successful teaching emotionally disturbed students than the Sensing/Thinking personality, but they will experience some of the same difficulties. A major problem area for both Sensing/Thinking and Sensing/Feeling teachers is their need to have orderly daily patterns, which often get thwarted in classes of disturbed students. These teachers' needs to feel successful based upon the students' success is dangerous. Often we go for a very long time with these students before we see even small gains in learning and behavior. In fact, many teachers of emotionally disturbed students never get to see the fruits of their labor. Because of family dynamics, many of these students move out of the school or the district before the teacher can know whether improvement has been accomplished. Often, they are put back into the regular classroom as soon as their surface behavior is under control. So special education teachers never know for sure if they had long-term impact on their students' lives. These are the ambiguities that we, as teachers of emotionally disturbed youth, have to endure. Those who cannot tolerate these unknowns burn out faster than other types.

3. The Intuitive/Feeling types view the role of the teacher as one who encourages, inspires, provides variety and creativity, and motivates youngsters. They get their ideas for teaching from the concepts of the content of the subject matter; taking college courses; reading, knowledge of student development, and "ideas from everywhere." They structure plans around general goals, themes, and students' needs, and adapt plans to the students' needs on a week-to-week basis if necessary. The Intuitive/Feeling teacher

uses a flexible pattern, depending on the topic and the students' needs. In evaluating students, these teachers use a number of factors (only one of which is grades), and they feel successful if the students' learning and participation increased, and they have the "feeling" of having made a personal contribution to the students' general education and welfare. This "feeling" comes from within based on several internal criteria and not on their students' grades.

Intuitive/Feeling teachers are most likely to use the interventions in this book. This type is most likely to succeed in teaching emotionally disturbed students because they are flexible and able to change plans based on student need. Most importantly, they have varied ways of evaluating student success. We have to be able to see small events as successes if we are going to teach these youngsters. This personality type "feels" successful based upon their own internal criteria, which is critical. If relying on grade change, behavior improvement, and the usual external feedback teachers expect from others is what makes one feel successful, then you will have many miserable days. This is the danger for the first two personality types but it is not an issue or problem area for the Intuitive/Feeling teacher.

4. The Intuitive/Thinking type views the teacher's role as one who encourages, inspires, and helps students develop as citizens and persons. They get their ideas from the concepts of the subject area, knowledge of students' needs and development, and a synthesis of ideas from many sources. They make their plans according to an overall yearly structure, organized by concepts and themes, and determined by details of students' levels. Intuitive/Thinking teachers have flexible daily routines that depend on topics and students' needs, with interaction based on expectations for order and learning. They use a number of factors to evaluate students, and they feel successful if they see increased involvement with learning from the students.

Intuitive/Thinking teachers are also likely to be very successful in teaching emotionally disturbed students—although not as completely comfortable or empathic as the Intuitive/Feeling type. The Intuitive/Thinking teachers' ability to sustain and feel successful will require that they have more structure in their classrooms. If they use the interventions in this book, they will have to be able to structure them in some kind of daily order because they are somewhat less able to "wing it" when necessary. There is some danger for them if their success is based entirely on developing good citizens and seeing increased involvement with learning from the students. This is the area where they may feel discomfort with these youngsters when that doesn't appear the way these teachers might expect. Again, internal feelings of success are of paramount importance in sustaining teachers in our work.

Nearly all college and university campuses have a counseling services center with someone who can administer the Myers-Briggs. Prospective teachers should find out their personality types before launching into a chosen profession, especially this one. The college student may find that they are suitable to teach other populations but not emotionally disturbed students, or they may find that teaching any population really doesn't fit with their personality at all. It is far better to find out ahead of time than to wait until student teaching, or worse yet, get on the job and find out that you wished you had done something else with your education and your life.

THE PROTOTYPE OF THE EMPATHIC TEACHER

In Chapter 3, I discussed the interpersonal qualities of an empathic teacher as described by emotionally disturbed children. Empathy is the affective component singled out because it is the primary personality trait that makes the interventions presented in this book work. Students describe empathic teachers as warm, caring individuals who could show affection openly to them. They were discussed as people who smiled frequently, spoke softly, appeared calm and relaxed, and had a sense of humor (Morgan, 1979).

Wakefield and Crowl (1974) found that the ideal special educator was a person who enjoyed analyzing others' behaviors and motives and predicting how they will act. This is necessary to use the interventions in this book. The desire to analyze behavior and the ability to predict how one will act are parts of empathy. Wakefield and Crowl also described empathic teachers as people who could sympathize and show affection for those in pain. They have little need to manifest their anger nor do they feel depressed when they cannot handle difficult situations. Morgan (1984) found that teachers who scored high on an empathy test were not overly sensitive to their own needs and feelings but could subordinate them for the benefit of others. These teachers were not inhibited in expressing their feelings behaviorally. This coincides with the description given by the emotionally disturbed children who said their empathic teachers were warm, caring, and could show affection openly. In Morgan's 1984 study, empathic teachers were described as being able to be spontaneous, which lines up with the children's description of their teachers having a sense of humor, which comes from spontaniety. They have feelings of self-worth and self-regard without any strong need to display anger, hostility, or aggression. This lines up with Wakefield and Crowl's description. Morgan (1984) found that they were sensitive, as did Wakefield and Crowl, but not to the extent that they were overwhelmed and could not function. In the 1979 study by Morgan, the children described these empathic teachers as relaxed and calm. Thompson's 1984 study described the Intuitive/Feeling teacher as one who encourages, inspires, motivates students to develop, adapts to their needs, and who want to make a personal contribution. Morgan's 1984 study found that empathic teachers received their greatest satisfaction by meeting the emotional needs of the children. DeNovellis and Lawrence (1983) found that teachers high on the Feeling dimension gave students more positive verbal and nonverbal feedback and attended more closely to students, several at the same time, and had them centrally involved in activities. Intuitives moved more freely in their classrooms and allowed more individual activity. Carlyn (1976) found that Intuitives enjoyed working with students in small groups and used independence and creativity in teaching. Those high on the dimension of Feeling had greater interest in children in the lower grades and a high commitment to teaching. Finally, Morgan (1984) found that the empathic teacher did not view emotionally disturbed children as being that deviant or different from other children. These teachers accepted them. If all of the information from the above cited studies is distilled, then a set of characteristics of the empathic teacher can be listed. The empathic teacher is:

1. Warm.
2. Caring.
3. Affectionate.
4. Friendly (smiles frequently).
5. Soft-spoken.
6. Calm.
7. Relaxed.
8. Humorous.
9. Analytical of behavior and motives.
10. Able to predict how another will act.
11. Able to sympathize.
12. Not easily incited to express anger.
13. Not easily depressed under difficult circumstances.
14. Able to subordinate their own needs and feelings for another's benefit.

15. Spontaneous.
16. Balanced in feelings of self-worth and self-regard.
17. Encouraging.
18. Inspiring.
19. Motivating.
20. Adaptable to the needs of others.
21. Altruistic (desires to make a personal contribution).
22. Able to give both positive verbal and nonverbal feedback.
23. Conscientous in attending to students' needs.
24. A person who does not have to be the center of attention.
25. A person who makes others centrally involved.
26. A person who is independent and creative.
27. Totally accepting of individual differences but does not focus on deviance.
28. A highly intuitive and feeling being.
29. A person who does not feel a great need to control all people and events.

Few people will have all of the characteristics shown, but to be considered *highly* empathic they should have most of these traits. To have all of them would be expecting a paragon of virtue, which is not realistic. To end this chapter it is important to give some attention to the syndrome referred to as burnout.

THE INTERACTION OF PERSONALITY, EDUCATIONAL PREPARATION, AND BURNOUT

In a recent study, Morgan and Krehbiel (1985) found that teachers who were not humanistic (i.e., not trained or using the interventions in this book) in their teaching approach with emotionally disturbed children were burned out and had significantly more dissatisfaction and frustration. These teachers reported much greater tension, anxiety, anger, hostility, and feelings of depression and dejection. In fact, their scores on these dimensions were even greater on a mood indicator test than participants in another study who had been diagnosed as neurotic (McNair & Lorr, 1964). There was no evidence that environmental conditions caused their feelings and their burnout because all participants in this study were assessed at the same time. Other teachers who were not burned out were working in the same environment, with the same administrators, under the same circumstances, and with the same type of pupils. It is important then to question whether the burned out teachers were individuals who were not personally suited to teaching these children in the first place. Obviously, a certain personality combined with an incompatible job creates more stress and exacerbates an already-existing predisposition to emotional problems.

The empathic teacher did not have feelings of anger, hostility, and depression. In many respects, the problems associated with teaching disturbed children are more akin to those experienced by counselors and psychologists than to those experienced by regular classroom teachers. There are excessive demands on the energy, strength, and personal resources of those teaching these children. Relationships develop quickly and center around highly emotionally charged fantasies and reality-based conflicts. Throughout the school year, there are extreme highs as disturbed children show motivation and periods of improvements, followed by intense lows, accompanied by frequent and common feelings of helplessness when the children relapse or resist all of the teacher's intervention skills. To tolerate these expansive mood swings, the teacher must have understanding and empathy to cope. There is research evidence (and it just makes common sense) that if people are not personally suited to their chosen profession, then when the going gets tough they are bound to burn out. This brings us back to an earlier suggestion in this chapter; the prospective teacher should get some career counseling before entering the profession.

In another study on burnout (Morgan & Reinhart, 1984), teachers who had been trained only in special education, with no regular education background, were less likely to burn out. They felt more respected in the community and received more system support. Those without a regular education background identified on a minimal level with the teaching profession as a whole. They viewed themselves as professionals with varied backgrounds, goals, and missions. They saw themselves as therapeutic agents who, only incidentally, do their work in the schools. As they perceive it, their support system comprises a very different group than those with a regular education background. They respect and value to a greater degree the opinions and feedback they receive from their students' psychotherapists, counselors, social workers, physicians, and parents.

On the other hand, the burned-out teachers, with a regular education background, look for support in the system from their principals, fellow teachers, supervisors, and persons in the central administrative offices. Those who had gone through regular elementary teacher training thought that, for the most part, their college curriculum had been inconsequential. The majority of burned-out teachers stated that most of their regular education courses did not provide a foundation for their jobs. They felt identity and job confusion in their roles as teachers of disturbed children and in what could or should be implemented from the training received in regular and special education.

The teachers in this study (Morgan & Reinhart, 1984) who were not burned out reported that additional training and experience in another area of special education, other than emotional disturbance, was most helpful. These teachers did not have feelings of frustration, helplessness, confusion, and bewilderment. They believed that if they did begin to feel burned out in teaching emotionally disturbed children, they would still want to stay in special education but teach a different population of handicapped youngsters for a short while.

So personality suitability alone is no guarantee against burn out. It appears that personality and educational preparation in combination is the best preventative for this syndrome. As a conclusion to this chapter, a final issue needs discussion. It is the issue of *control*, which can prevent teachers from effectively using the interventions in this book and which can also lead to burnout.

THE STRUGGLE FOR CONTROL

A number of times I have been asked by school districts to talk to teachers of emotionally disturbed students about what they referred to as "power struggles." Control is a big issue in our society. Control is a word that comes up in conversation frequently. How often do you hear people say things such as, "I am not in control of the situation. I have no control over my job. I cannot control my children, spouse, dog, and so on. Our financial situation is out of control. I feel out of control. I wish I had more control over such and such."

THE TEACHER'S EXPERIENCE

As I have spent more time with teachers and with disturbed youngsters, I have come to look at this issue differently. Instead of trying to gain more power, or as Dreikurs and Cassel (1972) believe, that the child misbehaves to get attention, I believe that what each person is trying to achieve is mastery over themselves, their incompetencies, and their environment. Before going into what the child is feeling, experiencing, and being motivated by, I want to talk about what some teachers are feeling, experiencing, and some of their motivations for getting caught up in the struggle for control.

We should begin with two examples of where the struggle for control can begin: (1) A child's refusal to work or defiance of your request for something; and (2) tantrums that seem to come out of nowhere or over seemingly insignificant matters. Some feelings and fleeting thoughts occur to teachers during these moments.

1. **Anger** because your authority is threatened.
2. **Rejection** because the children make you feel inadequate.
3. **Confusion** because the incident makes you question your own competence.
4. **Anxiety** about losing prestige and feeling humiliated.
5. **Fear** that your expertise will be questioned and that you will be attacked by other authorities and colleagues, and your job will be in jeopardy.

Here is where we start the struggle for control: not the child's, but the teacher's. Before anything constructive can take place, the teacher must get these feelings placed into perspective and reality-bound. Calm down and mentally take yourself through each feeling.

1. Anger over threatened authority. You must stop and think whether you are *really* without authority and power to do anything about the child's behavior. The answer is no! You have many options. Some of your feelings come from external factors that impinge on your emotions. There seem to be so many others in the school system who have more authority and power than you do: principals, assistant principals, coordinators, supervisors, parents, school board, psychologists, social workers, the courts, and public opinion in general regarding teachers. However, in the microcosm of your classroom, and a particular interaction with a child, you have power and authority to do many things. You are *not* helpless, weak, or impotent.
2. Rejection of the child for making you feel inadequate. Here again you have lost perspective on reality. At this point, you are only concentrating on the momentary situation and bringing with it all of your past real and fantasized feelings of failures. You are seeing the momentary confrontation as a lost cause, expecting to fail and allowing this incident to confirm a fear that you are a failure. We have all failed at something one time or another. We have all experienced not doing something as well as we wanted to or not accomplishing something that was important to us. This child–teacher incident brings that to the surface, and at this moment in

time you are frozen with feelings from past experiences. You are not remembering that there have been many successes and triumphs. You have forgotten how well you actually teach this or that; how well you handle all other situations; how you have helped other children improve; all of your special moments of being a winner.

3. Confusion about your competence. Again, your reality is distorted. You are now caught up in what I call the Perfect Teacher Syndrome (the teacher who is able to conquer all with perfection). None of us can be perfect in all aspects of our jobs, at every moment of the day, every work day of the week, month, year. But at this point, you are chastizing yourself because this one thing is not going as prescribed in those textbooks you studied—the ones that presented tough cases and then showed the ideal solution, and there was a perfect solution. You think you should have the beautiful curriculum, manage all inappropriate behavior, help all the children excel beyond belief in all of their academics, have decided mental health improvement, be ready to mainstream in one year or less, work extraordinary wonders with the parents, have insight into the children that no one else has, make your principal the happiest and most grateful human on earth, be appreciated, admired, and liked by all of your colleagues, and on and on. The fact is there will be some children (for every teacher) whom you cannot help. Allow yourself the frailties we all have.

4. Anxiety by feeling humiliated because you lost prestige. There are two things at play here. First, were you humiliated in front of other children or other faculty? Do you worry that if the other children see you momentarily unable to control another child, they will all mutiny and all will be lost? This will not happen. The things that ordinarily work to improve behavior will hold and are still important to the other children. They do not want themselves to be so out of control. Are you worrying about the stories they take home to their parents? If questions do arise, they will come later when you are calmer, and you will be able to make them understand the situation. The thing that upsets you here is the image of trying to explain at that moment in time when you have all these feelings operating. As for other faculty: Are you thinking you are a bad teacher, unable to control children, and not doing a job that they surely could do? You have lost perspective again. We have all seen some adult with a child out of control (e.g., a crying, tantruming child in the store or restaurant), and if you are like me, we think little of it except we are sorry for the adult at that moment that he

or she has to put up with such an unplesant situation. Even though you know better, you envision other teachers as doing a better job, that these things are only happening to you and never happen to them because they have some expertise or magic you do not. Again, reality is blurred for you during these high-tension moments. These things happen to every teacher, even in the regular classroom. In fact, it happens to the principal, the psychologist, counselor, nurse, parent, and any adult who has contact with children.

5. Fear for your employment. This is the most difficult issue to resolve. But once more, this comes about from not hanging on to a strong reality base. You are forgetting *you* are the expert in your job, not the principal or anyone else on the outside looking in. Only you know your class situation, all the components of the incident, and no one knows the children as you do. You are the one with the training and experience.

THE CHILD'S EXPERIENCE

Now let's look at the child's side of the struggle for control. If you understand what is going on with the child, it is much easier to cope with the situation, empathize, and gain control over your own feelings. I do not agree with Dreikurs that power struggles are for attention only. That is too simplistic and paints a negative picture of a willfully malicious child. It is usually much more complicated than that.

I will agree with the attention component in this way: The child is trying to tell you something is seriously wrong, and this is a disturbed, maladjusted way to right things, to elicit from you some direction, interpretation, or explanation.

Now the more important consideration: Many of these youngsters come from environments that are, for the most part, out of control. They do not have the most reliable, dependable, or stable home lives. Decisions are made for them and imposed constantly and almost always without explanation or understanding. Things just happen and often not in their best interest. Painful things happen which are out of their control: a divorce and a parent goes; the child is forced to be with one parent and not always the favored one; they are moved away from friends, their school, everthing they know, and they have no choice, or say, or control over these matters.

So, when big, important things are wrenched from them and they have no control over these matters that causes them real suffering, even the smallest thing takes on great importance. They need to feel they have some control somewhere over some, however small, part of their lives.

When they do not have this at home, then the logical place to test their ability to control something is at school, and especially with you. If you think about this, you will feel flattered and will not have all of those other feelings. It does show their trust in your relationship. They are willing to go that far because they know you are not going to knock them across the room, even though in the heat of the moment you might feel like you want to. Through trust, children learn it is safe to be dependent upon someone, and strangely enough, independence grows out of the knowledge that we can be dependent safely. In this sense, these struggles for control are healthy signs. They indicate that the youngsters trust you enough to be dependent upon you for their psychological needs, and now they feel that with you they can strive for, and move on to independence, or growth.

APPROACHES

Once you have joined the battle, you have lost it. First realize that you cannot demand changes from the child as long as you are determined to fight it out. Admit openly you will not fight. There is no challenge to your authority if you do not feel challenged. Try to offer reasonable options to students so that they feel they have some control. If they accept one of your options, then you both have control and you both win. Continue with your system and do not respond to their verbal bantering.

Allow the youngster to own his or her behavior. In the case of tantrums, how many times have you seen adults rush in and try to put a stop to the tantrum—grabbing youngsters and pinning them down to the floor or yelling or telling them to be quiet and stop crying? Have you ever seen that tactic work? I have not! Remember some mothers in the store with a tantruming child. They just keep pushing their carts down the aisles and ignoring their screaming children, not giving in and not struggling. Maybe it is not soon enough to suit everyone, but eventually the child stops, if for no other reason than sheer exhaustion. Tell the youngster, "Okay, this is your tantrum, not mine. You may scream and cry all you want. You own your feelings. I will not let you hurt yourself or anyone else hurt you." Then stay nearby to make sure they are not hurt, but do not comment on how they are behaving. Go on as best you can with the other students, commenting on how well they are doing whatever they are doing. Later, you can sympathize with tantruming children in the sense of commenting on how upset they felt and how it must have made part of their day miserable.

Finally, you need to educate the people in your environment. They need reassurance that things are under control. They need to know that at least you know what you are doing and why, even if it is not the most pleasant thing to witness, listen to, or teach next to. People will accept just about anything if they think you know what you are doing and if you help them understand the child's behavior and your behavior.

CONCLUSION

This book is an eclectic approach to teaching students with emotional disorders. The philosophy is heavily humanistic. The intention was to give to teachers and prospective teachers as many intervention skills as possible because it is a known fact that one approach does not work all of the time, with all students, under all circumstances. Interventions were presented for students of all ages: the primary-level child, the middle-elementary-age youngster, and the adolescent. An attempt was made to assist the prospective teacher and teacher trainer in identifying those who may be best suited for this profession. Finally, information was discussed regarding factors contributing to teacher burnout. The enormously important issue of the struggle for control was discussed as one possible preventive for teacher burnout.

We hope that this book will be useful to teachers, no matter what theoretical approach they study or adhere to. The driving force to all interventions is the ability of teachers to be empathic, whether they are using behavior modification or psychodynamic approaches.

REFERENCES

Aichhorn, A. (1925). *Wayward youth*. Vienna: International Psychoanalytic Press.

Carlyn, M. (1976). The relationship between Myers-Briggs personality characteristics and teaching preferences of prospective teachers [Doctoral dissertation, Michigan State University]. *Dissertation Abstracts International, 37*, 3493A. [University Microfilms No. 76–27, 081].

DeNovellis, R., & Lawrence, G. (1983). Correlates of teacher personality variables (Myers-Briggs) and classroom observation data. *Research in Psychological Type, 6*, 37–46.

Dreikurs, R., & Cassel, P. (1972). *Discipline without tears*. New York: Hawthorn Books.

Dunn, L. M. (1963). *Exceptional children in the schools*. New York: Holt, Rinehart, & Winston.

Dobson, J. K. (1970). Predictions of individual student teacher behavior in classrooms for emotionally disturbed children. Unpublished doctoral dissertation. Ann Arbor, MI: University of Michigan.

Lee, G. C. (1971). The changing role of the teacher. In W. C. Morse, & G. M. Wingo (Eds.), *Classroom psychology*. Glenview, Ill.: Scott, Foresman.

McNair, D., & Lorr, M. (1964). An analysis of mood patterns in neurotics. *Journal of Abnormal Social Psychology, 69,* 620–627.

Morgan, S. R., & Krehbiel, R. (1985). The psychological condition of burned-out teachers with a nonhumanistic orientation. *Journal of Humanistic Education and Development,* 24(2) 59–67.

Morgan, S. R., & Reinhart, J. A., (1984). Training as a factor contributing to burnout in teachers of emotionally disturbed children. *Education,* 106(2), 185–192.

Morgan, S. R. (1984). An illustrative case of high empathy teachers. *Journal of Humanistic Education and Development,* 22(4), 143–148.

Morgan, S. R. (1979). A model of the empathic process for teachers of emotionally disturbed children. *American Journal of Orthopsychiatry,* 49(3), 446–453.

Morgan, S. R. (1977). Personality variables as predictors of empathy. *Behavioral Disorders,* 2(2), 89–94.

Myers-Briggs, I. (1987). *Myers-Briggs type indicator (Form G—self scorable report form).* Palo Alto, CA: Consulting Psychologists Press.

Myers-Briggs, I., & McCaulley, M. H. (1985). *A guide to the development and use of the Myers-Briggs Type Indicator.* Palo Alto, CA: Consulting Psychologists Press.

Piaget, J. (1979). The relation of affectivity to intelligence in the mental development of the child. In S. Harrison & J. McDermott (Eds.), *Childhood psychopathology* (pp. 156–182). New York: International Universities Press.

Smith, S. A. (1967). An educational program for emotionally disturbed children. *Psychology in the schools, 4,* 280.

Thompson, L.L. (1984). An investigation of the relationship of the personality theory of C. G. Jung and teachers' self-reported perceptions and decisions. Unpublished doctoral dissertation, Ohio State University.

Wakefield, W., & Crowl, T. (1974). Personality characteristics of special educators. *Journal of Experimental Education, 43,* 86–89.

Index

33,740

940.54 Collier, Richard
COL
    The war in the
       desert

B+T 1295

DATE		
SEP 13	DEC 23 1998	
JUN 4		
AUG 1 3	JUL 26 2001	
SEP 1 7	APR 2 0 2002	
MAR 1 8	MAR 0 4 2005	
JUN 1 5		
APR 1 0		

A German panzer crewman, emerging from the turret of his immobilized tank with his hands up, surrenders to bayonet-wielding British infantry soldiers in October 1942, during one of the desert war's most hard-fought and decisive actions, the Battle of El Alamein.

THE WAR IN THE DESERT

Other Publications:
THE EPIC OF FLIGHT
THE GOOD COOK
THE SEAFARERS
THE ENCYCLOPEDIA OF COLLECTIBLES
THE GREAT CITIES
HOME REPAIR AND IMPROVEMENT
THE WORLD'S WILD PLACES
THE TIME-LIFE LIBRARY OF BOATING
HUMAN BEHAVIOR
THE ART OF SEWING
THE OLD WEST
THE EMERGENCE OF MAN
THE AMERICAN WILDERNESS
THE TIME-LIFE ENCYCLOPEDIA OF GARDENING
LIFE LIBRARY OF PHOTOGRAPHY
THIS FABULOUS CENTURY
FOODS OF THE WORLD
TIME-LIFE LIBRARY OF AMERICA
TIME-LIFE LIBRARY OF ART
GREAT AGES OF MAN
LIFE SCIENCE LIBRARY
THE LIFE HISTORY OF THE UNITED STATES
TIME READING PROGRAM
LIFE NATURE LIBRARY
LIFE WORLD LIBRARY
FAMILY LIBRARY:
   HOW THINGS WORK IN YOUR HOME
   THE TIME-LIFE BOOK OF THE FAMILY CAR
   THE TIME-LIFE FAMILY LEGAL GUIDE
   THE TIME-LIFE BOOK OF FAMILY FINANCE

Previous World War II Volumes:
Prelude to War
Blitzkrieg
The Battle of Britain
The Rising Sun
The Battle of the Atlantic
Russia Besieged

WORLD WAR II · TIME-LIFE BOOKS · ALEXANDRIA, VIRGINIA

BY RICHARD COLLIER
AND THE EDITORS OF TIME-LIFE BOOKS

THE WAR IN THE DESERT

WORLD WAR II

Editorial Staff for *The War in the Desert*
Editor: William K. Goolrick
Picture Editors/Designers: Thomas S. Huestis,
Raymond Ripper
Text Editors: Jim Hicks, Anne Horan,
Henry Woodhead
Staff Writers: Susan Bryan, Richard W. Flanagan,
Henry P. Leifermann, Abigail Zuger
Researchers: Christine M. Bowie, Jane Coughran,
Peter Kaufman, Helga Kohl, Karen L. Mitchell,
Robin Richman, Phyllis K. Wise
Editorial Assistant: Dolores Morrissy

Editorial Production
Production Editor: Douglas B. Graham
Operations Manager: Gennaro C. Esposito,
Gordon E. Buck (assistant)
Assistant Production Editor: Feliciano Madrid
Quality Control: Robert L. Young (director),
James J. Cox (assistant), Daniel J. McSweeney,
Michael G. Wight (associates)
Art Coordinator: Anne B. Landry
Copy Staff: Susan B. Galloway (chief), Victoria Lee,
Barbara F. Quarmby, Celia Beattie
Picture Department: Alvin L. Ferrell

Correspondents: Elisabeth Kraemer (Bonn);
Margot Hapgood, Dorothy Bacon, Lesley Coleman
(London); Susan Jonas, Lucy T. Voulgaris (New
York); Maria Vincenza Aloisi, Josephine du Brusle
(Paris); Ann Natanson (Rome). Valuable assistance
was also provided by: Leny Heinen (Bonn);
Colleen Mitchell, Karin B. Pearce (London); John
Dunn (Melbourne); Carolyn T. Chubet, Miriam
Hsia, Christina Lieberman (New York); Mimi
Murphy, Deborah Sgardello (Rome).

The Author: RICHARD COLLIER, born in London
in 1924, served as a war correspondent in the Far
East. Formerly a feature writer for the London *Daily Mail*, he is the author of more than a dozen
books, including *Ten Thousand Eyes, The Sands of
Dunkirk* and *Duce!*, a biography of Benito Mussolini. He lives at Burgh Heath in Surrey, England.

The Consultants: COLONEL JOHN R. ELTING, USA
(Ret.), is a military historian and author of *The
Battle of Bunker's Hill, The Battles of Saratoga* and
Military History and Atlas of the Napoleonic Wars.
He edited *Military Uniforms in America: The Era
of the American Revolution, 1755-1795* and *Mili-
tary Uniforms in America: Years of Growth, 1796-
1851*, and was associate editor of *The West Point
Atlas of American Wars.*

MARTIN BLUMENSON, a former lieutenant colonel in the U.S. Army Reserve, was educated at
Bucknell and Harvard, and served in Europe in
World War II and later in the Korean War as a
historical officer. He was a senior historian at the
Army's Office of the Chief of Military History and
then held chairs in military and strategic studies
at Acadia University, the Naval War College, the
Citadel and the Army War College. He is the author of 12 books, notably *Kasserine Pass* and the
two volumes of *The Patton Papers.*

For information about any Time-Life book, please write:

Reader Information
Time-Life Books
541 North Fairbanks Court
Chicago, Illinois 60611

CONTENTS

ITALY'S REACH FOR GLORY

Smartly uniformed Italian antiaircraft crews in Libya, their machine guns mounted on a truck, exude confidence prior to the invasion of Egypt in September 1940.

THE DUCE'S PLANS FOR A ROMAN EMPIRE

"Italian people, rush to arms and show your tenacity, your courage, your valor," shouted dictator Benito Mussolini to the cheering crowd that filled the immense square beneath his famous balcony *(left)*. It was June 10, 1940, the day that Italy entered the War against the Allies. Hitler was rapidly completing his conquest of Western Europe, and the Duce, not to be outdone, determined to make some flashy conquests of his own and in the process triple the size of his empire on the continent of Africa. Mussolini already held Libya in the north, and Eritrea, Italian Somaliland and Ethiopia to the southeast. Now that Great Britain was fighting for its very existence, it seemed a fine time to grab off British interests in the Mediterranean area.

On June 28, Mussolini ordered the invasion of Egypt, "that great reward for which Italy is waiting." Britain had only 36,000 men in Egypt; opposing them in Libya were nearly 250,000 Italians. Still, preparations for the attack dragged on for two and a half months. Through the summer, the Italian High Command fueled the fires of enthusiasm on the home front with grandiose pronouncements of victories elsewhere in Africa. Mussolini's armies seized posts along the Egyptian-Libyan border, drove into Kenya, penetrated the Sudan and took British Somaliland. In the heart of Rome, the Italian advances were charted on a huge map *(right),* and people throughout Italy were soon telling themselves: "We are a revived nation. We can fight."

Finally, on September 13 the Italians launched their expedition into Egypt, hoping to make a clean sweep to the Suez Canal. Across the Libyan border they streamed, 80,000 strong. There were five infantry divisions, seven tank battalions. When the smoke and dust of the first attack cleared, the British were amazed to see a large part of this formidable force arrayed before them as though on review—first the motorcyclists, then the light tanks, then the other vehicles, all drawn up in neat rows. The outnumbered British fell back, but not before—in Prime Minister Winston Churchill's words—"our artillery took its toll of the generous targets presented to them."

From the marble balcony of his office in Rome's Palazzo Venezia, a belligerent Mussolini announces he has declared war on Britain and France.

While a worker on a ladder adds the finishing touches, passersby in Rome scan a map erected to trace the successes of the Italian Army in North Africa.

Trim and cocky, goose-stepping Italian Blackshirts pass a saluting Marshal Rodolfo Graziani in Benghazi on August 14, 1940, on their way to the Libyan front.

Sun-helmeted Italian foot soldiers, carrying rifles and shouldering light machine guns, trudge across the desert during their September 1940 offensive. The greater part of the Italian Army was made up of infantrymen, who were of little use against the more mobile British.

SETTING FORTH ON THE ROAD TO DISASTER

As the Italian troops advanced into Egypt, they appeared to be a formidable fighting force. But the reality was otherwise. Their tanks were so flimsy they split apart under fire. Their solid-tired trucks were no match for desert boulders and shook to pieces. And many soldiers were poorly trained.

Nevertheless, at the start of the campaign, all went well. Four days out, the Italians occupied Sidi Barrani—a 60-mile advance uncontested by the British. Here they halted to consolidate their gains before the final push and here they had their first real taste of the desert. The land was barren and the life spartan. The officers were contented. They were well fed and slept on sheets; to them, victory seemed sure and adversity worth bearing. But the enlisted men had poor food and dismal living conditions, and their morale sagged. "This is an evil that must pass quickly," wrote one. Others began to wonder why they were there. One commented: "This is a European war fought in Africa with European weapons against a European enemy. We take too little account of this. . . . We are not fighting the Abyssinians now."

On December 9 the storm hit. The British, who had used the respite to build up their forces, launched a counterattack—and the Italians were suddenly routed.

A phalanx of Lancia trucks, loaded with Italian artillerymen, draws up on the Libyan sands, waiting for

orders to advance. Officers ride in a small Fiat convertible (right); the vehicle with the oversized wheels at far left was used for pulling guns and field kitchens.

As artillery shells explode in the background, Italian infantrymen charge across the Western Desert in a December 1940 attack on British positions. Such heroics

did little to stem the tide of the British counteroffensive, which wiped out three Italian divisions at Sidi Barrani and then swept over the stronghold of Bardia.

An endless stream of Italian captives, reflecting the demoralization of defeat, marches toward a detention area after the fall of Bardia in early January, 1941. By this

time, less than a month after the British counteroffensive had been launched, some 80,000 Italians in the Western Desert had surrendered or been taken prisoner.

1

At dawn on September 13, 1940, a fanfare of silver trumpets sounded across the barren landscape of the North African desert. From Fort Capuzzo, just inside Libya's border with Egypt, streamed a long line of tanks in single file, followed by three infantry regiments, an artillery regiment, a machine-gun battalion, and engineer and mortar companies. At the head of the column, in the flamboyant style of an earlier war, marched the black-shirted shock troops known as Arditi, armed with daggers and hand grenades. And in the wake came trucks loaded with marble monuments, which were intended to mark the triumphal progress of Italian fighting men as they swept across Egypt and wrested it from Britain's control.

Such, at least, was Benito Mussolini's fond hope. For a year, since the start of World War II, Italy's dictator had enviously watched his Axis partner, Adolf Hitler, achieve one conquest after another across Europe. Now, in the late summer of 1940, final victory in the West appeared within Hitler's grasp. Only Britain remained to be crushed, and an intensifying German air assault on its cities promised to hasten that end.

Mussolini, calculating the probabilities, foresaw an outcome not at all to his liking. Unless he put on his own show of military might while there was still time, he could hardly make a case for sharing the fruits of Axis victory. "To be able to attend the peace conference as a belligerent," he told Marshal Pietro Badoglio, Chief of the Italian General Staff, "I need a few thousand dead."

The thesis had been pretested in France, though with dispiriting results. In June, with France about to fall to the Germans, Mussolini had suddenly declared war on the Allies and sent troops into the corner of France that bordered on Italy. The foray had earned him widespread derision as a jackal trying to feed upon a corpse and had gained him only a sliver of territory—Hitler would allow him no more.

Africa, however, offered a rosier prospect. In moving to seize Egypt, the Italians would start with certain advantages. One was the current plight of the British. Though they had long dominated Egypt, first under a protectorate and more recently under a treaty that permitted British troops to be stationed there, they were now preoccupied with defending their own island. With their resources of men and

A GAMBLE FOR HIGH STAKES

matériel stretched thin, they could ill afford to reinforce their Middle East bastion.

A second advantage to the Italians lay in their own years of entrenchment in Africa. Libya, with nearly 1,000 miles of strategic frontage on the Mediterranean, had been in Italian hands since 1911, Eritrea and Italian Somaliland on Africa's eastern coast even longer. To his East African possessions Mussolini had recently added Ethiopia. Libya lay immediately to the west of Egypt; and Ethiopia abutted on the British colonies in East Africa. Britain's domination of the area could thus be challenged on two fronts.

Behind his bravado, Mussolini knew that his forces' quick victory over Ethiopian tribesmen in 1936 was not likely to be duplicated in combat with the well-trained British troops in Egypt. Still, given Britain's dilemma of the moment, the gamble looked possible. And it would show Hitler that the Duce was pressing the Axis cause with proper fervor.

The man chosen by Mussolini to lead Italy's North African forces was the 58-year-old Marshal Rodolfo Graziani, a much-bemedaled veteran of earlier African campaigns against rebellious natives, who was known out of earshot as "The Butcher" for his mode of dealing with his adversaries.

Graziani had expected that his task would be largely defensive—to guard Libya against British inroads from the east and against attack from French-controlled Tunisia on the west. But the fall of France had removed the threat from Tunisia. On taking up his post, Graziani was appalled to learn that he was expected to advance 300 miles into Egypt and capture the great British naval base at Alexandria. At once he flew home to Rome to plead with both Mussolini and Chief of Staff Badoglio.

His forces, Graziani argued, would be no match for the British. He had transport for no more than four battalions. Some of the weapons at his disposal were better suited to a war-surplus dump: cannons and rifles dating from the 19th Century, rusting machine guns. He was also short of up-to-date equipment—planes, tanks, antitank and antiaircraft guns, even mines. At places along the Egyptian border Italian soldiers on night patrols were forced to defuse and steal British mines to sow their own minefields.

The bleak picture Graziani painted could not have surprised Mussolini and Badoglio. The military ventures of recent years—notably the Ethiopian campaign and the in-

tervention in the Spanish Civil War—had sapped Italy's military strength.

Then, in April 1939, Italy had invaded tiny Albania, its neighbor across the Adriatic, as a rival gesture to Hitler's take-over of Czechoslovakia. Though Albania had given up without a fight, the Italians were compelled to maintain a large occupation force there, using men and arms that might otherwise have been put at Graziani's disposal.

But Mussolini hungered for some sort of victory in North Africa, and Graziani's protests proved unavailing. All he could get from the Duce was soothing syrup. "I am not fixing precise territorial objectives," Mussolini assured him. "I only ask you to attack the British forces opposing you." Egypt, the Duce predicted, would be a rich prize, its seizure "the final blow to Great Britain."

A disconsolate Graziani returned to Libya with only one tangible promise. Soon, Badoglio pledged, he would send 1,000 tanks—the weapon most effective in desert terrain. The promise was never to be kept, though for a time it gave Graziani a logical excuse to delay the invasion while awaiting the tanks' delivery. Meanwhile, hostilities with the British were confined to border skirmishes, resulting in an unequal toll that reinforced the marshal's forebodings: 3,500 Italian casualties, 150 British.

Increasingly irked as Graziani stalled, the Duce set a deadline. Ready or not, Italian forces were to move into Egypt when Hitler's presumably imminent air victory over Britain's home island brought the first German soldier stepping onto British soil. By early September, Mussolini was no longer willing to wait for this landing to materialize. He ordered Graziani to get going in two days—or be replaced.

At first Graziani's pessimism seemed unfounded. Four days after his troops left Fort Capuzzo, they were 60 miles inside Egypt and holding the coastal settlement of Sidi Barrani (map, page 27). Except for its mosque and police station, this village was little more than a collection of mud huts. But Rome Radio lost no time boosting the victory to improbable heights. "Thanks to the skill of Italian engineers," it announced, "the tramcars are again running in Sidi Barrani."

What the elated Italian listeners could not know was that the British had withdrawn from Sidi Barrani according to plan, falling back 80 miles deeper into Egypt to the sponge-fishers' village of Mersa Matruh. Once known as Paraetonium, where Anthony and Cleopatra had frolicked in the blue sea waves, Mersa Matruh was now the terminus of a narrow-gauge railroad from Alexandria. It gave the British an advantage. If the Italians continued their advance, their supply lines would be extended and exposed to attack while the British, close to their own sources of supply, could wait for an appropriate moment to launch a counteraction.

Graziani, however, was unwilling to dispatch his troops farther into Egypt. Not only their left flank, but also the flow of their supplies along the only coastal road from Libya lay open to bombardment from British warships in the Mediterranean. Graziani chose to have his men dig in at Sidi Barrani.

From his headquarters some 300 miles to the rear in the Libyan town of Cyrene, he ordered his commander on the ground, General Mario Berti, to fan out the Italian forces in a semicircle of seven defensive camps. Over the next three months these outposts took on the leisurely air of a peacetime cantonment, down to such refinements as colognes and silver hairbrushes in the officers' quarters, engraved glasses in their clubs, tinned hams and Frascati wines at their tables. Everywhere, on walls and gateways, were blazoned rallying cries from Mussolini's speeches, wryly inappropriate for an army already beginning to tire of the quest for a latter-day Roman Empire: *Chi se ferma è perduto* (He who hesitates is lost) and *Sempre avanti* (Ever forward).

The British too dug in, under the command of Lieut. General Richard Nugent O'Connor, a shy, birdlike little man with a self-effacing manner. In the long weeks of waiting, Mersa Matruh became a town of troglodytes as O'Connor's troops—fed a spartan diet of corned-beef stew and strong, sweet tea—carved trenches and dugouts in the limestone rock beneath the sand.

At British headquarters back in Cairo, the Commander-in-Chief, Middle East, General Sir Archibald Wavell, also bided his time, waiting for troop reinforcements and for a shipment of tanks designed specifically to work in close support with advancing troops. The British "I" (for infantry) tank,

THE ROYAL DUKE'S EAST AFRICAN DEBACLE

While his armies in Libya girded for the invasion of Egypt that touched off the desert war, Mussolini set in motion the other half of his scheme of African conquest: a strike at the British in East Africa. To lead that campaign he chose the Duke of Aosta, cousin of King Victor Emmanuel III and governor general of Italian East Africa.

Aosta was popular with his British neighbors in East Africa. They liked his charm, his polished manners, his "Englishness." When Mussolini ordered him to attack, in June 1940, he did so reluctantly but dutifully. In two months, parts of the Sudan and Kenya and all of British Somaliland fell to his troops. By a year later, however, the British had recouped their losses, and also controlled Italian East Africa. The Duke was captured in the Ethiopian mountains and died the following year from tuberculosis and malaria while a prisoner of war in Kenya. But his former friends treasured a token of his gentlemanly ways. Before fleeing his headquarters in Addis Ababa, he had penned a courteous note thanking the British in advance for protecting the city's women and children, "thereby demonstrating that strong bonds of humanity and race still exist between our nations."

The Duke of Aosta, in his capacity as the viceroy of Ethiopia, receives the homage of an Ethiopian dignitary in the throne room of the exiled Emperor Haile Selassie.

dubbed the Matilda, weighed some 30 tons. Its three-inch armor was impenetrable to Italian guns, while its own gun, a 2-pounder, could penetrate the best tank the Italians had.

But more than weapons would be needed in order to prevail in this parched and desolate land. Both sides would have to contend not only with each other but also with the unique challenges presented by the terrain. The Western Desert—originally a designation for western Egypt alone, but later expanded to include eastern Libya—encompassed a roughly rectangular area about 500 miles long and 150 miles wide. Behind a sandy plain that bordered on the Mediterranean lay a high desert plateau, much of its dun-colored expanse strewn with boulders and pebbles. Despite the havoc the stony stretches played with tank treads and truck springs, crossing the plateau was fairly easy; but getting to it was not. Between it and the coastal strip loomed an escarpment with cliffs as high as 500 feet and with only a few places passable by wheeled or tracked vehicles.

From a military standpoint, the worst aspect of the Western Desert was its lack of distinctive landmarks. Traversing it, except along the one coastal road, was like sailing an uncharted sea, navigable only by sun, stars and compass.

The analogy between desert and sea warfare was vividly drawn by the Australian writer Alan Moorehead, then a correspondent in Egypt for the London *Daily Express*. "Each truck or tank," he wrote, "was as individual as a destroyer, and each squadron of tanks or guns made great sweeps across the desert as a battle-squadron at sea will vanish over the horizon. . . . When you made contact with the enemy you maneuvered about him for a place to strike much as two fleets will steam into position for action. . . . There was no front line. : . . Always the essential governing principle was that desert forces must be mobile. . . . We hunted men, not land, as a warship will hunt another warship, and care nothing for the sea on which the action is fought."

Something intangible was also required: a "desert sense" that told a man never to try to tamper with this formidable environment but to use or circumvent it as best he could. The seasoned men in charge of Britain's Western Desert Force had acquired this sense, and correspondent Moorehead described some of the ways they put it to work:

"Always the desert set the pace, made the direction and planned the design. The desert offered colors in browns, yellows and grays. The army accordingly took these colors for its camouflage. There were practically no roads. The army shod its vehicles with huge balloon tires and did without roads. Nothing except an occasional bird moved quickly in the desert. The army for ordinary purposes accepted a pace of five or six miles an hour. The desert gave water reluctantly, and often then it was brackish. The army cut its men—generals and privates—down to a gallon of water a day when they were in forward positions."

In sum, Moorehead wrote: "We did not try to make the desert livable, nor did we seek to subdue it. We found the life of the desert primitive and nomadic, and primitively and nomadically the army lived and went to war."

To the Italians, settled in comfort at Sidi Barrani and hoping for no more than a static war, the British way of accommodating to the desert was thoroughly distasteful. They would learn its advantages, at heavy cost, beginning in December of 1940.

Before that time, two events with direct implications for the North African campaign occurred elsewhere in the Mediterranean. One was to be of immediate benefit to the British; the other spelled protracted trouble for them.

On November 11, night-flying torpedo bombers from the British aircraft carrier *Illustrious* swooped in on Taranto in southern Italy, home base of the Italian fleet, and crippled three battleships at their moorings. The raid substantially reduced the Italian naval threat to British supply convoys bound from Gibraltar for Egypt. It also enabled Britain's Mediterranean fleet, under Admiral Sir Andrew Cunningham, to turn more attention to harrying Italian convoys on their far shorter run from Sicily to Libya. For the next few months, the Mediterranean lived up to its Royal Navy nickname, "Cunningham's Pond."

The other event had occurred a few days earlier. On October 28, Mussolini suddenly embarked on another foreign adventure, dispatching his occupation troops in Albania to invade next-door Greece; piqued at getting no advance notice of a German move into Rumania, a new convert to the Axis cause, he had decided, as he put it, to "pay Hitler back in his own coin."

Mussolini's invasion of Greece posed a problem for the British. Though it soon met with savage resistance, it also confronted Britain with the need to make good on a pledge to the Greeks—given in April of 1939 by Winston Churchill's predecessor as Prime Minister, Neville Chamberlain—to help them with arms and men if they were attacked. Despite Britain's badly depleted resources, Churchill felt that the British were bound to honor the commitment. He wired Greek Premier Ioannis Metaxas: "We will give you all the help in our power."

At first Metaxas, fearing that British involvement would bring Hitler in to shore up the faltering Italians, rejected Churchill's proposal. But the Greeks' reluctance was only temporary, and their eventual acceptance of Churchill's chivalrous offer was destined to prolong the war in North Africa. Aid to Greece could come only from Britain's reservoir of strength, such as it was, in the Middle East.

Some of the men around Churchill were dismayed by what they deemed a rash and ill-advised gesture on his part. "Strategic folly," Secretary of State for War Anthony Eden noted in his diary. The view was unanimously shared by the

trio charged with protecting Britain's Middle East dominion by land, sea and air: General Wavell, Admiral Cunningham and Air Chief Marshal Sir Arthur Longmore, area commander of the RAF. Wavell, as overall head of the Middle East forces, was especially dismayed. From now on, he had to plan his counterattack against the Italians in North Africa as a race against time and amid renewed Churchill demands for action to save Greece.

Adding to the problem was the basic incompatibility of the two men—a clash of chemistries that was in time to lead to Wavell's removal from his post. Churchill was outspoken and articulate, Wavell withdrawn and taciturn. Once, asked by Australian Premier Robert Menzies for an appraisal of the Middle East situation, Wavell replied, "That is a complicated matter," then lapsed into a brooding 10-minute silence. Churchill assessed Wavell as "a good average colonel." Wavell detested politicians who meddled in military affairs. A veteran of World War I campaigns in Palestine and in France—where he had lost his left eye—he did not regard

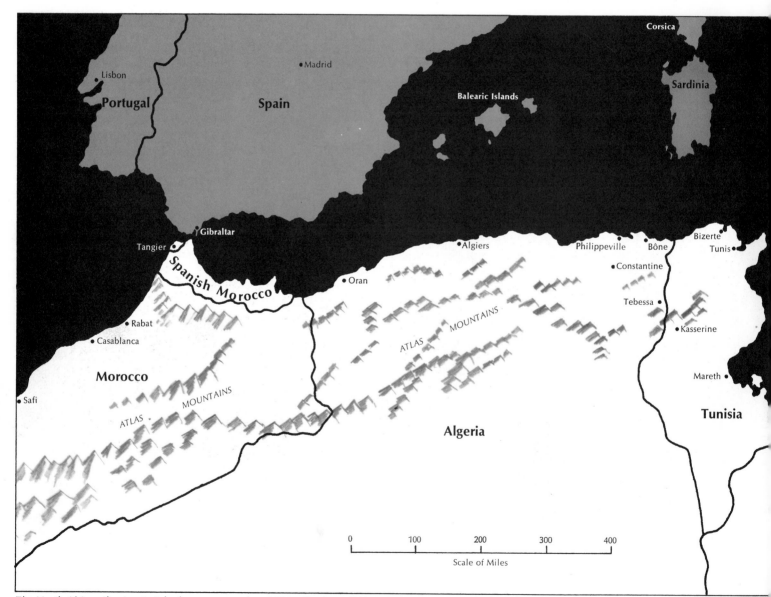

The North African theater stretched across more than 2,000 miles from El Alamein in Egypt to south of Casablanca in Morocco. The war seesawed in the Western

Churchill's own short tours of duty in the Sudan and in France during the First World War as grounds for claiming military expertise.

Throughout the fall of 1940, Churchill kept up a barrage of advice, comments and criticism, which Wavell succinctly summed up as "barracking"—an Australian term for the heckling engaged in by spectators at a sporting match in order to disconcert the players. Though aware that Churchill had begun to suspect him of being less than resolute, Wavell was determined not to attack in the desert until he felt his preparations were complete. He was also determined not to reveal, except to key subordinates, the plan that was taking shape in his mind.

But a visit to Cairo by Anthony Eden forced Wavell's hand. The Secretary of State for War proposed to drain off so much matériel for the Greeks that, as Wavell put it, "I had to tell him what was in my mind to prevent my being skinned to an extent that would make an offensive impossible." Eden was so impressed by what Wavell told him that

he scribbled a note reading, "Egypt more important than Greece," and conveyed the secret plan back to Churchill in London. To Wavell's astonishment, it utterly charmed Churchill. On hearing its details, the Prime Minister was to recall, "I purred like six cats."

The plan hinged on a piece of information reported by scouts and confirmed by aerial photographs: the Italians had left a 15-mile gap, unpatrolled and unfortified, between two of the seven outposts they had set up as a shield for Sidi Barrani. The camps in question were Nibeiwa, south of Sidi Barrani on the coastal plain, and Rabia, perched on the escarpment to the southwest. The fortified side of all the camps faced eastward toward the British. If the British could pass undetected through the Nibeiwa-Rabia gap, they would then be able to wheel about and fall upon the Italians from the undefended rear.

As refined by Wavell and his commander in the field, General O'Connor, the plan called for the use of the two

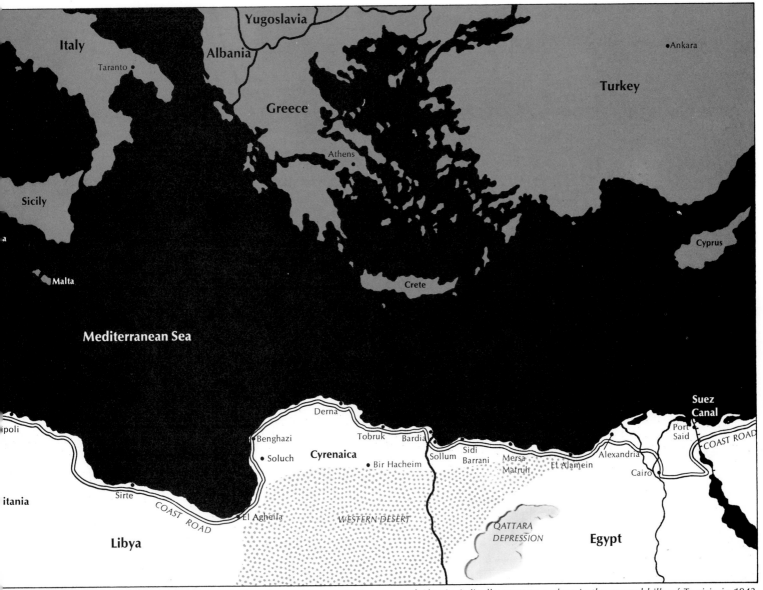

Desert until late 1942, and then focused upon the beaches and towns of Morocco and Algeria. It finally came to a close in the rugged hills of Tunisia in 1943.

In flier's cap and goggles, Italo Balbo gets his military pilot's wings from the Duce in 1927.

Balbo is showered by New York's ticker tape.

Before beginning his 43-day air journey from Italy to Chicago and back, Balbo inspects his Savoia-Marchetti seaplane with its fore-and-aft propellers.

A MAGNIFICENT FLIER'S FALL FROM GRACE

Italian flier Italo Balbo was everything Benito Mussolini wanted to be: a handsome, flamboyant, international hero. In 1933 the bearded aviator led an armada of 24 twin-hulled seaplanes on a sensational 12,000-mile round-trip flight between Italy and the World's Fair in Chicago. Landing on Lake Michigan, Balbo was welcomed by more than 100,000 admirers, many waving the red, green and white flag of Italy. In New York, Mayor John P. O'Brien gave him a ticker-tape parade and said Balbo's name would be coupled with that of Columbus and Marconi. And in Washington, the flier lunched with President Roosevelt.

The transatlantic triumph and the world fame that it brought Balbo were not without price—the jealous Duce's secret and dangerous enmity. Mussolini gave Balbo a publicly warm welcome-home kiss on the cheek and the gold eagle insignia of Italy's first Air Marshal, but three months later the hero was packed off to be governor of the Italian colony of Libya. The post was an ignominious quasi exile for a man of Bal-

bo's public stature and popularity, but he was stoic about it. "I obey orders," he said. "I am a soldier."

Although Balbo was an ardent Fascist—he was a founding member of the movement and was reported to have devised new methods of torturing anti-Fascists—he did not share the Duce's enthusiasm for the War. His objections undoubtedly irritated Mussolini. When the Duce warmed to an alliance with Hitler, Balbo protested: "You are licking Germany's boots." He was convinced that the Italian troops in Libya were no match for the British forces in Egypt. But he would not live to see himself proved right.

Flying over Tobruk on June 28, 1940—only 18 days after Italy declared war on Britain—he was shot down and killed by his own antiaircraft guns. Italian gunners had mistaken Balbo's plane for the enemy. (A British plane did fly over the city later—but only to drop a note of condolence from Middle East RAF Commander Sir Arthur Longmore.) Suspicion persisted that high-flying Italo Balbo was killed not by accident but on secret instructions from the resentful Duce.

Balbo and Italian King Victor Emmanuel III (left) review troops in Libya in 1938.

Seeking the dead hero's personal effects, a soldier combs the wreckage of Balbo's plane after it was mysteriously downed by Italian antiaircraft fire.

divisions in the Western Desert Force, the 4th Indian and the 7th Armored. Both divisions would move through the Nibeiwa-Rabia gap. Then the 4th Indian, supported by the 7th Royal Tank Regiment, would turn north and take Nibeiwa from the rear. After that the 4th would strike farther north to take three other camps on the coastal plain as well as Sidi Barrani itself. A frontal attack along the coast by British troops from the Mersa Matruh garrison, supported by gunboats of the Royal Navy, would take the coastal camp of Maktila and help mop up Sidi Barrani. Most of the 7th Armored Division, after moving through the gap, would head northwest for Buq Buq, a point on the coast road between Sidi Barrani and the Libyan border, to prevent the Italians from bringing up reinforcements. The rest of the 7th Armored, meanwhile, would swing westward onto the escarpment to prevent any interference from Rabia and from Sofafi, the other camp there.

Wavell did not contemplate a major offensive. He planned no more than a five-day raid, with Buq Buq, 25 miles west of Sidi Barrani, as the ultimate British halt line. His objectives were threefold: to test the Italians' fighting mettle in battle rather than in mere skirmishes, to secure a few thousand prisoners and—above all—to strike a decisive blow before the Germans moved to intervene in Libya.

Against some 80,000 Italians, General O'Connor had only 30,000 men—a polyglot force of Englishmen, Ulstermen, Cameron Highlanders, Sikhs, Pathans and Hindus.

At 7 a.m. on December 6, the two divisions moved out, tanks and gun carriers and trucks spaced 200 yards apart on a 2,000-yard front. Rocks and camel's-thorn often slowed them to a crawl. They had some 75 miles to cover before engaging in battle, but the desert-wise O'Connor, aware of the great strain imposed by the terrain, had planned accordingly. For one entire day and night, his 30,000 men would pause and lie out in the open, midway between Mersa Matruh and the Italian camps. Though they would be at the mercy of Italian spotter planes, as little as possible had been left to chance. O'Connor had even ordered windshields stripped from the trucks, lest the sun's reflections catch the eye of an enemy pilot.

Ahead of the advance, supplies lay buried deep in desert cisterns—planted there by patrols in the style of the warring Saracens more than 1,000 years earlier. Enough food, gasoline and ammunition had been stored to last the full five days until the projected return to Mersa Matruh.

Most of O'Connor's men thought they were on a routine training exercise. Briefings by the few officers in on the secret were noncommital: tank commanders were simply told that they would drive for some distance, pause for the night, then drive on the following day to an unspecified objective. The officers of the 7th Queen's Own Hussars were so certain of a speedy return to base that they dispatched a priority order to Alexandria: a special holiday feast for Christmas Day.

On the night of December 8, the troops moved on. Their way was now lit by a chain of beacons sited by patrols so as to be invisible from the Italian camps: gasoline cans, cut in half and facing toward the oncoming vehicles, shielded the steady glow of hurricane lamps. At 1 a.m., a few miles to the rear of the Italian camp at Nibeiwa, the British halted.

They were unaware of how well their luck was holding. Earlier that day, they had been spotted—by none other than Lieut. Colonel Vittorio Revetra, chief of the Italian fighter forces, while he was on a routine flight from a coastal airfield. Revetra promptly signaled Marshal Graziani at headquarters, reporting that he had seen "an impressive number of armored vehicles" moving up from Mersa Matruh. To his stupefaction, Graziani calmly ordered him to "let me have that in writing." The marshal later claimed that he had notified his subordinates in the field. But no action was taken against the British columns.

At 5 a.m. on December 9, the British awoke to darkness. In silence, the men breakfasted on canned bacon and hot tea, topped by a "fighting dram" of rum. The Muslims among them, forbidden alcohol, sucked on oranges. To the east, the fortified camp at Nibeiwa was gently astir. At 7:15 a.m., the first British tanks moved out. Incongruously, as they advanced some of the men could smell the tantalizing fragrance of hot coffee and rolls: the Italians were preparing breakfast.

It was never to be eaten. Rank upon rank of tanks came rumbling in. Riding on their flanks were Bren gun carriers, their machine guns uptilted in high-angle fire against the startled sentries on the ramparts. Then came a sound unfamiliar to Italian ears: the wild skirling of bagpipes sounding

Starting at Fort Capuzzo, Italian forces (red arrows) advanced eastward 60 miles to Sidi Barrani in Egypt, where they built seven fortified camps (red circles). The British (black arrows) withdrew to Mersa Matruh. They launched a counteroffensive three months later, moving along the coast and through an undefended gap that lay between Nibeiwa and Rabia, steadily pushing the Italians back. Most of the remaining Italian forces surrendered at Beda Fomm, nearly 300 miles inside Libya.

the charge as the Cameron Highlanders sprinted in, the rising sun shimmering from the steel of their bayonets. In the confusion, Italian cavalry horses took fright and stampeded screaming through the drifting smoke.

The Italians stood no chance. Twenty of their tanks were parked outside the camp perimeter. The Matildas shot them into smoking scrap metal and churned on. The defenders fought back with machine guns and grenades; many died bloodily beneath the Matildas' tracks. The tanks forged on, as one man would later recall, "like iron rods probing a wasp's nest."

Other men were to retain other memories: the stench from bursting creosote barrels; Italian officers, swathed in heavy blue cavalry cloaks, trying to rally their men; a litter of uneaten food and unused ammunition scattered among the tents. To Second-Lieutenant Roy Farran, the pell-mell speed of the attack was akin to "a gold rush on the Klondike." Private Jimmy Mearns of the 2nd Camerons fired as in a dream at an African manning a machine gun; standing over the fallen black soldier as the blood pulsed from a hole in his throat, Mearns felt the shock of taking his first life and retched helplessly.

On both sides there was savage determination. Nibeiwa's commander, General Pietro Maletti, sprang from his tent, firing a machine gun; then he fell, still firing, shot through the lung. Lieutenant James Muir, medic for the 1st Argyll and Sutherland Highlanders, his shoulder and pelvis smashed to pulp, lay on a stretcher under shell- and machine-gun fire, advising the stretcher bearers on how to treat the wounded.

By 9 a.m. the fighting was over. The first of the Italian outposts had fallen in only three hours. Against all expecta-

tions, the attack had yielded 2,000 prisoners. As the battle moved on toward Tummar East and Tummar West, two other enemy camps 10 miles north of Nibeiwa, a sense of euphoria seized the British. It was as if, like gamblers hitting a winning streak, they could not fail now. One captain whose truck had broken down was determined not to abandon it; he had himself towed into battle backward, his soldier-servant sitting impertubably beside him. A section of the 1st Royal Fusiliers advanced on Tummar West kicking a soccer ball, until an Italian bullet burst it between their feet. Alongside them, cheering frenziedly, raced the New Zealand drivers of their troop carriers—men allotted no part in the battle plan, yet loath to miss a fight.

There were many bizarre moments. Lieut. Colonel Eustace Arderne of the 1st Durham Light Infantry, advancing with his men on the Italians' camp at Maktila, prepared to attack. But after only two bursts from Arderne's machine gunners, one of his officers shouted: "There's a white flag, sir!" "Nonsense!" Arderne snapped. But it was true. Inside the fort, a brigadier and his 500 men stood rigidly at attention. "Monsieur," the brigadier greeted Arderne in diplomatic French. "Nous avons tiré la dernière cartouche." ("Sir, we have fired our last cartridge.") Beside him, as he spoke, was a heaping pile of unspent ammunition.

The sweep to Sidi Barrani took two days, at one point through a sandstorm so blinding that the Argylls mistakenly fought a brisk skirmish with the Camerons. The town was quickly taken, and again it was much the same story as before—the British had achieved total surprise. So headlong was the Italian rout that as the first Matildas entered the gutted streets, still smoking from the shells of the prearranged British naval bombardment, a hospitalized appendi-

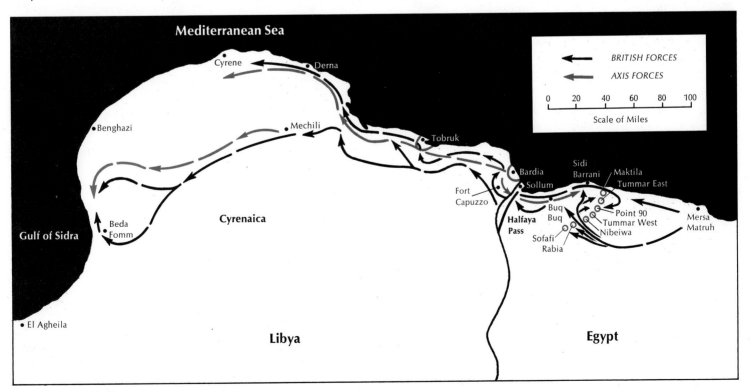

citis victim, already cut open, was found abandoned on the operating table.

By December 12, three days after the attack began, 39,000 Italians had surrendered or been captured. The British had expected 3,000 at most, and were acutely embarrassed. One tank commander radioed: "I am stopped in the middle of 200—no, 500—men with their hands up. For heaven's sake, send up the bloody infantry." A battalion commander estimated his prisoners at "five acres of officers, 200 acres of other ranks." Unending lines of Italians in dusty green uniforms choked the road to Mersa Matruh. There, the officers in charge, astonished at the size of the prisoner bag, furnished the arrivals with wood and barbed wire and set them to building their own stockade.

A disenchantment with Fascism and the Duce was quickly apparent. At Nibeiwa, captured Italian engineers, seeing British gunners set to work on a new forward gun emplacement, promptly brought picks and shovels and pitched in to help. Other prisoners showed some of their captors how to cook spaghetti and tomato sauce. One Pittsburgh-born Italian summed up the mood of many of his comrades: "If I could get my hands on that goddamned bastard Mussolini, I'd kill him right now."

In Cairo, Wavell was fast realizing that his "five-day raid" had acquired the irresistible momentum of a major campaign. Late on December 11, a message from the field reported: "We have arrived at the second B in Buq Buq"— where the British offensive had originally been supposed to stop. O'Connor's men kept going.

By December 16, a week after the fighting had begun, they had taken Sollum and Halfaya Pass and also moved into Libya to take Fort Capuzzo, Sidi Omar and other strong

points that the Italians had set up on the escarpment near their stronghold at Bardia.

As fast as Wavell's planning staff could produce studies on the next phase of the combat, O'Connor, whose shyness hid a terrier-like tenacity of purpose, rendered them out of date. Conducting Admiral Cunningham on a tour of the war room at Cairo headquarters, Wavell confessed with characteristic candor: "You know, I never thought it would ever go like this."

Churchill was jubilant. Not long before he had been voicing the suspicion that Wavell might be "playing small." Now he cheered on his commander in the Middle East with the text of Matthew 7:7—"Ask, and it shall be given you; seek, and ye shall find; knock, and it shall be opened unto you." But the amity between the two men was to be short-lived. Even as O'Connor's main force, now far beyond Buq

Buq, swept on to besiege Bardia, one battalion had to be left behind on the battlefield. Its task, which was ordered by Churchill, was to salvage Italian guns and vehicles—to be sent to the Greeks when they finally accepted the offer of British aid.

The relationship between Graziani and Mussolini was also worsening. In a "man-to-man" telegram the marshal accused Mussolini of never having listened to him and of pushing him into a futile adventure. Graziani also called for massive German air support, protesting that "one cannot break steel armor with fingernails alone." Mussolini, as always when military disasters threatened, blamed his fighting men. "Five generals are prisoners and one is dead," he said to his son-in-law, Foreign Minister Count Galeazzo Ciano. "This is the percentage of Italians who have military characteristics and those who have none."

For the immediate future, the Duce was pinning his faith on a fighting soldier of the line: Lieut. General Annibale Bergonzoli, commander of Bardia, whose flaming red beard had earned him the nickname "Electric Whiskers." No cardboard general, Bergonzoli was a Spanish Civil War veteran who disdained luxury, ate and drank with his men, and slept in a noncom's simple tent.

"I am sure that 'Electric Whiskers' and his brave soldiers will stand at whatever cost," Mussolini exhorted Bergonzoli. The general's reply was suitably dramatic: "In Bardia we are, and here we stay."

He had good reason to be confident. Bardia perched 350 feet above a circular harbor, had a garrison of 45,000 men and was ringed by a 18-mile belt of defenses. Its capture required tanks, and a shortage of spare parts had temporarily robbed O'Connor of all but 23 Matildas. The brunt of the assault on Bardia would have to be borne by infantry; they would have to secure a bridgehead across a 12-foot-wide antitank ditch, and the minefields beyond it, to provide a safety lane for the lurching Matildas.

Few men were better fitted for the task than the men of the 6th Australian Division, newly sent in from Palestine to replace the 4th Indian Division. On the troop ships that had brought them to the Middle East, the Anzacs—as the Australians and New Zealanders were informally and collectively known—had made their officers' lives a hell, swimming

Burning fuel-dumps still cast a pall of sooty smoke over Tobruk, a key Italian port in Libya, two days after its fall. Australian forces overran the town on the 22nd of January, 1941—some of them making use of captured Italian tanks that they emblazoned with leaping white kangaroos so that their own comrades would not mistake them for the enemy.

ashore half-naked in Ceylon to caper in the streets, raiding Cape Town's breweries for a mammoth jag, kissing every woman in sight. Now these stalwarts thirsted for one thing only: to fight.

On January 2, Air Chief Marshal Longmore's Wellington bombers thundered in over Bardia. Along the landward arc of the defenses, a nonstop rain of bombs gouged at pillboxes and machine-gun nests and set ablaze tanks and supply dumps. All night the RAF kept up the pounding; then, at dawn on January 3, the Australians moved in. Engineers dynamited the antitank ditch to create crossing sites, sliced at the wire surrounding the minefields, then flung grenades to detonate the mines. It was a complicated plan, requiring complicated logistics; 300 pairs of gloves for the wire cutters, flown overnight from Cairo, were doled out only as the men moved up. Behind the wire cutters came waves of Anzacs, boisterously singing "We're off to see the Wizard, the wonderful Wizard of Oz" and clad against the cold in sleeveless leather army jerkins that the terrified Italians took for some sort of armor. By noon the Anzacs had driven a wedge into the defenses 12,000 yards wide and 3,000 yards deep.

Meanwhile, Bardia lay under intensive bombardment by a Royal Navy force that consisted of three battleships, including Admiral Cunningham's flagship, the *Warspite,* and seven destroyers. When the bombardment was over, the gunboats *Ladybird* and *Aphis* and the monitor *Terror,* a heavily armored warship that was used chiefly for coastal action, glided toward the shore. At point-blank range they began to lob shells at the defenses beyond the cliff on which Bardia was situated.

By dawn on January 4, a heavy cloud of black smoke hung over the battered town. Then a whole section of the cliff gave way and slid roaring to the sea, wiping out many of the defenders' gun positions at one stroke.

As the day wore on, Bergonzoli saw that his position was hopeless. The bombing had cut off his water supply and wrecked his food depots. With a handful of troops, he slipped out of Bardia dressed as a private, passing close enough to the British lines to smell their cooking fires.

Bundled against the early-morning chill, Lieut. General Richard O'Connor (left), commanding Great Britain's desert forces, and General Sir Archibald Wavell, Commander-in-Chief, Middle East, confer near Bardia the day before the Italian stronghold fell to their offensive.

Hiding in caves by day and traveling by night, Bergonzoli escaped toward Tobruk, 70 miles west.

At sunset on January 4, the Italian flag was hauled down from Bardia's Government House, and the British had more than 40,000 new prisoners of war.

Tobruk, a major port, was the next target. O'Connor's tanks and trucks swept on like a battle fleet, their sides adorned with proud emblems—the leaping white kangaroos of the 16th Australian Infantry Brigade, the scarlet desert rats of the 7th Armored Division. Captured Italian trucks, emblazoned with such slogans as "Benito's Bus," were also in the ranks, rumbling past freshly posted road signs that read: "If you lika da spaghetti KEEP GOING. Next stop TOBRUK—27 kms."

But even as O'Connor's forces reached Tobruk's perimeter—120 miles beyond their original goal—Wavell, in Cairo, had a new reminder that the campaign was operating on borrowed time. Churchill again urged the Greeks to accept British aid. Metaxas again demurred, but Churchill remained adamant. In a message to London, Wavell questioned the Prime Minister's policy toward Greece; "nothing we can do from here," he said, "is likely to be in time to stop the German advance if really intended."

Churchill's reply was a stinging rebuke. "Nothing must hamper capture of Tobruk but thereafter all operations in Libya are subordinated to aiding Greece," he informed Wavell, adding acidly: "We expect and require prompt and active compliance with our decisions."

Throughout the autumn of 1940, Adolf Hitler's thoughts about the Mediterranean theater of war had been meticulously recorded in the diary of the Chief of the German General Staff, Colonel General Franz Halder. An entry for the 1st of November read: "Führer very much annoyed at Italian maneuvers in Greece . . . not in a mood to send anything to Libya . . . let the Italians do it themselves." And on November 3: "Führer stated that he has written off the Libyan affair."

But Britain's raid on Taranto eight days later, and a warning by Grand Admiral Erich Raeder that the British "had assumed the initiative at all points in the Mediterranean," changed Hitler's mind. Early in December he ordered that a number of German air units be transferred to bases in southern Italy to take part in attacks on British shipping in the Mediterranean.

This decision, put into effect less than a week after the Italian defeat at Bardia, was to alter the course of the desert war. The Luftwaffe's intervention conferred virtual immunity on Axis supply convoys and spelled deadly peril for those of the British.

The results were quick, dramatic and devastating. On January 10, 1941, Lieut. General Hans-Ferdinand Geisler, commander of the Luftwaffe's X Air Corps, was barely settled in his headquarters at the splendid Hotel San Domenico in Taormina, Sicily, when word came of the sighting of a British convoy with a large escort of warships. They were en route eastward from Gibraltar with troops and planes for the island of Malta, Britain's vital air and sea base in the mid-Mediterranean.

Among the warships escorting the convoy was the 23,000-ton Illustrious, whose torpedo bombers had struck at Taranto. One of Britain's newest carriers, she boasted an armor-plated flight deck. She was a terrible threat to Italy's supply convoys, and Geisler received a succinct message from Berlin: "Illustrious muss sinken."

At 12:28 p.m. Captain Denis Boyd, on the bridge of the Illustrious 100 miles west of Malta, was anxiously scanning the sky. Minutes earlier, a flight of his Fulmar fighters had zipped off toward Sicily, pursuing two Italian Savoia torpedo bombers. On the flight deck, another group of Fulmars, engines turning over, were due to take off in seven minutes. Boyd briefly debated whether to get them airborne sooner, then decided against it.

In those seven short minutes the fate of Britain's Mediterranean fleet swung like an overweighted pendulum. Boring toward the convoy at 12,000 feet came 30 to 40 Junkers-88 medium bombers and Stuka dive bombers. The Stukas, plummeting in a perfectly coordinated attack, screamed down on the Illustrious. Six 1,000-pound bombs struck the carrier. One sliced through the flight deck and burst in the paint store, sending sheets of flame clawing skyward. Another burst on the No. 2 starboard gun, wrenching it from its mounting and killing the crew. A third struck the lift platform, blasting a plane and its pilot to smithereens. Other bombs burst in the heart of the ship, disintegrating the fire screens and punching the stricken hangar into the shape of a giant arch. A torrent of fire swept through the *Illustrious*.

Boyd now faced the crisis all carrier commanders dreaded: with his flight deck out of service, not one of his planes could either land or take off. Biting down on an empty pipe ("to stop my teeth from chattering with fright," he explained later), Boyd made for Malta at 21 knots with the *Illustrious* belching inky clouds of smoke and listing to starboard. Three times on the way, Axis planes—Savoias, Stukas, then Savoias again—swooped to attack, rekindling the carrier's fires and ripping apart her sick bay and wardroom. But by 10:15 p.m. she had docked at Malta's Parlatorio Wharf, hailed by a band and a sea of waving hands.

Her ordeal was not over. Repeated Stuka attacks greeted the carrier at the wharf, piercing her below the water line and flooding her boiler room. Two weeks later, with the repair scaffolds still swinging at her sides, she slipped out of Malta at dusk and eventually reached Alexandria—still afloat but operationally useless for 11 months.

The bombing of the *Illustrious* signaled the start of an intensified aerial assault on Malta that would last almost two years and make the island one of the most bombed targets in the War. More than 14,000 tons of bombs would fall on the Maltese before the nightmare ended.

By January 20, O'Connor was poised before Tobruk. His men had smashed eight Italian divisions; only about 125,000 poorly armed enemy troops—out of the original North African force of some 250,000—remained. But unless he could decisively break the Italian Army in Libya within a month and put the entire eastern province of Cyrenaica under British control, the Germans were likely to intervene.

Tobruk's more than 30 miles of perimeter defenses were breached in a day and a half. Advancing through a sandstorm that forced some of them to don their gas masks, the Australians wedged explosives beneath the wire entanglements and blasted them to shreds. By sunset on January 21, the first units had pushed on eight miles to Tobruk itself. One Australian who had served in Palestine commented: "The police in Tel Aviv give us a better fight than this." As

they drove for the center of town, a greeting from an Australian airman the Italians had captured set the tone of the day: "Welcome pals! The town's yours."

Derna, 100 miles west of Tobruk, fell eight days later. O'Connor, tense and edgy and racked by stomach trouble, now faced the most critical test of all: Could he catch the Italians before they evacuated Cyrenaica? They were fast retreating along the southward-curving coast road from Derna through Benghazi toward Tripoli. If he moved quickly enough he might be able to cut them off before they could escape. Furious that a strong force of Italian tanks had escaped an attempted British trap at Mechili, a fort inland from Derna, O'Connor gave vent to a rare burst of temper. He stormed at Major-General Sir Michael O'Moore Creagh, commander of the 7th Armored: "You are going to cut the coast road south of Benghazi, and you are going *now*, repeat *now!*" Shortly, the word passed through the ranks: "The code word is Gallop."

At daybreak on February 4, the 7th Armored, now down to 50 cruiser and 80 light tanks, moved out of Mechili across the interior wasteland of Cyrenaica to try to cut off the retreating Italians beyond Benghazi. For some 30 hours, striving to cover 150 miles, men jounced in tanks and trucks over rocky, bone-jarring ground, harried by blinding squalls and vomiting from sheer fatigue. Racing in their wake came O'Connor and Brigadier Eric Dorman-Smith, Wavell's envoy with the Western Desert Force. Alarmed by the spectacle of abandoned broken-down British tanks that marked the way, O'Connor had sudden doubts. "My God," he burst out to Dorman-Smith, "do you think it's going to be all right?"

But at noon on February 5 came the signal that all his men had awaited, from an armored car near the village of Beda Fomm south of Benghazi. The road was cut. Thirty minutes later, trailing a plume of dust, the first trucks of the retreating Italian column loomed on the road from the north. O'Connor had sprung his trap with half an hour to spare.

For a day and a half a battle raged. Time and again the Italian tanks charged en masse, in a desperate attempt to break through; but they had only one wireless set for every 30 tanks, and coordination proved almost impossible. During lulls in the fighting a bizarre note intruded: local Arabs, their camels grazing peacefully nearby, would appear to sell eggs to both sides.

By February 6, with one British brigade down to 15 cruiser tanks, bluff began to count as much as armor. When a noncom complained that his gun barrel was bent all out of shape, his tank commander suggested that he stay put and simply *look* dangerous.

At first light on February 7, O'Connor received word that Marshal Graziani had decamped to Tripoli and that the army he had abandoned was surrendering; it could fight no longer. In their car, O'Connor and Dorman-Smith crossed a battlefield strewn for 15 miles with the debris of war. Every rise was littered with burned-out tanks. Softly shifting sand covered the dead; desert birds circled overhead. "Dick, what does it feel like to win a complete victory?" Dorman-Smith asked. O'Connor replied quietly, "I'll never believe I'm a successful general until I've commanded my forces through a retreat."

All through the day, in the battlefield mess tent and at O'Connor's new headquarters near Beda Fomm, there was a strange sense of anticlimax. Some men wondered whether the fighting was really over. Told that 400 Italians were ready to surrender, Lieut. Colonel John Combe of the 11th Hussars remarked wearily, "Tell them to come back in the morning." Sipping a victory drink, O'Connor apologized politely to one captured Italian general for the makeshift accommodations, commenting that not since 1911, when he had attended a particularly resplendent international gathering in India, had he seen so many Italian generals in one place. Among them was General Bergonzoli. Sheepishly, Bergonzoli pronounced what might have served as the campaign's epitaph: "You were here too soon."

Everywhere were reminders that the Italians had paid a terrible price for Mussolini's North African dream. Second-Lieutenant Roy Farran and his men, detailed to bury an enemy tank crew, found the task beyond them. All four of the Italian crew had been decapitated by a shell while sitting in their action stations; the stench inside the tank was unbearable. Suddenly, in a ghastly parody of combat, the tank rolled downhill, its engine turning over, a dead man's foot still jammed on the accelerator. Appalled, Farran and his men at last approached the tank, laid a trail of gasoline, and set fire to it.

On February 12, Brigadier Dorman-Smith was back in Cairo on an important mission: to persuade his commander in chief to approve O'Connor's request to drive on toward the Libyan capital of Tripoli. But even as he entered Wavell's map room he knew the answer. The desert maps had vanished from Wavell's wall, replaced by maps of Greece.

Wavell swept an arm toward them. "You see, Eric," he said wryly. "You find me busy with my spring campaign." Premier Metaxas of Greece had died suddenly, and his successor, Alexander Koryzis, had finally accepted Churchill's offer of help.

There was another bitter irony for Wavell. In two months O'Connor had advanced 500 miles and taken 130,000 prisoners, some 400 tanks, more than 1,000 guns and the major fortresses of Bardia and Tobruk. But he had defeated the Italians too quickly. Four months later, all of Hitler's resources would have been irrevocably committed to his obsessional attack on Russia, and other military ventures would have been out of the question. Now the seeds of trouble had been sown for the British in Africa.

On Sunday, February 9, Major General Enno von Rintelen, German military attaché in Rome, arrived at Mussolini's 40-room mansion, Villa Torlonia, with news that left the Duce beaming. A panzer division and a light mechanized division were to be dispatched from Germany to serve as a blocking force in Tripolitania, the Libyan province to the west of Cyrenaica.

Germany was now coming to the rescue of the Italians in North Africa.

THE DESERT FOX

Lieut. General Erwin Rommel, sporting a jaunty plaid scarf and a pair of captured British sun goggles, leads his panzer troops through the North African desert.

A LEGENDARY SOLDIER WITH A SIXTH SENSE

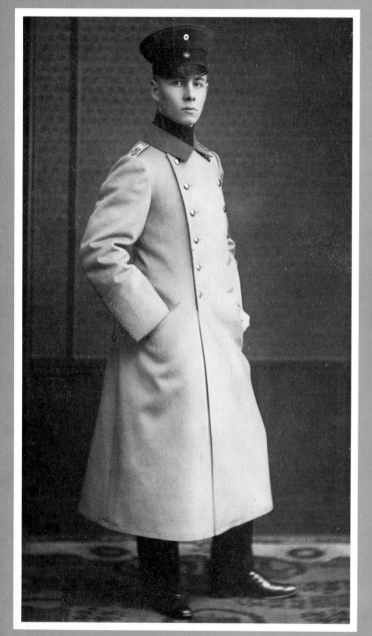

As an instructor of Army recruits in 1912, the youthful Lieutenant Rommel was a sober, serious man who was fascinated by military minutiae.

In January of 1942, as Allied forces in the North African desert struggled to regain ground lost to the Germans, Prime Minister Winston Churchill stood in the House of Commons and paid a singular tribute to one of Britain's most determined foes: "We have a very daring and skillful opponent against us, and, may I say across the havoc of war, a great general."

That general was Erwin Rommel, an aggressive, indefatigable and audacious soldier, whose exploits in North Africa earned him the nickname "Desert Fox" and made him a legend among his enemies. As commander of the Afrika Korps, Rommel applied blitzkrieg tactics to warfare in the desert with a mastery that awed the British. Among the troops opposing him his name came to be synonymous with success—so much so that any British soldier who performed well might be described by his comrades as "doing a Rommel."

Born the son of a schoolmaster in the German village of Heidenheim, Rommel joined the Army at the age of 18 and won high honors for his courage and skill in combat against the French and Italians in World War I. By the time he was 25, senior officers were seeking his advice on battlefield tactics. Two decades later, by then a major general, Rommel drove a panzer division through France in an operation so successful it made him a German national hero.

In the desert, Rommel's pace was as furious as a driving sandstorm. He directed his panzers from the front lines, oblivious to crackling shellfire and the threat of capture, protected by what his soldiers called *Fingerspitzengefühl,* "an intuition in the fingers," a sixth sense. "No admiral ever won a naval battle from a shore base," he said, fond as he was of comparing desert combat to warfare at sea. His split-second ingenuity under fire often violated textbook principles of military tactics and threw his enemy into confusion. He was a master of the unexpected, with a gift for improvisation. Outside of waging war, he had few interests. "He was 100 per cent soldier," recalled a general who served under him. "He was body and soul in the war."

In a portrait made by Hitler's chief photographer, Heinrich Hoffmann, Rommel displays the field marshal's baton awarded by the Führer in September 1942.

Rommel, outfitted in his new German Army uniform, displays a stony countenance in a 1910 photo with his younger brothers, Gerhard and Karl, and his older sister, Helene.

The 24-year-old Lieutenant Rommel manages an air of insouciance during a lull in combat in 1915 in France's Argonne Forest. He had only recently recovered from his first wound.

QUIET MOMENTS ON THE RISE TO FAME

"My Dearest Lu," began the letters Rommel wrote nearly every day to his wife from the far-reaching battlegrounds of his fighting career. Apart from military matters, Rommel's concerns in life were limited to his wife, Lucie Maria Mollin, whom he married in 1916, and Manfred, their son. As a soldier of the old school, Rommel had no taste for the heady revolutionary maneuverings that took place in Germany between the world wars. Although devoted to Hitler, Rommel never joined the Nazi Party. He disliked the Führer's SS troops and in time came to regard most of the Hitlerian entourage with disdain.

In 1937, Rommel published a book on infantry tactics. Hitler read and admired it, took an interest in its author, and assigned Rommel to his personal staff. As the Führer's protégé, Rommel was assured a key role in the war soon to come.

A decorated Rommel poses with his wife, Lucie, in 1917, following his greatest triumph of the First World War—the capture of an Italian mountain and its 9,000 defenders.

During the Second World War, on leave from the campaigns, Rommel visits his wife and son, Manfred, at home in Wiener Neustadt, a town in the mountains to the south of Vienna.

Poring over a battle map, Rommel ponders tactics with his staff officers in northern France in the late spring of 1940. During the pell-mell drive of his 7th Panzer Division through the French countryside to the Atlantic coast, he exposed himself repeatedly to frontline action and narrowly escaped capture.

THE GHOST DIVISION STALKS NORTHERN FRANCE

"What do you want?" Hitler asked Rommel a few months before the German invasion of France in 1940. "Command of a panzer division," Rommel quickly replied.

The Führer's resultant gift—the 7th Panzer Division—played a devastating role in the defeat of France. Rommel crossed the Belgian border on the 10th of May, 1940, and charged steadily ahead for five weeks, his panzers firing on the move, their turrets roving like those of battleships. Called the "Ghost Division" because of its sudden and unexpected appearances, the 7th Panzer surprised barracks full of French soldiers, overran retreating French detachments and terrified unsuspecting civilians. Patting Rommel's arm, a villager asked him if he was English. "No, Madam," he replied. "I am German." "Oh, the barbarians!" she screamed, fleeing home.

The Ghost Division pushed to the English Channel, then swooped west along the coast to capture Cherbourg, covering as much as 150 miles in a day. Rommel's calculated boldness in waging tank warfare had set the stage for his brilliant performance in North Africa the next year.

On a rocky French beach, Rommel plants his comb.

boot symbolically in the waters of the English Channel. "The sight of the sea with the cliffs on either side thrilled and stirred every man of us," he later wrote.

The first soldiers of the Afrika Korps to arrive from Germany stand at parade rest on a street in Tripoli.

FROM VICTORY IN FRANCE
TO PALM-STUDDED SANDS

"It's one way of getting my rheumatism treatment," Rommel wrote his wife before leaving for arid Libya in February 1941. It was his coded message to her that his two-year desert campaign was beginning.

In his role as commander of the Afrika Korps, Rommel tended to be impatient and abrupt with his senior officers, but kind and understanding with the younger soldiers, who bore the brunt of combat. He shared their hardships and earned their respect. In his dashes about the front he ran the same risks his troops did. Tough-

ened by mountaineering and skiing in his youth, he subsisted on snatches of sleep and the basic rations—canned meat and black bread—of common soldiers. He appeared impervious to the harsh desert life.

Almost immediately after he had arrived in Africa, Rommel began to shove the British eastward through the sands toward the gates of Alexandria. On June 21, 1942, he led his men to their most spectacular victory when the British fortress of Tobruk fell to his panzers. Later that same year, however, hamstrung by supply shortages and the German High Command's disinterest in the desert war, Rommel's forces began their slow slide to ultimate defeat.

Rommel rides in a procession in Tripoli beside

General Italo Gariboldi, the Italian commander in North Africa. Later, the Desert Fox would say of many of the Italians: "Certainly they are no good at war."

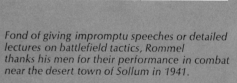

Fond of giving impromptu speeches or detailed lectures on battlefield tactics, Rommel thanks his men for their performance in combat near the desert town of Sollum in 1941.

The ever-present binoculars dangling from his neck, Rommel strains to help his officers free his staff car from the desert sand. He was not above dirtying his hands alongside his men.

Although he possessed no pilot's license, Rommel was an eager and confident amateur aviator who often took to the air for desert reconnaissance missions.

In field headquarters set up at the site of an old well in May 1941, Rommel uses a telephone to direct the siege of Tobruk on the Libyan coast. Tobruk's stout

defenses would frustrate the Desert Fox for an entire year, until, on June 21, 1942, the town finally fell to him after only a single day of concentrated attack.

HELL'S OWN BATTLEGROUND

In a howling desert wind, an Italian soldier ventures forth from a command post near Sidi Barrani. The horn on the stick at left was meant to be a good-luck charm.

THE WESTERN DESERT: A SECOND FOE

Late in April 1941, on the edge of the Western Desert, infantrymen of Lieut. General Erwin Rommel's Afrika Korps captured a desolate ridge south of Tobruk. Shortly thereafter a British artillery barrage pinned them down. In their attempt to dig in, the Germans found they could not make even a dent in the desert's underlying limestone layer. All day they lay motionless beneath a scorching sun as they tried not to draw more British fire. Swarms of black flies viciously attacked them. Darkness only increased their misery as the temperature plunged and left them shivering throughout the night. The following day the sky blackened and a sandstorm raged over them.

For soldiers in the desert war these were not unusual experiences. The Western Desert, where much of the fighting occurred, formed a rectangle 500 miles long and 150 miles wide. Although fringed by a fertile coastline, its inner reaches were a wasteland devoid of almost all life except for a few Bedouin nomads and such drought-adapted species as poisonous scorpions and vipers, and prickly camel's-thorn. Water could be obtained only from widely scattered cisterns or by drilling deep into the ground. Every item a soldier needed or wanted had to be brought in by truck.

The desert's torments were many. Temperatures fluctuated as much as 60 degrees in a single day. Sand that was as fine as talcum powder routinely clogged rifle breeches and inflamed eyes, and when driven by the hot southerly wind, it filled nostrils, permeated cracks in vehicles and tents, buried food and equipment, and reduced visibility to a few yards. On clear days mirages played tricks with vision, and concealment in so bleak and featureless a land became a conjurer's art.

And yet the desert was uniquely suited to the waging of war. The open spaces and the lack of natural obstacles made it ideal tank country. So did the absence of permanent human settlements. As Fred Majdalany, chronicler of the British Eighth Army's exploits, put it: "There was absolutely no one and nothing to damage except the men and equipment of the opposing army."

Afrika Korps troops advancing into the desert wear tight-fitting goggles to protect their eyes from flying sand churned up by wind and vehicles.

Partially concealed behind a hastily improvised rock shelter, a German forward observer peers through a periscopic instrument used to adjust artillery fire.

A STINGING MENACE BORNE BY THE WIND

The British called it *khamsin,* Arabic for the hot wind that blows out of the Sahara; the Germans used another Arabic word for it, *ghibli.* Most frequent in spring, the wind raised temperatures by as much as 35°F. in a couple of hours and sapped friend and foe alike. Bedouin tribal law permitted a man to kill his wife after five days of it.

As the wind roared in, it swept up sand and sent grains billowing across hundreds of square miles. Visibility dropped to zero, and soldiers gasped for air through makeshift sand masks while gusts of hurricane force overturned trucks and whisked telephone poles from the ground. Whirling particles of sand created electrical disturbances that drove compasses crazy. On the Gazala line south of Tobruk, in May 1942, such storm-generated electricity during a *khamsin* was blamed for an explosion that destroyed an ammunition dump.

Goggles and a mask were issued to early Afrika Korps troops for protection against sandstorms. Later in the war, the helmet was replaced by a cloth cap.

A swirling sandstorm advances on trucks and men southeast of El Alamein in September 1942. Such desert storms blotted out the sun, raised the temperature

and sometimes stopped battlefield movements for days, pinning down troops, halting tanks and grounding planes. Their winds raged up to 90 miles an hour.

MAKING DO IN A LAND OF EXTREMES

The most precious item in the desert war was water. When the Afrika Korps attacked the Gazala line, 350 miles west of El Alamein, in the summer of 1942, it carried with it only a four-day supply: three quarts for each man per day, four quarts for each truck and eight quarts for every tank. If the water ran out before the battle was over, the soldiers would have to survive on whatever they could capture or find—or die of thirst. Fortunately for the Germans, the battle soon ended—in victory.

The lack of water in the outlying desert areas posed a major challenge to both armies. Not a drop could be wasted. Dirty water was hoarded and filtered through cloth into radiators. Obtaining fresh supplies was a matter of critical importance. The British copied a sturdy German water can—theirs leaked—and called it the jerry can after the enemy, known as "Jerry" to two generations of British soldiers. Loaded with these four-and-one-half-gallon receptacles, fleets of trucks crisscrossed the desert to bring water to thirsty outposts.

Water that was distilled from the salty Mediterranean and chemically treated left much to be desired. The British boiled it for tea, but found that when they added milk it curdled and went to the bottoms of their cups in big lumps.

Pausing on the march to Benghazi in spring 1941, German soldiers strip to the skin for a rare bath at a desert cistern. Such reservoirs caught and held rain water, but since rains were infrequent, the cisterns were often empty and the armies used them as storage tanks.

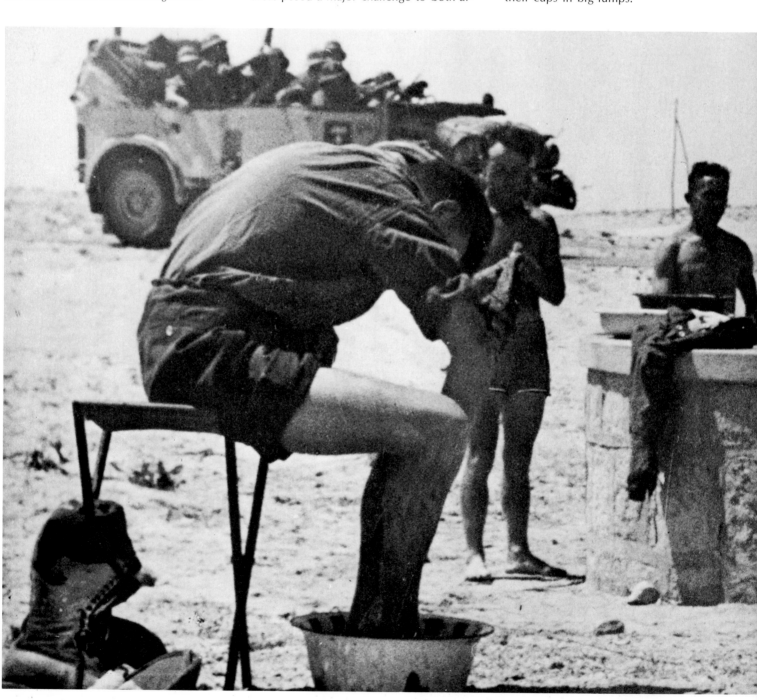

Lacking water, a German soldier scrubs his uniform with sand to rid it of salt, oil and grime. The British often used gasoline as well as sand to clean their clothes and save water. Without such makeshift methods, clothes would become stiff from dirt and salty sweat.

Swathed in head nets to protect their eyes, nostrils and mouths from swarms of flies, German troops tackle another desert hazard: dust and grit in their weapons.

Gauze dressings like those on the legs of the two men to the right were essential to keep sand away from even the smallest sores, which otherwise would not heal.

A German desert warrior fries eggs on the sun-heated hull of a tank. Cooking in this way was more a stunt than normal practice, but metal that was exposed to direct sunshine was sometimes hot enough to inflict serious burns on bare skin if tankers or others accidentally touched it.

Huddled in a slit trench and bundled up against the desert's chill night air, a British soldier sleeps with his gear close at hand. Such trenches not only provided protection from anything short of a direct hit by bomb or shell, but also offered their occupants a modicum of warmth.

2

It was a spectacle designed to awe Tripoli's Italian population and impress any British spies who might be watching. Across the city's main piazza rumbled a seemingly endless column of formidable 25-ton Panzer III and Panzer IV tanks, painted in the newly fashionable desert-camouflage shade of sand yellow. The tank commanders, wearing tropical uniforms much the same color as their vehicles, stood at attention in their turrets, as impassive as the death's-head badges adorning their lapels. Taking the salute on the reviewing stand was the man who had ordered this parade as a display of armored power, a short and muscular German lieutenant general with clear blue eyes: Erwin Rommel, commander of the newly formed Afrika Korps.

Standing near Rommel a young aide, Lieutenant Heinz-Werner Schmidt, watched the continuous line of tanks clattering through the square and out a side street with growing amazement. "I began to wonder at the extraordinary number of panzers passing by," he later recalled. After some 15 minutes, when he noticed a Panzer IV with a distinctive faulty track and realized he had seen it earlier in the procession, Schmidt chuckled. In a speech to German officers the previous evening, Rommel had stressed the importance of deceiving the enemy about the weakness of the Afrika Korps, which was still awaiting the arrival of most of its forces from Europe. Now, Schmidt realized, his chief was running the tanks around a few blocks to stretch a panzer regiment to the proportions of an armored corps.

The date was March 12, 1941. Rommel, who had arrived in North Africa only four weeks earlier, was already demonstrating his mastery of audacity and deception, qualities that were to play as great a part as real armored power in the next phase of the desert war. They were qualities the British had yet to master or learn to cope with. Even Rommel's identity had been successfully hidden from the British until the past few days. Before March 8, General Wavell's staff could only refer to the new German commander as "General X." Now, from their intelligence, they knew it was Rommel, and the knowledge caused some uneasiness in Cairo.

Rommel had the reputation of being a fighting general with an intuitive sense of his enemy's weakness, dedicated to the twin concepts of speed and surprise. His maxim was *Sturm, Swung, Wucht:* attack, impetus, weight. As commander of the 7th Panzer Division—the "Ghost Division"—

ROMMEL'S STUNNING BLOW

in May 1940, Rommel had time and again outsmarted the British retreating across France, repeatedly turning up in strength where least expected.

A 49-year-old self-made man from a family without money or influence, Rommel was proud and strong-willed and did not always conceal his contempt for some of the German Army's top brass. He considered Field Marshal Walther von Brauchitsch, the Army's commander in chief, to be an overly sensitive, withdrawn patrician. Rommel viewed the Army Chief of Staff, the acerbic and ambitious Colonel General Franz Halder, as an ineffectual deskbound soldier. Rommel himself was a field man, who enjoyed action and little else. He did not smoke and drank very little. He wrote almost every day to his wife, Lucie, but apart from his family his only pleasure in life seems to have been fighting—and winning. Joyful as a schoolboy when victorious, he became angry and petulant whenever he lost.

This galloping exponent of the open-ended offense had been sent to North Africa to fulfill an assignment that was clearly limited. The Italians were holed up in Tripoli, expecting the British to move along the coast and attack the port city at any moment. Many had their bags packed, hoping to be ordered aboard evacuation ships for a one-way voyage to Italy. Although Hitler considered North Africa a low-priority theater, he nonetheless felt that Germany should not let its Axis partner be pushed out of the region. He had agreed to send help. But Brauchitsch had made clear to Rommel when briefing him that his task was strictly defensive; for the moment Germany would not be able to send sufficient forces to drive the British from Cyrenaica, Libya's eastern province.

One of the two divisions allotted to Rommel, the 5th Light, began its transfer to North Africa in mid-February, planning to complete it by mid-April. More formidable than its name, the 5th Light Division included the 5th Panzer Regiment, which had 80 medium tanks (Panzer IIIs and IVs) and 70 light tanks. By the end of May, Rommel was told, he would receive a full-fledged panzer division, the 15th. What was left of the Italian motorized forces in North Africa—chiefly the Ariete armored division with 60 obsolete tanks—would also be under Rommel's command. But for the sake of diplomacy, the German was to serve under 62-year-old General Italo Gariboldi, who had succeeded the defeated Marshal Graziani as the Italian commander in North Africa.

When Rommel arrived in Tripoli on February 12, he fully expected the British to resume their westward thrust soon. He knew that if they attacked immediately, before his reinforcements arrived, there was little chance of stopping them. Lacking the men and equipment for a strong defense, he put his faith in a strong show of defense. "It was my belief that if the British could detect no opposition they would probably continue their advance," he wrote later, "but that if they saw they were going to have to fight another battle they would first wait to build up supplies. With the time thus gained I hoped to build up our own strength until we were eventually strong enough to withstand the enemy attack."

Within a few hours of arriving in Tripoli by plane he was back in the air for a flying reconnaissance of the desert east of the city. He decided to establish a forward defensive position in the area of Sirte, a village on the coastal road about halfway between Tripoli and the place where the British had finally halted their advance, El Agheila. General Gariboldi was reluctant to risk his few remaining troops by moving them 250 miles in the direction of the enemy, but Rommel insisted. "I had already decided, in view of the tenseness of the situation and the sluggishness of the Italian command," he said, "to take the command at the front into my own hands as soon as possible."

The next day two Italian infantry divisions and the Ariete Division were put on the road to Sirte. On February 14 the first German troops—one reconnaissance and one antitank battalion—arrived at Tripoli, and left for Sirte the next morning. Meanwhile, "to enable us to appear as strong as possible and to induce the maximum caution in the British," Rommel resorted to a ruse. He had a workshop make dummy tanks of wood and canvas mounted on Volkswagen chassis. By February 17, Rommel was sufficiently happy with his hastily assembled little army, half substance and half shadow, to write to his wife, Lucie: "Everything's splendid with me. . . . As far as I am concerned they can come now."

But the British did not come. They were going to Greece instead. The expedition to Greece, launched on March 4, stripped British defenses in eastern Libya to the bone. Cyrenaica was now "a passive battle zone" policed by the

THE DESERT FOX AS CAMERA BUFF

Among the many talents that Erwin Rommel employed in North Africa was his skill at photography, a peacetime hobby. Just hours after arriving in Libya he flew off in his Heinkel-111, camera in hand, to "get to know the country" he was to defend. Rommel thus opened the African chapter of a wartime scrapbook that ranged in subject matter from aerial panoramas to destroyed British tanks. Over the months in the desert Rommel took thousands of photographs. Besides being mementos of his campaigns, they were intended to illustrate a postwar book he planned—and was fated never to write. But in amassing his visual record, Rommel carefully avoided one subject. As he explained to his son: "I don't photograph my own retreat."

With his Leica, Rommel snaps one of his own weapons, a camouflaged 150mm gun.

On his first reconnaissance flight over the Libyan desert, Rommel shot this photograph of an Italian antitank ditch east of Tripoli.

One of the general's pictures records the escarpment that separates Tripoli's coastal plain from the Libyan plateau farther inland.

"minimum possible force." In theory, this consisted of the 9th Australian Division and the 2nd Armored Division. But both had been cannibalized for the campaign in Greece. What was left amounted to little more than an ill-trained, badly equipped infantry division and a weak, inexperienced armored brigade with tanks that kept breaking down under desert conditions. The western flank of Britain's Middle East command was thus dangerously vulnerable.

Moreover, the one man whose battle intuition might have been a match for Rommel's, Lieut. General Richard O'Connor—badly in need of a rest after his victorious campaign against the Italians—had been promoted to command of British troops in Egypt. At February's end, he was replaced as commander in Cyrenaica by Lieut. General Philip Neame, a soldier known for his bravery, but an engineer unversed in desert warfare.

As Wavell later was to admit, he had miscalculated fatally in making arrangements for Cyrenaica's defense. Not until mid-March—"when it was rather too late"—did he make a personal reconnaissance of the Benghazi area and the forward British positions. With dismay he discovered that he had "an entirely erroneous idea" of the escarpment south of Benghazi. He had thought that it was a barrier to tanks that could be scaled in only a few easily defended places. "When I actually went out and saw the escarpment, I realized that it could be ascended almost anywhere and was no protection." He found Neame's tactical dispositions "just crazy" and ordered some redeployment immediately. "But the really alarming feature," he recalled, "was the state of the cruiser tanks of the 2nd Armored Division, which were the core of the whole force." Of 52 tanks, half were in the workshop and more were breaking down every day.

Wavell instructed Neame that if his frontline troops at El Agheila were attacked they should fall back to Benghazi, fighting delaying actions along the way. If necessary, Neame was to yield Benghazi itself and save his armor by pulling it up onto the escarpment east of Benghazi. "I came back anxious and depressed from this visit," Wavell said, "but there was nothing much I could do about it. The movement to Greece was in full swing and I had nothing left in the bag."

Still, Wavell did not think Rommel would be capable of attacking before May. Neither did the German High Command. On March 19, the day after Wavell returned to Cairo from his visit to the front, Rommel flew to Berlin. He had become aware of the "momentary British weakness" and believed it should be "exploited, with the utmost energy, in order to gain the initiative once and for all for ourselves." He asked permission to attack the British immediately. Brauchitsch's answer was a flat no.

The German High Command, Brauchitsch told Rommel, still planned no decisive strike in North Africa, and he could expect no reinforcements beyond the ones already promised. (Unknown to Rommel, there were prior demands on available German forces. Hitler was about to send troops to aid Mussolini against Greece and was secretly planning an invasion of the Soviet Union.) Perhaps at the end of May, after the Afrika Korps had been strengthened by the arrival of the 15th Panzer Division, Rommel might launch a limited attack against British forward positions, perhaps advancing as far as Agedabia (map, page 67), Brauchitsch said. Later he might be allowed to retake Benghazi. But there was to be no general offensive. Rommel pointed out "that we could not just take Benghazi, but would have to occupy the whole of Cyrenaica, as the Benghazi area could not be held by itself." Brauchitsch was adamant: Rommel was to do nothing before the end of May. Rommel listened to his orders and then returned to North Africa to disobey them.

Before leaving for Berlin, Rommel had instructed that part of the 5th Light Division that had already arrived in North Africa—chiefly, the 5th Panzer Regiment—to prepare to attack El Agheila on March 24. On his return he ordered that the attack should proceed. His rationale for defying the High Command's cautious directive was that British patrols from El Agheila had been harassing supply columns bound for a German-Italian outpost at Marada, 90 miles to the south. To maintain this outpost, he had to throw the British out of El Agheila.

El Agheila was not strongly defended, and the British soldiers there shared Wavell's feeling that they were not immediately threatened by the enemy. But, at dawn on March 24, Rommel launched his attack. Deployed across a 1,000-yard front, the tanks and armored cars of Major Irmfried von Wechmar's 3rd Reconnaissance Battalion bored toward El Agheila. Behind them groaned trucks whose drivers were doing their best to obey Rommel's order: "Rear vehicles to raise dust—nothing but dust." For the first time Rommel's tactic of deception was put to a test in the desert. Many of Wechmar's "tanks" were incapable of firing a shot; they were the Volkswagen-mounted dummies, now known as "the Cardboard Division." But their outlines in the swirling dust suggested a formidable fighting force. The British garrison of El Agheila swiftly withdrew, falling back on Mersa Brega, 30 miles to the northeast.

Learning of the German advance to El Agheila and hearing of no British counterattack, Churchill cabled Wavell on March 26: "I presume you are only waiting for the tortoise to stick his head out far enough before chopping it off." In a long, rambling reply Wavell detailed the travails besetting his forces in Libya, weakened as they had been by the siphoning off of troops to Greece, and explained that he had no reinforcements to send Neame. In any case he was convinced the Germans would not be launching a major offensive soon. On March 30, Wavell wired Neame not to be too concerned about the enemy; "I do not believe he can make any big effort for at least another month." The next day Rommel struck at Mersa Brega.

He had paused at El Agheila for a week, but he feared that if he sat there until his panzer division arrived in May the British would be able to fortify a defile that made Mersa Brega a natural strong point. The 5th Panzer Regiment, which was advancing along the coastal road, provided the main German thrust. British resistance at the defile was determined, and by the end of the afternoon the attack had ground to a halt. But late in the evening Rommel sent a machine-gun battalion through some high, rolling sand hills to the north of the road. They struck the defenders' flank and dislodged them from the defile. The British hurriedly abandoned Mersa Brega as the Afrika Korps charged through the town of shell-shattered white houses chanting

their battle cry, "Heia Safari!"—Bantu for "Drive onward!"

The next morning Rommel learned from the Luftwaffe that the British were still withdrawing to the north rather than preparing defensive positions for another stand. The gates of Cyrenaica seemed wide open. To Rommel, in spite of his instructions not to undertake a major engagement until the end of May, "it was a chance I could not resist."

He ordered the 5th Light Division to move on Agedabia. On April 2, after a short battle, Agedabia and the nearby port of Zuetina were captured. Gariboldi now tried to restrain Rommel, insisting that any further move would be in direct violation of orders. The German ignored him. "I decided to stay on the heels of the retreating enemy," Rommel said, "and make a bid to seize the whole of Cyrenaica at one stroke."

Rommel divided his forces, sending one group north along the coastal road toward Benghazi, another east toward Maaten el Grara and Ben Gania, and a third up a central route to Antelat and Msus (map, page 67). He did not have a rigid plan for his ad hoc campaign but probed the enemy here and there and pushed on as the British fell back. Soon Neame's forces were in general retreat.

At Rommel's advance headquarters near Agedabia runners scurried in and out with news of the advances as Major Georg Ehlert, the operations officer, busily scrawled the movements of German columns and the enemy on his map. Rommel himself spent much of his time in the air or on the road, checking on his forces and flogging them on. One commander, whose column was temporarily halted, was startled when a message was tossed from the cockpit of Rommel's Fieseler Storch spotter plane: "Unless you get going at once I shall come down. Rommel."

Rommel's desire for speed caused him to take great risks. On April 3 the 5th Light Division reported that most of its vehicles were extremely low on gasoline and needed a four-

day break to replenish. Instead Rommel ordered all the trucks to be unloaded and sent them back empty to the divisional depot, instructing the drivers to return within 24 hours with sufficient fuel, food and ammunition to see the campaign through. It was a dangerous gamble—24 hours when the division's men were stranded in the desert, powerless to move if attacked. But it meant that the 5th Light Division was out of action for only one day rather than four.

That day Gariboldi—by now almost apoplectic about Rommel's risk taking and contravention of orders—challenged the German once more. "He wanted me to discontinue all action and undertake no further moves without his express authority," Rommel recalled. "I had no intention of allowing good opportunities to slip by unused. The conversation became somewhat heated."

That night the Germans occupied Benghazi, which had been evacuated by the British. In a letter to his wife, Rommel's boyish ecstasy was mixed with some doubts about the reaction of his superiors: "Dearest Lu, We've been attacking since the 31st with dazzling success. There'll be consternation among our masters in Tripoli and Rome, perhaps in Berlin too. I took the risk against all orders and instructions because the opportunity seemed favorable. No doubt it will all be pronounced good later. . . . The British are falling over each other to get away. . . . You will understand that I can't sleep for happiness."

Rommel was not overstating the British reaction. The general's rapid and unpredictable movements were producing exactly the effects he desired in Neame's command: confusion and panic. The Axis breakthrough at Mersa Brega had touched off a week-long, 500-mile British retreat. With gallows humor, some British soldiers later dubbed their hurried withdrawal "The Tobruk Derby" or "The Benghazi Handicap." More typical perhaps was the reaction of Roy Farran, a second lieutenant, who described that week as seven of the most inglorious days in the British Army's history. Lacking instructions to stand and fight, the British fell back in disorder—packed ignominiously 30 to a truck, nerves at breaking point from lack of sleep, faces thick with yellow dust that made them look like jaundice victims.

The traditional British qualities of a cool head and a stiff upper lip suddenly seemed to be in short supply. At Antelat,

a panicky corporal screaming "Mass retreat! The Jerries are coming!" was silenced only when Lieut. Colonel Crichton Mitchell threatened to shoot him. In Msus, one captain, told that an enemy column was approaching, blew up an entire divisional fuel dump to keep it from falling into Axis hands—and then recognized, too late, that the "enemy" was a patrol of the British Long Range Desert Group.

Neame, from his headquarters in Barce, 50 miles northeast of Benghazi, vainly tried to restore order with a series of telegrams to his subordinate commanders, but he made no attempt to visit the front. On April 2, Wavell went to Barce to assess the crisis. "I soon realised that Neame had lost control," he said later. He sent for O'Connor to come out and take over the command. On April 3, O'Connor arrived and diffidently suggested that Neame should keep the command while O'Connor acted as Neame's advisor, because "changing horses in midstream would not really help matters." Tact was not O'Connor's sole motive for demurring. He wrote later: "I cannot pretend that I was happy at the thought of taking over command in the middle of a battle which was already lost."

O'Connor's presence was not enough to alter the course of events. Rommel had developed his *Swung*—impetus—and was relentlessly maintaining it. "It was becoming increasingly clear that the enemy believed us to be far stronger than we actually were," Rommel said, "a belief that it was essential to maintain, by keeping up the appearance of a large-scale offensive." He let no opportunity pass. As the British 2nd Armored Division, losing numerous tanks in small actions and breakdowns along the way, fell back on Mechili, Rommel made that tiny desert fort the new focus of his multipronged advance. Three German columns churned toward Mechili on converging courses: the main body of the 5th Light Division and the Ariete Division from Ben Gania and Tengeder, the 5th Panzer Regiment reinforced by 40 Italian tanks through Msus, and the 3rd Reconnaissance Battalion from Benghazi via Charruba.

A fourth Axis group advanced along the coastal road toward Derna, to which the 9th Australian Division had retreated in hopes of making a strong stand there along a wadi, or dry stream bed. By April 6 the enemy forces gathering to the south around Mechili and the Axis column advancing along the coast road posed too great a threat to the 9th Australian Division, and forced a hasty withdrawal from Derna. It was so hasty, in fact, that only the rumble of departing transport alerted Lieut. Colonel E. O. Martin's Northumberland Fusiliers, who were also in Derna, to the bitter truth that they were being left behind. They hurriedly packed up and joined the retreat to the east.

That evening Neame and O'Connor, having lost touch completely with the 2nd Armored Division and realizing that their personal situation was perilous, decided it was time to withdraw from their headquarters. The two generals were among the very last to leave. In Neame's staff car they headed for Tmimi, some 100 miles to the east. During the night they took a wrong turn and ended up on the road for Derna. At about 3 a.m., Neame, who had been sleeping in the back seat, awoke to find they were in the middle of a halted convoy on the outskirts of Derna. From the darkness came shouts in a foreign language, and Neame's driver volunteered: "I expect it's some of them Cypriot drivers, Sir." Seconds later the generals were staring into the leveled barrels of German submachine guns. They would spend the next three years as prisoners of war in northern Italy.

In the immense, almost trackless desert arena, confusion did not beset the British alone. Rommel's leading units soon had outdistanced his command radio at Agedabia, and he spent hours every day in his Storch aircraft trying to find them and coordinate their movements. Frequent sandstorms threw the German columns off course and temporarily grounded Rommel's plane and other aircraft that could have guided them. Colonel Herbert Olbrich's 5th Panzer Regiment advancing from Msus was lost for more than a day. Frantically searching for it, Rommel himself came close to making a premature exit from the war. Seeing what he thought was Olbrich's column, he had his pilot circle while troops below spread out a large cloth landing cross on a

smooth patch of ground. Just before the aircraft touched down, Rommel saw by their helmets that the soldiers were British. The plane banked into a climb in a shower of machine-gun fire, but was hit only once, in the tail.

In spite of straying forces and a worsening shortage of gasoline, by April 7 the Germans and Italians had surrounded Mechili. Trapped in the ring were what remained of the 2nd Armored Division, the 3rd Indian Motorized Brigade and a handful of other British units that had failed to make their getaways. Rommel sent a demand for surrender to the senior British officer, Major-General Michael Gambier-Parry, commander of the 2nd Armored Division. "Of course he refused," Rommel recorded, without surprise. On the morning of April 8 the British tried to break out at the same time that the Axis forces began a general attack. In the confusion a few Britons managed to escape, but by noon Mechili had fallen and Gambier-Parry was added to the retinue of captive high-ranking officers.

An elated Rommel watched the British general's command truck being unloaded, and reached forward to annex an oversized pair of sun-and-sand goggles. "Booty—permissible I take it, even for a general," he said, grinning as he adjusted the goggles over the gold-braided rim of his peaked cap, where they would appear in numerous photographs taken of him during the next 22 months. The legend of the Desert Fox was in the making.

On that same day, in a water-front hotel in Tobruk, Wavell announced a crucial decision to a conference of senior officers: Tobruk must be held. The 9th Australian Division, which had slipped out of Rommel's net by withdrawing from Derna, was to take up defensive positions in this coastal city, joining the British and Commonwealth units already stationed in Tobruk.

None present at the conference challenged Wavell's logic. Rommel was bound to continue his advance to the east,

but as long as Tobruk was in British hands he could not go far. Holding Tobruk denied him the use of the only suitable port in Cyrenaica east of Benghazi. His troops needed 1,500 tons of water and rations a day; without Tobruk all of these supplies would have to be carried across the desert from Benghazi or Tripoli. Holding Tobruk would not be easy. Rommel would surely make every effort to drive the defenders into the sea. All their food, ammunition and replacement equipment would have to come in by ship under the bombs and guns of the Luftwaffe, which controlled the air space over the city. But there was no other choice. Noting on a map the few remaining British units scattered across 450 miles of desert—at Bardia, Sidi Barrani, Mersa Matruh—Wavell told his Tobruk officers dryly: "There is nothing between you and Cairo."

No one was more sharply aware of this than Rommel. In the next few days his Afrika Korps, bypassing Tobruk, pushed east along the coast, taking Fort Capuzzo, Sollum and Halfaya Pass, but it was futile to go farther as long as the British in their stronghold still posed a threat to his flank and rear. Tobruk was to become a thorn in his flesh, an obsession that was to dog him for seven months. Rommel, who was now intent on conquering Egypt and the Suez, found himself halted on the threshold of triumph by a single impudent British garrison.

"We must attack Tobruk with everything we have—before Tommy has time to dig in," Rommel told one of his divisional commanders. But Tommy had already dug in. The British had begun reinforcing Tobruk's old Italian defenses in mid-March, and the 220-square-mile enclave was more formidable than Rommel supposed. The 30-mile perimeter, called the Red Line, was marked by tangled whorls of barbed wire and bristled with 140 strong points, concrete-shielded dugouts holding up to 20 men apiece. Two miles behind the Red Line lay the Blue Line, a thickly sown minefield crisscrossed with more barbed wire and studded with strong points situated 500 yards apart.

Even after German tanks probing the perimeter on April 11 and 12 were beaten back by artillery, Rommel was sure that Tobruk would fall to the full-scale armored assault planned for Easter, April 14. "Dear Lu," he wrote early that day, "Today may well see the end of the Battle of Tobruk." German troops expected that the enemy would retire as soon as the panzers approached. Heartened by Rommel's belief in a quick victory, one battalion even tagged its administration truck to the rear of the assault column.

Such confidence did not seem misplaced as the battle got under way. At 5:20 a.m. the first wave of the 5th Light Division's tanks bulled unmolested through a gap blasted in the wire south of Tobruk. The Australians manning the perimeter posts made no attempt to engage the tanks—but as the German infantry passed the strong points, murderous fire hit them from the rear. Oblivious to the carnage taking place behind them, the panzers ground on. Soon they were two miles inside the perimeter—moving deeper by the minute into a deadly and elaborate trap.

Suddenly the panzer crews found themselves in a corridor of heavy fire. Field artillery, rushed from nearby sectors, was firing from both flanks at a range of only 600 yards. One hit tore the massive turret of a Panzer IV tank clean from its mountings. German Lieut. Colonel Gustav Ponath, who had driven brashly into battle in his staff car, was killed when the vehicle was blown to pieces by an antitank shell. The panzers milled about in confusion as smoke and dust obscured the vision of drivers and gunners. Finally ordered to retire, they had to fight their way back to the perimeter through the same gauntlet. The Germans lost 17 tanks in the melee—at least one of them immobilized by an Australian who rammed a crowbar into a tread sprocket. The 8th Machine Gun Battalion suffered 75 per cent casualties. The

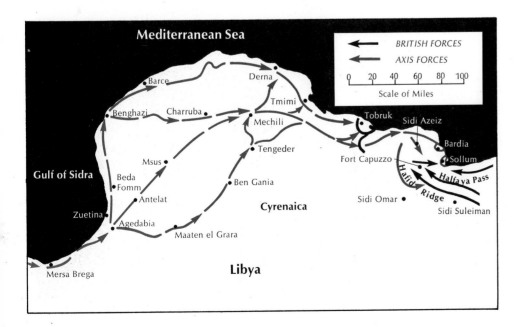

With his finger fixed on a point near the coast, Rommel (far left) pores over a map of Cyrenaica during his first offensive. Starting from west of Mersa Brega, his advance (red arrows) drove the British, except for a garrison at Tobruk, out of Libya by mid-April. Goaded by Churchill, British General Wavell in June mounted the Battleaxe counteroffensive, whose thrusts (black arrows) were repulsed by Rommel.

battle was a "witch's cauldron," a German tank commander wrote later. "We were lucky to escape alive."

Rommel was furious that he had been beaten. He raged at Major General Johannes Streich, commander of the 5th Light Division, saying his panzers had not given their best. He charged that both Streich and Olbrich, commander of the 5th Panzer Regiment, had "lacked resolution."

Two days later, on April 16, Rommel tried again. This time he personally took command, using the Ariete Division and an Italian infantry division against Tobruk's western defenses. As soon as they were fired on, the Italian tanks took refuge in a wadi and Rommel could not induce their commanders to resume the attack. Italian infantry, taking the brunt of an Australian counterattack, quickly surrendered. One of Rommel's officers saw a lone British scout car herding a whole Italian company into captivity. He fired on the car to give the Italians a chance to run. They did run, Rommel noted ruefully, "toward the British lines." More than 800 Italians were captured during the two-day attack; the Ariete Division lost at least 90 per cent of its tanks—to breakdowns. On April 17, Rommel called off the attack.

He still believed that when proper reinforcements arrived he would be able to take Tobruk. He consistently underestimated the determination of its defenders. There were 35,000 soldiers within the Tobruk perimeter—Anzacs, Britons, Indians—led by an Australian commander fully as tenacious as Rommel himself.

Major-General Leslie James Morshead, 51, was known to his troops as "Ming the Merciless," after a villain in the *Flash Gordon* comic strip. His concept of his task was simple. "There'll be no Dunkirk here," he told his staff. "If we have to get out we shall fight our way out. There is to be no surrender and no retreat." When an Australian newspaper ran a headline that said, "Tobruk Can Take It," Morshead was enraged. "We're not here to take it," he stormed. "We're here to give it."

Every night he sent out 20-man patrols to launch surprise attacks against the enemy. Soon Rommel was made aware of their deadly efficacy. Approaching an Italian sector of his line one morning he stopped short in amazement at the sight of hundreds of discarded helmets decorated with the cock's plumes of a crack Bersaglieri rifle regiment. An entire battalion had been seized during the night. Not all of Morshead's troops bothered to take prisoners. A patrol of Rajputs, warrior-caste Hindus from Jodhpur, rebuked for overestimating its enemy dead, returned some nights later with two small sacks of evidence: 32 human ears.

Since to stir aboveground during the day was to court snipers, the men guarding Tobruk's perimeter turned their daily routines upside down. They breakfasted at 9:30 p.m., ate lunch at midnight and dinner at dawn. Concealment was the key to life. Men entering camouflaged dugouts smoothed their footprints behind them with camel's-thorn switches so enemy bombers would not be led to the dugouts by the tracks. They had to fight not only the enemy but boredom, sunburn, lice, sand fleas and dysentery.

The Luftwaffe kept up its attacks on supply vessels. The harbor was soon littered with rusting wrecks of supply ships destroyed by German Stukas. It was with good reason that the Western Desert Lighter Flotilla, which brought food and equipment from Alexandria, contended that its initials stood for "We Die Like Flies."

On the perimeter, a consciousness of hardships shared bred a certain wry camaraderie between besiegers and besieged. Both sides endured the same desert privations—water that "looked like coffee and tasted like sulphur," as one of Rommel's officers noted, and canned meat that the Germans called "Mussolini's ass." There were fleeting relaxations of tension. Sergeant Walter Tuit, a British stretcher-bearer, seeking casualties in no man's land after one engagement on the perimeter, was assisted by Germans who delivered British wounded and dead and told him other wounded Britons had been sent to a German field hospital. They then gave him a fresh lemon drink before both sides retired to their own lines. And each night, promptly at 9:57 p.m., Britons no less than Germans turned in to Radio Bel-

The "rats of Tobruk"—the derisive Axis term for the British troops under siege in the Libyan port—make the best of their beleaguered state. An Australian soldier (right) cools off in an abandoned bathtub as his comrades wait their turn. Other amenities included mimeographed newspapers, daily church services, and meals served in one of Tobruk's many caves (far right) to avoid the danger of swooping Stuka dive bombers.

grade, to hear Lale Andersen sing—in German—the sad and sensuous lament about the girl who waited underneath the lamplight by the barracks gate, "Lili Marlene." It became the unofficial anthem of all the desert warriors.

By April 30, Rommel had been reinforced by enough of the 15th Panzer Division to try again. At 6:30 p.m. the Germans began their most furious attack on Tobruk so far. Stuka dive bombers and artillery pounded a hill called Ras el Medauer on the stronghold's southwest perimeter while German tanks burst through defenses north and south of the prominence. Within three hours the Germans had taken the hill and the panzers had penetrated two miles inside the perimeter. But they had failed to eliminate a number of fortified outposts manned by Australians who fought, Rommel said, "with remarkable tenacity. Even their wounded went on defending themselves and stayed in the fight to their last breath." These strong points were still active the next morning, harassing the German advance from behind as the British retaliated with artillery and counterattacks.

The seesaw struggle of thrust and counterthrust raged for three more days. Blinding dust storms made tactical control difficult for both sides. In the frenzied chaos, few could grasp with certainty who was winning—or for how long. One German medic, approaching the wire in an ambulance, furiously berated the Anzac who drew a bead on him; convinced that Rommel had taken Tobruk, the medic had arrived to treat the German wounded. (Seized as a prisoner, he treated both sides impartially.)

It was Rommel's most costly engagement to date. He lost more than 1,000 men in the battle. On hand to witness the slaughter was Lieut. General Friedrich Paulus, a cool and precise general staff officer who had arrived on April 27 on an urgent mission from Army High Command to somehow hold Rommel in check. (Colonel General Halder said Paulus was chosen because he was "perhaps the only man with enough influence to head off this soldier gone stark mad.") Paulus was appalled by the casualties and the fact that the German troops were "fighting in conditions that are inhuman and intolerable." He advised Rommel that there was no chance of taking Tobruk. Still, when the British broke off their last unsuccessful counterattack early on May 4, the Germans had managed to occupy a portion of the perimeter some three miles wide by two miles deep.

At about the same time an angry ultimatum arrived from Brauchitsch. The commander in chief forbade Rommel to attack Tobruk again, or to advance farther into Egypt. Rommel must hold his position and conserve his forces. The commander of the Afrika Korps was bitter at being compelled to take a defensive stance instead of being allowed to conquer Egypt. But he was soon to prove as consummate a practitioner of the defense as of the offense.

At Churchill's insistence, the British were about to launch their own Cyrenaican offensive. The groundwork had been laid on April 20, when the Prime Minister had conceived a bold, typically Churchillian idea. At the time a convoy carrying 295 tanks to aid Wavell was making ready to sail for Suez via the Cape of Good Hope. Churchill proposed that the ships cut 40 days off the trip by turning at Gibraltar and running the Mediterranean gauntlet to Alexandria.

British convoys had not dared to make the passage across the length of the Mediterranean since early January, when

the Luftwaffe had demonstrated its domination of the air there by badly damaging the carrier *Illustrious*. But Churchill, knowing that Rommel was being reinforced by a full panzer division, thought the risk worth taking. If Wavell could get the 295 tanks before the new German armor was fully operative in North Africa, the recent disastrous course of battle might be quickly reversed. "If this consignment gets through," the Prime Minister, with unflagging optimism, cabled Wavell, "no German should remain in Cyrenaica by the end of June."

In fact "Tiger Convoy," as it was dubbed, lost only one ship—to an enemy mine; it delivered 238 tanks at Alexandria on May 1. On the day it arrived, Churchill quoted from 2 Corinthians 6:2 in a message to Wavell: "Behold, now is the day of salvation." Wavell was not so certain. The tanks arrived in sorry shape, with cracked gearboxes, unserviceable tracks and no sand filters for their engines, so essential in the desert. Action before mid-June, Wavell told London, was out of the question.

Churchill reacted with anger and disappointment, but Wavell was not displaying any lack of initiative. On May 15, even without the new tanks, he set into motion Operation *Brevity*, a limited campaign designed to secure a jumping-off position for the major offensive to follow. Under the command of Brigadier W. H. E. Gott, the British threw three assault columns across the Egypt-Libya border. Two ascended the escarpment that ran parallel to the coast, one to sweep west and north toward Sidi Azeiz, the other to regain Fort Capuzzo west of Sollum. The third was to storm Halfaya Pass, a gash in the escarpment leading up onto the Libyan Plateau. The pass controlled access to the plateau as well as the coastal road to Sollum and points west.

The British quickly took Capuzzo and Halfaya Pass and were advancing on Sidi Azeiz when Rommel counterattacked, pushing them back in the early hours of May 16. Gott withdrew to the pass, which, if he could hold it, by itself would have been worth the losses of Operation *Brevity*—till then, 18 tanks and 160 casualties. But on May 27 a superior German force drove the British out of the pass, at a cost to Wavell of 173 more casualties and five more tanks. *Brevity* had gained nothing.

Churchill, aware that Rommel was strengthening his defenses every day, badgered Wavell about the need for haste in getting the big attack moving. The Western Desert offensive was not the only problem on Wavell's mind, however. Almost everywhere he looked he saw only trouble. The British had been thrown out of Greece at the end of April, and now Crete—the refuge to which most of the troops from Greece had been evacuated—was threatened by the Germans. In the meantime Wavell was being committed to campaigns in Syria and Iraq by the activities of pro-Axis puppet governments in those countries. Like a juggler frantically trying to manipulate too many colored balls, Wavell was beginning to falter.

But on June 15 at 2:30 a.m., Wavell finally got the Cyrenaica offensive—code-named Operation *Battleaxe*—under way. The plan was similar to that of Operation *Brevity*, but on a larger scale. An infantry brigade group (a reinforced brigade) with one and a half squadrons of tanks was to seize Halfaya Pass. At the same time an armored brigade and an infantry brigade were to move on Fort Capuzzo as a reinforced armored brigade swept wide to the west toward Sidi Azeiz, protecting the other British forces from the Axis troops in Sidi Omar.

The anchor of Rommel's defense, an artillery battalion in Halfaya Pass, first heard the throb of British tank motors at 6 a.m. on June 15. These defenders were known to the British as "seven-day men" because they were supplied with a week's worth of ammunition, food and water at a time and knew they had to fight to the last shell and the last drop of water. Their commander was 50-year-old Captain Wilhelm Bach, in civilian life an Evangelical minister from Mannheim, who would become known to his unswervingly loyal troops as "the pastor of Halfaya."

Through field glasses, the portly Captain Bach watched the British tanks approaching, about two miles away. "Under no circumstances fire," he told his men. "Let them come on." As the advance continued, the tanks began firing and shell craters soon pitted the biscuit-brown heights of the pass. Still Bach's men and an Italian battery under Major Leopoldo Pardo held their fire.

At 9:15 a.m., British Lieut. Colonel Walter O'Carroll, near the rear of the column moving into the pass, heard with satisfaction a radio code message: "Pink Spots"—the action was under control and going well. Then the appalled last words of Major C. G. Miles, in the lead tank, poured from the radio: "Good God! They've got large caliber guns dug in and they're tearing my tanks to pieces."

From concealed emplacements all along the cliffside, 88mm antiaircraft guns, leveled for use against the tanks, were firing 22-pound shells that could tear holes as big as basketballs in a Matilda a mile distant. In a few minutes, 11 of the 12 leading tanks were blazing like blowtorches. Five times the British tried to storm the pass and five times Bach's guns repulsed them. From that day forward, Halfaya would be known to the British army as "Hell-Fire Pass."

Up on the escarpment, meanwhile, British tanks in the center of the advance managed to drive the Axis troops back from the Fort Capuzzo area and then turned east to move on Sollum. But to the west the left arm of the British advance was stalled at Hafid Ridge by German defense emplacements that included more of the deadly 88s in use as antitank weapons. And during the day Rommel brought up reinforcements from the Tobruk area, including the 5th Light Division and part of the 15th Panzer Division.

On the morning of June 16, Rommel unleashed these reserves. The 15th Panzer Division hammered at the British at Capuzzo, but was beaten back and broke off its attack before noon. At the same time Rommel's 5th Light Division circled to the south and struck the British left flank near Sidi Omar. After a fierce battle with tanks of the British 7th Armored Regiment, the 5th Light Division broke through and began rolling east toward Sidi Suleiman. "This was the turning point of the battle," Rommel said. Here was a chance to cut right across the rear of the enemy, trap him and crush him. Rommel ordered most of the 15th Panzer Division to leave the Capuzzo area, circle to the southwest, and join the 5th Light Division in its eastward drive. Early in the morning of June 17 these units reached Sidi Suleiman and Rommel ordered them on to Halfaya Pass, happily contemplating the destruction of the British forces.

But at 11 a.m. Major-General F. W. Messervy, commander of the 4th Indian Division, unable to reach headquarters for approval, took it on himself to order a withdrawal of British forces in time for most to escape the trap. Later, on a desert airstrip, Messervy confronted a grim-faced Wavell. He recalled that Wavell stared at him for long minutes without speaking. "I thought he was going to sack me," Messervy said. Finally Wavell spoke: "I think you were right to withdraw in the circumstances, but orders should have come from Western Desert Force."

All told, Operation Battleaxe cost the British about 90 tanks, more than 30 aircraft (by great effort the Royal Air Force had maintained air superiority throughout the battle), almost 1,000 men and the chance to restore morale through a desert victory. Rommel thought Wavell's planning had been "excellent" but said that the British general was "put at a great disadvantage by the slow speed of his heavy infantry tanks, which prevented him from reacting quickly enough to the moves of our faster vehicles."

Some in London were not so understanding when they received Wavell's terse admission of defeat: "Am very sorry for failure of 'Battleaxe.'" Sir Alexander Cadogan, who was Permanent Under-Secretary to the Foreign Office, summed up one of the prevalent opinions: the German Army simply had better generals. "Wavell and suchlike are no good against them. It is like putting me up to play Bobby Jones over 36 holes."

Churchill's own feeling was already well known. As early as mid-May he had discussed replacing Wavell in an exchange of assignments with Lieut. General Sir Claude Auchinleck, commander in chief in India. Churchill told Field Marshal Sir John Dill, Chief of the Imperial General Staff, that he did not want Wavell hanging around London, living in a room in his club. The Prime Minister said that in India Wavell would "enjoy sitting under the pagoda tree." Early on the morning of June 22, Wavell's Chief of Staff, Lieut. General Sir Arthur Smith, arrived at his commander's house in Cairo. Wavell was in the bathroom shaving, his cheeks daubed with lather, razor poised. Quietly Smith read out a message that had just arrived from Churchill: "I have come to the conclusion that public interest will best be served by appointment of General Auchinleck to relieve you in command of armies of Middle East."

Wavell stared straight ahead. With no apparent emotion, no visible sign of regret, he said, "The Prime Minister's quite right. This job needs a new eye and a new hand." Then he went on shaving. It was a characteristic tribute from a large-hearted gentleman to his successor. But there was no assurance that the new hand would be any more capable of outdealing Rommel than the old one had been.

EMBATTLED MALTA

Malta's capital, Valletta, is silhouetted against the smoke of bomb explosions in this still from a newsreel that was filmed during the heavy blitz of spring 1942.

HEROIC ORDEAL OF A ROCK-BOUND ISLAND

A Maltese laborer widens the mouth of one of the hundreds of tunnel-like air-raid shelters that were carved by civilians into Malta's soft limestone.

One of the most heavily bombed targets in the War was neither a great industrial complex nor a munitions arsenal. Tiny British Malta was a flyspeck in the middle of the Mediterranean, with three small, ill-equipped airfields and a superb natural harbor. But in 1941 that speck of rock became the keystone of British defense in North Africa—and a major stumbling block of the Axis desert campaign.

As long as the island's air and submarine bases were operating, the convoys that sustained Axis armies in Africa were easy prey for British attacks. By November 1941, Malta-based crews were destroying more than three fourths of all Rommel's shipping. In desperation, Reich Marshal Hermann Göring called for the island to be "Coventrated"—destroyed from the air as completely as the English city of Coventry had been in 1940.

Only 70 miles from the airfields of Sicily, Malta was a readily accessible target for the hundreds of Luftwaffe bombers dispatched to neutralize the island. During the first months of 1942, bombs plummeted down on Malta's airfields and docks, and on the capital, Valletta, an average of eight times a day. In April alone, Malta withstood 6,728 tons of bombs, 13 times the amount that had shattered Coventry. During those months virtually every British convoy carrying supplies to the island was destroyed, and food and munitions grew desperately scarce.

But Malta's plucky defenders refused to give up. RAF crews repaired the airfields daily, sending fighters up to battle the Germans whenever possible. The 280,000 native Maltese learned to endure severe rationing and mounting casualties. Then, in April 1942, during the grimmest days of the siege, King George VI conferred on the whole island the George Cross, Britain's highest civilian award for gallantry. Their morale buoyed by this tribute, the Maltese gritted their teeth and persevered. Gradually, as fortunes shifted in North Africa, the siege lifted. The Luftwaffe moved its planes from Sicily to the Russian and North African theaters, and by late fall, battered but exuberant, Malta resumed its critical role as a base for attacks on German shipping.

Queen Victoria's statue sits indomitably amid the rubble in Queen's Square in central Valletta. At right are the ruins of the lion-bedecked Governor's Palace.

Playing on the wreckage of a German dive bomber, Maltese children seem inured to a landscape of devastation. Like many of their elders, they seized every

chance to escape the dank underground air-raid shelters where, for the worst of the siege, they slept, prayed, had classes and ate most of their meager meals.

Maltese islanders examine the ruins of Valletta's Royal Opera House, one of approximately 37,000 buildings destroyed or damaged during the course of the siege.

Soldiers clear rubble from Kingsway, Valletta's main thoroughfare, on the morning after a raid.

The silver George Cross and the King's framed citation were conferred as the British Empire's formal salute to Malta's fortitude.

BUCKINGHAM PALACE

The Governor
Malta.

To honour her brave people
I award the George Cross to the
Island Fortress of Malta to bear
witness to a heroism and devotion
that will long be famous in history.

George R.I.

April 15th 1942.

Honoring Malta's triumph over its attackers, King George VI salutes a throng of cheering islanders on June 20, 1943, during a tour he made of the Mediterranean.

3

General Sir Claude Auchinleck seemed to be just the man for the job when he took command of Britain's Middle Eastern forces. At 57 he neither knew nor sought any other life than that of a British Army officer. He had risen steadily since graduating from the Royal Military College at Sandhurst, serving in the Indian Army in peacetime and in various campaigns of World Wars I and II.

Besides his formal credentials, "The Auk," as he was affectionately known to his troops, possessed essential qualities of leadership. To begin with he had a quick grasp of strategic and tactical problems—an urgent necessity now, in the face of an enemy personified by the seemingly invincible Rommel. With Auchinleck's jutting jaw and steady gaze went a stern self-discipline that made him impose on himself the same austerities his men endured (because his officers were barred from bringing their wives to Cairo, he left his own wife in New Delhi). He had a resolute will that inspired trust in those whom he commanded. He also possessed powers of persuasion that enabled him to have his way with superiors as well—as no less a figure than Winston Churchill learned when Auchinleck held out against the impatient Prime Minister, insisting that the next British offensive must not be prematurely launched in summer, but must wait until November when Auchinleck would have sufficient reinforcements.

Hidden behind his formidable assets, however, was one crucial failing: Auchinleck was a poor judge when choosing subordinate commanders. Once he had placed his trust in someone, he took it for granted that his orders would be carried out without the need for any follow-up supervision. And when he chose poorly, a combination of stubbornness and misplaced loyalty sometimes made him slow to rectify his own mistakes.

The first task that Auchinleck found himself called upon to accomplish when he reached Cairo was to reorganize the Western Desert Force and find a commander for it. The force was more than tripled in size—Churchill had authorized the build-up in North Africa because he was determined to make gains there while Hitler was preoccupied with the war in Russia—and was renamed the Eighth Army. Auchinleck's choice for a commander was Lieut. General Sir Alan Gordon Cunningham—and a likely choice it seemed. The 54-year-old Cunningham, who had both a quick temper

TRIUMPH ELUDES THE BRITISH

and a ready smile, had distinguished himself in early 1941 in East Africa by soundly defeating the Italians, led by the Duke of Aosta *(page 20),* in only eight weeks.

"I asked for Cunningham," Auchinleck wrote later, "as I was impressed by his rapid and vigorous command in Abyssinia and his obvious leaning towards swift mobile action. I wanted to get away from the idea, which seemed to be prevalent, of clinging to the coastal strip, and to move freely and widely against the enemy's flank and communications." Unfortunately, Cunningham had never commanded tanks and was not innovative by nature. In the face of the quicksilver moves of the unorthodox Rommel, these were to be serious liabilities. Moreover, Cunningham was enduring a personal deprivation that was to have effects far beyond its apparently petty nature. A constant smoker, he had been ordered by his doctor to give up his pipe for reasons of health. Under the pressures of the coming months, the loss of his comforting pipe was to play havoc with his nerves.

Cunningham's first major assignment as commander of the Eighth Army was to direct Operation *Crusader,* the greatest offensive the British had yet launched in the desert. *Crusader's* objectives were no less than to engage and destroy the enemy's armor, to relieve the British garrison at Tobruk from the Axis siege that had been going on since April, to reconquer all of Cyrenaica and, eventually, to move on and take Tripoli.

In mid-November on the eve of Operation *Crusader,* Cunningham was buoyantly optimistic, and so were his fellow officers and men. They had every reason to be; the War Office had spared no effort to assure the operation's success. The new army had a total of 118,000 troops, more than 700 tanks, 600 field guns, 200 antitank guns, and was equipped with a wealth of other vehicles and weapons. And it had the support of the newly strengthened Desert Air Force, which now had nearly 650 aircraft.

On the Axis side, Rommel appeared to be not nearly so well off. While he had managed to create a new division—called the 90th Light, or Africa Division—from smaller units already in North Africa, he had received no reinforcements from Europe since June. The old 5th Light Division was renamed the 21st Panzer Division, but without any change in strength. Rommel's command had been given a new designation: Panzer Group Africa. It included the Afrika Korps (now consisting of the 15th and 21st panzer divisions, and the 90th Light Division) and two Italian corps numbering six divisions. Rommel had about 119,000 troops, but he had only 400 tanks (150 of them obsolete Italian vehicles), some 50 of which were undergoing repair when the British launched *Crusader.* Moreover, the Axis air forces, with fewer than 550 planes in Cyrenaica, were now outnumbered by the British. Rommel would be hard put to get additional reinforcements from Hitler, because the campaign in Russia, which had begun with rapid success in June, was by this time showing ominous signs of trouble.

Cunningham's ambitious plan called for the armored XXX Corps, under Lieut. General C. W. M. Norrie, to advance westward from Eighth Army headquarters at Fort Maddalena, about 50 miles south of the coast, and swing around behind the German defenses running south from Bardia on the coast to Sidi Omar *(map, page 84).* Once the XXX Corps outflanked the Germans, two of its units, the 22nd and the 7th armored brigades, would move northwest to Gabr Saleh, about halfway between Maddalena and Tobruk. Gabr Saleh's only value was that it lay astride the Trigh el Abd, an inland road that was expected to be Rommel's main route of advance as he responded to the British thrust. Cunningham hoped that Rommel would send his panzers to Gabr Saleh, where the British armor would engage and destroy them. Then the British would be free to swing either northeast to Afrika Korps headquarters at Bardia or northwest toward beleaguered Tobruk.

Meanwhile, the 4th Armored Brigade—also part of the XXX Corps—would veer northwest behind German lines. It would have the dual task of supporting the right flank of the 7th Armored Brigade rolling on to Gabr Saleh and the left flank of the XIII Corps, primarily infantry, under Lieut. General A. R. Godwin-Austen, who had served with Cunningham in East Africa. The XIII Corps itself would stay south and east of the Axis front line, harassing the Italian units holding the frontier until Norrie's armored units had eliminated Rommel's tanks. Only then was the XIII Corps to join the advance on Tobruk, where it would dispose of Rommel's infantry and lift the siege of the fortress. The garrison in Tobruk would attempt a breakout to coincide with the XIII Corps' attack on the Axis siege lines around the city. All this, Cunningham hoped, would take no more than a week.

Rommel, of course, had plans of his own. He had finally won grudging assent from the German High Command for another assault on Tobruk. Since spring he had left the task of maintaining the siege to the Italians. By early November he was beginning to move his German divisions from the Egyptian frontier toward Tobruk. He planned to strike on November 21.

The British were ready before him. At dawn on November 18 the XXX Corps' brigades crossed the frontier at Fort Maddalena and fanned out across the desert. Cunningham went along, riding with Norrie's headquarters staff to command the action from the field. Meeting little opposition on the way, the 22nd and 7th brigades reached their positions in the vicinity of Gabr Saleh by evening.

Cunningham had a long and uneasy wait for Rommel's reaction. The German, at his headquarters in Bardia, was preoccupied with his proposed assault on Tobruk. He had received no forewarning at all of the British attack, because

of poor German air reconnaissance and excellent British concealment of troop movements during the weeks before the offensive began. Rommel not only was caught off guard by the arrival of the British, but also was uncharacteristically slow to grasp the nature of their advance. Lieut. General Ludwig Crüwell, commander of the Afrika Korps—who was sometimes a better tactician than Rommel—advised his chief that he sniffed an offensive and urged that the two panzer divisions be moved south to counter the thrust. But Rommel was reluctant to change his plans; he thought the British were only making a cautious probe.

Cunningham, still without any real reaction from the enemy, the next day sent columns probing west to Bir el Gubi and north to Sidi Rezegh. At that point Rommel began to doubt his original assessment of what his enemy was up to. He yielded slightly to his advisers and allowed some of his panzers to move south to meet the British columns. The result was a series of heated, isolated engagements that cost the British about 50 tanks and the Axis some 30. But so far

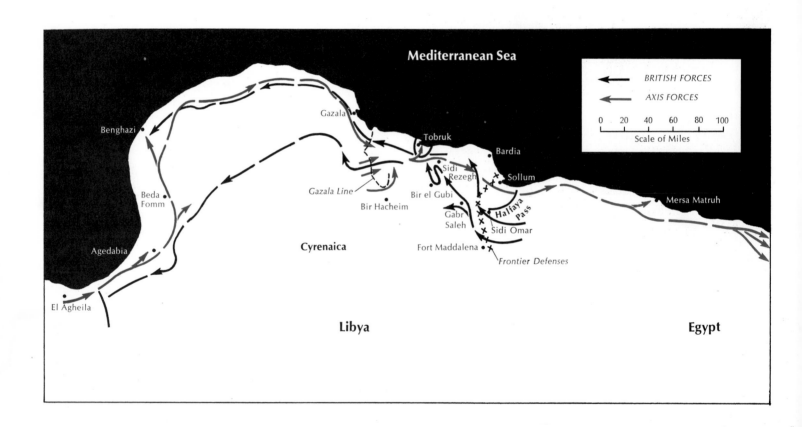

In Britain's Crusader offensive of November 1941, the Eighth Army (black arrows) relieved the siege of Tobruk and dogged Rommel across Cyrenaica to El Agheila. When the Axis forces (red arrows) rebounded in January 1942, the Eighth Army retreated to a chain of fortifications known as the Gazala line. In June, Rommel crushed these fortifications, captured Tobruk and drove the British across Egypt to El Alamein.

nothing had occurred that resembled the major confrontation of armor that Cunningham sought. The fighting did leave the British holding an airfield at Sidi Rezegh, along with 19 enemy aircraft captured on the runway. With Sidi Rezegh in the bag and no big counterblow from Rommel seemingly in the offing, Cunningham returned to his headquarters at Fort Maddalena on November 20, concluding that the operation was going well enough.

He was mistaken. Rommel, finally convinced that the British were involved in a serious offensive, had shelved his plans for seizing Tobruk and done an about-face. On November 22, some 70 tanks of the 21st Panzer Division sprang on the British 7th Armored Brigade at Sidi Rezegh. The British 22nd and 4th armored brigades rushed to the scene, but they arrived separately and too late to make much of a difference. At the end of the day the 15th Panzer Division showed up to add to British woes. It overran 4th Armored Brigade's headquarters and captured the brigade commander. The outcome of the day's fighting was that the British lost the airfield, more than 100 tanks and some 300 men.

This was only a foretaste of what they were to suffer the next day, November 23—which happened to be *Totensonntag*, "Sunday of the Dead," when Germans traditionally honored countrymen killed in World War I. Early that morning Rommel hurled his massed tanks on the British units that were scattered around Sidi Rezegh; he took them on one after another, and one after another he knocked them out. When night came the area was lighted by the flames of hundreds of blazing vehicles. Virtually every British formation took heavy punishment. Worst hit was the 5th South African Brigade, an infantry outfit that was part of the XXX Corps; it lost 3,400 of its 5,700 men. All in all Totensonntag accounted for the heaviest casualties yet endured by the British in the desert war.

Rommel was clearly the winner of the first phase of Operation *Crusader*, and he knew it. That night he wrote to his wife, Lu: "The battle seems to have passed its crisis. I'm very well, in good humor and full of confidence." Though he

General Sir Claude Auchinleck, who led the Crusader offensive, spent three years of his early childhood as well as most of his professional life in India. Unconventional and bold, he had a healthy respect for India's fighting men and lobbied to mechanize their Army at a time when some feared giving the Indians guns. His confidence in them was confirmed by the reliability of the Indians who fought under him in the desert war.

had been outnumbered and had suffered heavy losses, including perhaps a dozen senior officers and some 250 tanks, he had given the British a lesson in tactics. By consolidating his forces—massing his tanks and coordinating their attacks with infantry, antitank guns, artillery and air support—he had succeeded in achieving effective numerical advantage with a smaller force. "What difference does it make if you have two tanks to my one when you spread them out and let me smash them in detail?" he was later to ask a captured British officer. "You presented me with three armored brigades in succession."

At Eighth Army headquarters the radio had broken down and Cunningham waited anxiously for reports. When late on Totensonntag he learned the enormity of the disaster that had befallen the British, he was shattered. He thought that perhaps he should count *Crusader* lost and retreat into Egypt. There, at least, he could reorganize his forces in relative safety. Wrestling with his nerves and indecision, he sent an urgent plea for help to Auchinleck in Cairo, suggesting that the commander in chief come to see the front for himself. Auchinleck promptly flew to Fort Maddalena and

made a swift appraisal. "I thought Rommel was probably in as bad a shape as we were," he later wrote, "and I ordered the offensive to continue." Auchinleck's resolve remained firm. He told Cunningham to "attack the enemy relentlessly using all your resources even to the last tank."

In fact, not all the British plans were going awry. Two days earlier Cunningham had authorized the XIII Corps—comprising the New Zealand Division, the 4th Indian Division and a tank brigade—to begin its advance without waiting for the outcome of the armored struggle in the west. The XIII Corps moved north behind the Axis lines on the frontier as far as the coast northwest of Bardia, taking Fort Capuzzo and cutting off the garrisons at Bardia and Halfaya Pass from the bulk of the Axis forces to the west.

To relieve this pressure on his frontier forces, Rommel, heady with his successes, now embarked on a daring adventure. "Speed is vital," he told his leading officers. "We must make the most of the shock effect of the enemy's defeat." On the morning of November 24, while the British around Sidi Rezegh were still staggering, he brazenly led the entire Afrika Korps and two Italian divisions on a dash to the east,

ITALIAN UNDERWATER RAIDERS

To challenge Britain's control of the Mediterranean in late 1941, the Italian Navy resorted to employing midget submarines that were little more than manned torpedoes. On the night of December 19, three midget subs slipped into Alexandria harbor. Their mission: to destroy the only British battleships in the Mediterranean, the *Queen Elizabeth* and the *Valiant*, and set the harbor aflame by exploding a tanker.

Two of the crews attached their warheads to the hulls of the *Queen Elizabeth* and the tanker, then scuttled their subs and swam ashore. The third crew was captured in the water near the *Valiant*, after leaving its time bomb on the seabed beneath the ship. Thrown into the ship's hold a mere 15 feet above the explosive device, the Italians held their silence for two and a half hours, then warned the captain.

Minutes later three explosions rocked the harbor. The *Queen Elizabeth* and the *Valiant* listed crazily; the tanker went up in flames. The battleships were repairable, but while they were out of action, convoys with desperately needed supplies would reach the Axis forces in North Africa intact.

In this Italian wartime painting, frogmen on a midget sub cut an antisubmarine net.

straight through enemy lines. His purpose was to get beyond the frontier and threaten the British rear, a tactic that he hoped would force Cunningham to give up the offensive and withdraw. He rashly disregarded the costly losses he had sustained and the counsel of General Crüwell, who thought that prior to doing anything else the Germans should finish off the battered British forces remaining near Sidi Rezegh.

The sudden thrust was so unexpected and swift that the British rear echelons panicked and fled. It was like a replay of Rommel's first offensive in Cyrenaica. Units of both sides raced east for six hours and in their haste found themselves so hopelessly confused that many had no idea where they were or whether friend or foe was next to them. At dusk a British military policeman directing traffic suddenly realized that the vehicles he was now controlling were German. Rommel himself, along with General Crüwell, spent much of the night in the midst of British troops. No one noticed: the Germans were riding in a big, enclosed command vehicle that had been captured from the British, and its German markings were not discernible in the dark.

In making his bold move to the east Rommel had correctly perceived the Eighth Army's disarray—but he had failed to reckon with its hidden strength in the person of Auchinleck. Had Cunningham been acting on his own, the sudden Axis drive might well have induced him to call off *Crusader*. But Auchinleck stayed at Fort Maddalena for two days, propping up the troops as well as the flagging Cunningham. Auchinleck told his men that the enemy "is trying by lashing out in all directions to distract us from our object, which is to destroy him utterly. We will not be distracted and he will be destroyed." He said of Rommel: "He is making a desperate effort, but he will not get very far. That column of tanks simply cannot get supplies. I am sure of this."

He was right. Rommel penetrated some 15 miles inside Egypt, but on November 26 his panzers had to retire to Bardia to refuel. Ironically, during his rapid advance he had passed right by two huge, well-camouflaged supply dumps where the Eighth Army kept food, fuel and water for its *Crusader* forces.

In the final reckoning his dash proved to be an expensive detour. When Rommel began the raid, the balance of battle was tipping decidedly in his favor. But by the time the momentum of his dash was spent, the British had taken the offensive again. On the night that Afrika Korps tanks were refueling in Bardia, the New Zealand Division of the XIII Corps drove through the Axis forces surrounding Tobruk and linked up with troops from the beleaguered garrison who were fighting their way out. For the moment at least, Tobruk had been relieved. Farther south, the 4th and 22nd armored brigades had taken advantage of Rommel's absence to regroup and salvage some of the disabled tanks that had been abandoned at Sidi Rezegh. When Rommel's refueled panzers left Bardia on November 27, heading west to aid the hard-pressed Axis forces around Tobruk, British armor hammered them to a standstill. Only when the British withdrew to set up camp and rest for the night were the Germans able to push through the west.

After returning to Cairo on November 25, Auchinleck had made two difficult decisions. It seemed to him and to his colleagues at general headquarters that Cunningham's inclination to fall back after Totensonntag had been a sign of timidity unwarranted in view of the enemy's high losses. Lieut. General Sir Arthur Smith, Chief of the General Staff in Cairo, believed Cunningham had "lost his grip. He was not himself—he was not Cunningham." To leave him in charge would be to risk the existence of the Eighth Army and the whole British presence in North Africa. Yet to remove him might lower the morale of the already confused British troops and at the same time raise the spirits of the enemy; surely the Germans and Italians would look upon Cunningham's dismissal as an admission of defeat. Nevertheless, Auchinleck decided "it had to be done—rightly or wrongly." On November 26 he relieved Cunningham of command of the Eighth Army. Cunningham went reluctantly into a Cairo hospital, where he was found to be suffering from mental and physical fatigue.

To be Cunningham's successor, Auchinleck chose—or, in his own word, "pitchforked" into the job—Major-General Neil M. Ritchie, who had served in Cairo as deputy chief of Auchinleck's General Staff. Ritchie was familiar with Auchinleck's plans and could be counted on to know the mind of his chief.

At 44, Ritchie was the British Army's youngest general. He was handsome, wealthy and prone to take a rosy view of things, even in the worst circumstances. General Godwin-Austen, commander of the XIII Corps, said that Ritchie was "a very confident fellow—thought he was the goods." But, he added thoughtfully, universal agreement on this point was lacking. Ritchie had not led troops in combat since World War I, when he was a battalion commander.

It did not really matter. Auchinleck was virtually in command himself, with Ritchie functioning as his deputy. Auchinleck went out to Maddalena again on December 1 and stayed 10 days. With the commander in chief at Ritchie's elbow—and after that no farther away than the radio link to Cairo—the Eighth Army pulled itself together and continued Operation Crusader. Rommel still did not make it easy for the British. Although his tanks now were outnumbered 4 to 1, he succeeded in laying siege to Tobruk again on November 30. But without fresh supplies and replacements for his lost tanks and weapons, he could not stand up to sustained pressure from the Eighth Army. In a week the British forced him 40 miles west to Gazala, where, earlier, the Axis had prepared a fall-back defense line.

Rommel's defensive position extended some 40 miles to the southwest from Gazala on the coast. On December 15, Ritchie attacked the line from the east while sending an armored brigade sweeping around its southern end in an attempt to get behind the enemy and cut off his retreat. Rommel was determined to save what remained of his forces to fight another day. Although the Italian commanders, fearing that their nonmotorized infantry would be left

Racing headlong across the sand, French soldiers sally forth from Bir Hacheim in June 1942. In an epic 14-day struggle, the besieged Free French brigade gallantly defended the outpost that blocked Rommel's drive toward Tobruk. Determined to redeem the honor of the French Army, which had been tarnished in the fall of France, the stubborn garrison scorned surrender three times and finally fought its way out.

behind, objected strenuously, on December 16 he ordered a withdrawal, and slipped out of the trap before the British could close it. For three weeks the Axis retreated over the same ground they had crossed during their triumphant advance nine months earlier. Despite hot British pursuit, the withdrawal—including that of the Italian foot soldiers—was orderly and Rommel managed to avoid any further substantial damage to his forces as he fell back to El Agheila. In fact, on December 28 he seized an opportunity to attack a lone British armored brigade near Agedabia, inflicting a loss of 37 tanks on the enemy while losing only seven of his own.

However skilled his retreat and however determined his resistance in defeat, there was no escaping the fact that Rommel had suffered his first serious reverse. Operation *Crusader* had provided a sensational victory for the British. Early in January, Axis troops left behind on the Egyptian frontier, at Bardia and Halfaya, finally capitulated. Between November 18 and mid-January the British had taken about 33,000 Axis prisoners and destroyed 300 enemy tanks. They had lost more tanks than the Axis, but had suffered only half the number of personnel losses. Moreover, they had regained Cyrenaica—and driven Rommel back to the very point at which he had started in the desert in March 1941. "Here then we reached a moment of relief," wrote Churchill, "and indeed of rejoicing, about the Desert war."

In December 1941, events thousands of miles away suddenly exerted a powerful influence on the war in the desert. Japan's attack on British territories in the Far East forced London to divert to that area men and matériel earmarked for North Africa. Then around the end of the year, intensified Luftwaffe bombing of Malta and the arrival of German submarines in the Mediterranean—as well as successful raids by Italian midget submarines on Alexandria harbor (*page 86*)—worsened British supply problems at the same time they eased those of the Axis. On January 5, Rommel received by convoy 54 new tanks and a large supply of fuel. Now he felt strong enough to launch an attack on forward British positions, which he knew to be weak.

Setting out from his base at El Agheila on January 21, the Axis forces—now bearing a new, elevated designation, Panzer Army Africa—pushed north. Rommel quickly took Agedabia and Beda Fomm as the British fell back before him.

What began as a spoiling action to forestall any new British advance soon grew into a full-scale offensive. On January 29, Rommel entered Benghazi, which the British had abandoned, and there helped himself to large stores of booty, including 1,300 trucks. By February 6 he had pushed the British, who were now hurting badly for want of supplies, to Gazala—halfway back across Cyrenaica. In two weeks Ritchie's forces had lost 40 tanks, 40 field guns and some 1,400 officers and men.

The mounting crisis was compounded for Ritchie: his top subordinates had begun to lose faith in him. Godwin-Austen found to his discomfort that Ritchie "had a tendency to ask your advice and having received it to act in the opposite way," and—worse—that Ritchie bypassed him to issue orders to the officers of Godwin-Austen's corps. As a result, in early February, Godwin-Austen asked to be relieved of command of the XIII Corps. Auchinleck obliged, and Major-General W. H. E. Gott was pulled from the 7th Armored Division to take Godwin-Austen's job.

Other officers found the new Eighth Army commander no more reassuring than had Godwin-Austen. "Ritchie was all haywire by then," recalled Major-General F. W. Messervy, who took over Gott's post with the 7th Armored Division. "All for counterattacking in this direction one day and another in the next. Optimistic and trying not to believe that we had taken a knock. When I reported the state of 1st Armored Division to him at a time when he was planning to use it for counterattack, he flew to see me and almost took the view that I was being subversive."

Scenting trouble all the way from Cairo, Auchinleck sent Brigadier Eric Dorman-Smith, an old friend and trusted adviser, to investigate. On his return Dorman-Smith told Auchinleck that Ritchie was "not sufficiently imaginative" for his post and recommended that he be replaced. Although disturbed by the report, Auchinleck said no. "I have already sacked one army commander," he replied. "To sack another within three months would have effects on morale." He left Ritchie where he was.

Through the rest of the winter there was a lull in the fighting. Right into the spring, the Axis and British forces stayed on their own sides of the Gazala line, a 60-mile-long chain of defenses built by the British. From Gazala on the coast the line ran a jagged course southeast for about 40 miles, and then elbowed to the northeast for another 20 miles. The line was densely sown with mines, and scattered at wide, irregular intervals along it and to the east of it were a series of strongholds, each a mile or two square, called "boxes" by the soldiers who manned them. There were about six boxes in all. Some, like the one at Bir Hacheim, were known by Arabic place names surviving from early settlements; others, thrown up on unoccupied sites in the wasteland, were dubbed by the British soldiers with names such as "Knightsbridge" and "Commonwealth Keep."

Each of these boxes was girded on its perimeter with mines, barbed wire, slit trenches and pillboxes, and each had stores enough to withstand a week-long siege. Between the boxes, British tanks roamed freely. Their assignment was to intercept any tanks of Panzer Army Africa that might advance across their sector and also to race up or down the line to the aid of any box that might be attacked.

By late May, Rommel was ready to resume his offensive. While Axis infantry and some tanks launched holding attacks against the northern part of the Gazala line to preoccupy the divisions there, Rommel planned to lead the Afrika Korps and an Italian division south around Bir Hacheim, the box that formed the line's elbow. He would then swing north to chew up the British armor and attack the rest of the line from the rear. After that, he had planned a special treat for himself: the seizure of Tobruk.

The Axis struck in the north on May 26. Early on May 27 Rommel led his 10,000 vehicles around the British flank south of Bir Hacheim, leaving some Italian units to attack that box, and fanned out to the north and east. In his first encounter, about five miles northeast of Bir Hacheim, he quickly scattered the 3rd Indian Motor Brigade. By midday his forces had disposed of three more armored and motorized brigades.

But that afternoon he ran into an unwelcome surprise. The British had recently received a shipment of U.S. tanks—new 28-ton Grants, which were equipped with 75mm guns capable of firing high-explosive shells that could pierce the German armor.

By nightfall of the second day, thanks to a combination of dogged British resistance and the lethal new Grants, the two panzer divisions had lost a third of their tanks and had been

stopped outside the Knightsbridge Box, some 10 miles behind the main Gazala line and midway between Bir Hacheim and the coast. The Axis forces backed into a semicircular patch of some 100 square miles with British boxes and mines all around its perimeter—an area that would come to be known as "The Cauldron" for the seething battles that took place there. While Rommel regrouped, Italian engineers opened a new supply line to him from the west, through the minefields, but British artillery fire made resupply by this route difficult. Immobilized, the Axis troops were fair game for Ritchie. Now was the time for him to mass his armor and crush Rommel. Auchinleck, perceiving this from Cairo, dispatched a message urging Ritchie to take the offensive immediately, adding, "we must be ready to move at once, whichever way the cat jumps."

Ritchie was not ready. He went into a huddle with his two corps commanders, Norrie and Gott, to consider, committee style, various plans of action. For two days the British generals deliberated, and while they did, Rommel regrouped his forces. On June 1 he smashed a bigger hole through the Gazala line, ensuring easy access to his supplies. In the process he destroyed more than 100 British tanks, took 3,000 prisoners, eliminated the 150th Infantry Brigade and knocked out the box they held. Ritchie, his irrepressible optimism still undaunted, reported to Auchinleck: "I am much distressed over the loss of 150th Brigade after so gallant a fight, but still consider the situation favourable to us and getting better daily."

Rommel now turned south to deal with Bir Hacheim, simultaneously fending off some futile British assaults from the north. Bir Hacheim, the southernmost box in the Gazala line, was crucial to the British defense—and it was more strongly defended than Rommel had expected. The Italians who had begun attacking it on May 27 had made no headway. Bir Hacheim's 3,600 troops, mostly Free French, were under the command of Brigadier General Pierre Koenig, a tall, blue-eyed Frenchman known to his soldiers as "The Old Rabbit." Rommel expected to capture Bir Hacheim in 24 hours; instead it took him more than a week. "Seldom in Africa was I given such a hard-fought struggle," he recorded in his journal.

Between June 2 and June 10 the Luftwaffe flew 1,300 sorties against Bir Hacheim, while on the ground Rommel's

German gunners wheel a deadly 88mm gun into position near Tobruk. White rings painted on its barrel, like notches on a gunslinger's six-shooter, tally the number of British tanks the formidable gun has destroyed. Originally used as an antiaircraft weapon, the 88 was turned against the armor of the Eighth Army with harrowing effect. "It could go through all our tanks like butter," one awed Englishman later attested.

surrounding forces kept up a steady bombardment day and night. Several times Rommel asked Koenig to surrender, and every time Koenig curtly refused to do so. By June 10 the fort was down to its last reserves of food, and on orders from Ritchie the defenders evacuated Bir Hacheim. Koenig led the way himself, and 2,700 of his 3,600 soldiers fought their way through Rommel's forces that night. When the Germans stormed the fort on the following morning, they found only the wounded and some equipment that had been left behind.

After subduing Bir Hacheim, Rommel moved north along the Gazala line. One by one he knocked out the remaining boxes. By his quick maneuvering he nullified the advantage of the enemy's new tanks and destroyed so much British armor that by the third week in June he had achieved a 2-to-1 edge in tanks.

With the Gazala line a shambles, Rommel turned his attention to Tobruk.

The Tobruk of June 1942 was a far weaker fortress than the bastion that had withstood Rommel's assault the previous year. This was partly because men, ships and aircraft were needed elsewhere and partly because the Eighth Army had placed unfounded faith in the Gazala line. Furthermore, Auchinleck had no plans for another last-ditch defense of the fortress. As early as February 4 he had issued orders saying that whatever developed from Rommel's advance "it is not my intention to continue to hold Tobruk once the enemy is in a position to invest it effectively." He explained that he could not afford to have a full division penned up inside the defensive perimeter. His plans went uncontradicted by London, and he went ahead with preparations to evacuate Tobruk and destroy its stores if an Axis attack made such steps necessary.

Now, in June, the garrison had a new commander, South African Major-General H. B. Klopper, who had about 35,000 men, consisting mostly of South Africans but in part of Britons and Indians. Most of the troops, like Klopper himself, were recent arrivals, and few had combat experience. Many of the mines that had earlier protected the town had been removed when the beleaguered troops had sallied out during *Crusader* the previous November. Others had been lifted and resown along the Gazala line during the winter, when Tobruk seemed to be out of danger.

In the calamitous days of early June, as the boxes of the Gazala line fell and the Germans pressed farther north every

day, the troops at Tobruk made some frantic last-minute efforts to reinforce their defenses. But even as they did so, they did not know whether they should make plans to hold the fort at all costs or to evacuate it. No word came from Ritchie to guide them.

Britain's top commanders were as uncertain as the garrison. On June 15, after the last of the boxes had fallen, Auchinleck received a telegram from Churchill that read, "Presume there is no question in any case of giving up Tobruk." When, after a few more messages, this assumption of Churchill's grew to be an order, Auchinleck replied: "Ritchie is putting into Tobruk what he considers an adequate force to hold it."

Ritchie was trying to protect Tobruk by holding a new line extending some 30 miles south from the fortress. But on June 16 he authorized the British units in this line, which were suffering punishing panzer attacks, to withdraw to the Egyptian frontier to escape destruction. They fell back the next day and on June 18, Tobruk was once more under siege as Axis forces gathered around its perimeter.

"To every man of us," Rommel wrote later, "Tobruk was a symbol of British resistance, and we were now going to finish with it for good." The Afrika Korps and the XX Italian Corps—with the crucial assistance of the Luftwaffe—began to assault Tobruk on June 20. Throughout that day some 150 bombers flew 580 sorties. "They dived on the perimeter in one of the most spectacular attacks I have ever seen," wrote Major Freiherr von Mellenthin, Rommel's intelligence officer. "A great cloud of dust and smoke rose from the sector under attack and while our bombs crashed onto the defenses, the entire German and Italian artillery joined in with a tremendous and well-coordinated fire. The combined weight of the artillery and bombing was terrific."

As soon as a path was cleared through the mines that the Tobruk troops had hastily planted in the last few days, German and Italian infantry swarmed in, engaging in hand-to-hand combat with the British troops. Then the tanks rolled in behind the infantry.

Late in the afternoon, when the collapse of Tobruk appeared imminent, Klopper set about blowing up millions of dollars' worth of stores that had been meant to sustain the British desert effort. In the process he also knocked out most of his own telephone and telegraph lines—with the result that he could no longer keep in touch with his troops. At about 9 p.m., however, on one of his few remaining lines, Klopper did manage to communicate with Ritchie at Eighth Army headquarters. "Situation not in hand," Klopper wired. "All my tanks gone. Half my guns gone." Then he concluded on a plaintive note: "If you are counterattacking, let me know."

There was to be no counterattack. Ritchie's last message to Klopper, at 6 a.m. the following morning, read: "I cannot tell tactical situation and must leave you to your own judgment regarding capitulation."

At 9:40 a.m. on June 21, Klopper surrendered to Rommel. Ironically, the demolition that had cramped his own communication and movement was too little and too late to cheat the enemy. When Rommel took Tobruk, he won a rich prize—2,000 vehicles including 30 serviceable British tanks, 400 guns, enough fuel to fill up his panzers and start the drive for Egypt, 5,000 tons of provisions and large quantities of ammunition.

It had taken Rommel scarcely more than 24 hours to achieve this coup—the goal he had sought so long. "Tobruk! It was a wonderful battle," he wrote his wife that day. It was reported that, smiling broadly, he told a group of captured British officers, "Gentlemen, for you the war is over. You have fought like lions and been led by donkeys." The next day he learned that Hitler had rewarded his efforts by making him a field marshal. Later, when Rommel actually received his field marshal's baton from the Führer, he told his wife, Lucie: "I would much rather he had given me one more division."

The fall of Tobruk was a heavy blow to the Allies. Prime Minister Churchill later called it a "shattering and grievous loss." He was in Washington, conferring with President Roosevelt, when he heard the news. His only comment at the time was a laconic, "Rather disconcerting." But General Sir Hastings Lionel Ismay, Churchill's Chief of Staff, who was also present, recalled the moment as the first time he ever saw Churchill wince.

Churchill had reason to be alarmed; his own political future was at stake and—more important—so was the survival of his country. When he returned home he had to face a vote of censure in the House of Commons on his conduct of the War.

He won the vote by a wide margin, but the nation's dilemma was not so easily solved. The road to Egypt was now wide open, and Rommel was rolling along it full blast. To his troops he predicted that they would reach the Nile in 10 days. Within a week of taking Tobruk, he got as far as Mersa Matruh—140 miles beyond the Libyan border, and almost halfway to Alexandria.

As Rommel pressed deeper into Egypt, Alexandria and Cairo began to prepare for invasion. A pall of ash and smoke hung over the British Embassy and general headquarters, as officials hastily burned records. Automobiles and trucks clogged the roads leading away from the cities, and trains were packed with fleeing refugees. In Alexandria, Barclay's Bank paid out one million pounds in a single day to customers who feared a financial crash. In Cairo merchants tried to capitalize on the disorder. One, seeking the business of those who were fleeing the city, piled his windows high with luggage. Another, wooing stay-at-homes, touted bandages as a wise precaution against air raids. The only person who seemed to remain unperturbed in the crisis was the jovial, portly British Ambassador, Sir Miles Lampson. He threw a dinner party for 80 people at the Mohamed Ali Club. "When Rommel gets here," Sir Miles said, "he'll know where to find us."

Auchinleck, however, was of a different mind. On June 25 he flew to Mersa Matruh, relieved Ritchie of his command and took over the Eighth Army himself. From Mersa Matruh he retreated to El Alamein—a site that British troops had fortified in advance. El Alamein was 240 miles inside the Egyptian border and only 60 miles from Alexandria. But it stood in a neck of land that, as desert locations went, was defensible, because it was bordered on the north by the Mediterranean and on the south by hills that formed the lip of the impassable Qattara Depression, 700 feet below.

Here Auchinleck dug in. For the next six weeks, he lived among his troops, sleeping under the open sky and eating spartan rations. With his calm self-assurance Auchinleck tried to pump new spirit into the demoralized Eighth Army. Throughout July, Rommel hammered at the El Alamein line, but by a deft combination of offensive and defensive tactics Auchinleck held him at bay.

For Churchill's Cabinet in London, however—and for the British public—this was not enough. Auchinleck had to take some of the blame for the Eighth Army's losses over the past months, and for Ritchie's command in particular. Churchill and the British public were slow to forgive, and Auchinleck's reputation was clouded by the shortcomings of those he had placed in command under him. Churchill felt he had to boost public morale by bringing about another change in the desert command.

In August, therefore, two new British figures arrived on the desert stage. One was General Sir Harold Leofric Rupert Alexander, a veteran of Dunkirk, where he had been the last commander off the beach. He was wealthy, imperturbable, the possessor of a first-class military mind. It was said that during the perilous retreat from Dunkirk, Alexander, a stickler for proprieties even in the gravest of crises, sat down to a breakfast at a table set with a spotless cloth, serenely eating his toast and marmalade. Now he was given Auchinleck's post as commander in chief of the Middle East.

The other new arrival was Lieut. General Bernard Law Montgomery—eager, prickly, voluble, ruthless and unconventional. In character Montgomery was poles apart from the patrician Alexander, but that did not prevent the two from rapidly attaining an effective working relationship.

On August 12, the day before Montgomery was to take over Ritchie's post as commander in chief of the Eighth Army, he met with Alexander over afternoon tea in the mosquelike splendor of the lounge of Shepheard's Hotel in Cairo. There Alexander issued only one order to the Eighth Army's new commander. "Go down to the desert and defeat Rommel." Montgomery, at 54 about to take over his first important command, set off determined to do just that.

LIGHT RELIEF IN CAIRO

On the terrace of Shepheard's Hotel—one of Cairo's most popular watering places—British officers relax among civilians, some of whom often were Axis spies.

BEER, BATHS AND ANCIENT MONUMENTS

To the parched and exhausted desert fighters of the Allied armies, furlough in the Egyptian capital of Cairo meant more than a respite from combat. Cairo was a rare oasis of unaccustomed luxuries ranging from the simple to the exotic, from a hot bath and a cold beer to an evening spent watching the undulations of Madame Badia's belly dancers. Soldiers momentarily forgot the war as they roamed the teeming, noisy streets of this city on the Nile, searched for bargains amid the raucous Arabic cries of vendors, or rented camels for a ride around the Pyramids nearby. Officers, off duty from staff jobs at British General Headquarters or on leave from the desert, avoided the grit and flies of Cairo proper to play polo, golf or cricket on the sporting fields of the fashionable Gezira, a verdant island in the Nile.

The grimness of war barely touched Cairo. Among the few reminders of the bitter battles being fought in the sands to the west were the ambulance convoys arriving from the desert with fresh casualties, the recuperating wounded with their bandaged limbs, and the Cairo stock exchange, where prices dipped in response to each Axis victory.

Through this atmosphere of idle complacency ran a current of innuendo and intrigue. Communications between Cairo and the desert were spotty; the truth about the progress of combat came late to the city, and in its absence, rumor prevailed. In the bars and nightclubs, gossip about the war flowed as freely as liquor. Axis spies haunted Cairo nightspots favored by British officers to garner information that might prove useful to Rommel on his drive toward the city. Although Egypt had broken off diplomatic relations with Germany, it had not declared war, and in the native population of Cairo was a vocal, if ineffectual, contingent of Axis sympathizers. Students held rallies in support of the German advance, chanting "Press on, Rommel!" And in the Egyptian Army, a cabal of officers who were bent on ending the British presence in their country waited impatiently in Cairo for Rommel's invasion of the city—an invasion that was never to come. In the meantime, Cairo remained an ingratiating host.

New Zealand soldiers, armed with whisks to fend off the flies that swarmed in Cairo's narrow and dirty streets, peruse the offerings of a bazaar.

A smiling British Army woman and her companion take time off from the war to relax and wander about one of Cairo's nearby tourist attractions, the Sphinx.

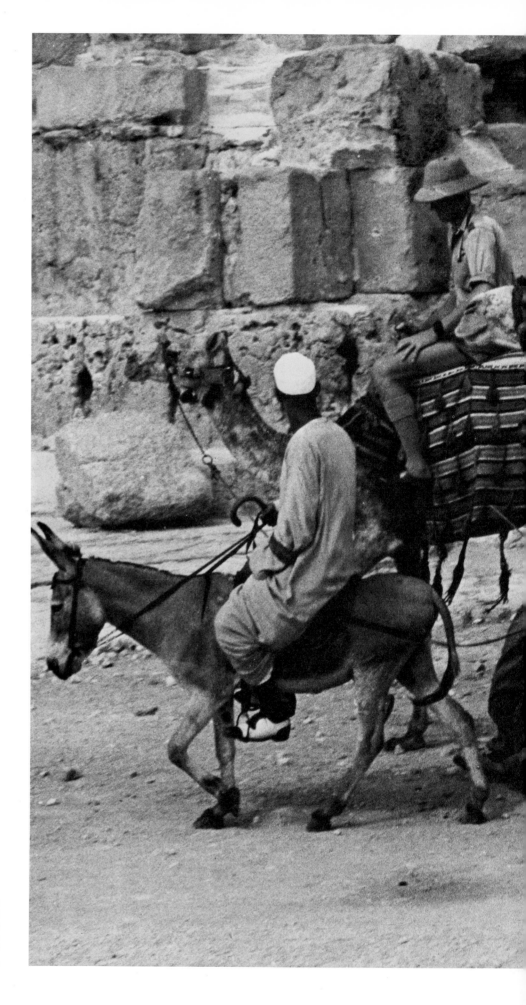

An Egyptian guide astride a donkey leads two
South African soldiers on a camel-back
expedition around the Cheops Pyramid close to
Cairo. The purses of guides and peddlers in
the city were fattened by the wartime influx of
British and Commonwealth soldiers.

Egypt's most famous belly dancer, the supple Hekmet, performs for British admirers. Hekmet was later arrested and accused of being a German spy.

A SOCIAL WHIRL UNTROUBLED BY WAR

In the evenings, as a cooling breeze drifted in from the green River Nile, the mood of Cairo mellowed, turning gay and romantic. The officers and their ladies went dancing at the roof garden of the Continental Hotel or at Shepheard's, a Swiss-operated hostelry with grand accommodations and sumptuous meals. Soldiers of lesser rank or gentility released wartime tensions in haunts like the Melody Club, where the band was protected from brawlers by a barbed-wire fence. The highlight of an evening's revelry was often a performance by the belly dancer Hekmet (left).

As the desert war raged on—even while Rommel's panzers were less than 100 miles away—Cairo lacked no amenity for the soldiers. Its steaks were tender, its wines French and its companionship warm.

A party of officers and their companions enjoys one of the nightly dinner dances held at Shepheard's Hotel, a social headquarters for the British in Cairo.

101

For a fee of four cents a month officers bound
for combat in the desert war could leave
their personal belongings in the storeroom
at Shepheard's Hotel. Many of these trunks and
bags eventually went unclaimed after their
owners met their fate in the sands to the west.

Although Cairo was not subjected to invasion, evidence of the war raging not far away was dramatically visible in the presence of wounded soldiers, such as this Free French officer making a slow descent with his comrades down the front steps of Shepheard's Hotel.

4

By the late summer of 1942 everyone sensed that the big push was coming. The question was: when? In the bars of Alexandria and in the Eighth Army's vast tented camp that had sprung up at El Alamein, 60 miles west of Alexandria, the British traded rumors endlessly. Only one thing was certain: the battle about to be joined would eclipse any the desert had seen before.

The Axis forces at El Alamein were dug in only a few thousand yards from the British lines, in a defensive position running from a rocky hummock on the coast to the Qattara Depression some 40 miles to the south. This position—the so-called Alamein line—could not be outflanked. If the British were to overrun it, they would have to do so by a massed frontal attack.

Day after day, from August to October, British reinforcements streamed to El Alamein: 41,000 men, 800 guns, more than 1,000 tanks, including 300 of the new 36-ton Shermans that Roosevelt had promised Churchill following Tobruk's fall. The tank commanders pinned their faith on the Shermans. With their 75mm guns, the Shermans could outshoot any Axis tanks except the Panzer IVs that had been fitted with new long-barreled guns—and of these Rommel now had no more than 30.

Despite the crushing reverses of the past seven months, and the formidable Axis defenses, few among the British were pessimistic. Within days of his arrival on August 13, Lieut. General Montgomery—already "Monty" to his troops—had instilled a new mood of confidence. Under his incisive leadership, the disillusioned men of the Eighth Army had swiftly grasped one salient truth: there would be no more retreating. To show that he meant business, Montgomery threw out Auchinleck's contingency plans for withdrawal to a secondary line of defense along the Nile Delta if Rommel broke through at El Alamein. "That's no plan," Montgomery growled. "By the time they have retired 10 yards," he said of his troops, "they will have lost half their fighting value." He announced that he was going to burn the plans. He took other convincing measures. He found a group of Tommies laboring on slit trenches to the rear and told them: "Stop digging there at once—you'll never need them." He sent the trucks on which any withdrawal from the front line would have depended lurching to the rear. Then, to all ranks he issued a blunt ultimatum: "From now

THE CRUCIBLE OF VICTORY

on the Eighth Army will not yield a yard of ground to the enemy. Troops will fight and die where they stand."

Montgomery was a stern disciplinarian who expected unquestioning compliance with his orders. "I want no belly-aching," he said. Moreover, he refused to tolerate sloppiness or low standards of discipline even in small matters. Staff officers soon learned to appear for meals spruce and on time in a brand-new mess tent fitted with laundered table linen and burnished cutlery. A slovenly army, in Montgomery's view, was an army halfway defeated.

Not all of his officers became Monty fans overnight. Some were irritated by the general's cocksureness and his mannerism of high-pitched repetition—"Bought it for the desert, bought it for the desert," he exclaimed of a new picnic basket. Deprecatory Monty jokes were heard here and there. In one a psychiatrist is summoned to heaven by St. Peter: "God's not feeling well. He thinks he's Monty." Someone later was to coin a heraldic motto for Montgomery: "In defeat, indomitable; in victory, insufferable." But the new desert general, borrowing a politician's techniques, scored resoundingly with the lower ranks. With his black Tank Corps beret ("worth two divisions," he said) and his cricket metaphors ("We've got to hit the enemy for six"), he proved to be a tonic for the bruised and bemused Eighth Army. Their job was to kill Germans, he told the troops, "Even the padres, one per weekday and two on Sundays."

But there was more to Montgomery's impact than salesmanship and wit. The quality that frontline troops most admire in their commanders is the ability to win battles. When Montgomery took over, the Eighth Army had endured a series of lackluster commanders who had repeatedly been outsmarted by Rommel. What they needed now was a demonstration that the new commander could lead the army to victory against the Axis forces. The opportunity was not long in coming.

On the night of August 30, Rommel launched his last attempt to smash the Eighth Army and break through to Cairo and Alexandria. The plan called for a large part of his forces, including four armored divisions, to attack in the south near the Qattara Depression, then to veer and cut off the Eighth Army from its bases by lunging north to the sea.

The operation depended on speed for its success. But the British had heavily mined the area where the assault was launched, and Rommel's troops spent the entire night clearing a way through the minefields. When they finally broke out, Rommel changed his plan and aimed his attack at a dominating topographical feature to the northeast called the Alam el Halfa Ridge. There, having anticipated the shift, Montgomery had dug in his American Grant tanks. Rommel's tanks and trucks were mercilessly shot up by the British armor and heavily bombed for two days and nights by the RAF. By September 3, after he had lost 49 tanks, Rommel fell back.

The Eighth Army now knew that it had a leader who could hold his own with the Desert Fox. But it soon became apparent that Montgomery was to take his own good time in getting ready for a decisive encounter with the Axis forces. The slowness of his preparations exposed him to some high-level criticism in London. Prime Minister Winston Churchill was impatient for the start of the big battle. "My next trouble will be to stop Winston from fussing Alex and Monty and egging them on to attack before they are ready," noted General Alan Brooke, Chief of the Imperial General Staff. Brooke was right. Churchill was urging a September attack, stressing the need to defeat Rommel before the autumn. On November 8 a mass Anglo-American invasion, under the code name Operation *Torch*, was to take place in French Algeria and Morocco. Churchill felt a victory at El Alamein would ease the way for the invasion by obliging the Vichy French in North Africa to take a more cooperative view toward the Allied effort. Moreover, Churchill was extremely eager for the Eighth Army to relieve the pressure on the embattled island of Malta—now under intense aerial bombardment for its role in the War as a British air and naval base—by capturing Axis airfields to the west of El Alamein.

But Montgomery categorically refused to move before October. If Churchill ordered a September attack, he would have to find someone else to command it, the general made clear. "It was blackmail," he later admitted, but it worked: no more was heard about a September attack.

Montgomery had a good reason for not attacking sooner. Even though the desert war had been going on for two years, he felt that the Eighth Army was not ready for the climactic battle. There were too many new recruits and improperly trained soldiers in its ranks. Montgomery was determined to make the army over into a top-notch fighting force. He pulled units out of the line, dispatched them to the rear, drilled them in the fundamentals of desert warfare and put them through field exercises on ground exactly like the terrain around the Alamein line. Six new antitank ranges were set up along the coast; there rookies fired 6-pounders at dummy tanks mounted on a moving assembly line. Nearby, a minefield-clearance school was established, and teams from 56 different engineer units were trained in mine-removal techniques.

For his part, Montgomery concentrated on tactics. His plan was to strike in the north, at the Alamein line's most heavily defended sector. To ensure complete surprise, one of the most elaborate plans of deception and concealment

in British military history was adopted. Under Lieut. Colonel Charles Richardson, of Montgomery's planning staff, an elaborate bit of fakery was contrived to dupe the Germans into believing that the British intended to strike in the southern part of the line.

In order to deceive Axis air reconnaissance, three and a half dummy field regiments of heavy artillery were constructed from timber and canvas—and manned by dummy gunners. Dummy soldiers were even positioned squatting on dummy latrines. A dummy water pipeline, simulated by empty gasoline cans, was begun, running 20 miles south to a portion of desert dotted with 700 stacks of dummy supplies. The ongoing construction was deliberately calculated to suggest to the enemy that the attack would not come

Wearing a jump suit and toting a parasol against the blistering sun, British Prime Minister Winston Churchill tours the Egyptian desert near El Alamein in August 1942, accompanied by his leading commanders. The Prime Minister, who regularly pestered his officers with advice and queries from London, relished the trip. "Now for a short spell I became 'the man on the spot,'" he wrote. "Instead of sitting at home waiting for the news from the front I could send it myself. This was exhilarating."

until after the pipeline was finished. At last the British were learning from—and improving on—Rommel's own successful use of deception.

To the north, a massive calm appeared to prevail among the British forces. But under cover of darkness, almost 2,000 tons of gasoline were concealed in 100 slit trenches near Alamein Station, on the coastal rail line. Food supplies were trucked in and draped with camouflage nets. And on the eve of battle, tanks were moved from staging to assembly areas and disguised as trucks with detachable canvas covers. Before dawn, to conceal the transfer, Richardson's men replaced with 400 dummy vehicles the real tanks that had left the staging areas.

Montgomery picked the night of October 23 for the assault. The training of his troops would be completed by then, and there would be a full moon, which would help the sappers clear paths through the enormous minefields that Rommel had laid in front of his position. Between the British front line and the Axis' rear headquarters the minefields stretched five miles deep and 40 miles long—500,000 deadly mines arranged in horseshoe patterns that Rommel called "The Devil's Gardens." In the eight hours before dawn the sappers were supposed to neutralize the mines, and the infantry and armor to push on through the fields.

As the zero hour approached, the Eighth Army could count on a 2 to 1 superiority over its panzer army opponent in almost every respect. Its troops outnumbered the Axis forces by 195,000 to 104,000, its medium tanks by 1,029 to 496. The British could also claim an almost 2 to 1 superiority in antitank guns and artillery. And the Eighth Army was well supplied. The Axis forces, by contrast, were suffering from critical shortages. Rommel's supplies had to be transported long distances from Axis-held ports—300 miles from Tobruk, 600 from Benghazi, 1,200 from Tripoli—making them vulnerable to air attack all along the way. In three short months, British submarines and bombers had cost the Germans and Italians 20 supply ships. Against the monthly 30,000 tons of supplies Rommel had demanded as a minimum, he had received no more than 6,000 tons.

To further compound the problems besetting the Axis, the Desert Fox had fallen ill. Throughout the summer Rommel had been driving himself to the edge of endurance. At last, on September 23, he could hold out no longer. Stricken by chronic stomach and intestinal catarrh, in addition to circulatory troubles and nasal diphtheria, he was forced to quit the front to undergo treatment 1,500 miles away in Semmering, Austria. General Georg Stumme, a paunchy veteran of the Russian campaigns, afflicted by acute high blood pressure, had taken his place.

Still, no one among the British saw the coming fight as an easy one—and the details of Montgomery's plan made all too plain how brutally difficult it was going to be. Under cover of a massive artillery bombardment, four infantry divisions of Lieut. General Oliver Leese's XXX Corps would move through the minefields, rooting out enemy machine-gun and infantry positions. Sappers would then clear lanes for the tanks of Lieut. General Herbert Lumsden's X Corps, which would then pass through and smash the Axis defenses. A secondary attack in the south by Lieut. General Brian Horrocks' XIII Corps would pin down German panzers in that sector to confuse the enemy further as to the Eighth Army's true objective. Meanwhile, British and American planes would bomb enemy positions and attack forward airfields in the Western Desert to prevent Axis planes from interfering with the Eighth Army's advance.

By the night of October 23 everything was in readiness. A skilled stage manager, Montgomery had overlooked few details. To the rear, 2,000 military policemen, in white gloves and red caps, stood by to shepherd the tanks to their objectives along six separate routes—and to direct the forward movement of water carts that would sprinkle the sand and hold down the dust. Medics double-checked their supplies of bottled blood and plasma inside refrigerated trucks, which were identified by the sign of a giant vampire bat. Sappers assembled their cumbersome paraphernalia: 500 long-handled mine detectors, like flat disk-shaped vacuum cleaners, 88,000 lamps to mark the minefield gaps for the advancing armor and 120 miles of marker tape to delineate cleared paths.

It was an unsettlingly quiet night, the silence broken only by the eerie call of night birds. The wide, golden moon, hanging low over the desert, was so bright that noncombatants to the rear, courting sleep, tugged blankets over their heads in order to blot out the light. Among the men who would soon be chancing death, reactions varied. Lieut. Col-

THE EIGHTH ARMY'S INTREPID DESERT COMMANDOS

In the fall of 1942, during the lull preceding the Battle of El Alamein, a handful of Eighth Army soldiers were waging a very different kind of war with the enemy. They were members of the Long Range Desert Group and the Special Air Service, two small bands of trained desert commandos.

The Long Range Desert Group was a reconnaissance force based deep in the Sahara, far behind enemy lines. Like a tribe of Bedouin nomads in British uniforms, its members had learned to survive in the desert—often on only half a pint of water a day—and to navigate the trackless wilderness with instinctive precision.

Such skills made these men invaluable as guides for the Special Air Service (SAS), a ground-based force that was so named because it originally was composed of paratroopers. SAS men were daredevils who wreaked havoc in lightning raids on Axis depots and airfields. They slipped into enemy strongholds by night, blowing up equipment and killing personnel, and then faded into the desert like a mirage when they were pursued. With help from the Long Range Desert Group's expert navigators, they made seemingly impossible treks hundreds of miles to and from their camps with remarkable ease.

Joint teams of Desert Group guides and Special Air Service commandos harassed the Axis unmercifully. They destroyed enemy aircraft, sometimes entering airfields on foot, sometimes donning German uniforms and boldly speeding past sentries in trucks with German markings. They apparently enjoyed their work and spread terror with cheerful liberality. One SAS officer recalled with relish tossing a bomb through the window of a German staff office as he shouted to the officer inside, "Here, catch this."

But their love of the theatrical did not impair their effectiveness. By the end of 1942 their relentless harassment had made such a dent in Axis supplies and morale that they received a kind of tribute from General Rommel himself, who in his diary said they "caused us more damage than any other British unit of equal strength."

A patrol of Special Air Service raiders, looking stern behind their machine guns, returns from a three-month sortie into enemy territory in September 1942.

onel Jack Archer-Shee and the officers of the 10th Hussars changed into formal dress for dinner, then proposed a toast to King George's health with vintage wine. The elegant Lieut. Colonel E. O. Kellett, of the Nottinghamshire Yeomanry—"Flash" to his men—set his servant to pressing and starching his best pair of breeches. If he was to be killed in battle, at least he would die looking his finest. Almost everyone wrote a letter home or made entries in a diary. Major-General Leslie Morshead, commander of the 9th Australian Division, warned his wife: "A hard fight is expected, and it will no doubt last a long time. We have no delusions about that. But we shall win out and, I trust, put an end to this running forward and backward."

Montgomery retired early to bed in his trailer. On the wall was a portrait of Rommel, beside which he had pinned a quote from Shakespeare's *Henry V:* "O God of battles! Steel my soldiers' hearts."

Five miles across the minefields, Stumme had no idea that the battle was at hand. Montgomery's ruses had worked. The Germans expected the attack to come in the south—and not until early November, after the water pipe the British were so busily laying was completed. The notion must have given Stumme some relief. He lacked gasoline for the 500 tanks that were supposed to support his infantry along the 40-mile Alamein line, and without sufficient fuel he could ill afford to shift his panzers back and forth to contain a British attack.

At 9:30 p.m., from far overhead came a faint throbbing: British bombers were moving up from the east to strike enemy positions and airfields. Then, briefly, there was silence. On the ground, all along the British front, gun commanders checked the snail-paced hands of their watches.

At 9:40 p.m., all along the line, the order was given: "Troop, fire!" Nine hundred guns spoke with an earsplitting, earth-shaking roar, and the entire front erupted in flame. The barrage—unequaled since World War I—poured a storm of fire onto the Axis positions; the explosions could be heard in Alexandria 60 miles away. Soon the British gunners were deaf from the thunder, and their thick gloves were burned through by the red-hot gun barrels. One Anzac officer reported feeling the ground vibrating under his feet "like the skin of a kettle drum." New Zealander Pe-

ter Llewellyn, who was a supply-corps driver, conceived a weird fancy—"giants were striking matches as big as pine trees on the rough desert, and a roaring wind was blowing out the flames."

Confusion reigned along the entire Axis line. The officers of the German 164th Division had been drinking with their commander, General Karl Lungershausen, in the huge dugout that served as tactical headquarters. With the first explosions a soda siphon rolled to the floor with a crash. One of the staff officers lunged forward to save a teetering bottle of wine. Peering through the slits of the dugout, Lungershausen could see the sky lit with brilliant flashes. He said incredulously, "The attack has started."

As the shells burst among the Axis strong points, acres of mines went skyward, spewing geysers of rocky sand and jagged lengths of barbed wire. Under the murderous roar of 900 rounds a minute, blockhouses crumbled and dugouts caved in; German and Italian soldiers dropped dead from the concussion of the exploding shells, with not a mark on their bodies.

Few men were more confused than Stumme. Within seconds of the start of the barrage, shells had torn his communications to ribbons. Stumme was cut off from every division, every regiment. He determined to head for the front line. Along with a staff officer, Colonel Büchting, and a driver, he set off for the battlefront early the next morning.

Jouncing through shellbursts, Stumme's staff car suddenly came under a hail of fire from Australian machine gunners. Büchting, mortally wounded, slumped forward. Now the driver reversed the car furiously—too intent on evasive action to see that Stumme was groping from his seat, fighting for breath, his face gray and mottled, pain gripping his breast. Stricken by a fatal coronary, he vainly tried to scramble from the car, then crumpled and fell.

The Axis forces were temporarily leaderless—and the battle was only a few hours old.

Montgomery's infantry had started moving up soon after the barrage began. One man who watched them, Captain Grant Murray, of the Seaforth Highlanders patrolling the line of departure, was never to forget it—"line upon line of steel-helmeted figures, with rifles at the high port, bayonets catching in the moonlight . . . gave us the thumbs-up sign. We watched them plod on towards the enemy lines which were by this time shrouded in smoke." They moved as they had been taught to move, three yards between men, covering a steady 50 yards a minute. In the Highland Division, in the northern sector of the line, each infantryman carried not only his small pack, two grenades, 50 rounds of ammunition, a day's rations and a full water bottle, but also a pick or shovel for digging slit trenches and four empty bags to fill with sand for protection. Each backpack was marked with a white St. Andrew's cross to orient those following.

Ahead of each battalion moved the navigating officers, compasses in hand, counting the paces, until the wire girdling the first minefields loomed into view. As one battalion of the Black Watch Highland regiment neared the wire, a voice called out to a company barber, who had charge of the wire cutters. "Get a bloody move on, Jock," it said. "You're no' cuttin' hair now."

From the first, the sappers faced a nightmare task. Although thousands of mines had already been exploded by the barrage, to clear all the mines was an impossible feat, and they did not attempt it. Instead, they tried to clear several lanes of up to 24 feet in width to allow the tanks to advance two abreast. They "deloused" antitank mines by feeling for and removing the igniters. Deadly S-mines, which were no larger than a can of beans and fired a lethal spray of shrapnel when stepped on, were disarmed by inserting nails into the small holes that had housed the safety pins before the mines were laid. Finally each gap, when cleared, was marked by white tape and orange and green pin-point lights—a signal that tanks and trucks could move up. Using detectors that reacted to metal objects underground with a sharp "ping" in the earphones, the sappers could clear up to 200 yards an hour.

Despite these heroic efforts, in the hours before dawn thousands of booby traps and mines took a gruesome toll. One section officer, forging ahead, had three trucks blown from under him in eight minutes. Miraculously he survived, but other men lay where they had fallen, torn apart by S-mines and fat, black Teller mines. A murderous 250-pound aerial bomb planted as a mine ripped a platoon of 30 men into bloody fragments. In one Black Watch battalion, mines killed or maimed seven navigating officers before dawn.

Yet a savage determination prevailed. Lieutenant Bruce Rae of the Gordon Highlanders, coming under fire, felt "as though I had had a couple of bottles of champagne." Lieut. Colonel Reg Romans, of the 5th New Zealand Brigade, somehow finding himself three quarters of a mile inside enemy territory with no enemy in sight, called out to his adjutant, "We can't stop here—we haven't fought yet!" He stumbled on until shellfire forced him to take cover.

Out of the maelstrom, men would carry with them scenes of surreal horror: a dead German signals officer with a telephone still cupped to his ear; another with a cigarette clutched in one hand, matches in the other; a severed white hand in the moonlight; blood seeping from the tight-shut door of an ambulance. Alaric Jacob, a war correspondent of long experience, could take no more than a few minutes at Dressing Station 86 of the 11th Australian Field Ambulance. "In one cubbyhole a doctor was amputating an arm, in another men lay gasping on trestle tables having fresh blood pumped into them. . . . Men with faces like soiled cardboard were slopped on a bench. The doctors worked like overworked butchers on a Saturday night."

Now a shortage of mine detectors slowed the advance literally to a crawl. Many of the detectors had proved defective, and others had been broken or destroyed in battle. The sappers had to prod the sand with bayonets; the rate of progress became that of a man on his hands and knees, listening, peering, probing. Anxiety spread from sector to sector. Could the mines be lifted fast enough for the oncoming armor to achieve its goal—a salient 10 miles wide, five miles deep—by dawn?

The answer was all too obvious. Struggling through the minefields, the advancing army was pinned down by Axis fire. In spite of the intensive artillery barrage and the efforts of the infantry, most of the Axis defensive positions remained intact. At dawn, in the north, British tanks unable to move forward were jammed together behind the infantry, motors running, radiators boiling. One man described the scene as resembling "a badly organized car park at an immense race meeting held in a dust bowl."

For all the fighting spirit of his troops, Montgomery had demanded too much of them.

All through the morning of October 24, as the sappers advanced yard by painful yard, with the armor stalled behind them, Montgomery, chafing in his headquarters, grew increasingly skeptical of their valor. "The X Corps Commander was not displaying the drive and determination so necessary when things begin to go wrong," he said later. He ordered the armor to push ahead regardless of whether the way had been cleared.

The top armor commanders were fearful that such an advance would mean heavy tank losses, not simply from the undetected mines, but from German antitank guns as well. Lieut. General Lumsden was appalled by the concept. One had to understand how to fight with armor, he said. "If you don't take your time you will get run through the guts. It is not for tanks to take on guns."

On the night of the 24th-25th what Montgomery was later to call "the real crisis of the battle" occurred. The tanks,

under Montgomery's orders, once more inched forward under cover of darkness. At about 10 p.m. a cluster of Luftwaffe bombs struck several supply trucks of the Nottinghamshire Yeomanry. In the tight column, truck after truck caught fire, and soon a wavering orange curtain of flame from 25 blazing trucks lighted up the night. Using the flames as a ranging point, field artillery, antitank guns, even lone bombers, loosed a rain of death on the tanks.

One regiment, the Staffordshire Yeomanry—sturdy brewers recruited from the Bass Brewery at Burton-on-Trent—came under the blowtorch fire of 88mm guns. An eyewitness, Major John Lakin, watched 27 tanks "go up in sheets of flame, one by one, just as if someone had lit the candles on a birthday cake." The Staffordshire's commanding

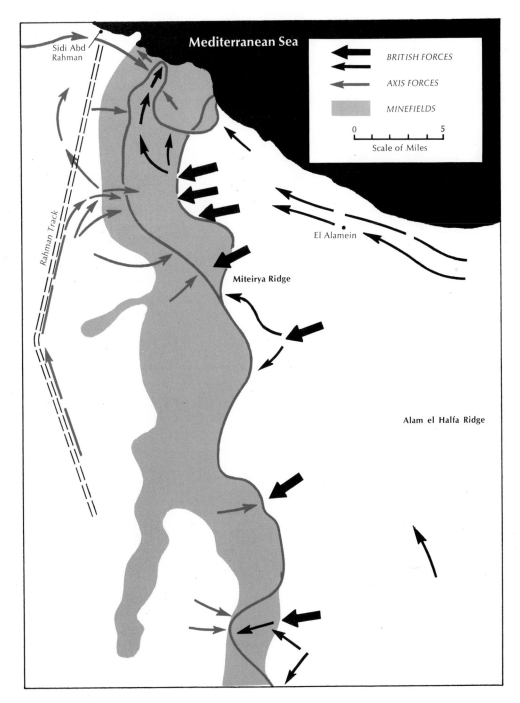

The Battle of El Alamein began on the night of October 23 with a British assault (black arrows) all along the front. Forcing their way through the enemy's minefields (shaded area), the British made moderate gains in spite of intensifying Axis resistance (red arrows). On October 31, British troops reached the coast, but the turning point of the battle did not come until November 2, when British armor, battering Axis defenses along the Rahman Track about 10 miles south of the coast, forced Rommel to break off and withdraw to the west.

officer, Lieut. Colonel James Eadie, broke down and wept.

Lumsden sent an urgent message to Montgomery's chief of staff, Brigadier Francis de Guingand: it was time to call off the attack. De Guingand acted swiftly. Despite Montgomery's deeply rooted aversion to being awakened at night, de Guingand, after first summoning Lumsden and Leese, commanders of the X and XXX corps, to a small-hours conference, aroused Montgomery to tell him.

At 3:30 a.m. on October 25, in Montgomery's trailer, the army commander listened in silence as Lumsden voiced his objections. The operation, Lumsden argued, should be abandoned; those few tanks that had already crossed Miteirya Ridge, a high strong point in the Axis line seven miles south of the coast, should be withdrawn before first light. Facing them just beyond the ridge, Lumsden warned, lay batteries of Axis artillery.

Montgomery shook his head. His plan must be followed through to the end: a withdrawal was out of the question. If Lumsden and his subordinates were unwilling to push ahead, others would be found to carry out the assignment.

Montgomery was giving his commanders a concept of warfare new to them. He reasoned with clinical logic that tanks, 900 of which were still operative, were expendable. But his infantry reserves were low; more than 6,000 men had fallen, dead or wounded, in the battle thus far.

Back to the raging fight on October 25 flew a weary Rommel. Although he knew that "there were no more laurels to be earned in Africa," he had been urged to return from his sickbed by an alarmed Hitler, who was still in the dark as to why Stumme had vanished. (In the heat of battle Stumme's disappearance had been reported but not his death.) Arriving at his headquarters just before nightfall Rommel now learned the worst from General Ritter von Thoma, commander of the Afrika Korps, who had taken temporary charge of Panzer Army Africa. Barely enough gasoline remained on the Axis side for three days' all-out fighting.

Rommel, who had distrusted the Army High Command but had retained his faith in Hitler's word, now realized for the first time the emptiness of the promises of the Führer. As recently as the end of September at his headquarters in Rastenburg, East Prussia, Hitler had assured Rommel, "Never fear, we are going to get Alexandria, all right." He had

expanded, weaving a web of military fantasy: a fleet of shallow-depth ferries, already in mass production, would rush gasoline across the Mediterranean by night and solve the supply problem; a brigade of new Nebelwerfer multi-barreled rocket launchers and 40 Tiger tanks, also in production, would be flown to Africa.

The reality was something else again. Not only were Rommel's fuel and ammunition supplies dangerously low; promised weapons had not appeared. The fighting in the desert had boiled down to a struggle of attrition, the kind of battle that the outnumbered Germans could not hope to win. Men fought with insane tenacity for a stony hill, for a hole in the ground, for a length of barbed wire. "Rivers of blood were poured out over miserable strips of land which, in normal times, not even the poorest Arab would have bothered his head over," Rommel later said.

During the first hours of fighting the Axis had managed to prevent a decisive breakthrough, but Montgomery was wearing down Rommel's forces piecemeal. The 15th Panzer Division, which had taken the brunt of the offensive in the north, had lost all but 31 of its 119 tanks. Rommel made desperate attempts to restore the old Axis line by counterattacks; they failed. The morale of the Germans and Italians alike had plunged. Rommel himself was feeling the pressure. "A very hard struggle," he wrote to his wife on October 27. "No one can conceive the burden that lies on me."

Montgomery was not one to admit to such doubts—but he too had reason for concern. His plan had been designed to achieve a dramatic victory over Rommel. But by October 26, the third day of the battle, most of his forces were still short of the objectives that he had originally expected them to reach in eight hours' fighting. Unless a new thrust could be developed and the stalemate broken, he realized, the British might well lose their momentum and their will to win. He spent most of the day closeted in his trailer—and emerged with the outline of a new plan.

Monty's best progress thus far had been made in the north, where the 9th Australian Division had penetrated most of the five-mile minefield and defense zone, and was now moving northwestward toward the coast. On the way it captured a piece of high ground that afforded a good view of the coastal road and railway. Montgomery now considered assembling a huge assault force to exploit the Austra-

SURVIVAL OF THE FITTEST IN ARMORED WARFARE

"The armor is the core of the motorized army," said Rommel, "everything turns on it." And the desert, with its flat, open terrain, provided the setting for armored warfare in its classic form. The result was a technological race between the protagonists to equip their armies with tanks that could outshoot, outmaneuver and outlast those of the foe. The tanks—some of the most widely used of which are displayed here—ranged from fast, light models for reconnaissance to heavily armored types for assaults on fortified positions.

At the start of the war, British armor, including the "Matilda," crushed the flimsy Italian M 13/40. But the balance shifted when Rommel arrived in early 1941 with his Panzer IIIs and IVs, two mobile tanks with excellent firepower. The panzers later were fitted with thicker armor and longer-barreled, more powerful versions of their already formidable guns.

The British forces were outgunned until they received American-built M3 medium Grants in May 1942. It was said that British crews manning the Grants shed tears of joy when they first found themselves overpowering panzers. The Grant's successor, the rubber-tracked M4 Sherman, a rugged fighting machine that was possibly the finest all-round tank in the North African war, arrived in time to be a key factor in Montgomery's victory at El Alamein.

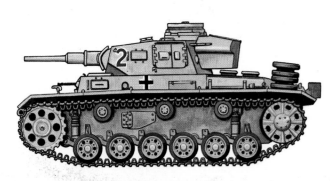

The unreliable Italian M 13/40 was dubbed the "mobile coffin" by the Axis forces because its armor plate was weak and it kept breaking down.

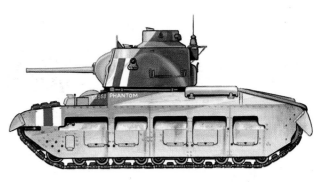

The 30-ton British Matilda, with a 2-pounder turret gun and a top speed of 15 mph, could withstand heavy fire because of its 78mm-thick armor.

The Panzer III, speedy and maneuverable, was highly effective in tank duels. Plated with 30mm armor, the 22-ton tank carried a 50mm gun.

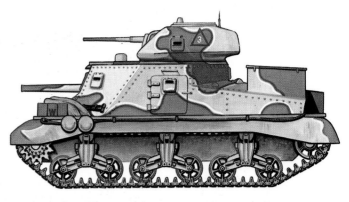

The Grant tank boasted both a 37mm turret gun and a 75mm gun, but the larger weapon was mounted on the hull, which restricted its arc of fire.

The 25-ton Panzer IV, a general-purpose medium tank, took on machine-gun nests, tanks, infantry and antitank guns with its 75mm turret gun.

Although the M4 Sherman tank had 62mm armor and weighed 36 tons, it could travel at 25 mph and had a 75mm gun in a power-driven turret.

lians' gains; if the coastal road could be seized, Rommel's supplies would be completely cut off. He began to pull the weary New Zealanders out of the line for rest and refitting: they would head up the new offensive.

Rommel, well aware of the dramatic Australian gains, brought his 90th Light Division in from reserve, and the 21st Panzers were moved some 30 miles from the south to the northernmost sector of his line. It was an irrevocable decision: he knew the gasoline shortage would not allow him to move the panzers south again if the necessity arose. But he could not afford to worry about that possibility; he must stop the British drive in the north.

In London, Churchill was puzzled. He feared that Montgomery might be giving up the attack when he pulled his troops from the line. "What is your Monty doing now, allowing the battle to peter out?" he demanded of Brooke. From Cairo, Richard Casey, Churchill's Minister of State in the Middle East, was sped to Montgomery's headquarters to investigate. He spoke to de Guingand, Montgomery's chief of staff. If Montgomery was to break off the attack, Casey suggested, perhaps a message should be sent to Churchill preparing him for the worst. "If you send that signal," declared the outraged de Guingand, "I will see that you are hounded out of political life!"

In actuality, Montgomery was hardening his battle plan. When he learned that Rommel was shifting his elite German troops to the north he decided to switch his main effort about five miles farther south. The Australians would continue to mount their attacks in the north. But the big push would be made through the vulnerable juncture where the German defenses abutted on the Italian part of the line. The initial objective, some four miles beyond, would be a powerful concentration of Axis field artillery along a section of undeveloped road known as the Rahman Track. The XXX Corps would carry out the attack, led by part of the highly respected 2nd New Zealand Division under Lieut. General Bernard Freyberg, a battle-scarred veteran of Gallipoli, the Somme and, more recently, Greece and Crete. The New Zealanders would be augmented by two British infantry brigades. Preceded by a thunderous artillery barrage, the infantry would attack to within 2,000 yards of the Rahman Track. Then the 9th Armored Brigade and the 1st Armored Division would pass through the infantry, overrun the Axis artillery positions along the track and break out into the clear. Rommel's panzer army would finally be destroyed— or so it was hoped.

The operation—under the code name of *Supercharge*—inevitably would surpass in its ferocity any action the men had seen so far in the battle, a fact that the British commanders, following Montgomery's stern rebuke of Lumsden, somberly accepted. At a conference before the battle, Brigadier John Currie, in command of the 9th Armored, noted that his brigade's task might mean 50 per cent losses. Freyberg replied quietly, "It may well be more than that. The Army Commander has said that he is prepared to accept 100 per cent."

At 1 a.m. on the 2nd of November, 360 guns opened fire simultaneously on the minefields beyond Miteirya Ridge, and the cold, blue desert night seemed to split apart. Like a steel shield advancing 100 yards every three minutes, the barrage poured a creeping cataract of fire upon mines and trip wires. It was so dense and so accurate, one officer later remarked, that his men "could have leaned on it." Indeed, some trod so close in the wake of the bursting shells that the first casualties turned out to be men suffering extreme dizziness from the bitter fumes of high explosives.

The infantry reached their objectives by 5:30 a.m. The tanks then passed through the infantry, but they had fallen a crucial half hour behind schedule, having been held up by mines and blinding dust. Forewarned by the bombardment, Rommel had time to set up a screen of antitank guns, even more murderous than the field artillery the British expected to face. The sky was beginning to brighten to the east, and the black silhouettes of the 9th Armored's lead tanks were plainly visible to the Axis troops manning the heavy guns on the other side of the Rahman Track. Tank after tank was hit and burst into flame, the crews bailing out through inky torrents of smoke and rolling frenziedly through the sand to stifle the flames that licked at their clothing.

But some tanks broke through to the gun pits, and as they lumbered forward the German gun crews were crushed under the tanks' treads or slaughtered by machine-gun fire. Some of the defenders turned and ran, others stood and fought, and died in the sand. A few Germans, like Lieutenant Ralph Ringler of the 104th Panzer Grenadiers, even tried to tackle the tanks singlehandedly. Ringler lobbed a hand grenade at a Sherman's turret and saw it bounce off harmlessly. Standing in the turret, the British tank commander called out, "Near miss!"

The toll mounted heavily on both sides. Within an hour, 70 British tanks were knocked out. Although Currie's 9th Armored never made it all the way through the enemy positions, a dent had been made, and now the tanks of the 1st Armored Division's 2nd and 8th brigades took up the assault. A furious counterattack ensued, as Rommel's 21st and 15th panzer divisions desperately tried to wipe out the British advance by hitting it from both sides.

The battle raged through most of the day. By evening Rommel was down to 35 German tanks. Almost 100 Italian tanks remained, but they had proved ineffective in the battle. A grim but inescapable fact was staring Rommel in the face: His panzer army had been decisively defeated. Rommel ordered gradual disengagement and withdrawal 60 miles to the west.

But the next day an order arrived from Hitler. "In the situation in which you find yourself," the Führer said, "there can be no other thought but to stand fast, yield not a yard of room and throw every gun and man into battle. . . . It would not be the first time in history that a strong will has triumphed over the bigger battalions. As to your troops, you can show them no other road than that to victory or death."

Rommel instructed his troops to stop their withdrawal, but he was aghast. "This crazy order has come like a bombshell!" he exclaimed to Field Marshal Albert Kesselring, who arrived to visit the front on the morning of November 4. Rommel, schooled in implicit obedience, was extremely reluctant to disobey the Führer's order. But throughout November 4 he saw more and more of his forces being destroyed, and finally decided he had no alternative. The Afrika Korps' Thoma put it even more strongly. "This order is a piece of unparalleled madness," he said. "I can't go along with this any longer." Sadly, Rommel ordered the withdrawal to the west to resume, "to save what still can be saved." He had lost an estimated 32,000 men, more than 1,000 guns, at least 450 tanks. A day later, Hitler authorized the withdrawal.

Now, as Rommel's shattered forces fled, an unnatural quiet descended upon the battlefield. For mile upon mile the sand was strewn with smouldering, gutted tanks. All around were gray-white Afrika Korps caps, empty shell cases, tar barrels, barbed wire and—incongruously—postcards. The dead, already blackening with decay, were surrounded by the last letters of loved ones. "We are so glad you have left that awful desert and are now in beautiful Egypt," read a message from a German mother. Scrawled in an Italian woman's handwriting were the words: "Always be a brave soldier, my dearest, and may Saint Dominic protect you."

Many British commanders were bitter over the cost: in 12 days, 13,500 troops killed, missing or wounded. The 51st's Major-General Douglas Wimberley, watching as the bodies of his Highlanders were carried from the field, swore, "Never again!" The 9th Armored Brigade's John Currie, asked where his armored regiments were, pointed grimly at the 12 tanks left to him: "There are my armored regiments."

Montgomery, however, was elated. Attired in a gray knit sweater and khaki pants, a silk scarf knotted at his throat, he told the war correspondents grouped around him, "It was a fine battle. Complete and absolute victory." Then, using the old World War I term for the Germans, he added, "Boches are finished—finished!"

It was almost—but not quite—true. In the driving rain that now engulfed the desert, Rommel was struggling to save the remnants of his army. But now there could be no real escape. As he retreated westward, his army's fate was already being sealed.

A BRUTAL POUNDING OF THE AXIS

The nighttime blaze of a 900-gun barrage on Axis positions at El Alamein silhouettes British infantry troops who are waiting to charge following the rain of shells.

BLOODY EL ALAMEIN: THE TURNING POINT

As a golden strip of fire flashed into the night over the El Alamein line on October 23, 1942, Field Marshal Erwin Rommel's Panzer Army Africa was taken by surprise. The artillery fire signaled the start of the biggest British attack of the desert war. In the days ahead, Lieut. General Bernard Law Montgomery threw in everything he had to crush the German-Italian army once and for all.

Although outnumbered almost 2 to 1 in men, guns and tanks, the Axis forces clung bitterly to their battered lines and faced some of the worst combat of the war. Lieutenant Ralph Ringler, in command of a company of panzer grenadiers, described a British tank assault he witnessed: "The first tank had reached the machine-gun position. It drove over the position and came to a stop with a squeaking of its tracks. It turned and buried the crew alive." Rommel himself described the fate of the Italian Armored Corps: "Tank after tank split asunder or burned out, while all the time a tremendous British barrage lay over the Italian infantry and artillery positions." After 12 days, Rommel had lost some 90 per cent of the 500 tanks with which he had begun the battle.

Facing annihilation, the Desert Fox had no choice but to order a complete withdrawal on November 4. His immediate goal was the Sollum and Halfaya passes on the coast near the Libyan frontier some 270 miles west of El Alamein. If he got there before the British did, he could block the passes with rear guards, whose staging action would enable him to escape with the rest of his army over the high plateau and along the coastal road west of them. In a race against time, the once-proud Afrika Korps and the remnants of Rommel's other units began their retreat. Along the coastal road, the tattered column stretched 40 miles long.

The fleeing army left behind more than 30,000 soldiers—captured and marched off to barbed-wire stockades around Alexandria. But Rommel's survivors did beat the British to the vital passes. With Montgomery's Eighth Army snapping at its heels, Panzer Army Africa fled 1,400 miles across Libya, reaching the sanctuary of Tunisia's hills in January 1943.

A line of British Crusader tanks rushes into the desert to hound Rommel's defeated Axis army from El Alamein westward across Egypt and Libya.

Tough Australian infantry troops, with their bayonets fixed for hand-to-hand combat, sneak over the smoke-filled battlefield to storm an Axis strong point.

A near-miss explodes into a column of sand and smoke, jarring a British heavy tank as it advances on Axis positions through a hailstorm of artillery fire and antitank shells.

Under an enemy artillery barrage on the front line, British soldiers of the Middlesex Regiment—automatic-weapons experts—man their machine gun during the El Alamein assault.

British soldiers, threatened by shellfire as they pursue the enemy across the open desert, crouch behind a German tank, hit and abandoned in the earlier fighting.

After the battle, German soldiers shoulder a stretcher carrying one of their wounded. The British estimated that 10,000 Axis troops were killed and another 15,000 were wounded.

LIMPING AWAY TO SAFETY IN HILLS TO THE WEST

Carrying as many of their wounded with them as they could, the beaten Axis army offered the British a chance to deliver the final blow as it crawled painfully westward along the coastal road northwest of El Alamein. At 2:45 a.m. on November 6—the retreat's second day—pilots of the British Desert Air Force reported a solid mass of enemy vehicles on the coastal road. Since the British commanded the skies, this appeared the perfect opportunity to cut up Rommel's forces.

But, to the pilots' complete surprise, the Eighth Army—whose coordination with its air force was suffering from the confusion of battle—called for air strikes only five times on that crucial day. In the following days the retreating column was bombarded intensely. But the British pilots lacked the strafing ability that they would develop later in the War, and thus a larger number of men and vehicles survived than might have. The opportunity was lost completely by November 12, when the only German or Italian soldiers left in Egypt were prisoners of war.

Australian troops, emerging from a dust cloud on the debris-strewn El Alamein battlefield, help a wounded German soldier who was captured during the fight.

A bomber's-eye view of the Egyptian coastal road, choked with German and Italian vehicles fleeing El Alamein, reveals (inset) a portion of the 40-mile traffic jam

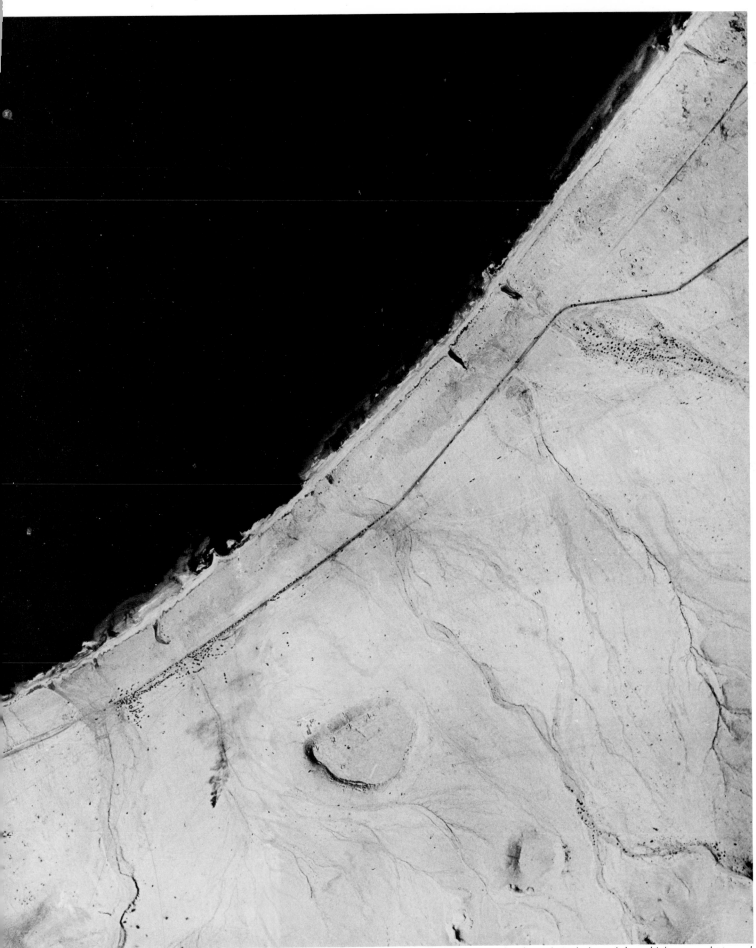

nearing the Halfaya and Sollum passes. The British dropped 170 tons of bombs on the road in just two nights, but relatively few of the vehicles were destroyed.

Discarded clothing and an abandoned truck mark the frenzied Axis retreat from El Alamein.

Having survived the bloody battle at El Alamein, this

German soldier was riding his bicycle westward, in an attempt to catch up to the retreat along the coastal road, when he was spotted and killed by a British sniper.

MONTY AT THE HELM

Primed for his first encounter with Rommel, Lieut. General Montgomery (center) discusses tactics with officers of the Eighth Army on the 15th of August, 1942.

A MAN TO TURN THE TIDE

Bernard L. Montgomery, the Eighth Army's commander at the Battle of El Alamein, was a paradox. Brusque, overbearing and rigidly uncompromising, he was almost everything the British people instinctively dislike. Yet he commanded not only the respect of his men in the field but the adoration of millions at home.

The Bible-reading, teetotaling son of a bishop, Monty—as his men liked to call him—was a natural leader who hated to be a follower. His childhood was a prolonged contest of wills with his mother and her iron Victorian discipline. At school he excelled at sports but refused to play unless he was made captain of the team. In the Army he gained promotion because of his single-minded devotion to soldiering. The senior officers who recommended him for advancement always groused that he was a bit too erratic and opinionated, and Montgomery himself admitted that he was a hard man to get along with. "One has to be a bit of a cad to succeed in the Army," he said early in his career. "I am a bit of a cad."

But Monty was more than a cantankerous eccentric. Beneath the flamboyant façade was a dedicated professional with a keen understanding of how to inspire combat soldiers. To the bedraggled force in the desert that had been outwitted and badgered by Rommel for more than a year, he was a refreshing change. Small and wiry, with searing blue eyes, he rode around dressed in a pull-over sweater and khaki pants, waving to his men instead of saluting, and tossing cigarettes to them as he passed.

He made a point of visiting frontline units, gave pep talks to the troops, instituted a rigorous new training program and let it be known that henceforth the Eighth Army would move only forward.

Everywhere he went, this brisk, decisive, relentlessly exacting general left the air charged with self-confidence. God and right were on his side, and victory was just around the corner. "We will finish with Rommel once and for all," he promised his men, and he never doubted that his prophecy would be fulfilled.

Wearing short pants, Montgomery at the age of 14 aims a gun while hunting rabbits in Tasmania, where his father served as bishop for 12 years.

Sporting the black beret that became his trademark, Monty nonchalantly leans against an American-made Grant tank as a shell explodes behind him in 1942.

Montgomery takes a jump using the backward-seat technique fashionable during his days as a gentleman cadet at the Royal Military College at Sandhurst. The fractious Montgomery got into trouble with authorities there when he set another cadet's shirt on fire as a prank, but he still managed to graduate in 1908.

Boots muddied from a tour of the trenches in France, Brigade-Major Montgomery (at right) and his commanding officer lean on their canes near the Arras front in 1916. Fourteen months earlier Montgomery had been wounded and almost left for dead on the battlefield.

Major Montgomery was 39 when he married Betty Carver (above left). She was a gentle pacifist and appeared an unlikely match for the proud career soldier, but Monty was devoted to her. Ten years after their marriage Betty died of an infection caused by an insect bite; Montgomery, plunged into despair, vowed that he would never remarry.

Four years after his wife's death, Montgomery visits his son, David, a schoolboy of 13 in 1941. Monty was a dedicated father; to make sure David had a home while he was away he asked the headmaster of the boy's school to raise David as a member of his own family.

Monty takes tea with tank men of the 6th Royal
Tank Regiment during a brief pause in their
pursuit of Rommel across the desert after the
victory at El Alamein. He let himself be
known to his men and regularly stopped to talk
tactics with the lowliest foot soldiers.

At an informal conference, Monty congratulates
New Zealand and English armored troops
who participated in the swift outflanking
movement that forced Rommel to abandon the
Mareth Line in southern Tunisia. By then,
Monty and his men were a highly successful
team, full of pride and mutual respect.

The dust-covered commander of the Afrika Korps, General Ritter von Thoma, salutes Montgomery after being captured during the final day of fighting at El Alamein. Cordial but professional, Monty invited the general to dinner, verbally refought the battle with him and made a tape of their conversation.

From the turret of his Grant tank, Montgomery beholds the outskirts of Tripoli, the last unconquered Italian port in North Africa. Tripoli fell to him on January 23,

138

1943, adding to his unbroken string of successes: in the three months following El Alamein he pushed the Axis forces back across 1,400 miles of North Africa.

5

Six miles off the coast of French North Africa, the ships rode quietly at anchor under a new moon. Only muffled sounds broke the stillness of the night: the muted squeal of winches as boats were lowered, the muttered curses of fighting men, each laden with 60 pounds of equipment, as they grappled down rope ladders into bobbing landing craft. Soon the first of the craft, their screws churning the water to a silvery froth, were gliding shoreward.

The time was shortly before 1 a.m., November 8, 1942—just four days after Montgomery's defeat of Rommel in the desert at El Alamein. Now, at diverse points along a greener and more populous stretch of coastline far to the west of Egypt, a new hammer blow at the German forces in North Africa was in the making, beginning with an amphibious operation on a scale never before attempted.

More than 107,000 troops—three fourths of them American, the rest British—were to go ashore on a mission of unique complexity. First they were to secure a foothold at nine key coastal points spread over a distance of some 900 miles. Next they were to take control of three of French North Africa's biggest port cities: Casablanca in Morocco, Oran and Algiers in Algeria. Then they were to speed eastward into Tunisia to seize Tunis and Bizerte before these major ports, the closest to the enemy's bases in southern Europe, fell into Axis hands.

The sheer magnitude of this venture—which was the first major joint Anglo-American operation of World War II—was daunting, but it was off to a good start. Astonishingly, the armada of more than 500 American and British ships, setting out from harbors as far apart as Portland, Maine, and Loch Ewe in Scotland, had traveled over the Atlantic unmolested by German submarines. Not until noon on November 7, less than 13 hours before the first landing craft were supposed to head for shore, did the Germans conclude that a massive enemy movement was under way—and even then they mistook its destination.

Because of the distances separating the three focal points of the landings—600 miles from Casablanca to Oran, 250 miles from Oran to Algiers—the Allied armada had been organized into three task forces: Western, Central and Eastern. Casablanca, objective of the Western force, lay on Morocco's Atlantic seaboard, directly accessible from the ocean. But in order to reach the Mediterranean ports of

AN ALLY JOINS THE WAR

Oran and Algiers, respectively the goals of the Central and Eastern forces, the transports had to travel through the Strait of Gibraltar.

German agents on the Spanish side of Gibraltar had reported an unusual number of Allied ships offshore as early as November 3. At that moment, however, Hitler had other things to worry about: not only Rommel's imminent disaster at El Alamein, but also the monumental battle in which German forces were locked with the Russians at Stalingrad. The enemy ships in the western Mediterranean, the Führer decided, were no more than a heavily guarded convoy bound for the island of Malta. By November 7, with Rommel retreating toward Libya, Hitler changed his mind. The Allied ships, he concluded, were indeed bent on invading the African coast—probably at the Libyan ports of Benghazi and Tripoli.

A deliberate feint by the Allies had encouraged both of Hitler's conjectures. Steaming due eastward, the Central and Eastern task forces had in fact appeared to be bound for Malta or beyond it for Libya. But sometime after dusk on November 7 both forces wheeled south and under cover of darkness took up stations off Oran and Algiers, even as the Western Task Force arrived off Casablanca.

Operation *Torch*—a code name suggested by Winston Churchill to replace the earlier, less lyrical choice of Operation *Super Gymnast*—was about to face its first critical test.

Aboard the transports, men waiting their turn to climb over the side squinted under dim red lighting designed to adjust their eyes to night vision and tried not to dwell on the dangers ahead. For most of the Americans, this would be their first taste of combat. Some shored up their courage with flippancy, others affected nonchalance. On the H.M.S. *Royal Ulsterman* off Oran, Sergeant Walter S. Sieg of the U.S. 1st Ranger Battalion devoured a last-minute hamburger, quipping: "At least we get something American in our stomachs before we die." Sergeant Gene K. Elzas listened intently to a short-wave broadcast from home of the Army-Notre Dame football game. Aboard the cruiser U.S.S *Augusta*, Major General George S. Patton Jr., commander of the Western Task Force, was deep in a paperback whodunit, *The Cairo Garter Murders*.

Other commanders were moved to exhortation. Major General Charles W. Ryder, in charge of the Eastern Task Force off Algiers, offered dubious comfort to his men: "Some of you will not make the beaches—but you will be immortal!" An infantry colonel from Minnesota struck an earthier note, counseling his troops to "light out like stripey-assed baboons up the wharf until you can get some cover—then fight like hell."

For the men who were already nearing the shore in the first wave of assault craft, the time for exhortation was past. Instead, they heard only their own loudspeakers repeatedly booming shoreward over the dark waters: "*Ne tirez pas. Ne tirez pas. Nous sommes vos amis. Nous sommes Américains.*" ("Don't shoot. Don't shoot. We are your friends. We are Americans.") Then, in sudden response, the horizon ahead was marked by what looked like sheets of lightning— the flashes of 75mm coastal guns, manned by French crews. The word spread: "They're fighting."

The planners of Operation *Torch* had known that its first big hurdle would be of French rather than German making. Though defeated at home, the French still controlled their overseas empire. The men in charge in the colonies differed widely in their sympathies toward the Allied cause. Some fervently favored it; some were pro-American but implacably anti-British; others, swayed by the smashing German triumph over the French homeland, regarded any aid to Germany's foes as both foolhardy and futile.

Whatever their personal views, French North Africa's administrators were officially answerable to their superiors at Vichy, seat of the government that had been formed after the fall of France to rule the part of the country not occupied by the German victors. In turn, the Vichy regime was answerable to Berlin. Hitler had exacted a price for allowing the French to retain control of their African possessions: Vichy had pledged that the French themselves would defend these territories in the event of an Allied invasion.

How stubborn the defense would be was a question that had occupied the planners of *Torch* during months of inconclusive probing. Because Vichy had severed ties with Britain, the task of sounding out the French had fallen mostly to the Americans—who still maintained relations with Vichy—and to one American in particular: a craggy, affable career diplomat named Robert D. Murphy. As counselor of the American Embassy in Paris and more recently in

Vichy, Murphy had acquired a host of French friends and a feel for the intricacies of Gallic thinking.

Secretly assigned by President Roosevelt as his personal representative in North Africa, Murphy shuttled about the area discreetly ascertaining the private sentiments of military officials and influential civilians, gauging the potential worth to the Allies of various anti-Vichy and anti-Nazi underground groups, appraising the help or hindrance that might come from Arab nationalists who hoped in time to rid their lands of all Western rule.

One of Murphy's myriad assignments involved a carefully concealed trip to England two months before the invasion to brief the man who was to direct the Allied Expeditionary Force, an American then so little known to his countrymen that some newspapers back home had at first spelled his name wrong. He was Lieut. General Dwight D. Eisenhower.

As Murphy recalled: "From questions asked I could see that Eisenhower and some of his officers had mental pictures of primitive country, collections of mud huts set deep in jungles. I assured them that French North Africa was more like California than a tropical wilderness, and I described briefly the creature comforts of Algiers and Casablanca. Eisenhower then prudently inquired whether winter underwear would be necessary, and I told him it was, especially on the high plateau in eastern Algeria. Thousands of American soldiers appreciated that the following winter."

To the key question—the sort of reception that would greet the landings—Murphy offered two possible answers. If the French perceived *Torch* as an American operation, they would be less inclined to resist, for the tradition of Franco-American friendship died hard. But if they perceived *Torch* as a British affair, they would fight bitterly.

Still rankling the French were two instances of what they regarded as their former ally's perfidy. In an attempt to keep the French fleet from Hitler's grasp after the fall of France, the Royal Navy had shelled and sunk or disabled four French warships at Mers el Kebir, near Oran, killing more than 1,200 sailors. To cap matters, the British had given haven to a "Free French" government-in-exile led by an arrogant general, Charles de Gaulle, whom many of his compatriots viewed as a traitor.

But there were two other Frenchmen whose support, if won by the Allies, could lessen if not eliminate resistance to the landings. One was General Henri Giraud, a North African expert and brilliant soldier in both world wars, held in high esteem in the French Army. Though he had found sanctuary in Vichy after escaping from German captivity, he had not—unlike other top-ranking French officers—sworn an oath of allegiance to Vichy's aged chief of state, Marshal Henri Philippe Pétain.

The second, if fainter, hope of the Allies rested on a five-star admiral, Jean François Darlan, who served Vichy as commander in chief of all French forces—naval, land and air. A sometime admirer of the German war machine, Darlan had given recent signs of a change of heart, hinting to Murphy that North Africa would take up arms against the Axis—if given the help of 500,000 American troops.

Just 16 days before the landings were to begin—some convoys had already sailed from the United States—a secret parley took place in an isolated villa on the Algerian coast. Arranged by Murphy at Eisenhower's request, the meeting brought together three American officers led by Major General Mark W. Clark, Eisenhower's deputy commander, and a group of French officers led by the ardently pro-American Major General Charles Emmanuel Mast, deputy commander of French ground forces in Algiers and a staunch supporter of General Giraud. Little was accomplished except a vague

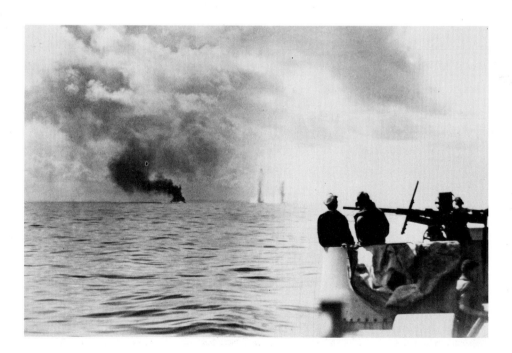

During Operation Torch, gunners aboard the U.S.S. Augusta watch the splash of salvos fired by the French battleship Jean Bart from her moorings about 12 miles away in Casablanca harbor. (The smoke on the horizon is a screen laid by two French corvettes.) Soon thereafter U.S. bombers hit the Jean Bart (far right) and opened a 75-foot gash in her hull.

promise—never kept—to put Giraud, eventually, in charge of the Allied forces. Because the Americans were under orders not to mention the British role in *Torch* or to reveal the impending date of the landings, the French got the impression that *Torch* was months away, giving them time to prepare to help it succeed.

The meeting had unexpected elements of slapstick. Local Arabs, noting the unusual stir at the villa, suspected smugglers; hoping for a reward, they notified police, whose arrival forced the American officers to hide in the wine cellar while Murphy, upstairs, feigned a drunken stupor. Clark, too, had his moment of discomfiture; en route back to the British submarine that had stealthily deposited him on Africa's shore, he somehow managed to lose his trousers.

The invasion planners' concern with secrecy was to lead to more serious problems. Murphy was forbidden to alert the pro-Allied French underground until four days before the landings, thus reducing the chances for concerted action with the one source of French support on which the Allies could absolutely rely. More than 20 tons of small arms and walkie-talkies intended for these clandestine groups, and due to be landed by British submarine, never did arrive—largely, Murphy suspected, because the British doubted the ability of either the French or the Americans to keep a tight lip. Forced to depend on such antiquated weapons as were at hand, the Allies' strongest sympathizers were to prove no match for the well-equipped Vichy loyalists.

In Algiers, the indefatigable Murphy made one last effort to ensure that the fighting would be minimal. Word of the start of the landings had reached him over a small radio receiver-transmitter flown from Washington by way of Lisbon in a sealed diplomatic pouch; the code message, contained in a BBC broadcast in French from London, said simply: "*Allo Robert. Franklin arrivé.*" At once Murphy sped

to the suburban villa of his good friend General Alphonse Pierre Juin, commander in chief of all of French North Africa's ground forces. Roused from bed, sleepy and rumpled in pink-striped pajamas, Juin reacted to the news of the landings with shock. Although he was bitterly anti-German, his only concern now was that French lives lay in jeopardy. But as Murphy pleaded with him to order his troops not to fight, Juin shook his head. Any such order, he pointed out, could be countermanded by Admiral Darlan, who outranked him.

By pure chance, Darlan was in Algiers, summoned from Vichy to the hospital bedside of a son who had been stricken with polio. At Murphy's urging, Juin telephoned Darlan. In less than 20 minutes the admiral appeared—only to turn purple and explode as Murphy broke the news. "I have known for a long time that the British are stupid," Darlan shouted, "but I always believed Americans were more intelligent. Apparently you have the same genius as the British for making massive blunders!" The invasion, he went on, was "premature," and "not at all what we have been hoping for."

Murphy retorted: "It is your responsibility to arrange that no French blood will be shed by senseless resistance to the American landings already in progress."

Pacing the room and puffing furiously on a pipe, Darlan seemed torn by indecision. "I have given my oath to Pétain and preserved allegiance to the Marshal for two years," he said. "I cannot revoke that now." Murphy kept talking and kept pace, tactfully adjusting his long stride to the pint-sized Darlan's shorter steps. Finally, Murphy asked if the admiral would cooperate if so authorized by Pétain. Darlan agreed, and drafted a message to the Marshal.

But in the message, reporting the situation as Murphy had outlined it, Darlan also took pains to note—as if to signal

Vichy that he had not forgotten—that the 1940 armistice terms with Germany required the French to defend their territories. The admiral was cannily hedging his bets, waiting to assess the strength and mettle of the invasion force.

The answer to that question was even then being spelled out on beaches and airfields, docks and streets throughout Darlan's sphere of command.

The Allies' tactical plan called for each of their three main objectives to be taken the same way: by landing troops at points on both sides of the objective, then encircling it. In addition, the inner harbors of Algiers and Oran were to be seized by special detachments to head off sabotage of the port installations by the defenders; the shipping facilities of these cities, much closer than Casablanca to the Allies'

ultimate goal, Tunisia, would prove invaluable in the Allied drive eastward.

Algiers was the first objective to be taken, though the assault on the port itself failed dismally. Nearing the Bay of Algiers in the predawn darkness, the British destroyers *Malcolm* and *Broke,* packed with more than 600 American infantrymen, made several passes before finding the harbor entrance. Then, caught in the searchlights, the two ships came under withering shellfire from the heights above the bay—from batteries equipped with infrared thermal detectors and range finders. The *Malcolm,* badly hit, had to withdraw. The *Broke* managed to slice through the barrier booms, berth at a quay and unload 250 men. But on her way out in the early morning light she was so heavily pounded that she later sank. Though the members of the landing

GIs wearing combat garb and Moroccans dressed in djellabahs mingle at the gatehouse of the Hotel Miramar on the outskirts of Casablanca, where Major General George S. Patton set up his headquarters on the second day of Operation Torch. "Very nice," commented Patton of the Miramar, "but it had been hit several times so there was no water nor light and only cheese and fish to eat and champagne to drink."

party secured a power station and oil storage tanks, they were soon pinned down by machine-gun fire and captured.

Behind the harbor another key move went awry. General Mast, despite the ambiguous answers he had been given by General Clark at their secret meeting two weeks earlier, had irrevocably thrown in his lot with the Allies. At his direction, anti-Vichy groups seized police stations and Radio Algiers. But as morning came and American troops did not appear, Mast's people were overpowered by Vichy loyalists.

Mast's efforts proved more effective among friendly fellow officers at military installations outside the city. The landings were virtually unopposed; Fort Sidi Ferruch, on the coast 12 miles west of Algiers, surrendered without a shot. From three sets of beaches designated as Apples, Beer and Charlie, men and tanks and armored cars moved on past fishing hamlets and seaside resorts, through olive groves and vineyards, meeting only minor pockets of resistance.

Inland, Algiers' main airfields, Maison Blanche and Blida, yielded quickly. Patrolling over Blida, the leader of a flight of planes off the British carrier *Victorious* noticed white handkerchiefs fluttering on the field; he landed and got the French commander's written permission for Allied planes to fly in. American ground troops reinforced by British commandos took Maison Blanche, soon followed by two squadrons of Hurricanes from Gibraltar; though they had no way of knowing when taking off that the field would be in American hands, the RAF pilots had risked making the flight from the Rock without enough fuel to get back.

By mid-afternoon, Allied forces were on the high ground overlooking Algiers and a cease-fire was being arranged by General Juin—with Admiral Darlan's approval. At 7 p.m. on November 8, less than 20 hours after the landings began, American troops moved in to occupy the city.

Oran held out longer and fought harder; memories of Great Britain's devastation of French warships and crews at nearby Mers el Kebir were still fresh, and General Robert Boissau, the area commander, ordered that a stern resistance be shown to the invaders.

The element of surprise was also lost. As some of the ships of the Central Task Force prepared to lower boats for a run to a beach west of Oran, their path was crossed by a small French convoy inward bound. By the time of the Allied frontal assault on the inner harbor of Oran, sirens had sounded a general alarm throughout the city and a blackout was in effect. Attempting to land troops and antisabotage personnel, the U.S. Coast Guard cutters *Walney* and *Hartland*—transferred to the Royal Navy under Lend-Lease, but flying the American flag—met a rain of fire both from shore batteries and from French destroyers and submarines in port. The *Walney,* raked by broadsides, was soon a blazing hulk; drifting helplessly, she eventually rolled over and sank. The *Hartland* was blasted by a shore battery that wiped out her gun crew. Then she was hit at point-blank range by a French destroyer; the shells burst in her engine room and amid troops massed to land. The dead were heaped so thickly on deck that the survivors could not get at the hoses to fight the fires. As the *Hartland* drifted about the harbor, all power gone, flames funnel-high, her captain, blinded by a shell fragment, gave the order to abandon ship. More than half of the 600 men on the two cutters were lost; most of the rest were taken prisoner.

Calamity also attended the initial attempts to take the key airfields at La Senia and Tafaraoui, south of Oran. Troops moving inland from the beaches were to have been joined by paratroops flown directly from Cornwall, on England's Channel coast. Storm and fog en route broke up the formation of 39 planes. Seven of them never made it to Algeria; 12 planes dropped their troops more than a day's march from the objectives; the remaining 20, short of fuel, landed close enough to take part in the action, but four were seized on the ground by the French.

It took a concerted attack by American armor and infantry, finally converging on Oran after having to fight most of the way, to force the city to surrender. Major General Lloyd R. Fredendall, Commander of the Central Task Force, received the formal capitulation shortly after noon on November 10—more than 48 hours after the first of some 39,000 troops had come ashore.

Yet despite the tenacity of the defense, scores of Allied units had learned at first hand that the French front against them was less than solid. U.S. Rangers, scaling one of the steep bluffs near Oran like mountain goats, had found the gunners of the French Foreign Legion garrison at Fort du Nord distinctly disinclined to shoot; after the Rangers' leader, Lieut. Colonel William O. Darby, agreed to an offer of "token resistance"—the firing of one rifle round skyward—the gunners came out with their hands up. During the battle in Oran harbor, Americans struggling in the water and trying to dodge the machine-gun fire from a circling French motor launch had watched other Frenchmen—in rowboats—braving the bullets in an effort to rescue them.

Similarly bewildering scenes had taken place all along the invasion coast. "The mix-up of French emotions was fantastic," wrote the American war correspondent Ernie Pyle. Even as some Frenchmen fought to the death, others—including many civilians—hailed the Allies as deliverers. American troops moving to seize the Cape Caxine lighthouse in Algiers had been intercepted by a joyful bistro keeper nearby, insistent on feting them first with champagne. Near Casablanca, one boatload of Americans, forced to take precipitately to the water after their craft had been ripped by a French destroyer's shells, were hauled ashore by dozens of sympathetic civilians, who wrapped the dripping soldiers in their own coats.

But the powerful French naval contingent at Casablanca was less kindly disposed. The most celebrated of the warships in the harbor was the 35,000-ton battleship *Jean Bart;* under construction at a base on the Bay of Biscay when France fell, she had been sent to North Africa to prevent her seizure by either the British or the Germans. Though still unfinished, and unable to leave her moorings, the *Jean Bart* was capable of wielding her four formidable 15-inch guns. In the first daylight hours of the invasion, she opened up on the covering warships of the Western Task Force, dueling with them at 12- to 17-mile range. It took eight hits from the battleship *Massachusetts* and strikes by U.S. bombers to put the *Jean Bart* out of action.

Meanwhile, under cover of a smoke screen, seven French destroyers and eight torpedo-bearing submarines, followed by the cruiser *Primauguet,* slipped out of Casablanca harbor on a bold mission of their own: to attack the American transports as they unloaded their landing craft off the small nearby port of Fedala. Of the three landing points in Morocco selected by the planners of Operation *Torch,* Fedala was the closest to Casablanca, only 14 miles away. The French attackers appeared, came under fire and withdrew. But they returned again and again—finally to encounter the heavy guns of the cruiser *Augusta* and other covering warships. All but one of the French ships were sunk or forced to beach.

The battles off Fedala and Casablanca cost the French Navy the lives of some 500 sailors. Among the fatalities were wounded men who had been lying helpless on the deck of the *Primauguet,* and who had been savaged by fear-crazed pigs broken loose from their pen in the ship's hold.

One grim-faced witness to the clash off Fedala was General Patton, on the *Augusta;* his diary that day was to record a landlubber's awe at the American ships "all firing and going like hell in big zig-zags and curves." When the French appeared, Patton and some of his staff had been about to take off for the Fedala beachhead; a landing craft had been stowed with his gear, including his cherished brace of ivory-handled pistols. The craft, still swinging from davits, was blown to bits by a muzzle blast from the *Augusta's* rear turret—but someone had thought to retrieve the general's pistols in time.

Patton had less reason to rejoice when, on the morning of November 9, he made a tour of the Fedala beaches. Confusion reigned. The planners of *Torch,* lacking any precedent for an amphibious operation of such magnitude, had overlooked many essential details. In the unloading of the supply ships, automotive transport had been given low priority; thus matériel brought in could not be moved inland, and lay heaped in the sand on the beaches. Army engineers, who should have been among the first ashore in order to organize exits from the beaches, had been unaccountably detained aboard their transports. Then mechanical failures beset some of the unloaded amphibious tractors, making it impossible to salvage many of the landing craft that had been swamped or stranded.

Similar mishaps had bedeviled the landings around Algiers and Oran, but Patton had two special problems to cope with. One was the pounding surf along the Atlantic shore, which made a mockery of unloading schedules. The other was the extent of the front assigned to the Western Task Force. It stretched almost 200 miles, from Safi, a small, deepwater port 125 miles southwest of Casablanca, to Mehdia, 70 miles northeast—the nearest approach to Port Lyautey, the site of French Morocco's best airfield.

Added to these complexities was another that Patton ran into only after he began roaming the Fedala beaches. A

High-ranking Allied officers and a guard of honor surround the coffin of Admiral Jean François Darlan, gunned down in his Algiers headquarters on Christmas Eve, 1942. The assassin was a young French Royalist named Bonnier de la Chapelle. Chapelle, summarily executed, apparently was enraged by the bargain that put Darlan in charge of civil affairs in French North Africa in return for his assistance during the Allied invasion.

warrior born, he was mortified to find men under his command who were plainly frightened by strafing French planes overhead. Under fire for the first time, they were more preoccupied with digging foxholes than with unloading supplies. Patton, short on patience and long on profanity, moved among the men cursing and exhorting, wading up to his waist in water as he guided in landing craft, dragging men from their foxholes, kicking the backside of any soldier who dared crouch down.

The final straw for Patton was a lack of adequate communications equipment, desperately needed to keep in touch with his far-flung subtask forces. By November 10, only one of the bulky SC-299 radio sets he had counted on had been brought ashore. Cipher machines had been landed far from the units that required them; vital items of signal equipment lay buried beneath piles of supplies still aboard the ships. As one Patton biographer later noted: "For once, the United States Army's most loquacious general had lost his voice."

One message, however, did come through to Patton on November 10. It was from Eisenhower, saying: "The only tough nut left is in your hands. Crack it open quickly." The shooting had stopped in Algiers and Oran. The two outermost objectives in Morocco, Safi and Port Lyautey, had been subdued. Casablanca alone still held out. Patton, without consulting his commander in chief, decided there was only one quick route to victory: an air and naval bombardment of Casablanca at daybreak the next morning, followed by a ground attack, to force the city's surrender.

But at 6:48 a.m. on November 11, Colonel Elton F. Hammond, Patton's signal officer, heard his walkie-talkie crackle

HIGH-LEVEL MATCHMAKING AT CASABLANCA

In January of 1943, as the Allies were closing in on the Axis armies in Tunisia, a top-secret meeting was taking place in a Casablanca hotel surrounded by barbed wire and bristling guards. President Roosevelt and Prime Minister Churchill had traveled to North Africa, where their armies were fighting side by side, to map out a grand strategy for the rest of World War II and to agree on a new objective: the "unconditional surrender" of the Axis powers.

At the same time, the Allied leaders tried to force a "shotgun marriage"—as Roosevelt put it—on the two leading figures in the tangle of French politics that imperiled stability in North Africa. General Henri Giraud, who had been made High Commissioner of French North Africa with Allied approval, came face to face with the politically ambitious General Charles de Gaulle, leader of the Free French.

At the end of the talks, Roosevelt got the two tall, proud Frenchmen to shake hands for press cameras. Their first touch was so fleeting and feeble that some photographers complained that they had missed the shot. The generals got up and shook hands again (below), then exited. Roosevelt called after them, "Bon voyage." Five months afterward, de Gaulle ousted Giraud through political maneuvering and took control of French North Africa.

Roosevelt and Churchill watch Giraud (left) and de Gaulle clasp hands for the cameras in the garden of the President's Casablanca quarters.

into life. "Call it off," came Patton's staccato voice. The French had capitulated—only minutes before the American attack was to begin. "It was a near thing," Patton wrote later to his wife, "for the bombers were over the targets and the battleships were in position to fire. . . . These hours were the longest of my life so far."

Later that day—the 24th anniversary of the signing of the World War I armistice, and Patton's 57th birthday as well—the commanders of the French naval, air and ground forces in Morocco arrived at Patton's headquarters at the Hotel Miramar in Fedala. He complimented them on the fight they had put up, read them the armistice terms, then added one condition of his own: they would have to join him in a toast—to the liberation of France by their combined efforts.

What had brought the hostilities to a sudden end was a cease-fire order applicable to French troops everywhere in North Africa—an order issued on the morning of November 10 by Admiral Darlan. Presumably it was issued in the name of Marshal Pétain, but the Vichy regime no longer mattered in any event. By midnight on November 10, Axis troops—10 German and six Italian divisions—had swarmed into unoccupied France, taking over full control.

Darlan's reward from the Allies was his appointment as High Commissioner of French North Africa, in charge of civil administration, with General Giraud under him as commander of the French ground and air forces. In America and Britain a storm of protest arose over the so-called "Darlan deal." Critics bitterly assailed the role bestowed upon a former Axis collaborator. In justification, President Roosevelt reminded questioners at a White House press conference of an old Balkan proverb: "My children, it is permitted you in time of grave danger to walk with the devil until you have crossed the bridge."

Ironically, the furor about Darlan was soon to become moot; before the end of 1942 he was dead at the hands of an assassin—a compatriot. But even his short-lived cooperation with the Allies relieved them of a heavy burden. They lacked officers who were versed in French or Arabic, and enough troops to police the region; they were in no position both to govern North Africa and press the next phase of their campaign—the sweep into Tunisia. They needed the assistance Darlan gave them, and the help of the 200,000 French fighting men he brought over to the Allied cause.

Buoyed by the success of the landings, the Allies confidently expected to reach Tunis and Bizerte, their main objectives in Tunisia, in a 450-mile dash from Algiers that they figured would take about two weeks. Speed, they knew, was essential. By November's end, northern Tunisia—the area of their projected operations—would begin to turn into a sea of mud, pelted by winter rains that would not let up before March. Nor was weather the only spur to swift action: Tunis and Bizerte had to be won before Axis forces got there in overwhelming numbers.

The Axis build-up was already under way. Hitler's indifference toward the Mediterranean theater, long a source of anguish to Rommel and farseeing German strategists, had vanished overnight. Suddenly, it had occurred to the Führer that more than the entrapment of Rommel's forces was likely if the Allies took Tunis and Bizerte. These cities, equipped with good port and airfield facilities and situated on the Mediterranean at its narrowest point east of Gibraltar, would serve as the best staging ground for an Allied move to breach Hitler's Fortress Europe where it was weakest, along its southern ramparts.

The vanguard of the Axis forces, 24 Stuka dive bombers and 27 Focke-Wulf and Messerschmitt fighters, landed at El Aouina airfield in Tunis on November 9, while the Allies were still fighting to take Oran and Casablanca. Scores more planes quickly followed; then came German ground forces, ferried in by air and sea at the rate of 750 per day. By the end of the month they would number some 15,000. Rommel, his own forces now wearily retreating toward Libya's border with Tunisia in a 40-mile-long column, was predictably bitter when he found out that some of the fresh troops in Tunisia had been drawn from reserves previously promised to him.

Only a few thousand men were initially available to the Allies for the drive toward Tunisia. As Eisenhower later explained it: "There still existed the fear that the Germans might thrust air forces down across the Pyrenees into Spain, to attack us from the rear." With the Western and Central task forces required for rear-guard duty, the responsibility for the Tunisian campaign fell primarily to British and American armor and to infantry of the Eastern Task Force, now renamed the British First Army under a new commander: Lieut. General Kenneth Anderson, a dour, unsmiling Scot nicknamed "Sunshine."

The troops left Algiers by sea, land and air on the evening of November 10, less than 72 hours after they had arrived there, and sped eastward. In accord with Anderson's plan, based on the need to shorten his supply lines, they took the eastern Algerian ports of Bougie, Djidjelli, Philippeville and Bône and swept inland to secure the highway towns of Sétif and Constantine before moving over the border into Tunisia. By November 16 they were at Souk el Arba, a railhead 80 miles southwest of Tunis.

Anderson had little to please him on his entry into Tunisia. In taking on his assignment, he had wondered aloud whether he should consider himself "an able general or an outright lunatic," and his forebodings now seemed justified. His hopes of expediting supplies by rail were dampened by the discovery that some of the railway lines were standard gauge, others meter gauge, creating delays in the transport of freight. Locomotives and rolling stock were old and inadequate, and there were no freight cars capable of accommodating medium tanks.

Even more discouraging was the terrain. Except for the coastal flatlands around Tunis and Bizerte, the northern part of the country was mostly mountainous, the eastern end of the great Atlas chain. For lovers of scenery, there was much to admire: red rock ranges ribbed by winding valleys and rivers, scattered with cork forests and with vineyards dappled in the scarlet and gold foliage of autumn. But military eyes noticed the narrow defiles through which tanks and troops would have to squeeze, the heights from which the enemy could observe their movements, the dense hillside shrubbery in which he could conceal his mortars.

For a time, however, Anderson's troops advanced largely uncontested; his opposite number, General Walther Nehring, had chosen to concentrate on his Tunis and Bizerte beachheads, steadily enlarging their perimeters against the Allied approach. On November 25, Nehring braced for a confrontation with the enemy. Word reached him that Allied tanks were within nine miles of Tunis. The report was false. What had happened, in fact, was one of the war's most extraordinary episodes: the triumph of tanks over grounded aircraft.

During a brush with the German garrison at Tebourba, 20 miles west of Tunis, Lieut. Colonel John K. Waters, commander of an American tank battalion—and Patton's son-in-law—had sent one of his companies to reconnoiter ahead. The tanks reached a low ridge above a newly established German airfield at a place called Djedeida. Carelessly guarded, it proved fair game for the 17 tanks of Company C. They rushed the field, destroyed 20 planes, shot up personnel and installations, and departed into the dusk.

Waters' satisfaction was short-lived. Next day, a few miles from Djedeida, his battalion took up positions on the slopes above a pass near the village of Chouigui. Then the whole countryside blew up. From what seemed at first to be some German mobile derrick equipment, near a farm about a mile to the north on a dirt road, shells came screaming in. The vehicles were the Germans' deadly Panzer IVs—13 of them. What had appeared to be boom spars were long-barreled 75mm guns.

In the battle that ensued—the first between German and American armor in World War II—the Americans learned that their M3 light tanks, so efficient and responsive in field maneuvers, simply could not match the brutal power of the panzers. A young second lieutenant, Freeland A. Daubin Jr., saw the shells from his 37mm cannon bouncing fruitlessly off a Panzer IV's 50mm plates. The panzer came on, closing from 150 yards to 75, while Daubin vainly pumped 18 more rounds at it. At 30 yards, the panzer launched a round that buckled the M3's front like tin plate and killed the driver. Daubin was blown from his turret by the concussion and hurled to earth, still stunned and uncomprehending as medics carried him off the field.

By the time the battle was over, five more M3s had been destroyed. The best the Americans were able to do was to put six Panzer IVs temporarily out of commission—not by penetrating them with direct hits but by chipping away at the engine doors and shooting at the tanks' tracks.

But the Americans could draw no comfort from this feat; the real implications of the battle were appalling. A Panzer

IV could totally wreck an M3; an M3 could merely disable a Panzer IV, permitting it to fight again. Other U.S. tank battalions were equipped with the medium General Lee, but in subsequent battles it too proved no match for the Panzer IV. If disaster was to be averted in Tunisia, the Americans there would need more powerful tanks.

On December 2, General Anderson informed headquarters that his troops were stretched thin, his communications imperiled, forward reserve supplies nonexistent and air cover wholly inadequate against relentless streams of German planes that were within quick striking distance from airfields in Tunis and Bizerte. General Eisenhower agreed to a breathing spell.

Two days later, the German army in Tunisia also paused—to receive a new commander far more aggressive than Nehring. The replacement was Colonel General Jürgen von Arnim, plucked by Hitler from the Russian front, where he had been commanding a corps.

The Allies' breathing spell, which was prolonged by worsening weather, ended a few days before Christmas. A thrust at Tunis was to be made by troops of the British 6th Armored Division; other troops were to protect their left flank by taking a number of positions in the hills above the valley of the River Medjerda. One position above all was prized: a hill two miles long and 800 feet high, known to the Arabs as Djebel Ahmera and to the Allies as Longstop Hill. Whoever held Longstop commanded the whole of the valley, which stretched all the way to Tunis, 25 miles distant.

At dusk on December 22, in a merciless rain, Lieut. Colonel W. S. Stewart-Brown's 2nd Battalion of the Coldstream Guards waded across sodden meadows to the slopes of Longstop. Clinging to saplings and bushes, they struggled upward. Then glittering sprays of tracer ammunition arched from the hillside above. Soon Britons and Germans were grappling in hand-to-hand combat across the rocky slopes, biting, gouging, kicking. But by 10 p.m. the Germans had melted into the night, and the Coldstream dug in.

Just before dawn on December 23 they were relieved by men from Colonel Frank Greer's 1st Battalion, 18th U.S. Infantry, and slogged the 12 miles back to base. At five that afternoon the Coldstream began slogging out to Longstop again: the Americans were in deep trouble. Unknown to the Allies, Longstop was a double peak. Beyond a gully on the far side loomed the second peak, almost 800 feet high—and in German hands. A surprise rush by the Germans had sent the Americans back down Longstop's slopes.

As the Coldstream Guards returned, the rains redoubled. The mud was now like some brute force, wrenching the rubber boots off men's feet. It was so thick that no vehicle could get within a mile of Longstop. Every grenade, every clip of ammunition, had to be passed by hand.

Pinned down on the lower slopes by mortar and artillery fire, the Allied troops fought through Christmas Eve to regain Longstop's crest. By 10 a.m. on Christmas Day, with 356 Americans and 178 Britons lying dead or wounded, an order came to withdraw. Longstop was lost; its jubilant German captors quickly renamed it Christmas Hill.

The Allied withdrawal had the unhappy consent of Eisenhower himself. During a personal inspection of the surrounding countryside the day before, the general had seen the appalling difficulties posed for his troops by the combination of weather and terrain. The hopelessness of a winter thrust toward Tunis, he was later to recall, was borne in on him by one incident in particular: "About thirty feet off the road, in a field that appeared to be covered with winter wheat, a motorcycle had become stuck in the mud. Four soldiers were struggling to extricate it but in spite of their most strenuous efforts succeeded only in getting themselves mired into the sticky clay. They finally had to give up the attempt and left the motorcycle more deeply bogged down than when they started."

Eisenhower now knew at first hand what would happen to any tanks that tried to push on. That evening, at Allied headquarters in a farmhouse near Souk el Khemis, he informed his assembled commanders of a "bitter decision"—a postponement of the campaign. The Allies had lost the race for Tunis. What lay ahead, instead of a pell-mell dash for the coastal ports, was a slow, months-long process of building up reinforcements and supplies.

TIPPING THE BALANCE

American infantrymen come ashore near the Algerian port of Oran on the 8th of November, 1942, carrying the Stars and Stripes into the North African action.

TORCH: A MASSIVE INVASION OF AFRICA

"This is the largest landing operation that has ever taken place in the history of the world," Hitler remarked with awe and envy as he received intelligence reports about hundreds of Allied transports and warships approaching North Africa on November 7, 1942. Operation *Torch,* a massive bid by the Allies to end the desert war, was under way.

Anything that floated—from a converted refrigerator ship to an ex-passenger liner—had been enlisted to transport more than 107,000 British and American soldiers to the Vichy French colonies of Morocco and Algeria. The ships came laden with 11,000 tons of food, 10 million gallons of gasoline and no less than 500,000 pairs of shoes. Early on November 8 the troops hit the beaches, weapons in hand—and equipped with mosquito netting, dust masks, water purifiers, sun goggles and salt tablets. Hoping to be welcomed by the French, the U.S. soldiers wore small American flags on their left sleeves and carried booklets that told them how to behave in North Africa. But as they soon discovered, the French reception was in most places anything but friendly.

Because of its scale, Operation *Torch* had its problems. Vehicles fell overboard, troops were landed on the wrong beaches and some soldiers wearing heavy packs drowned when their boats crashed onto reefs. At one landing site, ammunition reserves lay buried beneath tons of rations. And in a bit of tragicomedy, when the ramp of a landing craft was lowered too soon, an officer drove a jeep into eight feet of water.

Torch also had its share of resourcefulness and heroism. Shallow water stopped a ship carrying tanks more than 360 feet from the beach, but engineers hurriedly set up a pontoon bridge to get the vehicles ashore. When one American transport was crippled by a U-boat torpedo in the Mediterranean, the 700 infantrymen aboard piled into 24 landing craft and headed for the coast of Algiers—155 miles distant. The landing craft—designed for very short voyages—soon broke down, but the soldiers crowded aboard an escorting corvette and got to the scene of the fighting.

Aboard the carrier U.S.S. Ranger, crewmen carefully load a 1,000-pound bomb onto a U.S. Navy SBD dive bomber supporting the Torch landing.

While British sailors help to steady his descent, an American soldier climbs down the side of his transport into an assault boat for the run to Algeria's shore.

A U.S. Army 2½-ton truck, heavily loaded with supplies, splashes onto the Algerian shore from a landing craft to battle its way across the soft sand of the beach.

The wreck of a jeep that slipped from a swamped landing craft lies overturned on Morocco's Atlantic coast, where huge waves made the landing difficult.

American soldiers bend to the job of beaching an antiaircraft gun unloaded in Algeria, while other United States and British troops wait for orders to advance. Although Vichy French planes strafed such landing sites, their infrequent attacks did not succeed in stopping the flow of men and matériel coming ashore. Ironically, some of the attacking planes were American-made P-36s that had been sent to France before its fall.

To search a building in Algeria, specially trained U.S. assault infantrymen called Rangers kick in a door while a buddy covers them with a submachinegun.

158

THE ENEMY THAT BECAME A FRIEND

"It felt just like going into hell and back out again," recalled U.S. Sergeant Ralph Gower, whose ship had come under point-blank fire from a French vessel in the harbor at Oran, Algeria. Many American soldiers got their first taste of combat from the French forces who opposed the landings. Although the French resistance crumbled within a short time, it involved several fights that were among the bloodiest in the North African campaign.

Because the landings were near major cities, some of the battles took on the air of spectator events. As both sides blazed away at each other, townspeople moved outside their homes to observe the action. During one encounter, milkmen continued making their deliveries, despite the chatter of machine-gun fire around them.

In the ensuing weeks, after the North African French switched their allegiance to the Allies, American troops got acquainted with their new comrades-in-arms and the local people. The GIs handed out literally tons of candy, gum and cigarettes. Some units donated one half of their milk ration to local children. Many GIs tried to learn French, causing a run on English-French dictionaries in stores. Others shared their recreation facilities with French soldiers, who joined the Americans in community sing-alongs. And, in a crowning irony, a U.S. infantry detachment met with French Zouaves, whom they had been fighting only two weeks before, to participate in a joint flag ceremony.

A French soldier is interrogated by his captors. French troops, many with only three bullets in their rifles, were ordered to hold out against the Allies as long as possible. Officers who had sworn allegiance to the Vichy government felt bound by honor to fight to the last.

159

After encountering the real enemy—the Axis forces—a wounded U.S. Army Air Corps sergeant stands grim-faced amid the wreckage of a camp hit by German bombers at Youks les Bains, Tunisia, in December 1942.

In Tunisia a few weeks after the Torch landings, grinning American troops —young, green, confident and as yet untested in battle—pause while loading their General Lee tank to cheerfully display the shells fired by its 75mm gun. Before too long the soldiers would be grimly struggling against panzers manned by veteran German tank men.

6

General Dwight D. Eisenhower spent the entire day of February 13, 1943, inspecting the American sector of the Tunisian front, and shortly after midnight he left his car for yet another briefing at a desert command post near an oasis village called Sidi Bou Zid *(map, page 166)*. The air was still and the moon shone brightly. The front was quiet. But despite the disarming tranquillity of the setting, Eisenhower—now commander in chief of all Allied forces in North Africa—was upset. In the distance, the lumpy mass of a mountain range loomed dark against the sky. Eisenhower feared an attack from the Axis forces on the far side of the range. That day he had visited the American troops defending the passes in those barren mountains. And what he had seen on his inspection tour gave him little confidence that the U.S. II Corps was ready to deal with an Axis onslaught.

Most of the U.S. troops had never tasted combat. Among the inexperienced officers he found a complacency that led—as he put it—to an "unconscionable delay" in preparing strong defensive positions. Infantrymen who had been in the area two days had not yet laid minefields, which Eisenhower knew the enemy would have prepared in less than two hours. He found that the II Corps' commander, Major General Lloyd R. Fredendall, had isolated his headquarters in a remote and nearly inaccessible ravine 80 miles behind the mountain range defended by his men and, still anxious that the enemy might find it, had engineers tunneling shelters for him and his staff. "I quietly asked whether the engineers had first assisted in preparing front-line defenses," Eisenhower later recalled, "but a young staff officer said 'Oh, the divisions have their own engineers for that!' It was the only time, during the war, that I ever saw a higher headquarters so concerned over its own safety that it dug itself underground shelters."

To add to Eisenhower's concerns, Fredendall, a loud and opinionated man, was not the sort of commander who inspired loyalty among his officers. He distrusted the ability of his principal subordinate, Major General Orlando Ward, commander of the II Corps' 1st Armored Division, to such an extent that he bypassed Ward entirely, giving orders directly to his subordinates. But it was Fredendall's distribution of his troops that most concerned Eisenhower. Instead of maintaining a strong, mobile reserve, ready to plug the mountain passes wherever the Germans might attack, Fre-

AMERICANS TASTE THE FIRE

dendall had scattered his units piecemeal along the front. The American line was dangerously thin, maintained more by bluff than military muscle.

Eisenhower had turned his attention to the southern flank of the forces under his command after the Allied drive in the north to capture the port cities of Bizerte and Tunis had bogged down in the icy mud of the Tunisian winter. The Allied front had solidified along a harsh mountain backbone called the Eastern Dorsal, which ran for 200 miles in a north-south direction, parallel to Tunisia's eastern seacoast and some 60 miles inland. In the northern sector of this line were the British, who waited for spring and good weather to renew their offensive. The center of the front was manned by poorly equipped troops of the French XIX Corps. Below them, defending the passes at the southern end of the mountain range, in what Eisenhower considered "the most dangerous area," was the U.S. II Corps.

To the east of the range, on the coastal plain between the mountains and the sea, there were now two Axis armies, each under the command of a formidable German general. Colonel General Jürgen von Arnim of the Fifth Panzer Army —the force that Hitler had rushed to Tunisia after the *Torch* landings—had proved his mettle by stopping the Allied drive toward Tunis in December. And now Arnim had been joined by Rommel and the Panzer Army Africa. The Desert Fox had arrived in Tunisia in January after his 1,400-mile retreat across Egypt and Libya with the British Eighth Army on his heels. Hugging the Mediterranean coastline, he had funneled his army through a narrow passageway formed by the sea and an impassable range of hills, 100 miles inside the Tunisian border. This easily defended natural corridor was spanned by a series of old French fortifications called the Mareth Line, and there Rommel had left a contingent to protect his rear against Montgomery's Eighth Army. Then he was ready to take the offensive again. His professed aim was to instill in the Americans in the Allied line "an inferiority complex of no mean order."

Eisenhower foresaw that the Axis forces might attempt to bull their way through the American-defended passes of the Eastern Dorsal, sweep across the wide plain west of the mountains, penetrate the passes of yet another range, the Western Dorsal, and then drive northward toward the Algerian coast. Along their path would lie rich prizes—Allied airfields and supply depots just across the Algerian border.

What Eisenhower had not realized until his inspection tour of February 13 was how ill prepared the Americans were to resist such an offensive. As he left Sidi Bou Zid and began the drive back to Fredendall's headquarters at Tebessa, he resolved to issue orders for new dispositions of the II Corps' defenses. It was too late. When he reached II Corps headquarters at 5:30 a.m., Eisenhower learned that the Axis had struck. The Germans had launched an attack on Sidi Bou Zid only two hours after Eisenhower had left.

Accompanied by a canopy of screeching Stukas that gave most of the GIs their first taste of dive-bombing, the 10th Panzer Division surged through the Eastern Dorsal via the Faid Pass. Under the cover of a sandstorm, the panzers rumbled toward the village of Sidi Bou Zid, where the Americans blocked a road leading west. At the same time the 21st Panzer Division pushed through the mountains south of Sidi Bou Zid and raced north toward the village.

By midmorning, U.S. troops stationed on two hills to the north and south of Sidi Bou Zid were surrounded by German tanks. Fredendall, who depended more on maps than visits to the front for information, had deployed forces on the hills, named Djebel Lessouda and Djebel Ksaira, to create islands of resistance. The men on the hills were supposed to support American tanks and troops in the plains below. But Fredendall had made a grave mistake. The forces on the two hills were not strong enough to affect the outcome of the battle on the plains and were too far apart to support each other. As the enemy tide lapped at the islands of resistance the GIs on the hills were marooned.

From the slopes of Djebel Ksaira, Colonel Thomas D. Drake watched the battle unfolding on the plain below him. He saw that artillery units supporting the American tanks were cracking, and troops were fleeing from the battlefield. He telephoned the Sidi Bou Zid command post—itself under attack—to report the rout.

"You don't know what you're saying," his shocked superior replied. "They're only shifting positions."

"Shifting positions, hell," Drake responded. "I know panic when I see it."

By dusk, the Americans had retreated from Sidi Bou Zid and the Germans held the town. But Fredendall ordered a counterattack the following day to retake the village and rescue the 2,500 Americans trapped on the two hills. Shortly after noon on February 15, Lieut. Colonel James D. Alger led his battalion of tanks in parade-ground precision across the level plains toward Sidi Bou Zid. The Germans were ready with a trap. They allowed Alger's tanks to near the Axis position virtually unopposed, and then opened an artillery barrage accompanied by a savage Stuka attack. In the confusion, the Americans noticed too late that panzers were boring in on their flanks. Alger's tank was hit, and he was captured. His entrapped armor fought valiantly, exchanging point-blank fire with the Panzer IVs, but only four of the American tanks managed to escape the German vise. Alger's battalion was annihilated, losing 15 officers, 298 enlisted men and 50 tanks.

Realizing the futility of another rescue mission, Fredendall had an airplane drop messages to the marooned GIs on the two hills telling them to try to break out on their own. At 10 p.m. on Tuesday, February 16, Colonel Drake led his 1,600 men down the slopes of Djebel Ksaira to the plain. All went well under the cover of darkness. Drake and his men marched through a panzer bivouac without a challenge. But as the sun rose, they were spotted and surrounded by trucks full of German infantry. Drake formed his men in a defensive perimeter, but their position was hopeless. He stood in the center and directed the fire. German tanks soon arrived—"huge monsters with yellow tigers painted on their sides," Drake recalled. One broke through the circle and bore down on Drake, its commander shouting: "Colonel, you surrender."

"You go to hell," Drake replied, and turned his back, waiting to be run down or shot. The tank swerved at the last second. Realizing they were beaten, the Americans stopped firing. They were rounded up and herded away.

On the other hill, Djebel Lessouda, Major Robert Moore ordered a breakout for the same night, February 16. He had led his 900 men only a mile into the plain when a German voice called out from a clump of trees. Moore ignored it and kept walking. But his bluff failed. The quiet night erupted suddenly with machine-gun fire. "Scatter!" Moore shouted to his men. As the darkness pulsed with the eerie light of tracers and bursting flares, Moore alternately crouched and sprinted as far as he could, then rolled on the ground and lay still. Gradually the din subsided. Moore regained his feet and spent the rest of the night walking nine miles west to the American lines. He and 300 of his men escaped; the other 600 were killed or captured.

Stunned by the extent of its losses—two battalions each of armor, artillery and infantry—in just two days of combat, the Allied high command ordered a withdrawal of the II Corps and part of the French XIX Corps from the Eastern Dorsal to the Western Dorsal, 50 miles away. The exhausted and discouraged Americans streamed over the hills and through the cactus patches of the plain, their withdrawal slowed maddeningly by traffic jams. By night, their way was marked by the flicker of exhaust flames. The moist air was heavy with the stench of gasoline.

The Americans fled across the waist of Tunisia, pursued and harassed by Axis armor and planes, until they reached the slopes of the Western Dorsal. Here the weary men of the II Corps turned to confront their pursuers. This time, an unyielding defense was crucial. One of the corridors through the mountains, Kasserine Pass, was a gateway to Algeria and the town of Tebessa, a vital Allied communications and supply base. From Tebessa, roads led north, and there were few natural obstacles to hinder Rommel if he chose to sweep to the Algerian coast. There seemed to be little reason to think that he would not: he could sever Allied supply lines, attack the British from the rear—and the Allies would be forced to withdraw or face disaster.

The odds were against the Americans holding Kasserine Pass. The II Corps was weary and distraught. The retreat across the plain had been disordered and tinged with panic. Many officers felt their troops slipping out of control. Units had lost their commanders; soldiers had been separated from their units. To add to the confusion, Fredendall was on worse terms than ever with General Ward, commander of the 1st Armored Division. The personality conflict between the strident commander and his calm, quiet subordinate had burgeoned into acrimony. Fredendall had frozen Ward out of the chain of command and overruled him constantly, thereby perplexing Ward's divisional officers.

To the Allies' good fortune, bungling caused by a new and curious arrangement of Axis dual command at this point created a two-day breathing spell. Rommel and Arnim

To the skirl of a bagpipe the Eighth Army's Gordon Highlanders cross the Libyan border into Tunisia in mid-February, 1943. From El Alamein to Tripoli, pipers of the Eighth Army's Highland Division punctuated momentous occasions of the British drive westward with strains of Scottish melody, an eerie intrusion on the sand-muffled silence of the desert.

were on equal footing, but it was a status that neither enjoyed. Their tenuous union was marked by rancor and jealousy. Each had his own strategy; both answered to Field Marshal Albert Kesselring in Rome, who was too far away to adequately coordinate their actions. As expected, Rommel wanted to exploit his success by striking quickly toward the Allied communications and supply base of Tebessa. Arnim argued that supplies were too low for an extended maneuver. Already he was shifting some of his troops away from the Kasserine area, intending to strike farther north. Rommel suspected Arnim of withholding forces "for a private show of his own." Field Marshal Kesselring flew in from Rome to settle the dispute. He gave Rommel the authority to attack, but even after Kesselring's decision Arnim withheld units he was ordered to transfer to Rommel. While the Germans bickered, the Allies gained valuable time—Rommel would remember with bitterness.

Fredendall did not know which one of five passes the Axis would choose for their main attack; he was compelled to parcel out his troops wherever there was an opening in the mountain range. Even after some French and British units were thrown in as reinforcements, none of the passes were strongly defended. By February 18, Axis reconnaissance patrols at Kasserine Pass made Fredendall suspect that an attack of some weight was intended there. Fredendall felt that only an experienced combat officer could be left in charge of Kasserine's meager defenses. He phoned Colonel Alexander Stark, whose 26th Infantry Regiment was covering a pass to the south. "I want you to go to Kasserine," Fredendall told Stark, "and pull a Stonewall Jackson."

With this vague instruction, Stark headed for the pass, arriving the next morning, February 19, just before the squat dark shapes of advancing panzers loomed through the mist in the plains below. A swift survey of his positions gave Stark little confidence that he could hold the pass. The only troops initially available to defend it were one battalion each of infantry, artillery and tank destroyers, and Colonel Anderson T. W. Moore's 19th Combat Engineer Regiment. The engineers had never been under fire.

The Americans chose to allow the enemy entrance to the pass, but not exit from it. The configuration of the pass dictated this tactic. At its narrowest point the rocky corridor was only 1,500 yards wide. In their advance, the Germans would be increasingly constricted, like sand flowing through an hourglass. The road that threaded the pass split near the exit and emerged into a wide basin; one branch

went west to Tebessa, the other continued north to the town of Thala. The Americans set up their guns in the basin on both road branches. They would pound the Germans as they tried to funnel through the narrows of the pass.

On the afternoon of February 19, the Afrika Korps panzers of Brigadier General Karl Buelowius tried to storm through this natural bottleneck, only to be halted by a hail of artillery, antitank and small-arms fire. Then, as dusk fell, Buelowius resolved to seize by infiltration what he had failed to take by force. Afrika Korps infantry patrols worked their way up into the heights along the north sides of the pass, overran outposts on the ridges, then descended behind the defenders in the basin and took them by surprise. Some 100 Americans were captured on the Thala road.

On the Tebessa road, one company of Moore's engineers, unnerved by the phantom appearance of stealthy German night patrols, broke and ran. The panic became contagious. Several artillery forward observers, sent by Moore to direct fire on the Germans, abandoned their position after one announced: "This place is too hot." Though some troops were still holding out, others fled in fear and many were missing. By midnight on the 19th, Kasserine's defenses were close to disintegration. Only the arrival later that night of reinforcements—another battalion of U.S. infantry and a small British force with only 11 tanks—kept the Germans bottled up in the pass.

As the Allies continued to hold on the next morning, February 20, Rommel grew increasingly impatient. His time was running out. For on that same morning, far behind him on the other side of Tunisia, the advance elements of Montgomery's Eighth Army began to probe the German rear guard that screened the approaches to the Mareth Line. Rommel anticipated a major battle there within a matter of days. A victory at Kasserine must come soon, before Montgomery forced the Desert Fox to backtrack to defend his rear at Mareth.

Rommel exhorted Buelowius to apply more pressure to uncork the bottleneck at Kasserine Pass, and the German attack on February 20 was unusually fierce. The pass echoed to the screams of rockets fired from six-barreled launchers called Nebelwerfers. In the wake of the massive artillery barrage, waves of Axis troops crashed through the drifts of

Mountainous Tunisia (map) was the last North African stronghold of the Axis. Through the Eastern and Western Dorsal ranges, Axis troops mounted their final major offensive early in 1943, sending the Allies reeling. General Sir Harold Alexander (above), who commanded the Allied ground forces in North Africa, regrouped his armies and countered with a drive that pushed the enemy into a bridgehead in the northeastern corner of the country. In recognition of his brilliant role in the ultimate Allied victory in Tunisia, Alexander was made a lord. His new title: the Viscount of Tunis.

daisies and scarlet poppies growing on the floor of the basin. By midafternoon, the British force, which was defending the Thala road, lost its last tank. The American engineers on the Tebessa road fell back in disorder. Their commanding officer, Colonel Moore, barely escaped capture and appeared at Stark's headquarters to report that his 19th Engineers were faltering. Some 128 of them were dead, wounded or missing. The remaining troops withdrew down the road to set up another desperate defense.

At 4:30 that afternoon the Axis finally broke the bottleneck and Rommel watched the men of the Afrika Korps, the Italian Centauro Division and the 10th Panzers storm through the pass and pour into the basin. Italian tanks scouting along the road toward Tebessa reported no resistance. Nor did panzer reconnaissance troops find any opposition on the Thala road. Seeing the way clear for a drive deep into Allied territory, Rommel suddenly became cautious and halted the advance. He suspected that the Allies were planning a counterattack for the next day and he wanted his forces consolidated and well prepared. As Rommel paused, British and American reinforcements poured into the area to defend the roads to Tebessa and Thala.

When Rommel resumed his advance the next day, February 21, the newly strengthened American position held the Tebessa road but the vastly outgunned British force on the Thala road, pushed by the 10th Panzers under the command of Major General Fritz von Broich, gradually gave ground and finally dug into a ridge south of the village. Of all the reinforcements that fought in the battle for Thala, none played a more vital role than the artillery battalions of U.S. Brigadier General LeRoy Irwin's 9th Infantry Division. They arrived from western Algeria on the afternoon of February 21, after a feverish four-day march over muddy mountain roads. Irwin and his dead-tired soldiers spent the whole night getting their 48 howitzers into position. The impressive sight of the American guns heartened the small band of British holding out at Thala, and they abandoned their plans for an exodus. By dawn, Irwin was ready. As the morning mists rose from the valley on February 22, his artillerymen, although exhausted from their labors, pumped shells into the advancing panzers.

Irwin's first volley struck Broich's force as it was about to make its final assault on the village. The intensity of the bombardment startled the German commander; it convinced him that the Allies had been heavily reinforced during the night and that a strong counterattack was forthcoming. Halting the advance, Broich called Rommel and explained the situation. Rommel agreed that it would be wiser to assume a defensive stance and deal with the expected Allied thrust before proceeding with the assault on Thala. Broich waited all morning. The Allies were quiet. He informed Rommel that he would attack at 4 p.m.

The assault was never launched, for that morning Rommel's uncustomary caution mushroomed into grave doubt about the chances of his offensive succeeding. He had taken time out to examine captured U.S. war matériel: tanks, trucks, troop carriers and weapons. He had been amazed by the abundance of supplies and equipment, and the profusion of spare parts available to the Americans; he had been impressed no less by the speed with which Allied reinforcements had flowed into the Kasserine area. In contrast, his own forces were down to one day's ammunition and only six days' food. His vehicles had enough gasoline to travel only 120 miles.

On the verge of victory at Thala, Rommel came to the conclusion that the flow of Allied reinforcements was too great for his forces to check. If the Axis forces continued the drive, each day extending their already stretched supply line, they would surely be engulfed by the swelling tide of Allied strength. In addition, the Desert Fox was anxious to return his troops to the Mareth Line to stop the expected advance of the British Eighth Army, his old desert enemy.

Rommel's radical change of heart surprised his superior, Field Marshal Kesselring, who arrived at the front that afternoon brimming with optimism. "Nothing of his usual passionate will to command could be felt," Kesselring sadly observed later. In fact, Rommel was sunk in a pit of depression and suffering from jaundice and desert sores. On the next day, February 23, he pulled his troops back through the pass he had taken such pains to secure. He withdrew so discreetly that it was 24 hours before the Allies fully realized that he was gone.

Now the front shifted east again, back to the ridges of the Eastern Dorsal. Abandoning the towns and airfields between the mountain ranges they had taken during a week of fierce fighting, Rommel and his troops marched southeastward to a new arena of battle, the Mareth Line, to meet the Eighth Army.

The first major encounter between Axis forces and the Eighth Army since El Alamein, four months previously, came on March 6 near the town of Medenine, some 25 miles southeast of the Mareth Line. There, attempting to delay Montgomery's advance, Rommel launched a spoiling attack against the British. Warned of Rommel's advance by air reconnaissance, the British had time to superbly camouflage a line of antitank guns across his path. Cool British gunners held their fire until the panzers were within close range of the hidden emplacements, then loosed a holocaust of armor-piercing shells. One tank after another caught fire, their black-cross insignia disappearing in the flames. "Attack after attack was launched, but achieved no success," Rommel wrote later. The British used only one squadron of tanks at Medenine, but their antitank guns cost Rommel 52 of his panzers.

On that ignominious note, Rommel ended his two-year career in Africa. Three days after the battle he flew to Germany to try to persuade Hitler to abandon North Africa entirely and thereby save his soldiers from annihilation. Predictably, Hitler refused to listen to his argument, and then forbade the Desert Fox to return to his Tunisian command post. "Africa will be held," the Führer snapped, "and you must go on sick leave." General von Arnim would take charge of Army Group Africa, a newly designated command that included both his and Rommel's armies. Thus the Allies were rid of their once-formidable African adversary.

The departure of Rommel from the North African theater coincided with the arrival in southern Tunisia of a flamboyant American general whose aggressiveness matched that of the Desert Fox in his prime. The Allied high command had examined carefully the reasons behind the debacle that began with Sidi Bou Zid and continued through Kasserine. Many of the top brass—especially the British—attributed the failure to muddled leadership in the U.S. II Corps. Some suspected that Fredendall had lost control of his command, and they urged Eisenhower to replace him. Major General Ernest Harmon, who had seen Fredendall's performance firsthand, had counseled Eisenhower: "This is Rommel and

tank warfare at its latest—way above poor Fredendall's head." British General Sir Harold Alexander, commander of the Allied ground troops in Tunisia, expressed it more diplomatically: "I'm sure you must have better men than that."

The man whom Eisenhower chose arrived at II Corps headquarters in the little village near Tebessa amid a fanfare of screeching sirens. Arabs peering from the cover of doorways saw a convoy of armored scout cars and half-tracks bristling with machine guns, their fishpole radio antennas whipping in the wind, sweep into the dingy square. In the lead car, bolt upright like a Roman charioteer, stood Major General George S. Patton, a scowl on his face, his jaw straining against the web strap of his steel helmet.

Patton immediately cranked up an iron-fisted campaign of discipline to whip the discouraged men of the II Corps into fighting shape. Within days, one of his deputies recalled, "the II Corps staff was fighting mad—but at Patton, not at the Germans." A stickler for spit and polish, Patton quickly tightened uniform regulations. He wanted his men dressed by the book. Most had adopted the British Tommy's disregard for proper field dress; when not in combat, they removed their helmets and wore only the olive-drab liner beneath. To Patton, the helmet liner became the symbol of the II Corps' slovenliness. Coining a slogan, "Banish That Beanie," he levied fines—$50 for officers, $25 for enlisted men—on any soldier not impeccably clad in helmet, leggings and necktie. No one was immune. GIs musing in the latrine were rattled to be confronted by Patton yanking open the doors for a helmet check.

At 57, the volatile Patton was already a legend among the American soldiers. Fiercely proud of his warrior's reputation won in World War I, he sought to further it by practicing martial frowns in a mirror; on the other hand, his emotions often got the better of him—once he broke down weeping three times during the course of a staff conference. His oratory was flamboyant: "We won't just shoot the sonsabitches—we're going to cut out their living guts and use them to grease the treads of our tanks." Patton successfully used this combination of showmanship, bravado and severity to galvanize the sloppy Americans into a trim and effective fighting force.

He would soon get a chance to show the mettle of his revamped II Corps, which, in addition to its improved morale, now also had received some tanks that were a match for the Panzer IVs—new Shermans with 75mm guns. General Alexander still harbored doubts that the Americans were capable of mounting a major offensive against the Axis. So he gave the II Corps a secondary, though important task: to draw the Axis forces away from the Mareth Line while Montgomery tried to break through it. Patton was to probe the enemy's flank 90 miles northwest of Mareth through the oasis town of Gafsa and the mountain passes at El Guettar and Maknassy.

On the night of March 16, Patton assembled his staff for a last briefing in a dimly lit schoolroom that served as II Corps headquarters. Patton's apocalyptic message left his officers speechless. "Gentlemen," he said, "tomorrow we attack. If we are not victorious, let no man come back alive."

The advance began that same night. Initially, the ease of their progress deluded Patton's troops into dreams of imminent victory. Arriving at Gafsa, which had been abandoned by the Allies a month before during the retreat to the Western Dorsal, Major General Terry Allen's 1st Infantry Division met no opposition. The Italian garrison had pulled out and retreated into the hills beyond the date-palm oasis of El Guettar. "Jeez, General," a euphoric GI shouted to Allen, "aren't we doing swell?"

A few miles past El Guettar, the Americans had to pause. There, as they entered a vast green valley rimmed by ridges, the road leading east split in two; both branches disappeared through narrow passes in the high hills that blocked other exits from the valley. The Axis had converted these passes into fortified funnels sown with wide belts of mines backed up by aprons of barbed wire. The cliffs above them sprouted antitank and light and heavy machine guns.

The Americans recognized that a steep slope rising to the crest of the hill overlooking one of the passes might be climbed by a column of men moving in single file. A chain of gorges, crevices and saddles would serve as a rough path for their ascent. If they were able to gain the crest, they would be staring at the backs of the Italians whose guns were trained down on the pass.

On the night of March 20, a column spearheaded by 500 of Lieut. Colonel William O. Darby's U.S. Rangers set out over the path. They could not carry any sizable weapons; the terrain was too difficult. The success of their mission would depend instead on stealth, surprise and shock. They marched in silence, picking their way painfully over a carpet of loose stone and struggling through crevices. The blue steel of their rifle barrels glistened in the light of a rising moon. At intervals, their progress slowed to a crawl as they scaled 20-foot cliffs, passing their equipment up from hand to hand. It was nearing dawn when at last the Rangers reached the rocky plateau that overlooked the Italian guns.

A bugle call signaled the attack, and skirmish lines of Rangers, their faces black with burnt cork, surged down on the sleepy Italians. The Rangers screamed as they bounded from rock to rock, terrifying some of the unsuspecting enemy troops into immediate surrender. Many of the defenders who resisted were bayoneted or shot. The morning sun rose on scores of Italian dead and 700 prisoners. The Rangers' exultant leader radioed his superior, the 1st Infantry Division commander, General Allen: "You can send in your troops. The pass is clear."

Clearing the enemy from the ridges and hills that loomed over the other exit from the valley—the pass on the road to Gabes and Mareth—proved more difficult for Patton's troops, and their advance was stalled for three days. Then, at dawn on March 23, with a panzer division diverted from the Mareth Line, the Axis struck back through this pass.

Fifty tanks of Broich's 10th Panzers rumbled through the defile and onto the dusty floor of the El Guettar valley, followed by mobile guns and troop carriers full of infantry. Messerschmitts swarmed out of the rising sun to strafe the 1st Infantry's foxholes and gun emplacements. Patton, watching from his nearby observation post, saw that the enemy attack was devastating. But his troops seemed determined to stand fast. General Allen set the keynote. Sighting two panzers trundling perilously close to command headquarters, one of Allen's staff officers suggested a change of scene. "I will like hell pull out," Allen answered, "and I'll shoot the first bastard who does."

The Germans overran a number of infantry positions and two field-artillery battalions, and it appeared that another Allied disaster was in the making. But then the panzers ran full tilt into a well-concealed minefield in a wadi that traversed the valley. As the surviving German tanks turned tail in confusion, the American artillery and antitank guns

DISARMING THE DEADLY MEMENTOS OF A RETREATING ARMY

Engineers—called sappers by the British—scan a taped-off sector of a minefield with metal detectors.

A turbaned Sikh sapper gingerly defuses a mine.

Sappers of the 4th Indian Division of the Eighth Army gently probe with bayonets for wooden or plastic mines that might have eluded metal detectors.

As the German Army retreated west, its engineers grew diabolically adept at the art of sowing the desert with mines. By 1943, the Allied engineers clearing German minefields in Tunisia faced a complex, nerve-shattering task. Their basic tool was an electric detector that buzzed when it was passed over buried metal. The engi-neers scoured the ground for a range of buried explosives—from heavy, saucepan-shaped Teller mines, whose blasts could turn tanks upside down, to small, cylindrical S-mines that, when set off by a foot-step, sprang to shoulder height, then shot forth hundreds of tiny steel fragments.

Systematically, the engineers perfected intricate techniques for defusing delayed-action mines and carefully severing trip wires so that the unearthed mines would not explode in their hands. Among the most expert were the Indian engineers of Britain's Eighth Army, who became famous for the cool skill they brought to Tunisia's fields of hidden death.

covering the minefield blasted away at their targets. By 9 a.m. they had knocked out some 30 German tanks, and the rest of the enemy pulled back to reorganize.

At 4:45 that afternoon the Axis returned, this time in long skirmishing lines of infantry led by panzers. The American artillerymen had used the intervening hours to prepare well, and they coolly showered the incoming lines with shells. As the German infantry wavered and thinned, Patton, observing from a hillside, commented bluntly on the Axis commanders' use of their men. "They're murdering good infantry," he burst out. "What a hell of a way to waste good infantry troops."

As the Axis assault faltered, Lieutenant Heinz-Werner Schmidt, Rommel's former aide, detected a radical change in German will power. Three self-propelled assault guns, raked by fire from a squadron of Shermans that had moved onto the field, broke cover and sped by him toward the rear. As if to excuse his flight, the officer in charge called to Schmidt, "Tank attack! We must get back." Schmidt said to himself bitterly, "That would never have happened in Rommel's old Afrika Korps. We are facing defeat in Africa."

The bruised 10th Panzer Division retreated from the El Guettar valley and dug in to reinforce the Centauro Division in the mountains. Later the 21st Panzer Division, also dispatched from Mareth to meet the American threat, joined them. For three weeks Patton tried to hammer his way through the passes at El Guettar and farther north at Maknassy, but the Axis held fast in their mountain strongholds.

Yet, in a sense, Patton had already achieved his goal. He had revitalized the discouraged and bewildered II Corps. He had seen his novice troops acquit themselves well in tough battles—for the first time, at El Guettar, an American infantry division had taken on German tanks and won. Moreover, at a crucial hour, he had drawn two panzer divisions from the Mareth Line and diluted the opposition facing Montgomery and his Eighth Army.

Patton's jabs at the Axis from the west were timed to coincide with Montgomery's hammer blows from the south. On the same night—March 20—that Darby's Rangers assaulted the Italians at El Guettar, the Eighth Army attacked the Mareth Line south of Gabes.

Built by the French in 1939 to counter a possible Italian advance into Tunisia from Libya, the Mareth Line was a 25-mile chain of concrete blockhouses, gun emplacements, mines and barbed wire that was bounded by the sea on one side and the impassable Matmata hills on the other. Before they could take the fortifications, Montgomery's men would have to negotiate the Wadi Zigzaou, a ravine some 20 feet deep, running parallel to the line.

Montgomery had been planning his Mareth Line venture since early January, and he had concocted a maneuver to take the pressure off his frontal assault. In the second week of March he dispatched the 2nd New Zealand Division under Lieut. General Bernard Freyberg on an arduous 200-mile march that would take them up the western side of the Matmata hills. The New Zealanders then would drive through the Tebaga gap in the northern end of the range of hills and thrust at the Axis rear near the village of El Hamma, 30 miles behind the Mareth Line. Montgomery dubbed this flanking maneuver "my left hook."

Getting the left hook into position to strike took more than a week. The 25,600 New Zealanders first struggled through barren hills so riddled by wadis that their advance was often narrowed to a one-tank front. After several days the hills gave way to soft, powdery desert sand in which their trucks sank up to the axles. The long column crawled slowly northward, leaving a wake of billowing dust.

Once, Freyberg halted the advance after spotting German outposts on a spur of a mountain range that stood in his path to El Hamma. He summoned a Free French general in command of a unit providing cover for the New Zealanders, and asked him: "Do you think your chaps could clear the Germans off that mountain?" The French officer, a viscount whose name was Jacques Phillippe de Hautecloque but who used the name Leclerc, raised his eyebrows mildly and replied: "But of course—except that would it not be better to clear them off the whole range?" For the next two days, bayonet-wielding Senegalese troops led by French officers flushed the Germans from the crags and crevices of the mountain range, taking no prisoners. The path to El Hamma was again free of obstructions.

With his left hook ready to press through the Tebaga gap (and Patton's II Corps pushing from the west at El Guettar), Montgomery struck the Mareth Line with his right on the night of March 20. Under the cover of a British artillery barrage, sappers moved out to clear a path through the minefields for three divisions of infantry: the 50th Northumbrian leading, followed by the 4th Indian and the 51st Highland. From the beginning their attack was crippled. The noise of the artillery was so thunderous that the sappers could not hear the telltale "ping" in the earphones of their mine detectors, and the undiscovered mines claimed many victims among the infantry trying to rush the line.

Torrential spring rains had turned the Wadi Zigzaou in front of the line into a moat of muddy water, a tank trap. Engineers struggling to carpet the ravine with fascines—bundles of brushwood that would serve as crude roadbeds for the tanks—managed to create a single causeway over the wadi, but only four tanks were able to cross that night. The last to try smashed the fascines into the sodden floor of the ravine and sank up to its turret in muck and water, blocking the passage.

The infantry fared better than the armor in crossing the wadi. Using ladders, or forming human pyramids, British soldiers scaled the steep banks of the ravine and attacked the blockhouses with grenades. Despite heavy casualties—especially among the sappers—the infantrymen had won a bridgehead on the far bank by morning. But without armor and antitank guns it could not be held for long.

While the infantrymen broadened their bridgehead the next day, engineers worked feverishly to build a more substantial causeway across the ravine. This accomplished, the British commander made a costly error. Instead of sending antitank guns over first, he gave priority to lightly armed Valentine tanks. Forty-two made the crossing but churned up the causeway so badly it became impassable again.

And when the 15th Panzer Division counterattacked the next afternoon, March 22, the British infantry in the bridgehead on the other side of the wadi crumbled without antitank support. The British Valentine tanks were no match for the more powerfully gunned panzers and by dusk the bridgehead had all but disappeared. A few infantrymen clung to the sides of the wadi, making a feeble last stand.

The Allied command was stunned by this reversal, but Montgomery rallied with a new tactic. He decided to throw all of his weight behind his left hook. He sent Lieut. General Brian Horrocks and the British 1st Armored Division over Freyberg's long desert route to join the New Zealanders in their thrust through the Tebaga gap.

On March 26, as Freyberg's infantry and Horrocks' armor moved toward the entrance of the Tebaga gap, waves of 30 Allied bombers, paced 15 minutes apart, zeroed in on the Axis defenses in the valley passageway to El Hamma. The bombing and strafing lasted for three hours, and when at dusk silence again settled in the valley, Freyberg's New Zealanders, bayonets at the ready, poked into the gap. "If we punch the hole, will the tanks really go through?" Freyberg, who was skeptical of British armor, had asked. "Yes, they will," Horrocks assured him, "and I am going with them."

After the infantry led the way through the rim of the Axis defenses, it parted and let Horrocks' armor slide through and push on toward El Hamma in the moonlight. If the tanks did not clear the valley by dawn, however, they would be at the mercy of any German 88mm guns that might have survived the bombing of the hills rimming the gap.

As the 1,200 vehicles left the infantry behind and advanced on a single track, they passed almost unchallenged through the encampment where part of the 21st Panzer Division rested for the night. Crouched in the turret of his tank, Horrocks could see the occasional spatters of ill-aimed rifle fire. Even though the resistance was feeble, the progress of the gigantic column was agonizingly slow, impeded by frequent wadis. By dawn, the Germans had been able to scrape up enough 88mm guns to establish an antitank screen at the exit of the valley, three miles from El Hamma. They opened up on the 1st Armored Division and stopped its advance, keeping Horrocks at bay for two days.

But Montgomery's reinforced left hook had done its job. Fearing that Horrocks might break through at any moment and attack their rear in force, the Axis troops at the Mareth Line were compelled to retreat. They pulled out under cover of a sandstorm on March 26 and withdrew northward along the coast, settling finally for another fight at Wadi Akarit, 15 miles north of the port of Gabes.

Wadi Akarit was the last natural barrier that stood between the British and the Tunisian coastal plain. The Axis defensive line there bridged an 18-mile gap between the sea on the east and a range of ragged hills on the west. The wadi itself was a deep and formidable obstacle for only four miles of its length. Where it was shallow, the Axis had reinforced their line with a chain of minefields and antitank ditches.

Unlike the Mareth Line, Wadi Akarit lacked both concrete bunkers and pillboxes, and this absence of permanent fortifications contributed to the air of disillusionment among the Axis troops that had recently suffered defeat at Mareth. As they dug in at Akarit, a noncommissioned officer, intent on boosting the morale of his weary and bedraggled men, announced, "This is a much better line than Mareth." Private Giuseppe Berto, of the 6th Blackshirt Division, retorted sourly, "Then why didn't we come here in the first place?"

From the Allies' point of view, the most disturbing feature of the defense was the 900-foot-high Djebel Fatnassa that commanded the wadi from the rear. Four hours before the battle began, two battalions of the 4th Indian Division set out to infiltrate the Italian positions high on the hill.

In the lead were Gurkhas, doughty warriors from Nepal. Their principal weapon was the kukri, a long, curved knife with a blade sharpened on the inner edge. Shortly after midnight, on April 6, two sections of Gurkhas began scaling Fatnassa to secure the pathway leading along its ridgeline high above the wadi. One officer, waiting at the foot of the hill, recalled only silence until the Gurkhas reached the first Italian post. "Then," he remembered, "there came an eerie sound, an excited whimper not unlike hounds finding the scent." The Gurkhas charged grimly along the ridge through a sheet of machine-gun fire, leaping from rock to rock, hacking with their kukris. They secured the high ground, eliminating a key position of the Axis defense.

A few hours later, the British opened up with an artillery barrage described by the Italian commander, General Giovanni Messe, as an "apocalyptic hurricane of steel and fire." The 50th Division and the 51st Highland Division then struck at the center of the Axis line. Despite the forewarning of artillery, the Italians were surprised by the assault. They had expected their enemy to wait for a moonlit night to launch an attack. Instead it came in inky darkness, and the Italian defenders, thrown off guard, were quickly overrun. By 9:30 a.m. they were surrendering in huge numbers.

But the battle was far from over. The German 90th Light Division refused to yield its sector of the line. And that afternoon, as the British 8th Armored Brigade crawled cautiously around the base of a hill behind the captured Italian positions, its lead tanks were met head on and stopped by the guns of the 15th Panzer Division. All that afternoon, the 15th Panzer blocked a British breakthrough. Montgomery decided to wait until the next morning before trying to force the advance.

But that afternoon, the German divisional commanders brought discouraging reports to Messe: although they had blocked the British advance so far, they would not be able to hold out much longer. Messe agreed, and passed the word to Arnim. The Axis commanders then made a fateful decision: if the Italian forces were to be saved, they must pull back at once. The remaining Axis troops in the coastal region, at El Hamma and El Guettar, must also withdraw in mutual support to the north.

On April 7, the Eighth Army and the American II Corps discovered that the enemy had disappeared. Patton lashed his forces eastward to the coast for either "a fight or a bath." And that afternoon a symbolic encounter took place in the coastal plain southwest of the port of Sfax: a reconnaissance patrol of the British 12th Lancers, probing north, met up with an advance patrol from the American II Corps. On behalf of the Eighth Army, Sergeant William Brown, from Devon, said, "This is certainly a pleasant surprise." Replied Private Perry Searcy from Kentucky: "Well, it's good to see somebody besides a Nazi."

The Axis forces were now in full retreat up the coastal plain; no terrain would lend itself to a defense until they reached the high mountains ringing Tunis and Bizerte. And the two Allied armies, one hardened by desert warfare, the other learning quickly, would join in the pursuit and in the last, climactic battles that spelled the end of Axis domination in North Africa.

ONE MAN'S FOCUS ON THE WAR

STARING DANGER IN THE FACE

In North Africa as elsewhere, the War was thoroughly reported in words and pictures, and the people who covered it often faced the same dangers as the soldiers whose deeds they depicted. The job of combat photographers was especially risky, since a camera had to be where the action was to record it. One who braved those dangers in Tunisia was Eliot Elisofon of LIFE. During seven months in Tunisia he shot thousands of pictures, many in color—rare for that day. Some of the most striking appear on these pages. Along with excerpts from his reports to the magazine, they offer a remarkable, personal record of part of the hard-fought campaign that finally brought the desert war to an end.

At the front, Elisofon worked like an Old West gunslinger. "You shoot first and think afterwards," he said. "To delay is to lose the picture here." The two 35mm cameras he carried were always at the ready; if he didn't have time to focus, at least he could press the shutter release and hope. He aimed his lenses at all aspects of the war: at generals and GIs, at scenes of violence and the quiet moments in between.

Elisofon was enormously competitive and would do almost anything to get better pictures than his rivals. "Elisofon was afraid like the rest of us," said Ernie Pyle, America's best-loved war correspondent. "Yet he made himself go right into the teeth of danger." He shot photos from the bubble nose of a plane flying at 50 feet on a low-level bombing run and infiltrated German lines with infantrymen. Pinned in a slit trench for two hours by shellfire, he fumed because the barrage was so heavy he could not get up to take pictures of it. When a plane he was in crashed upon takeoff, Elisofon escaped just before it burst into flames, immediately began photographing the blazing wreck, and then fainted.

To Elisofon, who died in 1973, the picture was the crucial thing. "The great challenge," he said, "is to help the world to see."

Elisofon turns a basically mundane scene—two U.S. Signal Corps soldiers stringing telephone lines along a Tunisian road—into a dramatic picture.

PHOTOGRAPHER ELISOFON

TWO-FISTED ASSAULT ON AN ENTRENCHED ENEMY

"Nothing was lacking," said Elisofon, reporting back to his editors on an American attack on Axis positions near El Guettar in central Tunisia on March 30, 1943. "A tremendous amount of artillery of every type was brought into play. While all this artillery was working on the ridges, light tanks and half-tracks went in to feel out the enemy. After them came more than 100 medium tanks. The 155mm guns were firing away from a point so far back many soldiers attached to rear echelons wondered what they were firing at."

U.S. artillerymen hold their ears against the blast of their camouflaged 155mm gun, which, Elisofon said, could fire "20 rounds in less time than it took to shoot a dozen pictures."

American tanks grinding across El Guettar's sun-baked valley stir up clouds of dust. The murky conditions plagued Elisofon. "It is impossible to make pictures

without sand and dirt blowing into every part of your camera," he said. "I carry a shaving brush to clean the body of the camera and a small fine one for the lens

U.S. Signal Corpsmen try to track down a break in field-telephone wire caused by German fire.

IN PRAISE OF UNSUNG HEROES

"I feel that war should be shown in relation to people and I try to cover as many aspects as possible," Elisofon said. He particularly liked to turn his lens toward "people who were not usually photographed in battle." Among these unsung heroes were "the poor guys" who carried ammunition to the front. "They would drive a 2½-ton truck to within three miles of the shooting, cover it with a net and at night sneak it up to the guns."

Elisofon also greatly admired the courage of engineers who searched for and disarmed the thousands of mines sowed by the Germans. "They did this often under fire," he noted, "and a man wearing a headset to detect mines doesn't hear a shell coming."

He had no less admiration for the men of the Signal Corps, who had to work in dangerously exposed positions, and often alone, in order to keep vital communications open. "I remember," the photographer wrote, "one man walking along with a wire running through his hands looking for a break. One guy, pretty small in a very big landscape."

A group of American soldiers takes time out to watch the flaming remnant of an overturned armored vehicle still burning hours after the battle. It had been

A VALLEY LITTERED WITH THE WRECKAGE OF WAR

After a futile German counterattack at El Guettar, the floor of the valley resembled a graveyard for tanks, guns and half-tracks. Elisofon roamed the battlefield, taking pictures of the destroyed and captured equipment that littered the landscape.

He also indulged his insatiable curiosity, trying to discern something of the enemy's life and character from the debris of battle. A gourmet and avid cook, the photographer was fascinated to find in one German tank an unburned food box, and meticulously noted the contents: "It had three cans of sardines, two Portuguese and one Norwegian (from Stavanger), a can of German Limburger cheese, pressed meat, butter, black bread, fresh eggs (from the Arabs, no doubt), a can of British tea, sugar and dried milk."

destroyed either by a mine or by artillery fire. An American soldier inspects a German 150mm gun in a vast array of captured enemy weapons

Near a grainfield, wooden crosses mark a common grave for German dead.

COVERING THE AFTERMATH OF A LOST CAUSE

As the fighting at El Guettar progressed, scores of both German and Italian soldiers found their way into American prisoner-of-war compounds. "There were 897 prisoners taken the day I made my pictures," Elisofon recalled. "The Germans tried to hide from the camera and the Italians were strictly lens lice"—his way of saying that they competed to get into his shots.

Other Axis soldiers were less fortunate. Killed in action, they lay buried all over the valley *(above)*. Once Elisofon found "a magnificent German cemetery" containing 120 neat, stone-bordered graves. Some of the graves were decorated with helmets or marked with imposing replicas of the Iron Cross. A sign in the cemetery read: "These dead gave their spirits for the glory of Greater Germany." Elisofon was touched when he discovered an Italian grave, its headstone bearing a plastic-covered oval photograph of the dead soldier.

just adored being photographed," Elisofon wrote after making the picture.

7

On March 30, 1943, when General Siegfried Westphal, Kesselring's chief of staff, visited General von Arnim's headquarters in Tunis, he complained that Arnim's Army Group Africa, instead of concentrating on its job of fighting the Allies, was always looking over its shoulder. Yes, Arnim replied bitterly—looking for supply ships. "We are without bread and ammunition, as was Rommel's army before," he said. "The consequences are inevitable."

While Arnim's gloomy assessment would win him no good will from the German High Command or Hitler, who still maintained a façade of optimism about the outcome in North Africa, it was a true one. As the Allies drove Arnim's troops back into the northeast corner of Tunisia, their air and naval forces were devastating his lines of supply. Hitler himself had acknowledged that for the Axis forces to hold their Tunisian bridgehead they needed at least 150,000 tons of supplies a month. But since December, shipments had never averaged more than 75,000 tons a month, and in March they dropped to 51,000 tons. Besides suffering shortages of food and ammunition, Army Group Africa was running so dangerously low on fuel that soon it would have to save its gasoline for localized tactical operations and would be unable to make any major shifts in position.

Yet Hitler stubbornly insisted that the Axis presence in North Africa could and must be maintained. He had reasons for being so adamant. He deduced that the Allies would strike next at southern Europe (in fact, Allied planning for an invasion of Sicily was already under way). He recognized that such a move would be extremely difficult as long as Germans and Italians kept the Allies occupied in Tunisia and denied them the use of the valuable ports of Tunis and Bizerte. He also knew that the hold his ally Mussolini had on the Italian people was eroding. Workers demanding an end to the War and freedom from Fascism had already staged mass strikes in Turin and Milan. If Tunisia fell and the thousands of Italian soldiers there ended up in Allied prisoner-of-war camps, public reaction in Italy might lead to Mussolini's overthrow by anti-Fascists, dangerously exposing the southern flank of Hitler's Fortress Europe to an Allied onslaught.

The Führer's determination to hold the Tunisian bridgehead was faithfully translated into action on the ground by Arnim, who, despite his own doubts, was an obedient sol-

THE KNOCKOUT PUNCH

dier. While he privately conveyed his pessimism to the High Command, he addressed his officers and men in a spirit of optimism and admonished them to avoid defeatist attitudes. They had been pushed back from the Mareth Line and Wadi Akarit. But Arnim ordered that there be no retreat from the line held by Army Group Africa in mid-April, a ragged arc stretching from a point 25 miles west of Bizerte on the north coast to Enfidaville, below the Cape Bon peninsula on the east coast (map, page 166).

Along this 130-mile perimeter, the Axis dug in. While fending off sporadic attacks, Germans and Italians managed to mine passes and valley floors, fortify ridges and hillsides (sometimes using pneumatic drills to carve dugouts from solid rock), and place their artillery to command routes along which the Allies were most likely to make their major thrusts. The Axis troops worked with haste, knowing that those thrusts were sure to come soon.

Just which Allied forces would attack where had been a point of sometimes angry contention among the Allies since they had begun planning their big push. General Alexander, commander of Allied ground forces, had little confidence in the American troops (he had described them as "ignorant, ill-trained" and "mentally and physically soft") and had devised a plan that excluded most of them from the final action. The plan called for the major drives to be made by the British Eighth Army from the south and the British First Army—which had arrived in North Africa with the Torch invasion—from the west. One American division was to be detached from the U.S. II Corps and moved to the north of the First Army, under whose commander, Lieut. General Kenneth Anderson, it would serve. The main body of the II Corps, positioned between the two British armies, would take part in the initial attack but would be gradually pinched out of the offensive by the Eighth and First armies converging from the south and west.

On learning of Alexander's plan in mid-March, II Corps Commander George Patton and his deputy, Major General Omar Bradley, were enraged. Bradley flew to Algiers to protest to General Eisenhower, who as overall Allied commander in chief in North Africa could overrule Alexander. "I think we're entitled to function under our own command without being farmed out forever from ally to ally," Bradley told Eisenhower. "Until you give us the chance to show what we can do in a sector of our own, with an objective of our own, you'll never know how good or bad we really are. And neither will the American people." He suggested that Eisenhower move the entire II Corps to the north of the First Army, and let the Americans go after Bizerte by themselves.

After considering the problems of shifting the whole of the II Corps across the busy supply lines of the First Army, Eisenhower agreed and quietly commanded Alexander to revise his plan. The shift was masterfully coordinated—particularly considering that on April 15, just about the time it got under way, the II Corps had a change of command (Patton, detached to work on the plans for invading Sicily, was replaced by Bradley). Almost 10,000 vehicles carried 100,000 men and their equipment from the Tebessa area to the vicinity of Tabarka, a distance of more than 150 miles across the British rear, without significantly interfering with the First Army's supply operation.

Meanwhile, the British were undergoing some reorganization of their own. On April 11, Montgomery tried to get an armored division transferred from the First Army to his Eighth Army. Alexander replied that, instead, Montgomery would have to yield an armored division and an armored car regiment of his own to the First Army. Because the mountainous terrain made Axis defenses strongest in the south, Alexander explained, Montgomery's attack was to be secondary, a diversion to draw opposition away from the main drive to Tunis by General Anderson's First Army. Montgomery understandably regretted that the Eighth Army, which had struggled so long in the desert, should have any less than the leading role now. On April 16 he wired Alexander almost plaintively: "All my troops are in first class form and want to be in the final Dunkirk."

At least Montgomery's Eighth Army had the privilege of striking the first blow in the offensive, code-named Vulcan, on the night of April 19. Two strongly defended prominences close to the village of Enfidaville—Djebel Garci, 1,000 feet high, and a 500-foot hill named Takrouna—were among the Eighth Army's initial objectives.

The 4th Indian Division struggled up the slopes and gullies of Djebel Garci for two days, repeatedly repulsing brutal counterattacks and suffering heavy losses. The division had secured only the southern portion of the hill before being ordered by Montgomery to halt the attack.

The New Zealand Division tackled Takrouna and met similarly fierce opposition. Takrouna's slopes were riddled with small caves in which German soldiers and Italians of the Folgore Parachute Division were holed up. The battle was waged with bayonets, grenades, knives—even rocks, hurled down from above. The first New Zealanders to reach Takrouna's summit were fewer than a dozen Maori soldiers led by Sergeant J. Rogers and Lance Sergeant H. Manahi. Roped together like mountaineers with scraps of telephone cable that they had found along the way, they managed to scale 20 feet of sheer rock face while under fire to reach the final pinnacle. The New Zealanders suffered 536 casualties taking Takrouna. Lieut. General Brian Horrocks, who was commander of the Eighth Army's X Corps, commented later that the capture of Takrouna was the most gallant feat of arms he witnessed during the entire war. He said he was "bitterly disappointed" when Manahi was awarded only a Distinguished Conduct Medal instead of the Victoria Cross for his deeds.

As costly as the hills were to assault, neither Djebel Garci nor Takrouna were of major significance. Behind them stretched more than 20 miles of similar mountainous country, and the Eighth Army could expect every peak to be strongly contested by the Axis. Two days after beginning the attack, a discouraged Montgomery paused; he spent the next four days regrouping his forces.

Unfortunately, the Eighth Army's attack had ceased before accomplishing its primary goal—drawing Axis forces away from the First Army, which had not yet started its drive toward Tunis. Arnim was convinced that the major effort would come from the west and had kept his strongest forces there. (On April 20, he had even dared to launch a spoiling attack against the British near Medjez el Bab, a key town along the main road to Tunis from the west, causing some damage, but not enough to forestall the Allied offensive.) Now, with pressure easing in the south, he could bring yet more troops to this part of the front.

On April 22 the First Army began its slow and arduous advance, characterized by tough slugging matches between British armor and panzers for little patches of level ground and costly infantry struggles for the hills. One dramatic conquest was that of Longstop Hill—the notorious peak

that had claimed 500 British and American casualties when the Allies tried without success to take it in late December, 1942. Longstop, which controlled two roads to Tunis, could not be bypassed.

The British began pounding Longstop with artillery on April 22, but the defenders bided their time in the relative safety of well-stocked dugouts that ran deep into the hillside. That night, when two battalions of the 36th Infantry Brigade moved up the western slopes of the hill, the Germans emerged from their burrows just far enough to slow the attack with heavy fire. By dawn the British had secured

Hill 609, an Axis stronghold, dominates Tunisian terrain far different from the desert setting of earlier campaigns. Concerned that the Americans who were to take the hill would suffer high casualties, British Lieut. General Kenneth Anderson (inset, on left) suggested going around it. U.S. Major General Omar Bradley (inset, on right), believing it would be impossible to move troops past the hilltop guns, insisted on capturing it. When Hill 609 was finally taken, the British Eighth Army was being pinned down by other Axis positions on hills to the south. "Let's radio Monty," said Bradley, full of pride, "and ask if he wants a few American advisers."

only the lower slopes. On April 23 the 8th Battalion of the Argyll and Sutherland Highlanders took up the advance in broad daylight and were met by a sustained fusillade that exacted a stiff toll. After his commander was killed, a major named John Anderson stood up in the face of German fire and shouted "Come on!" Yelling, shooting, bayoneting and struggling through barbed wire, the Highlanders followed him up. When the battalion reached Longstop's western summit—ensuring the capture of the entire hill by the next day—it had been reduced to 30 men. Despite such courageous efforts, the First Army was able to advance its front little more than 10 miles in eight days of bitter fighting.

To the north the U.S. II Corps, which began its own advance on April 23, was soon engaged in a contest for another key hill. The battle for Hill 609—so called because French maps designated it by its elevation of 609 meters (about 2,000 feet)—dispelled doubt about the effectiveness of the GIs in North Africa. Known to Tunisians as Djebel Tahent, Hill 609 dominated not only lower surrounding hills but also the Tine River valley about five miles to the south. The valley—which soldiers called The Mousetrap because any force crossing it was easy prey for Axis artillery on the

heights—was a natural route to Mateur, a gateway to the Tunisian coastal plain. General Bradley wanted to move the 1st Armored Division through The Mousetrap but could not do so until the 1st Infantry Division, under Major General Terry Allen, had cleared the enemy from the hills along the valley's northern rim. And Allen's advance was being stymied by savage artillery fire from Hill 609, which was reducing many of his companies to the strength of platoons.

Bradley sent for Major General Charles W. Ryder, whose 34th Infantry Division had done especially poorly in an operation with the British in the south. "Get me that hill," Bradley told Ryder on April 26, "and you'll break up the enemy's defenses clear across our front. Take it and no one will ever again doubt the toughness of your division." For four days the Americans repeatedly tried to dislodge the Germans from Hill 609 and the nearby lower hills, suffering heavy casualties each time. The tenacious defenders threw bundles of grenades known as "potato mashers" at the GIs and answered almost every gain by the 34th Division with a determined counterattack, often before the Americans could dig in. Then Bradley had an inspiration. For an attack early on April 30, he offered Ryder the use of Sherman tanks as mobile artillery support. Bradley later recalled that Ryder looked at him with "mild surprise"—tanks were not usually employed against hill positions—but accepted.

With infantry following in their wake, 17 Sherman tanks groaned up the slopes of 609 and began blasting the German strong points with their 75mm guns. Simultaneous attacks were launched against two crucial nearby hills. By the end of the day, the Americans had gained the summits and a reputation for toughness that soon spread throughout the Allied forces—a reputation they reinforced by fighting off ferocious German attempts to retake the hills.

The Americans paid dearly for the victory: 200 dead, 1,600 wounded, and 700 captured or missing. But the tactical rewards were substantial. Axis forces to the north, foreseeing that the American armored penetration made possible by the capture of 609 could imperil their rear, quickly fell back some 25 miles to the east. On May 3 the 1st Armored Division rolled through The Mousetrap and into the undefended town of Mateur.

While Axis soldiers attempted to defend their perimeter against a well-equipped and well-fed adversary, their supply problems assumed ominous proportions. During April, Allied warplanes pounced repeatedly on the lumbering Junkers-52 and Messerschmitt-323 cargo aircraft ferrying Axis supplies across the Mediterranean, and destroyed more than 200 enemy planes. On April 18, over the Gulf of Tunis, British fighters downed 38 of the German aircraft in a single encounter. By the end of April, desperately needed munitions had such high priority on the few Axis ships and planes reaching Tunisia that almost no food at all was arriving. Many of Arnim's troops were obliged to subsist on two slices of bread a day each.

The Allies, however, had no intention of laying siege to the northeast corner of Tunisia and starving the enemy into submission. On the same day that Hill 609 was taken, April 30, Alexander set in motion a scheme to renew the offensive, which seemed to have ground to a halt in all but the American sector. The plan, code-named *Strike*, called for a sudden, massive push by the First Army straight across the Axis bridgehead to Tunis in an effort to split the enemy's forces and seize the city before the defenders could damage its port facilities. Haste was necessary also to prevent the Axis from withdrawing behind the hills stretching across the base of the Cape Bon peninsula, a good natural defense line. While the First Army raced for Tunis, the U.S. II Corps was to press with similar speed toward Bizerte and the coast between the two cities.

To build up the muscle of the First Army, which was to deliver its big armored punch on May 6, Alexander ordered Montgomery to yield three of his crack units to Anderson: the 7th Armored Division, the 4th Indian Division and the 201st Guards Brigade. Some 3,000 aircraft were to support the attack.

Arnim knew by the Allied build-up where the heaviest thrust would come—the Medjez el Bab sector—but his shortage of fuel prevented him from shifting sufficient reinforcements to the area. For a week before the main effort, Allied aircraft, including American B-25s, softened up enemy positions with bombing raids. On May 4 the French XIX Corps, to the south of the First Army, advanced to secure the right flank of the corridor through which the British tanks would charge, and the First Army's own V Corps moved out to secure the left flank. In between them, the

A victorious Montgomery—tilting back in his camp chair for an aside with an aide—consults with his captives, Italian Marshal Giovanni Messe (seated at left) and German Major General Frecken von Liebenstein (seated at right), on assembly points for Axis prisoners. As they talked on May 13, 1943, thousands of Axis troops had already thrown down their arms and were streaming along the Cape Bon roads toward the British line at Tunis, in a procession that was spontaneous, leaderless and 80 miles long.

IX Corps of the First Army was poised, ready to spring.

At dusk on May 5, Allied planes began the heaviest air attack of the North African war. In the following 24 hours they flew 1,958 bombing and support sorties. (General Henry H. "Hap" Arnold, Commanding General of the U.S. Army Air Forces, who followed the action from his headquarters in America, later boasted, "We blasted a channel from Medjez el Bab to Tunis.") That same night the fire of 600 guns exploded across a 3,000-yard front astride the road from Medjez el Bab to Tunis. The weight of fire was enormous: 16,632 shells in two hours on the sector facing the British 4th Division alone. The projectiles crashing down on Axis positions, Lieutenant Nigel Nicolson later recalled, "burst like the flowering of a field of ruby tulips."

At 3:30 a.m. on May 6, the IX Corps moved out. First, carving a path for the armor, came the infantry: the 4th Indian Division on the left and the 4th British Division on the right. Behind them roared tanks of the 6th and 7th armored divisions. By 11 a.m. the enemy's frontline defenses had been cleared, and the tanks rolled on through the infantry to begin their dash for Tunis—juggernauts hastening to the kill, grinding cactus hedges to pulp and scattering goats that wandered across their route.

In the American sector, the II Corps' 9th Infantry Division, which had begun its advance on May 4, overcame the last Axis stronghold between it and Bizerte on May 6. The remainder of the II Corps launched its attack—aimed at the Bizerte-Tunis road—on May 6 and made steady progress in spite of tough opposition. Major General Ernest Harmon, commander of the U.S. 1st Armored Division, advised Brad-

ley that he would have to sacrifice 50 tanks in order to break through the entrenched enemy to the coast. Bradley told him to go ahead. The final tally: 47 tanks lost. From the north, Major General Manton Eddy, commanding the 9th Infantry Division, complained that the road to Bizerte was "lousy with mines." Over his field phone Bradley was adamant. "Well then, get off your trucks and begin walking, but get the hell into Bizerte."

The urgency in the British sector was just as great. Alexander impatiently rebuffed Anderson's suggestion that, once the breakthrough was achieved, the First Army's armor should turn aside to mop up the battlefield. Both the 6th and 7th armored divisions, Alexander ruled, were to ignore any skirmishing on the flanks and drive for Tunis. "The rapier was to be thrust into the heart," he said later.

It was less a rapier than an inundation. The dam had collapsed and the Allied forces flooded toward Bizerte and Tunis. Hundreds of tanks sped for the two ports and the road between them—artillery and antitank guns, fuel and munitions trucks, and armored reconnaissance cars flowing with them. Down the Tunis road, swerving among the First Army vehicles, came Alexander driving his own jeep, his hands tight on the wheel, his face white with dust.

The Allied advance was so rapid that both sides were startled. As he hit Bizerte at 3:20 p.m. on May 7, American Lieutenant Gene Boutwell, in a jeep with two noncoms, discovered to his dismay that he had arrived 40 minutes ahead of the first Shermans. Two German submachine gunners he passed on the road were so taken aback that neither thought to open fire until the jeep was well past. "They must have been as scared as we were," Boutwell said.

In Tunis, which the British reached at 4 p.m., the confusion was great. Although it was raining, hundreds of Germans were moving about the streets or sipping drinks with their girl friends under the awnings of sidewalk cafés. In one barbershop some German soldiers jumped from their chairs, white cloths around their necks, chins lathered, to gape in awe at British armored cars rolling down the street.

There was scattered resistance in the Tunisian capital. British Colonel Freddie Stephens found himself besieged by French citizens pressing flowers, fruit and kisses on him— while the random stutter of machine-gun fire echoed across the city and rifle shots from snipers holed up in high build-

ings struck the pavement near his jeep. Some Germans were uncertain how to react: a major of the Hermann Göring Division, surprised just outside of Tunis, refused to believe the city had been taken until he was led to a radio set and heard the messages coming from the center of town.

Bizarre requests were made of the liberators. One officer was hailed by a Frenchman who asked him for chewing gum. "My wife is pregnant, and she has a craving for chewing gum," he explained. A beaming youngster told correspondent John MacVane: "We now can again see American films—Robert Taylor and Greta Garbo."

Inevitably, some citizens saw a way to turn a fast profit. Twenty-five troopers of the 15th Panzer Division, cut off by the River Medjerda from the 11th Hussars to whom they agreed to surrender, found the river too deep to wade. An Arab appeared with farm horses and offered to ferry the Germans across to their captors at 50 francs a head. The Germans reluctantly dug into their pockets and paid for their transport into captivity.

But the bulk of Arnim's forces, although disorganized and short of transport, fled toward the Cape Bon peninsula and the double line of defensible hills that ran across its base. If what was left of the Axis forces could get behind those hills and hold the two coastal passes that gave access to the peninsula—at Hammam Lif near Tunis on the north side and Hammamet on the coast to the south—Arnim might be able to delay the final Allied victory for months.

But Alexander struck swiftly to forestall this move. The 6th Armored Division rolled out of Tunis to Hammam Lif and with other British units spent two days forcing the pass there. On May 9 the division sped on toward Hammamet. This advance from Hammam Lif to Hammamet, which was reached on May 11, has been called one of the strangest and most impressive feats of arms in the entire war. Although the Axis had great numerical superiority in this area, they were stunned by the swiftness of the British armor. With no stops for taking prisoners, the 6th Armored's forces thrust through the surprised enemy, creating confusion among all who saw them. With the 6th Armored now holding the Hammam Lif-Hammamet line, the Axis forces were split, some bottled up on the Cape Bon side of the line while others were being surrounded to the west of it. With division cut off from division, regiment from regiment, the

Axis command structure broke down. Although dedicated German officers created ad hoc organizations to continue fighting, some men headed for the Cape Bon beaches seeking boats that might carry them to Italy.

In the bitter 11th hour, a stark order for Arnim arrived from Hitler: "The German people expect you to fight to the last bullet." Arnim conceived his own interpretation of "the last bullet." It would be the last shell fired by the last tank. Then the weapons would be destroyed and Army Group Africa would give up.

On May 11 the last seven tanks of the 10th Panzer Division, their desert-yellow paint peeling, ran out of fuel and fired a final defiant salvo toward the Hammam Lif-Hammamet line. The next day Arnim capitulated. Before surrendering he personally set fire to the big command vehicle Rommel had bequeathed him, captured from the British in the Western Desert two years before. To the German High Command, General Hans Cramer, the last commander of the Afrika Korps, dispatched a proud farewell message: "Munitions expended, weapons and war equipment destroyed. The Afrika Korps has fought to a standstill as ordered. The German Afrika Korps must ride again."

Surrender was a complex process, involving emotions as well as formalities. General Graf von Sponeck's 90th Light Division insisted on giving up to the New Zealanders, their doughty adversaries of two years' standing. To boost Italian morale, Mussolini promoted General Giovanni Messe, commander of the First Italian Army, to field marshal on the day he became a prisoner. Messe would surrender only to the veteran Eighth Army, not the fledgling First, and he was the last leading Axis commander to capitulate, on May 13.

To some fighting men this professional emphasis on protocol, following the slaughter of two and a half years, struck a jarring note. When the staff of Major General Fritz Krause, Afrika Korps artillery commander, arrived at General Harmon's headquarters wearing crisp dress uniforms and riding in Mercedes-Benz staff cars, Harmon commented, "You would have thought the bastards were going to a wedding." The men of the Hermann Göring Division, entrenched on a hillside, demanded a certificate saying that they were the last Germans to lay down arms on that front (it was not just pride; without communications, they were afraid they were being tricked into giving up while the fight continued elsewhere). Retorted an American battalion commander: "Brother, either you'll come down right now and cut out this monkey business or we'll carve that certificate on your headstone." The Germans came down.

In great sand-colored Wehrmacht trucks with the palm-leaf markings of the Afrika Korps, on bicycles and on burros, in horse-drawn gigs, some 275,000 Axis soldiers moved to areas designated by the victors as prisoner-of-war assembly points. Their feelings about surrendering varied widely. Major General Willibald Borowiecz, commander of the 15th Panzer Division, broke down and wept in General Harmon's headquarters. "I am a general without a command," he said. "My Panzers have been wiped out."

Some continued to display stubborn defiance. Private Tony Wittkop, a Philadelphia-educated Afrika Korps veteran, warned his captors: "Just wait until you try to land in Europe. We are not beaten yet, not by a long shot!" But many felt that the German High Command had let them down. On a Tunis street, one captured private took a portrait of Hitler from his pocket. "That's my Führer," he said as he tore the picture into pieces, "my Führer."

Troops on both sides were exhausted. After entering Tunis, some Allied soldiers simply lay down on the sidewalks and slept, despite the victory and liberation celebrations around them. They had only listless curiosity about the Axis troops streaming toward the prisoner-of-war camps.

No accurate calculation of Axis casualties in Tunisia has ever been made, but they probably totaled some 315,000—275,000 captured and 40,000 killed, wounded or missing in action. British losses, by contrast, numbered 35,940 dead, wounded or missing in action; American losses totaled 13,984; French, 16,180.

At 2:15 p.m. on the 13th of May, General Alexander sent a message from Tunis to Churchill that the Prime Minister had waited almost three years to receive: "Sir, it is my duty to report that the Tunisian campaign is over. All enemy resistance has ceased. We are masters of the North African shores."

Masters—and more. The Allies had become a strong and confident team. This strength and unity was already being counted as an asset by planners who looked across the Mediterranean to Europe where yet another kind of war was soon to begin.

GRAND FINALE IN TUNIS

A sign on a van proclaiming the Allies' next destinations to be the Axis capitals in Europe elicits cheers from the liberated populace as the victors enter Tunis.

JUBILANT WEEKS OF VICTORY AND LIBERATION

The struggle in North Africa was virtually over. By late afternoon Wednesday, May 7, 1943, the Allies' first major victory celebration of World War II was building to a grand revel on the sun-washed boulevards of Tunis. Without waiting for the last German or Italian to surrender—that happened six days later—the old French colonial city unfurled the tricolors and plunged into festivity.

Tunis' jubilant population, doubled by refugees from the fighting and the horde of exultant, victorious soldiers who at last were out of the harsh North African deserts and mountains, gave itself over to wine, song and dance. Dowagers on balconies screamed "Vive!" while younger women smothered marching British and Free French troops with kisses, and showered the victors' tanks and trucks with flowers of the season—roses, lilacs and poppies. The Hotel Majestic, where Axis officers had resided two days before, now accommodated Allied officers—with the staff's apologies for the lack of hot water and electricity, and, since the restaurant cupboards were bare, with offers to warm C rations in the hotel kitchen.

While Tunis celebrated, there were reports of riots in Berlin. A Swedish newspaper said the families of Panzer Army Africa soldiers took to the streets of the German capital when they were refused news of the fate of their men in Tunisia, and troops had to be called out to put down their protest. In fact, most of the Germans in Tunisia were willingly crowding into prison compounds: at the gates of one barbed-wire enclosure in a Tunis suburb, a German infantry band serenaded the arriving captives with strains of Viennese *Lieder*.

The revelry continued for two weeks until May 20, when the Allies staged an official victory parade. The Americans, who had taken Bizerte on the same day that the British and French entered Tunis, came to town to join the review. For two hours, American, French and British troops, including veterans of Tobruk, El Alamein and Hill 609, marched through the crowded streets in a grand finale to the North African campaign.

Accepting hands eager to shake his, a smiling soldier marches proudly down a Tunis boulevard as victorious columns pour into the liberated city.

Allied riflemen, part of the official victory review, parade past British, French and American commanders in Tunis at the end of the North African campaign.

Jubilant French civilians accompany a British armored car as it enters Tunis. A small girl rides with the Tommy in the turret while her father, on the running board, flashes the "V" for victory sign, and a saluting woman runs alongside.

Dressed up in spring hats and suits to welcome liberation, Tunisian women wave to passing Free French soldiers who cling to their trucktops in order to get a better view of the crowds that turned out to greet them in the capital.

A group of smiling French Tunisians gather around a truck carrying impassive Gurkha soldiers—celebrated knife-fighters from the 4th Indian Division.

A wildly gesticulating throng—French and native Tunisians cheering the end of Axis occupation—jams an intersection during the boisterous Allied welcome.

In this aerial view, some of the 275,000 German and Italian soldiers who surrendered at the end of the North African campaign pour into a prisoner-of-war compound west of Tunis, near Mateur. Many of them arrived driving their own trucks, with white flags in clear view. Eventually, they were interned in POW camps in Canada, Great Britain and the U.S.

BIBLIOGRAPHY

Agar-Hamilton, John A. I., and Leonard C. F. Turner, eds., *The Sidi Rezeg Battles.* Oxford University Press, 1957.

Aglion, Raoul, *War in the Desert.* Holt, 1941.

Altieri, James, *The Spearheaders.* The Bobbs-Merrill Co., 1960.

Austin, A. B., *Birth of an Army.* Victor Gollancz, Ltd., 1943.

Badoglio, Pietro, *Italy in the Second World War,* translated from the Italian by Muriel Currey. Greenwood Press, 1976.

Barclay, C. N., *Against Great Odds.* Sifton, Praed, 1955.

Barnett, Correlli, *The Desert Generals.* The Viking Press, Inc., 1961.

Bartimeus:
East of Malta, West of Suez. Little, Brown and Co., 1944.
The Turn of the Road. Chatto and Windus, 1946.

Beddington, William Richard, *A History of the Queen's Bays, 1929-1945.* Warren & Son Ltd., 1954.

Bekker, Cajus, *The Luftwaffe War Diaries,* edited and translated from the German by Frank Ziegler. Macdonald & Co., 1967.

Bergot, Erwan, *The Afrika Korps,* translated from the French by Richard Barry. Allan Wingate Ltd., 1972.

Blumenson, Martin:
Kasserine Pass. Houghton Mifflin Co., 1967.
The Patton Papers, 1940-1945. Houghton Mifflin Co., 1974.

Borghese, J. Valerio, *Sea Devils,* translated from the Italian by James Cleugh. Henry Regnery Company, 1954.

Bradley, Omar N., *A Soldier's Story.* Henry Holt & Co., 1951.

Bragadin, M., *The Italian Navy in World War II,* translated from the Italian by Gale Hoffman. U.S. Naval Institute, 1957.

Brownlie, W. Steel, *The Proud Trooper: Story of a Regiment.* Wm. Collins, Sons & Co., Ltd., 1964.

Bryant, Arthur, *The Turn of the Tide, 1939-1943.* Doubleday & Co., Inc., 1957.

Butcher, Harry C., *My Three Years with Eisenhower.* Simon and Schuster, Inc., 1946.

Bykofsky, Joseph, and Harold Larson, *The Transportation Corps: Operations Overseas.* Office of the Chief of Military History, 1957.

Cameron, Ian, *Red Duster, White Ensign.* Doubleday, 1960.

Canevari, Emilio, *Graziani mi ha detto.* Magi-Spinetti, 1947.

Carell, Paul, *The Foxes of the Desert,* translated from the German by Mervyn Savill. E. P. Dutton & Co., Inc., 1961.

Carver, Michael, *El Alamein.* B. T. Batsford Ltd., 1962.

Cary, James, *Tanks and Armor in Modern Warfare.* F. Watts, 1966.

Chamberlain, Peter, *Afrika Korps.* Almark Publishing Co., 1970.

Churchill, Winston S.:
The Second World War, Bantam Books.
Volume III, *The Grand Alliance,* 1962.
Volume IV, *The Hinge of Fate,* 1962.

Clarke, Dudley, *The Eleventh at War.* Michael Joseph Ltd., 1952.

Clifford, Alexander, *Three Against Rommel.* George G. Harrap & Co., Ltd., 1943.

Cocchia, Aldo, *The Hunter and the Hunted,* translated from the Italian by M. Gwyer. U.S. Naval Institute, 1958.

Collier, Richard, *Duce!* Collins, 1971.

Connell, John:
Auchinleck. Cassell & Company Ltd., 1959.
Wavell. Collins, 1964.

Cowie, Donald, *The Campaigns of Wavell.* Chapman & Hall Ltd., 1942.

Crisp, Robert, *Brazen Chariots.* Muller, 1959.

Cunningham, Andrew, *A Sailor's Odyssey.* Hutchinson, 1951.

Davy, G. M., *The Seventh and Three Enemies.* Published for the regiment by W. Heffer, 1953.

D'Arcy-Dawson, John, *Tunisian Battles.* Macdonald & Co., 1943.

De Guingand, Francis:
Generals at War. Hodder and Stoughton, 1964.
Operation Victory. Hodder and Stoughton, 1947.

Destruction of an Army. Her Majesty's Stationery Office, 1941.

Eden, Sir Anthony, The Earl of Avon, *The Reckoning: The Eden Memoirs.* Cassell, 1965.

The Eighth Army: September 1941 to January 1943. Her Majesty's Stationery Office, 1944.

Eisenhower, Dwight D., *Crusade in Europe.* Doubleday & Co., Inc., 1948.

The Encyclopedia of Sea Warfare. Thomas Y. Crowell Co., 1975.

Esebeck, Hanns Gert von, *Afrikanische Schicksalsjahre.* Limes Verlag, 1950.

Esposito, Vincent J., ed., *The West Point Atlas of American Wars, Vol. 2: 1900-1953.* Frederick A. Praeger, 1959.

Evans, Trefor E., ed., *The Killearn Diaries, 1934-1946.* Sedgwick and Jackson Ltd., 1972.

Farago, Ladislas, *Patton: Ordeal and Triumph.* Ivan Obolensky, Inc., 1964.

Farran, Roy, *Winged Dagger.* Collins, 1948.

Fearnside, G. H., *Sojourn in Tobruk.* Ure Smith Pty Ltd., 1944.

Felletti, Leonida, *Soldati senz'armi, le gravi responsabilità degli alti commandi.* D. de Luigi, 1944.

Fergusson, Bernard, *The Black Watch and the King's Enemies.* Collins, 1950.

Forty, George, *The Desert Rats at War.* I. Allan, 1975.

Freidin, Seymour, and William Richardson, eds., *The Fatal Decisions.* William Sloane Associates, Inc., 1956.

Gallagher, Wes, *Back Door to Berlin.* Doubleday, Doran & Co., 1943.

Gibson, Hugh, ed., *The Ciano Diaries, 1939-1943.* Garden City Publishing Co., Inc., 1947.

Graham, F. C. C., *History of Argyll & Sutherland Highlanders 1st Battalion, 1939-1945.* T. Nelson, 1948.

Halder, Franz, *Kriegstagebuch,* Vol. 5. W. Kohlhammer, 1962-1964.

Hastings, R. H. W. S., *The Rifle Brigade in the Second World War, 1939-1945.* Gale & Polden Ltd., 1950.

Heckstall-Smith, Anthony, *Tobruk.* Anthony Blond, 1959.

Hill, Russell, *Desert Conquest.* Jarrolds, 1944.

Holmes, Richard, *Bir Hacheim: Desert Citadel.* Ballantine Books, 1971.

Horrocks, Brian, *A Full Life.* William Collins Sons & Co., Inc., 1960.

Howe, George F., *Northwest Africa: Seizing the Initiative in the West.* Office of the Chief of Military History, 1957.

Howard, Michael, and John Sparrow, *The Coldstream Guards, 1920-1946.* Oxford University Press, 1951.

Icks, Robert J., *Tanks and Armored Vehicles, 1940-1945.* WE, Inc., 1970.

Ingersoll, Ralph McAllister, *Battle is the Pay-off.* Harcourt, Brace & Co., Inc., 1943.

Ismay, Hastings Lionel, *Memoirs.* Heinemann, 1960.

Jackson, W. G. F., *The Battle for North Africa, 1940-1943.* Mason/Charter Publishers, Inc., 1975.

Jacob, Alaric, *A Traveller's War.* Dodd, Mead & Co., 1944.

Jewell, Derek, ed., *Alamein and the Desert War.* Ballantine Books, Inc., 1967.

Jones, Vincent, *Operation Torch.* Ballantine Books, Inc., 1972.

Jordan, Philip, *Jordan's Tunis Diary.* Collins, 1943.

Kennedy, John, *The Business of War.* Hutchinson, 1957.

Keyes, Elizabeth, *Geoffrey Keyes.* G. Newnes, 1956.

Kippenberger, Howard, *Infantry Brigadier.* Oxford University Press, 1949.

Kirk, John, and Robert Young Jr., *Great Weapons of World War II.* Walker, 1961.

Lewin, Ronald:
Montgomery as Military Commander. B. T. Batsford Ltd., 1971.
Rommel as Military Commander. B. T. Batsford Ltd., 1968.

Lewis, P. J., and I. R. English, *The 8th Battalion, The Durham Light Infantry, 1939-1945.* J. & P. Bealls, Ltd., 1950.

Liddell Hart, B. H.:
ed., *The Rommel Papers,* translated from the German by Paul Findlay. Harcourt, Brace & Co., 1953.
The Tanks, Vol. 2: *1939-1945.* Frederick A. Praeger, 1959.

Lochner, Louis P., ed., *The Goebbels Diaries, 1942-1943.* Doubleday & Co., Inc., 1948.

Long, Gavin, *To Benghazi.* Australian War Memorial, 1952.

Macksey, Kenneth, *Beda Fomm.* Ballantine Books, Inc., 1971.

MacVane, John, *Journey Into War.* D. Appleton-Century Co., Inc., 1943.

Majdalany, Fred, *The Battle of El Alamein.* J. B. Lippincott Co., 1965.

Martineau, G. D., *A History of the Royal Sussex Regiment.* Moore & Tillyer, 1953.

Maughan, Barton, *Tobruk and El Alamein.* Australian War Memorial, 1966.

Maule, Henry:
Out of the Sand. Odhams Press, Ltd., 1966.
Spearhead General. Odhams Press, Ltd., 1961.

Mellenthin, Friedrich von, *Panzer Battles,* translated from the German by H. Betzler. University of Oklahoma Press, 1956.

The Memoirs of Field-Marshal the Viscount Montgomery of Alamein. The World Publishing Co., 1958.

Michie, Allan:
Honour for All. G. Allen & Unwin, Ltd., 1946.
Retreat to Victory. G. Allen & Unwin, Ltd., 1942.

Montgomery, Brian, *A Field-Marshal in the Family.* Taplinger Publishing Co., 1973.

Moorehead, Alan:
The March to Tunis. Harper & Row, Inc., 1943.
Montgomery. Hamish Hamilton, Ltd., 1967.

Morison, Samuel Eliot, *Operations in North African Waters.* Little, Brown and Co., 1975.

Murphy, Robert, *Diplomat Among Warriors.* Greenwood Press, 1964.

Mussolini, Benito, *Memoirs, 1942-1943,* edited by Raymond Klibansky and translated from the Italian by Frances Lobb. Weidenfeld & Nicolson, Ltd., 1949.

Neame, Philip, *Playing with Strife.* George G. Harrap & Co., Ltd., 1947.

Newton, Don, and A. C. Hampshire, *Taranto.* W. Kimber, 1959.

Nicolson, Nigel, *Alex: The Life of Field Marshal Earl Alexander of Tunis.* Weidenfeld and Nicolson, 1973.

North, John, ed., *The Alexander Memoirs, 1940-1945.* Cassell & Co. Ltd., 1961.

Onslow, William Arthur Bampfylde, Earl of Onslow, *Men and Sand.* Saint Catherine Press, 1961.

Parkinson, C. Northcote, *Always a Fusilier.* Low, 1949.

Phillips, C. E. Lucas, *Alamein.* William Heinemann Ltd., 1962.

Playfair, I. S. O., *The Mediterranean and Middle East,* Vols. 1-4. Her Majesty's Stationery Office, 1954-1966.

Poolman, Kenneth, *Illustrious.* W. Kimber, 1955.

Pyle, Ernie, *Here is Your War.* Henry Holt & Co., Inc., 1943.

Quilter, D. C., *No Dishonorable Name.* W. Clowes, 1947.

Rainier, Peter W., *Pipeline to Battle.* William Heinemann Ltd., 1944.

Rame, David, *Road to Tunis.* The Macmillan Co., 1944.

Ramsay, Guy, *One Continent Redeemed.* George G. Harrap & Co., Ltd., 1943.

Rissik, David, *The D. L. I. At War*. D. L. I. Dept., 1953.
Robinett, Paul McDonald, *Armor Command*. No publishers' information, 1958.
Rosenthal, Eric, *Fortress on Sand*. Hutchinson, 1943.
Roskill, S. W., *The War at Sea*, Vol. 2. Her Majesty's Stationery Office, 1956.
Schmidt, Heinz-Werner, *With Rommel in the Desert*. George G. Harrap & Co., Ltd., 1951.
Shirer, William L., *The Rise and Fall of the Third Reich*. Simon and Schuster, Inc., 1960.
Stamps, T. Dodson, and Vincent J. Esposito, eds., *A Military History of World War II*. United States Military Academy, 1956.
Stevens, W. G., *Bardia to Enfidaville*. New Zealand Department of Internal Affairs, 1962.
Strawson, John, *The Battle for North Africa*. Batsford, 1969.
Taggart, Donald G., ed., *History of the Third Infantry Division in World War II*. Infantry Journal Press, 1947.

Talbot, Godfrey, *Speaking from the Desert*. Hutchinson & Co., Ltd., **1944.**
Taylor, Henry J., *Men in Motion*. Doubleday, Doran & Co., Inc., 1943.
Tedder, Arthur, *With Prejudice*. Cassell & Co. Ltd., 1966.
The Tiger Kills. His Majesty's Stationery Office, 1944.
Tompkins, Peter, *The Murder of Admiral Darlan*. Simon and Schuster, 1965.
Truscott, Lucian K., *Command Missions*. E. P. Dutton & Co., Inc., 1954.
Verney, G. L., *The Desert Rats*. Hutchinson, 1954.
Walker, Allan S., *Middle East and Far East Australian Medical Services*. Australian War Memorial, 1953.
Walker, Ronald, *Alam Halfa and Alamein*. Historical Publications Branch, New Zealand Department of Internal Affairs, 1967.
Wellard, James Howard, *Man in a Helmet*. Eyre & Spottiswoode Ltd., 1947.
Wilmot, Chester, *Tobruk*. Angus & Robertson, 1944.
Yindrich, Jan, *Fortress Tobruk*. Ernest Benn Ltd., 1951.
Young, Desmond, *Rommel, the Desert Fox*. Harper & Brothers, 1950.

PICTURE CREDITS

Credits from left to right are separated by semicolons, from top to bottom by dashes.

COVER and page 1: Imperial War Museum, London.

ITALY'S REACH FOR GLORY: 6, 7—Istituto Luce, Rome. 8—Publifoto Notizie, Milan. 9—Bibliothek für Zeitgeschichte, Stuttgart. 10, 11—Istituto Luce, Rome. 12, 13—Istituto Italo-Africano, Rome, except inset, top left, Istituto Luce, Rome. 14, 15—Pietro Caporilli, Rome. 16, 17—Imperial War Museum, London.

A GAMBLE FOR HIGH STAKES: 20—Unedi, Rome. 22, 23—Map by Elie Sabban. 24—Roma's Press, Rome; Unedi, Rome—Stato Maggiore Aeronautica, Rome. 25—Roma's Press, Rome. 27—Map by Elie Sabban. 28, 29—Photo Trends. 30—Imperial War Museum, London.

THE DESERT FOX: 34, 35—Ullstein Bilderdienst, Berlin. 36—Courtesy Manfred Rommel. 37—Bundesarchiv, Koblenz. 38, 39—All courtesy Manfred Rommel. 40, 41—Bundesarchiv, Koblenz; courtesy Manfred Rommel. 42, 43—Süddeutscher Verlag, Bilderdienst, Munich; Bundesarchiv, Koblenz. 44—Bundesarchiv, Koblenz. 45, 46, 47—Ullstein Bilderdienst, Berlin.

HELL'S OWN BATTLEGROUND: 48, 49—Istituto Italo-Africano/Luce, Rome. 50—PhotoWorld. 51—H. Roger-Viollet. 52, 53—Camera Press, courtesy Imperial War Museum, London, except inset, top left, H. Roger-Viollet. 54, 55—Süddeutscher Verlag, Bilderdienst, Munich—Robert Hunt Library, London. 56, 57—Keystone. 58, 59—Camera Press, courtesy Imperial War Museum, London; Transit Film, Munich, courtesy Bundesarchiv, Koblenz.

ROMMEL'S STUNNING BLOW: 62—PhotoWorld—National Archives, Rommel Collection (2). 64—National Archives, Rommel Collection. 66—National Archives, Rommel Collection. 67—Map by Elie Sabban. 68—Australian War Memorial. 69—P. I. from Black Star.

EMBATTLED MALTA: 72, 73—From *Message from Malta*, Office of War Information, courtesy National Archives, Motion Picture and Sound Record Branch. 74 through 77—Imperial War Museum, London. 78, 79—Courtesy Associated News (Malta) LTD.; Imperial War Museum, London. 80, 81—Camera Press, courtesy Imperial War Museum, London, except inset, top left, Photo Trends.

TRIUMPH ELUDES THE BRITISH: 84—Map by Elie Sabban. 85—Imperial War Museum, London. 86—Lega Navale. 88—H. Roger-Viollet. 91—Photoreporters.

LIGHT RELIEF IN CAIRO: 94, 95—Bob Landry for LIFE. 96 through 100—George Rodger for LIFE. 101—E. Chamma for LIFE. 102, 103—Bob Landry for LIFE.

THE CRUCIBLE OF VICTORY: 106—Photo Trends. 108—Imperial War Museum, London. 111—Map by Elie Sabban. 113—George R. Bradford, courtesy Arms and Armour Press, London, and Squadron/Signal Publications, Michigan (6).

THE BRUTAL POUNDING OF THE AXIS: 116, 117—Camera Press, courtesy Imperial War Museum, London. 118—Imperial War Museum, London. 119—Wide World. 120 through 123—Camera Press, courtesy Imperial War Museum, London. 124, 125—British Official except inset, bottom left, Wide World. 126, 127—Dever from Black Star; George Rodger for LIFE.

MONTY AT THE HELM: 128, 129—Imperial War Museum, London. 130—Courtesy Colonel Brian Montgomery. 131—Imperial War Museum, London. 132, 133—Courtesy Colonel Brian Montgomery (5). 134 through 137—Imperial War Museum, London. 138, 139—Wide World.

AN ALLY JOINS THE WAR: 142, 143, 144—Navy Department, courtesy National Archives. 147, 148—U.S. Army.

TIPPING THE BALANCE: 152, 153—Imperial War Museum, London. 154—Navy Department, courtesy National Archives. 155, 156—U.S. Army. 157—Camera Press, courtesy Imperial War Museum, London. 158 through 161—U.S. Army.

AMERICANS TASTE THE FIRE: 165—United Press International. 166—Map by Elie Sabban; Imperial War Museum, London. 170—Eliot Elisofon for LIFE (3).

ONE MAN'S FOCUS ON THE WAR: 174 through 187—Eliot Elisofon for LIFE.

THE KNOCKOUT PUNCH: 190, 191—U.S. Army except inset, top left, Imperial War Museum, London. 193—Photo Trends.

GRAND FINALE IN TUNIS: 196, 197—Library of Congress. 198—Camera Press, courtesy Imperial War Museum, London. 199—Library of Congress. 200—U.S. Army (3). 201—Bob Landry for LIFE. 202, 203—U.S. Army.

ACKNOWLEDGMENTS

The index for this book was prepared by Mel Ingber. The editors of this book also wish to express their gratitude to Lieselotte Bandelow, Ullstein, Berlin; Bernard Bäter, Düsseldorf, Germany; Lieut. Colonel Oreste Bovio and General Rinaldo Cruccu, Stato Maggiore dell'Esercito, Rome; Commander Marc' Antonio Bragadin (Ret.), Rome; Rosario Casella, Rome; Commander Andrea Corsini, Rear Admiral Renato Fadda and Commander Leonardo Sansonetti, Stato Maggiore della Marina, Rome; Cecile Coutin, Curator, Musée des Deux Guerres Mondiales, Paris; Colonel Henri de Buttet, Saint Julien de Royaucourt, France; Admiral Luigi Durand de la Penne, Genoa, Italy; V. M. Destefano, Chief of Reference Library, U.S. Army Audio-Visual, Washington, D.C.; Edward Elisofon, New York, New York; Ulrich Frodien, Süddeutscher Verlag, Bilderdienst, Munich; General Adolf Galland (Ret.), Bonn-Bad Godesberg, Germany; Kyrill von Gersdorff, Deutsches Museum, Munich; Dr. Matthias Haupt, Bundesarchiv, Koblenz, Germany; Werner Haupt, Bibliothek für Zeitgeschichte, Stuttgart; First Lieutenant Heinz Hiltmann (Ret.), Koblenz, Germany; E. Hine, Department of Photographs, The Imperial War Museum, London; Julius C. Jefferson, Motion Picture Sound Recording Branch, National Archives, Washington, D.C.; Hans Klein, Bad Honnef, Germany; Dr. Roland Klemig, Director, Bildarchiv Preussischer Kulturbesitz, West Berlin; Franz Kurowski, Dortmund, Germany; Gustav Lamprecht, Clear, Alaska; Lieut. Colonel Brian F. Montgomery, London; Benedetto Pafi, Rome; Harry Postol, New York, New York; Helmut Regel, Bundesarchiv, Koblenz, Germany; Colonel Enrico Ripamonti, Captain Massimo Staccioli, Stato Maggiore dell'Aeronautica, Rome; Professor Dr. Jurgen Rohwer, Director, Bibliothek für Zeitgeschichte, Stuttgart; Manfred Erwin Rommel, Lord Mayor of Stuttgart; Joseph Schembri, Consul General and Carmel Sammut, First Secretary, Embassy of Malta, Rome; Jim Trimble, National Archives, Washington, D.C.; George Wagner, Archives Specialist, Modern Military Branch, National Archives, Washington, D.C.; General Siegfried Westphal (Ret.), Celle, Germany; Robert Wolfe, Chief, Modern Military Branch, National Archives, Washington, D.C.

INDEX

Numerals in italics indicate an illustration of the subject mentioned.

Printed in U.S.A.